MOUNT MARY
Milwaukee, W

W9-AEN-503

Technology
and the
Character of
Contemporary
Life

MOUNT MARY COLLEGE LIBRARY
Milwaukee, Wisconsin 53222

Technology

and the

Character of Contemporary Life

A Philosophical Inquiry

ALBERT BORGMANN

THE UNIVERSITY OF CHICAGO PRESS
Chicago and London

84-3243

ALBERT BORGMANN is professor of philosophy at the University of Montana. He has studied in Germany and the United States and has written extensively on philosophical issues raised by technology.

THE UNIVERSITY OF CHICAGO PRESS, CHICAGO 60637
THE UNIVERSITY OF CHICAGO PRESS, LTD., LONDON

© 1984 by The University of Chicago
All rights reserved. Published 1984
Printed in the United States of America
93 92 91 90 89 88 87 86 85 84 5 4 3 2 1

LIBRARY OF CONGRESS CATALOGING IN PUBLICATION DATA

Borgmann, Albert.
   Technology and the character of contemporary
life.

   Includes bibliographical references and index.
   1. Technology—Philosophy.   I.   Title.
T14.B63   1984   303.4′83   84-8639
ISBN 0-226-06628-2

303.483
B64

Contents

Acknowledgments

This book is the summary of work that has occupied me for over a decade.[1] I have received help from many people. From John Winnie I have learned to appreciate the power of the natural sciences. Henry Bugbee taught me to affirm in my thinking what matters to me in life. Carl Mitcham's friendship has been crucial to my working out a philosophy of technology. The staff, the faculty, and the administration of the University of Montana have supported my work generously. Finally, I am indebted to discussions with my students.

PART 1

The Problem
of Technology

Part 1 of this study is introductory. The main topics are presented in Part 2 and in Part 3. The first of these major topics is the character of contemporary life. The modern world and contemporary life particularly, so I will argue, have been shaped by technology, which has stamped them with a peculiar pattern and so given them their character. But although our world bears the imprint of technology, the pattern of technology is neither obvious nor exclusively dominant. It competes with and threatens to obliterate certain focal things and practices that center and order our lives in a profoundly different way. These focal concerns represent the other major theme of this inquiry. Part 2, then, is intended to clarify and explicate the pattern of technology and the prevailing character of our time. Given a clear and intelligent view of technology, Part 3 is to show how in the midst of technology we can become more conscious and confident of our focal concerns and how, against the background of technology, we can give them a central and consequential place in our lives.

These remarks must appear dubious and perhaps cryptic. They are so in part because they are brief, but partly also because they summarize views at variance with the common understanding of technology. A careful introduction is thus needed to connect the major concerns of this book with current thought on technology and to clear the ground for another way of approaching the problem of technology. This is the task of Part 1. It begins in Chapter 1 with a more detailed sketch of the contrast between the established views of technology and the position developed in this book. In particular, it provides introductory illustrations of what is meant by the pattern of technology, the pivot of Part 2, and by a matter of profound concern, the focus of Part 3. It presents brief surveys of those two parts and, at the same time, clarifies the significance of scholarship and method for the task before us.

In Chapter 2, the concept of technology that will guide this essay is tentatively sketched against the background of the presently dominant views of technology. The perspective on theories of technology is further elaborated in Chapter 3 through a comparison of the present classification with one developed by Carl Mitcham. This discussion points up more clearly and urgently the need for a fundamental and fruitful notion of technology; and it also suggests that the clarification of science and its connection with technology is the first task if that need is to be met. Accordingly, Chapter 4 considers what status science as a mode of viewing and explaining the world has in the technological society. This leads, in Chapter 5, to an examination of the structure of scientific explanation. Chapter 6, finally, develops and extends the understanding of science to include the problem of technology. It concludes that modern science is a necessary condition of modern technology and so is an understanding of one for the appreciation of the other; but science and technology are not the same thing nor essentially continuous with one another. Hence the character of technology requires an investigation and a method in its own right.

The chapters of Part 1 are brief, and some readers may find them a needless obstacle. That would be a misunderstanding. Strong and unusual claims of the sort that can be found on occasion in Part 2 and Part 3 are easily made by themselves. Even if one finds them immediately persuasive, or perhaps precisely when one does, one remains accountable to the established views, and one has an obligation to standards of thoroughness and circumspection in giving an account of one's views. Part 1, though not Part 1 alone, is intended to meet those requirements.

1   Technology and Theory

The advanced technological way of life is usually seen as rich in styles and opportunities, pregnant with radical innovations, and open to a promising future. The problems that beset technological societies are thought to be extrinsic to technology; they stem, supposedly, from political indecision, social injustice, or environmental constraints. I consider this a serious misreading of our situation. I propose to show that there is a characteristic and constraining pattern to the entire fabric of our lives. This pattern is visible first and most of all in the countless inconspicuous objects and procedures of daily life in a technological society. It is concrete in its manifestations, closest to our existence, and pervasive in its extent. The rise and the rule of this pattern I consider the most consequential event of the modern period. Once the pattern is explicated and seen, it sheds light on the hopes that have shaped our times, on the confusions and frustrations that we have suffered in our attempts to realize those hopes, and on the possibilities of clarifying our deepest aspirations and of acting constructively on our best insights.

Concrete, everyday life is always and, it seems, rightly taken for granted. It is the common and obvious foreground of our lives that is understood by everyone. Therefore it is almost systematically and universally skipped in philosophical and social analysis. But if the determining pattern of our lives resides and sustains itself primarily in the inconspicuous setting of our daily surroundings and activities, then the decisive force of our time inevitably escapes scrutiny and criticism. I want to argue that this is in fact so, and not only because everydayness in general seems inconsiderable but because of the particular way in which the ruling pattern of our time arose and came to be articulated.

The pattern of which I have been speaking inheres in the dominant way in which we in the modern era have been taking up with the world; and that characteristic approach to reality I call (modern) technology. Technology becomes most concrete and evident in (technological) devices, in objects such as television sets, central heating plants, automobiles, and the like. Devices therefore represent clear and accessible cases of the pattern or paradigm of modern technology. Giving these claims conviction will occupy us for much of the book. But the note of alarm in the foregoing remarks and their abstract and perhaps peremptory tone as well as the unusual focus of the perspective that they advocate make it advisable to provide an early illustration of the device paradigm. Surely a stereo set, consisting of a turntable, an amplifier, and speakers, is a technological device. Its reason for being is well understood. It is to provide music. But this simple understanding conceals the characteristic way in which music is procured by a device. After all, a group of friends who gather with their instruments to delight me on my birthday provide music too. A stereo set, however, secures music not just on a festive day but at any time, and not just competent flute and violin music but music produced by instruments of any kind or any number and at whatever level of quality. To this apparent richness and variety of technologically produced music there corresponds an extreme concealment or abstractness in the mode of its production. Records as unlabeled physical items do not bespeak, except to the most practiced of eyes, what kind of music they contain. Loudspeakers have no visible affinity to the human voice, to the brass or the strings whose sound they reproduce. I have little understanding of how the music came to be recorded on the disk and by what means it is retrieved from it. I have a vague conception at best of the musicians who originally performed the music; I may not even know how many there were, and in some cases I will not be able to distinguish or identify their instruments from the reproduction of their playing.

When we consider such a technological device and the things and practices that it replaces, varied and conflicting intuitions come to mind. What are the gains and what the losses in the rise of technologically recorded and reproduced music? If a consistent and revealing answer can be found to this question, does the finding have general significance? Is it an instance of a pervasive pattern? In the pursuit of an answer to these questions, we will have to pay attention to the sharp division between the commodious availability of music that a stereo set procures and the forbiddingly complex and inaccessible character of the apparatus on which that procurement rests. It is the division between the commodity, e.g., music, and the machinery, e.g., the mechanical and electronic apparatus of a stereo set, that is the distinctive feature of a technological device. An object that exhibits this central feature clearly is a paradigm of the technological device. I use "paradigm," however, not only in the sense of "clear case" but also for the pattern the clear case exhibits so well; and that pattern in turn can be drawn from various points of view and at different levels of abstraction. Obviously this definition of technology conflicts with many others that have been developed. It is helpful to consider these, and I will do so in Chapter 2. But it is not my purpose to establish the sense of technology that I have proposed as somehow superior or privileged. What the word "technology" should provide for this essay is a concept, a *conceptus,* in which the most helpful insights and experiences are gathered in a tentative, prereflective way.

Helpful for what? The chief concerns of this book are two, and they are interrelated as follows: The first is to provide a concise, illuminating, and, as far as possible, cogent description of the device paradigm. This description reveals a fatally debilitating tendency in the present rule of technology. But that aspect of its rule can be made intelligible only if we turn explicitly to those forces in our lives that are endangered by the rule of the device paradigm. I use "focal things and practices" as approximate terms for those forces. My second major concern is therefore with the nature of focal concerns. Here too an introductory sketch may aid the reader's orientation. A focal practice is one that can center and illuminate our lives. Music certainly has that power if it is alive as a regular and skillful engagement of body and mind and if it graces us in a full and final way. Our daily and mundane endeavors are then centered around music and invigorated by it. In such a practice the musical instrument occupies a privileged place. In many cases it embodies a long tradition of a craft, of a method, and of a musical literature. In it the melodious power of the world is gathered concretely. And it challenges humans to develop and exercise the finest bodily movements of which they are capable. In this sense a violin, for instance, is a focal thing. These observations will again evoke a variety of responses. We may applaud the value of music and yet wonder if musical practice can have a secure, a consequential, and a widely shared place in a technological setting. Still, it may have become apparent that there is a crucial connection between the rule of the device paradigm and the destiny of focal concerns. The present essay, at any rate, is primarily concerned with the explication of the technological paradigm and the elucidation of focal concerns.

These two major tasks are taken up in more specific or subsidiary investigations. The first of the latter are preparatory and methodological. Since I regard "technology" as the most appropriate and helpful title for what is characteristic of our lives, it is necessary to take account of presently available theories of technology. And since I am urging a shift in philosophical attention and description, reflection is needed on what it means to describe, explain, and evaluate something. There is a particular need to take account of natural science both because it sets new standards of description and explanation and because it is a crucial, though poorly understood, contributor to the rise of technology. These matters are taken up in Part 1, "The Problem of Technology."

Part 2, "The Character of Technology," turns to the central task of describing the concrete features and idiosyncrasies of technology. Though I claim that these are usually and even systematically overlooked, it would be most unlikely, and no one would reasonably assume, that what is most characteristic and consequential in our time has been altogether missed or ignored. It is possible, however, that a failure of focus has deflected, confused, or limited social and philosophical analyses of technological culture. My task, therefore, is not to reject or deny such inquiries but to point out how their best insights are rendered more incisive and consistent when the technological pattern of our time is clearly seen. Moreover, the investigations of social scientists have collected many data which, however limited or one-sided in perspective, have a strong claim to objectivity and generality. The kind of description and analysis that I propose is, roughly speaking, in a phenomenological style, and such analyses often run the risk of being anecdotal and parochial. For these reasons the description of the device paradigm must be tested and elaborated against pertinent work in philosophy and especially in the social sciences.

I regard scholarship as essential to a serious and credible inquiry. Still I have made no attempt to exhaust the scholarly material. Technology is at the intersection of so many currents and disciplines that the literature has become boundless in its extent. But the essential positions, I have found, appear to be limited in number. What can be expected from the treatment of scholarship is not exhaustiveness but a thorough consideration of some of the eminent and representative schools of thought and the possibility of extending fruitfully and consistently the major theses of the book to arguments and evidence that have been ignored. Though scholarship must be given its due, the esoteric features of its language and arguments are not needed in an essay of the present sort. Accordingly I have tried to write in a style that is accessible to any literate reader. I have tried to do this through simplicity of presentation and through the explanation and illustration of technical matters where the latter are unavoidable.

In Part 3, "The Reform of Technology," I turn to the focal forces whose predicament and dignity is what finally motivates my critique of technology. Here again, my concern in general is not unique. Just as there is an abundant literature devoted to the analysis of the technological society, so there is an abundance of pleas for the victims of technology and of reform proposals. But the lack of focus that I have claimed for the common analysis of technology infects the literature of accusation and reform more harmfully still. Since most writers fail to have a clear view of the pattern according to which we orient ourselves and take up with the world, their allegations are often misdirected and their proposals ineffective. The latter are so because they frequently play into the hands of what they oppose or they fail to connect with the real openings for reform.

Assuming that this essay accomplishes what it sets out to do, is it not one of social analysis and commentary? In what sense does it constitute a *philosophy* of technology? To begin with, I believe that there is no sharp dividing line between social science, or perhaps social studies, and philosophy. To be sure, this is to take philosophy in a sense which is not the dominant one in the modern era and is only now being recovered. It is a traditional one, however, and close to Aristotelian theory, to *theoria*, the calm and resourceful vision of the world.[1] *Theoria* was eclipsed with the rise of the modern period, and ambiguity befell all eminently theoretical endeavors. Language is negatively ambiguous if it exhibits a disorienting or debilitating plurality of senses. In the everyday world a pervasive negative ambiguity makes itself felt in the suspicion and diffidence with which ambitious questions and assertions are met.[2] Words of beauty are suspected of naiveté, words of salvation are thought to conceal egotism, words of profoundness are charged with obscurantism. The mere plurality of senses that attaches to every word is a prosaic matter, apparent in dictionaries, and normally counterbalanced by the resolving force of the context of discourse. But no such context seems to be at hand when weighty matters are at issue. Instead more and more claims pour forth, eroding and submerging all points of orientation.

Philosophers today try to gain firm ground and act on this ambiguity by turning to the antecedent and enabling conditions of thought, discourse, and argument. Attention is directed not to what is claimed to be shown and seen but to the grounds and possibilities of claims in general. Philosophy is not concerned with theory in the sense of a steady view of the world but with metatheory, the conditions of visibility.[3] This seems to be a plausible move beyond the common level of confusion. In fact it turns out to be an inconclusive enterprise. But that does not permit us to set it aside. It is for now simply a fact that the predominant response to ambiguity is not a desire to be open for what speaks with simple and salutary authority but the desire to gain authority over ambiguity by getting hold of its controlling conditions. The pattern and context of this response will become clearer precisely when we first take the metatheoretical turn and then move on to its final analysis where its insufficiency and the region beyond it become apparent.

There is a spectrum of attempts at taking the measure of our times. At one end are the concerns with immediately pressing and empirically quantifiable issues; at the other we find considerations of a radical and reflective sort. The present study is philosophical in belonging to the latter extreme. Though it pays more attention to substantive and empirical concerns than philosophy typically does, at least in this country, the present study has to draw on many of the concepts, methods, and insights of mainstream philosophy to obtain a reflective and radical view; and to that extent it is philosophical in the currently received sense as well.

2   Theories of Technology

Proponents of science and technology can respond to flamboyant accusations and proposals with superior silence. Modern science provides principled explanations and modern technology effective solutions of the problems that have troubled the human race from its beginning. This, at any rate, is the prevailing view, and it has a measure of accuracy. And from that viewpoint critics and competitors who fail to attain scientific rigor and technological efficacy are disqualified at the start. The strength of this view cannot be overcome by a colorful tour de force. One must at least begin by meeting it punctually and carefully. To be sure, one cannot overtake science and technology by their own standards. But care and precision of argument can make an opening for a truly alternative and viable kind of discourse, and in that universe of discourse deeper concerns can come to the fore which are eclipsed by science and technology. It is for the sake of these final aspirations that this essay sets out in what may seem an overly painstaking way.

Before a theory of technology as a vision of the world can be advanced, then, we must reflect on the possibilities of such a theory. They are best approached by starting from the theories of technology that have been developed in the literature. Each of these theories is guided by a certain sense of technology. The most common can be circumscribed as applied science and engineering. It designates an area of much sober and salutary work whose practitioners are entitled to fair and judicious treatment. If the word is not used in this sense, that must be made clear.[1] In fact, technology as applied science and engineering is not a suitable title and guide for a theory of technology.[2] To begin with, the subject matter covered by that title suffers from an overarticulation of its parts and seems to leave no areas for fruitful philosophical inquiry.[3] It is the result of singularly principled and systematic efforts. No sorting out seems to be necessary. Take the case of medical technology. It would be nonsensical to ponder the laws and methods that surgical procedures, for instance, are based on. At best one would come back to the explicit knowledge of anatomy, biology, chemistry, and so forth from which surgical techniques derive in the first place. On the other hand, the reduction of a practically successful but theoretically opaque procedure to scientific laws, say, in metallurgy, is doing technology; it is not philosophical reflection about technology. The same holds true when we turn to the narrowly technological *context* of medical technology. There is voluminous and explicit knowledge on how medicine by way of insurance is connected to the economy, how by way of medical schools to the educational establishment, how by way of the AMA to politics, and so on. All these problems are at least attended to by well-trained specialists, and no field of inquiry is left for the philosopher.

At the same time, there is a common intuition that the realm of research and development and of machines is characteristic of our era. Any fundamental investigation that ignores that part of our world must appear quaint. But to bring out the significance of technology in this larger sense one must turn to a larger context, to the antecedents and consequences of applied science and engineering. Often technology is kept as a designation for that wider field of study and its findings. Technology in this broader and stronger sense competes with other titles that attempt to catch the character of our times.[4] As said before, the contest of titles should be decided by the criterion of fruitfulness.

Philosophy at its best has always been concerned to provide an ontology, a vision of reality in its decisive features. One would therefore expect contemporary philosophy to have taken up the challenge of technology, to have inquired into the origin and fundament of the age of applied science and engineering, and to have furnished theories of technology in the wider sense. But most such theories have come from the social sciences. The philosophy of technology is just beginning to develop as a discipline. A theory, however, needs no philosophical hallmark to be appropriate. Let us look, then, at the theories themselves to examine their adequacy. Such a survey has scholarly precedents and can benefit from them. What follows here is not intended as a survey of all surveys of theories of technology. The intention is rather to gain entry to the problem of a theory of technology by way of looking at a few summaries of such theories.

These summaries distinguish a multitude of approaches, but all distinctions fit well one of three essential types: the substantive, the instrumentalist, and the pluralist views of technology. In the substantive view technology appears as a force in its own right, one that shapes today's societies and values from the ground up and has no serious rivals.[5] Hence that view is sometimes called the "sociological approach" or "technological value determinism."[6] The explicit proponents of the substantive view usually depict technology as a pernicious force, and so their position can be labeled "antitechnologist."[7] Implicitly, however, all the writers who speak of the "imperatives of technology" are committed to the substantive position though there is much inconsistency as regards such commitments.[8]

The substantive view is theoretically inviting because of its ambition and radicality. It seeks to give a comprehensive elucidation of our world by reducing its perplexing features and changes to one force or principle. That principle, technology, serves to explain everything, but it remains itself entirely unexplained and obscure. The most important example of this approach is given by Jacques Ellul. He paints the most comprehensive and somber picture of the omnipotence of what he calls the technical phenomenon which establishes itself through various techniques.[9] But his terminology is tellingly shifting.[10] Though the technical phenomenon is initially described as something very close to the essence of modern technology and a technique is defined merely as any methodical procedure to achieve an end, *technique,* nevertheless, comes to carry the entire explanatory burden. "technique" (sometimes qualified as "modern") is invoked as the autonomous and irresistible power that enslaves everything from science to art, from labor to leisure, from economics to politics.[11] How can technique, so generally defined, accomplish this? Ellul mentions two additional factors that must enter technique or technical operations to produce the technical phenomenon, namely, consciousness and judgment.[12] These are presumably human factors. But Ellul devotes the concluding part of his book to showing that humanity has lost control over technique and is overwhelmed by it. If that inconsistency were resolved, the qualified concept of technique would still suffer from a debilitating generality. A consciously applied method may be more powerful than an implicit one, but to what ends will it be applied? For Ellul the answer is provided by the notion of efficiency.[13] But efficiency is a systematically incomplete concept. For efficiency to come into play, we need antecedently fixed goals on behalf of which values are minimized or maximized. Those goals remain in the dark. From the omnipotence of technique we can infer, however, that whatever the goals may be they cannot be forces in their own right which could give guidance to technical developments. Technique is presumably its own end, and this is what the description of the characteristics of modern technique suggests.[14] But now we have come full circle in our search for the explanatory base of Ellul's analysis. Modern technique, a power in its own right, is put forward by Ellul as its own unexplained explanation.

Talk of such an obscure and pernicious power is easily dismissed as a demonizing of technology.[15] Ellul's important and fruitful observations are then lost along with his pivotal concept. Although he had anticipated the major points of Galbraith's *The New Industrial State*,[16] Ellul's theses found little resonance because the central obscurity of Ellul's book made them so easy to ignore.[17] That ease is accommodated by the availability of a much more familiar and seemingly more perspicuous view of technology, namely, instrumentalism. There is a continuous historical thread that leads from our ensemble of machines back to simple tools and instruments. We may think of both machines and tools as affording possibilities of which we can avail ourselves for better or worse. The extension of human capacities through artifacts is as old as humankind itself. A human being is, simply, a toolmaker and a tool user. Hence the instrumentalist view of technology is sometimes called the anthropological approach. A variant of the anthropological perspective is the epistemological view.[18] Here the focus is not on the development of humans and their tools but on the methodology that modern technology embodies as a way of taking up with reality, particularly in distinction to scientific procedure.[19] If technology is at bottom a mere instrument, the inquiry of *what guides* technology becomes a task in its own right. The determination of the guiding values is sometimes held to be a matter of rational inquiry. "Rational value determinism" is therefore by implication a species of instrumentalism.[20]

The notion of technology as a value-neutral tool or instrument is congenial to that liberal democratic tradition which holds that it is the task of the state to provide means for the good life but wants to leave to private efforts the establishment and pursuit of ultimate values.[21] In that view, technology appears to have a well-defined place in public policy. Radical critics generally accept the instrumentalist view of technology but claim that it is naive at best to disregard the ends technology serves in Western democracies. Those ends are said to be the welfare of the ruling elite and the exploitation of the working class. To ignore these issues is to cast a technological veil over social reality.[22] A penetrating inquiry of technology must inevitably be a social critique. This approach, sometimes called "politicized technology," is an important kind of instrumentalism.[23] Indeed, if one is persuaded that the political dimension is decisive in human endeavors, any analysis of technology can be evaluated as to its political salience, and it becomes possible to give an array of prominent analyses from left to right.[24]

The instrumentalist approach is in one way unassailable. Any concretely delimited piece of technology can be put forward as a value-neutral tool. But it is a shortsighted view. The availability of mere means is itself a remarkable and consequential fact. Historically, it is just in modern technology that such devices become available. As I will show later, it is an equivocation to speak indifferently of tools in a modern and in a pretechnological setting. A means in a traditional culture is never mere but always and inextricably woven into a context of ends.

If it is true that the presence of mere instruments in modern technology is consequential, then it must be misleading to continue to speak of ends and goals in a traditional manner. Putting technology in the context of political purposes is itself naive if one fails to consider trenchantly the radical transformation of all policies that technology may bring about. Indeed, Ellul and Galbraith who have been assessed and criticized within the political framework have forcefully challenged the adequacy of that framework, a challenge not always sufficiently met by their critics. The challenge, briefly, urges that traditionally radical distinctions, say, between socialism and capitalism, between union and management, have been eroded by modern technological or economic developments. Politics, then, is no longer the undisputed master science; it may well be in the thrall of a radically new and different force.

These questions will occupy us throughout this book. The present considerations suffice to show that in the instrumentalist view technology does not come fully into relief. Instrumentalism does not constitute a proper theory of technology. The failure that ambition suffers in the substantive view of technology and the obstacles that constrain common sense in the instrumentalist school of thought invite a more cautious and circumspective approach, one that takes account of the various evolving trends and complexities and of the many interacting forces. It has been called the "evolution and interaction" approach.[25] Essentially, it is a form of pluralism in that it meets all comprehensive approaches with reminders of counterexamples, unresolved problems, and disregarded evidence. The pluralist sees it all, the entire complex web of numerous countervailing forces. Against this picture any proposal of a great and consequential scheme must appear as a falsification of reality. Ironically, the pluralist view does very well with opposing theories, but it fails reality. Technology, in fact, does not take shape in a prohibitively complex way, where for any endeavor there are balancing counterendeavors so that no striking overall pattern becomes visible. It is intuitively apparent that in modern technology the face of the earth is transformed in a radically novel way; and that transformation is possible only on the basis of strong and pervasive social agreements and by way of highly disciplined and coordinated efforts. These crucial matters escape the pluralist's minute and roving scrutiny. The pluralist view is at bottom a learned reflection of the ambiguity we noted in Chapter 1.

Clearly, the theory of technology that we seek should avoid the liabilities and embody the virtues of the dominant views. It should emulate the boldness and incisiveness of the substantive version without leaving the character of technology obscure. It should reflect our common intuitions and exhibit the lucidity of the instrumentalist theory while overcoming the latter's superficiality. And it should take account of the manifold empirical evidence that impresses the pluralist investigations and yet be able to uncover an underlying and orienting order in all that diversity. It is the purpose of the paradigmatic explanation of technology to provide such an illuminating theory of technology. To avoid misunderstanding, let me repeat that my concern is with modern technology and its character. I will at times use the appropriate qualifier as a reminder. But often, in what follows, I will simply speak of technology when I mean modern technology. Now although the actual development of a fruitful theory of technology is a difficult task and of uncertain success, the program can be clearly laid out. It is a matter of discovering a basic pattern or paradigm that has been serving us since the beginning of the modern era as a blueprint or template for the transformation of the physical and social universe. If the pattern turns out to be clear and remarkable, it can serve as the pivot of a helpful theory of technology, one that would tell us more clearly what our goal has been, to what extent we have achieved it, and where we ought to turn should our achievements appear dubious to us. Perhaps such an ambitious goal is unattainable. It will be prudent in any case to take the first steps toward it carefully and to raise from another angle the question of what should guide the choice of a theory of technology.

3   The Choice of a Theory

Is it a sufficient recommendation for the classification proposed above that it is able to subsume so many others? It is easy to devise an equally or more inclusive scheme, either by moving to a higher conceptual level or by setting up sufficiently broad categories of classification. How is one to choose among competing classifications? All of them must meet the condition of internal consistency and of applicability to their subject area. But many will pass these tests, and there cannot be a sufficient condition of adequacy; for no classifying scheme can be exhaustive in taking explicit account of all properties and relations of an area. A classification orders an area in certain regards. It highlights certain features and obscures or suppresses others. It is necessarily selective; and once one is assured that a classification is consistent and applicable, one can pursue the question of adequacy only by asking, What are the concerns that have motivated the particular selection of features that are highlighted by the present classification?

We have touched on these methodological problems in Chapter 1, and we will have to return to them again. For now I want to put the question above to the classification system developed in the preceding chapter to characterize more closely the orientation of this investigation. We will obtain a tentative answer by comparing the present classification with one developed by Carl Mitcham.[1]

His is one of the most searching and comprehensive classifications, and it has been rightly praised for its rigor, originality, and exhaustiveness.[2] It begins by distinguishing (as I did above) between the narrow sense of technology (used by engineers) and the broad sense (used by social scientists). One might use this distinction to proscribe all philosophy of technology by insisting that technology, as its clear and narrow meaning suggests, be left to the experts, the people who truly know what technology is in its mechanical, chemical, and electrical aspects. But most of Mitcham's efforts are devoted to clarifying the phenomena located toward the broader end of the spectrum that spans the meaning of technology, and he attends to the philosophical tasks that are implied in those phenomena. These efforts assume that the way in which the products of technology in the narrow sense enter the everyday world is problematic and that this problem is perhaps more troubling and important than the technical problems that are internal to engineering. Mitcham's procedure is open to a more ambitious assumption, namely, that a profound problem of technology arises not just locally at the intersection of engineering products and the everyday world but that there is a global problem of technology; technology may be thought of as a force or an approach to reality that is all-pervasive. In that view engineering is not the origin and focus of technology and its problems but merely one and perhaps the clearest manifestation of a more inclusive and decisive phenomenon. It was to make room for this radical thesis that the distinction between the substantive and the instrumental sense of technology was introduced above.

Initially, at any rate, Mitcham rejects the radical thesis by defining technology as "the human making and using of material artifacts in all forms and aspects."[3] Technology so understood contrasts according to Aristotle's distinction with "human doing—e.g., political, moral, or religious action."[4] This point, as Mitcham stresses, is important for its force regarding philosophical practice. Philosophical analysis has traditionally ignored human making, and today, too, one will look in vain for philosophical reflections on technology in most textbooks and anthologies. But it is not clear that the Aristotelian distinction corresponds to a contemporary difference. Today it may be illuminating only in the remarkable fact of its disappearance. Human making has overgrown and suffocated human doing, truly political action in particular. That, at least, is the point of Hannah Arendt's influential book on *The Human Condition*.[5]

Mitcham then distinguishes three major dimensions within the full spectrum of the meaning of technology: the subject or material, the functional or structural, and the social or historical. It is the middle one that is further analyzed, and it is best understood from its complements. The material dimension lies close to technology in its technical or engineering sense. The social and historical dimensions are entrusted to historians and social scientists. To call the remaining dimension structural or functional is, it seems to me, simply to use cautious terms for "essential."[6]

But why the concern with the essence of technology? One answer might be that knowledge of the essence of technology would allow us to gain a firm grip on technology. Yet in one sense technology is nothing but the systematic effort to get everything under control.[7] And so the pursuit of the essence of technology would result in the unchecked advancement of technology—instead of what? Again the distinction between the substantive and the instrumental sense of technology makes room for an answer. If technology is thought of as a nearly irresistible instrument, the danger arises that we embark on an endless and aimless course of problem solving. If technology is said to be a force in its own right, we may pause and consider the ways of technology. In particular we will reflect on whether technology fulfills our deepest aspirations, and such reflections in turn may lead us to ask what in the world moves and sustains us most deeply. These questions are, of course, among the essential ones of traditional philosophy, and they, I am sure, are the basis of Mitcham's concern with the essence of technology.[8]

Though the substantive notion of technology opens up these questions, it also, as noted before, closes them too quickly and simply. Mitcham forces one to be more circumspect; he points out that the function or structure of technology displays three distinct aspects: "technology-as-knowledge, technology-as-process, and technology-as-product—or thoughts, activities, and objects."[9] Mitcham rightly insists that any definition (and theory, to be sure) of technology ought to be tested in light of these essential distinctions. They reflect a traditional *ordo essendi* in that the distinctions apply well to human technology from its first beginnings; and an *ordo cognoscendi* in that most scholarship is centered on one of these aspects of technology. Thus the distinctiveness of modern technology and the particular claims of a theory of technology have an appropriate background in the terms of Mitcham's distinctions. Particularly as regards the objects of technology, it is a fair if demanding requirement that a philosophical theory of technology have something to say about the machines and products that surround us daily, and to do this in a mode that undercuts and illuminates the language of engineering and economics in which we normally speak about the technological furniture of our age. In discussing technology as process or activity, Mitcham singles out making and using as the "root distinctions."[10] Here again the traditional cast of this distinction provides an adequate focus for a crucial phenomenon in modern technological societies, the fact, i.e., that the balance of making and using has been shifted to using in the mode of consumption. Membership in that society is typically exercised through consumption. The general participation in making, on the other hand, has declined in terms of expertise and responsibility. These too are matters on which a theory of modern technology must shed light.

Regarding technology as knowledge, the inevitable task of a contemporary theory is to come to grips with the relation of modern science and technology. This is perhaps the most basic task of an investigation of technology and the one that is most often neglected or ineptly treated. Mitcham distinguishes a fourth aspect in the structure of technology—technology as volition. Most philosophers would accept knowing, doing, and objects as phenomena or distinctions sufficiently well-grounded in the prereflective, everyday world to provide unobjectionable starting points for philosophical analysis. To be sure, people make everyday distinctions between knowing and willing as often but not as well. Many philosophers would protest this distinction from the start as being prejudicial or confused. Mitcham acknowledges the obscurity of the nature of willing.[11] And one should add that, while knowing in the general sense in which it designates the mental realm and contrasts with the realm of activity and of objects is fairly unproblematic, knowing when distinguished from willing becomes itself questionable in its outlines and boundaries. The reason why Mitcham persists with the problem of technology as volition is his insight that when the three preceding aspects of the structure of technology are attended to, there remains a troubling question about the ultimate springs and principles of technological activity.[12] In particular, he argues that attention to technology as volition can open the problem of how or indeed whether technological means do conform to our deepest aspirations, a problem that too often gets a facile treatment in terms of the selection and realization of one's values.[13] We return here to the issue that is approached from a different angle when one asks: Is technology a powerful instrument in the service of our values, a force in its own right that threatens our essential welfare, or is there perhaps no clear problem of technology at all, merely an interplay of numerous and variable tendencies?

The three parts of this question are raised and answered affirmatively by the instrumentalist, the substantive, and the pluralist schools of thought. That they cannot all be right at once is readily apparent. The more helpful lesson that we can learn from Mitcham's survey tells us that modern technology is evidently too complex and powerful a phenomenon to fit one of the answers above to the exclusion of the others. This point in turn leads us back to the task of discovering a fundamental pattern in technology that, when explicated, corrects and unites partial and, at first sight, incompatible views. One source of the inconsistency and confusion that one discovers in surveying the dominant views of technology is the lack of a principled understanding of science. Science and technology are usually named in the same breath when one tries to discern the character of our time. Science and technology are thought to be much the same or at least aspects of one and the same enterprise. This is a fatally misleading and confusing assumption as I now want to show.

4   Scientific Theory

Science is both the subject and the rival of the philosophy of technology. A theory of technology must talk about science to explain the relation between science and technology. But it is also true that a theory of technology, in attempting to outline a world view, is in competition with science since it is science that today sets the standard of explanation and is widely thought to give the most accurate description of our world.

We accept this privileged rank of science in our dealings day in and day out. When asked to explain an illness, the phases of the moon, or the rate of inflation, we will not resort to the wrath of God, a dragon in the sky, or the vices of people. Rather we attempt to give a physiological, astronomical, or economic analysis as best we can. When a well runs dry, a horse becomes lame, or a car breaks down, we demand that action be taken on the basis of scientific information. We talk seriously about the origin and the structure of the universe in scientific terms and save stories of creation and of the sun's chariot for special occasions.

It is difficult to establish whether such reflections accord with sociological fact, and the chief difficulty is this: one cannot presuppose, either with the public or among experts, a clear and common notion of what science is. There is no general agreement whether a sharp distinction must be made between science and technology. And among those who are willing to distinguish there is much controversy about the origin and status of scientific laws and explanations.

It is possible to measure the public's command of scientific facts, and it is deplorably weak.[1] Science as a whole seems to be a prohibitively complex and confusing phenomenon to the public, and its responses depend on what facets of the phenomenon and which inclinations of the respondents come into play. Science is sometimes confused or identified with technology.[2] But if the questions are suitably framed, a distinction is made.[3] Generally people's opinion of science and scientists is high.[4] In particular people respect and trust science more the better educated and the more acquainted they are with it.[5] The vociferous critique of science as an unprincipled and dehumanizing force is clearly not shared by the public at large. Do people therefore have a scientific view of the world? One very limited study suggests that this is so where people are in command of their situation and that they resort to religion for an explanation of their predicament when resignation is all that is left.[6]

We touch here upon a problem that will require more attention. It is of the first philosophical rank and concerns the question: With what degree of insight has the normal citizen of the technological society appropriated his or her world? An answer must aim at an equilibrium of reflection and empirical research.[7] The latter is required because the intuitions that guide our reflections are at times entirely at variance with more general facts. Yet the available data are always inconclusive because opinion surveys are of necessity directed by simple and brief questions which must elicit ambiguous responses. A survey as a rule cannot invite respondents to probe, clarify, and justify their responses. If today's typical world possession is of concern, one must boldly develop one's insights as an eyewitness and member of this society. But one is also bound to test these insights as far as possible against empirical findings.[8]

The entire exercise will of course be pointless if no attempt is made to expose today's normal world citizenship to criticism, to expose its inconsistencies and liabilities, and to free and strengthen its profoundest aspirations. As a first step in this direction, let us try to remove some of the confusions that beset the common view of science by separating three senses of (modern) science. These are (1) science as a human and social enterprise, (2) science as the body of well-established laws and theories, (3) science in its applications. Of these, the second sense is central. The laws and theories of science are the goal of science as a social enterprise and the basis of its applications. Science in its central sense gives a representation of the general structure of reality that, for the first time in human history, exacts universal assent. Whereas science as a human enterprise shows all the features of other human works— ambition, ingenuity, heroic effort, resignation, treachery, jealousy, failure— science as a body of laws and theories is objective and cogent. Again, in the application of science there is resourcefulness, imperialism, generosity, wastefulness, recklessness. But none of these is attributable to or sanctioned by science in its second meaning. It makes no difference to the validity of a scientific law whether it has been discovered by a Jesuit or a Communist and whether it is applied to kill or to cure.

To argue this way is to urge a distinction between science and technology. Science in its third sense should be called technology. And science in its first sense only is essentially dependent on or allied with technology. But it is dangerous to settle matters so quickly. Do all scientific theories have an equal claim to objectivity and cogency? How precisely do they establish a standard for explaining and understanding our world as was earlier said? How does technology fit into the scientific view of the world? Is it *merely* applied science? We need more detail and illustration to answer these questions. Let us look at an example of scientific explanation.

5   Scientific Explanation

Why does grape juice turn to wine? It has long been known that through the influence of yeast the sugar in the must is converted into alcohol. How does the yeast get into the must? Some have held that it is generated spontaneously. But beginning in the eighteenth century, experiments were conducted to show that yeast does not arise from nothing, only from yeast. Yeast is already present on the grapes or in the vats and casks. From the same must, it can produce wines that differ in alcohol content, color, and taste. "Yeast" is a collective term and covers many strains, some of which aid in the making of bread and beer. Most beloved of winegrowers is *Saccharomyces cerevisiae* var. *ellipsoideus*.[1] Like all yeasts, it consists of microorganisms as was first seen by van Leeuwenhoek in 1680 with hardly more than a good magnifying glass.[2]

How does yeast transform sugar into alcohol? Fermentation can be described by a formula, first reported by Gay-Lussac in 1810:

$$C_6 H_{12} O_6 = 2C_2 H_5OH + 2CO_2$$

One sugar molecule is converted into two alcohol and two carbon dioxide molecules.[3] But like "yeast," "sugar" and "alcohol" cover many kinds. Here we have glucose and ethanol. What role does the yeast play in this? Does the yeast bring about the transformation by rearranging the atoms in mechanical fashion? That view was put forward by Liebig in the nineteenth century.[4] Pasteur argued, however, that in fermentation the yeast ingests the sugar, releases the alcohol and carbon dioxide as waste products and retains a net gain of energy for growth.[5] It took many more decades to work out the links in the long chain of these reactions in which enzymes play a crucial role.[6]

Anyone would give an answer of this sort to the question of why must turns to wine and to the subsequent questions. We may not go so far into the history of science or into chemistry, but we would approve of the directions. No one would invoke the god Dionysus or insist on spontaneous change, that is, one that is not traceable to antecedent conditions in a lawful way. As the example shows, the drift to a scientific explanation is gradual and inescapable. More precisely, we move in the realm of scientific intelligibility from the start, and this becomes more evident as we pursue the explanation of a problem. Once we grant that yeast plays a role in fermentation, we cannot very well reject van Leeuwenhoek's invitation to look through his primitive microscope and to recognize that yeast consists of small organisms. And if Büchner succeeds in distilling a substance from yeast cells and finds that the substance alone brings about a kind of fermentation in a sugar solution, we have no good reason to withhold acceptance.[7] Then, if organic chemistry identifies that substance as a mixture of enzymes and isolates these catalysts and the reactions they make possible, this is but a further and consistent series of steps in the explanation of the change from must to wine. Finally, we might press on and explain organic chemistry in terms of physical chemistry, the latter in terms of physics, and we may end with a consideration of work at the frontier of physics, namely, in nuclear physics.

Along the explanatory route, there may be obstacles or dissent about this step or that. We have seen that this is historically so. But such controversy does not regard the direction and consistency of the explanatory course. If one accepts fermentation and yeast, one will accept cells, enzymes, chemical reactions, and so on down to our best current knowledge of subnuclear structures and processes. Such considerations amount to an argument in support of scientific realism, the view, in other words, that the directly unobservable elements and processes of which science speaks are just as real as the tangible phenomena from which it proceeds and to which it returns.

The opponents of this standpoint, the scientific instrumentalists, are struck by the differences between the point of departure, bubbling, frothing, brownish, sweet-sour must, and the final explanatory level of nuclear physics with its abstract formulas, intangible particles, and its austere language. So they want to draw a line between the tangible reality of the everyday world and the abstract objects of scientific explanation. But where can a principled line be drawn across the explanatory continuum that encompasses both extremes?

Still, the charge of artificiality in scientific explanations seems to be supported when we remember that the explanation sketch above ignores much that comes to pass in the change from must to wine: the development of the wine's bouquet and color, the maturing of the wine, the countless nuances and features lovers of wine recognize and cherish. Scientific explanation, however, is endlessly resourceful. Any challenge that is clearly advanced can be taken up scientifically. The great majority of past challenges has been met. It is a desperate move to try to secure a transscientific solidity for the everyday world by resting one's case on clearly stated but scientifically unsolved problems. Our common understanding of the world is always—and already—scientific. More precisely, everyone takes a protoscientific view of the world. The objects around us, large and small, are seen *within the range of scientific explanation.* Regardless of one's present competence or concern, most everyone admits that scientific scrutiny of any event or phenomenon is possible in principle; nothing falls beyond the scope of the sciences. The validity and also the ambiguities of this view will become clearer when we attend to *the structure of scientific explanation,* its validity in this chapter and its scope in the next.

To say that the world is real and intelligible is to say that it is lawful. Aristotle was the first to show in a resourceful way that we always and already move within a lawfully articulated world.[8] In particular, those who assert an endlessly shifting and unreliable reality can do so only to the extent that they tacitly take their position in a stable world. Much later and under very different circumstances, Kant argued similarly that there must be necessarily binding rules of structure and coherence if our individual experiences are to have objective validity.[9] From this it follows, as both Aristotle and Kant argue, that to render something intelligible is to place it explicitly in the matrix of laws and principles.[10]

One may find by simple inspection that must has turned to wine. But that process becomes intelligible only when it is seen as an instance of the law according to which, in the presence of yeast cells, the sugar of a solution is converted into alcohol. We can put this more formally, calling the phenomenon to be explained the *explanandum* and the principles and specifications that provide the explanatory insight the *explanans.*[11]

84-3243

MOUNT MARY COLLEGE LIBRARY
Milwaukee, Wisconsin 53222

explanans ⎰ Sugar, dissolved in water, is always converted into alcohol when
          ⎱ yeast cells are present in the solution.

          Must is a sugar solution, and yeast cells are present in must.

explanandum { Therefore must turns to wine.[12]

Or more generally:

explanans ⎰ laws
          ⎱ initial conditions

explanandum { event or process to be explained

And formally:

explanans ⎰ (lawlike) premises
          ⎱ (particular) premises

explanandum { (lawlike or particular) conclusion

This kind of explanation is called deductive-nomological since it can take the form of a syllogism where, from premises among which there is at least one empirical law (Greek *nómos*), a conclusion is deduced. The logical form a scientific explanation exhibits mirrors the cogent force of the latter. If the laws and conditions are accepted as true and the rules of logical inference are followed, then the truth of the proposition that refers to the event to be explained cannot be refused. Aristotle used the Greek word *apodéixis* as a technical term for this kind of compelling demonstration, and, when it is a matter of highlighting the cogency rather than the structure of scientific explanations, I will refer to them as apodeictic explanations.

To understand a particular event in seeing it within the framework of regularities is the common and pervasive way in which humans orient themselves in their world. To sow seeds is to act in view of the law of germination, growth, and fruition. To slaughter an animal is to proceed on one's general knowledge of the sustaining force of meat. Scientific explanation is not a novel assault on the world but the radical precisioning of a procedure that is as old as humanity. The procedures become precise through the sharpening of the laws to which phenomena are reduced. That must turns to wine is itself a rough sort of law. When we say that yeast, along with other factors, causes the fermentation, we say something more precise. But precision in one place requires precision everywhere else. The action of yeast produces alcohol. Yet the mere production of alcohol is not yet the production of wine. The development of colors and tastes is also involved; so are acids, tannins, and esters. Further, yeast cells require for their growth not only a sugar solution but also nitrogen, vitamins, minerals, and a certain range of temperature.

When we so analyze fermentation, we have already taken the standpoint of *modern* science. From that point of view, fermentation appears as a manifold and complex chemical process, and the terms "must" and "wine" designate stages that are selected for convenience, not for reasons that derive from the laws of chemistry. Indeed, "fermentation" itself has a selective function. It tells us, if we are *observers,* what to pay attention to and what to ignore when we follow the fate of the grape from the vine to the cask. What the word tells us if we are *practitioners* is a question that will later lead us to central problems in the philosophy of technology.

The seemingly opaque phenomena and processes of the everyday world become perspicuous in the matrix of scientific laws. Opacity gives way to perspicuity as the molar objects are analyzed into their microscopic components and events are subsumed under laws. The move from the molar to the microscopic is at the same time a move from diversity to sameness.[13] The laws of chemistry hold for baking bread as well as for fermentation, and for metallurgy as well as for organic processes. It is conceivable that the change from sugar to alcohol is a lawful but not further analyzable process. Any theory of explanation must end with such ultimate laws. But modern science has shown that the final structures of our world lie several stages removed from their tangible appearances.[14] Sugar is a compound, analyzable into molecules, these into elements, the latter into atoms, and those into particles and subparticles. And at one or another of these stages the lines of analysis that depart from bread or bronze converge and become one.

In part, the laws of modern science allow us to restate and explicate what we knew prescientifically. Winegrowers have always known that sunshine and well-drained soils are crucial for productive vines. Science elucidates these phenomena in terms of photosynthesis and minerals. In part, modern science corrects our prescientific views. Naively, we are inclined to overestimate the substance that is drawn from the soil since we are unaware of the carbon dioxide in the air as a raw material. Finally, modern science discloses entirely new phenomena. No one could know without science that air contains nitrogen which is in part captured by rain and so becomes a nutrient for the vine. Through such disclosures the network of relations that constitute the context of our world becomes richer and tighter. We come to see the cycle of the production of oxygen in photosynthesis and its consumption in respiration. We can follow the path of calcium from the soil to shrubs, to the antlers of a deer, to the rodents that consume the antlers. We see cycles in the course of water and in the weather; we see courses of development in geological formations.

Thus modern science gives us a more coherent and detailed view of the world. It lets us see more precisely what a phenomenon consists of, and it connects that phenomenon more definitely and more manifoldly to other phenomena. Science reveals detail because its theories ultimately treat of microparticles. Science is in one regard a microtheory. In constituting *one* microtheory for all the varied phenomena it discloses the many bonds of commonness among phenomena. This is the explanatory power of science: it explains everything more precisely and more generally than any prior mode of explanation. From this we should conclude that science can also provide a precise and general explanation of technology just as it has furnished one for fermentation. We know as a matter of fact that this has not been done. Is it to be expected? Is it a matter of principle or of practical circumstances that a scientific explanation of technology has not been forthcoming? What is the scope of scientific explanation?

6   The Scope of Scientific Explanation

A deductive-nomological explanation makes explicit how an event fits into the lawfulness of reality. It outlines the place of an event in the nomological network. Explanation in this sense brings into relief clearly and in some cases surprisingly an understanding of the world that is implicitly present all the time. To repeat: intelligibility is of one piece with lawfulness. To say that reality is lawful is simply to highlight the solidity and steadiness of the world. We could not be at home in the world if it changed in strictly capricious ways. Unforeseen events stand out against a world that is understood in its lawfulness, and, if an event that has exploded our nomological network and taxed our understanding is at all of concern to us, we will not rest until its relation to the laws of nature is understood.[1]

Subsumption under laws, be it explicit or implicit, is surely necessary for an explanation and understanding of events. Scientific explanation is the clear and ideal case of such explanation, and Hempel and his followers contend that any kind of explaining is valid only to the extent that it approximates this ideal. Of course in many situations an approximation is all that is needed or possible. But is subsumption under scientific laws also sufficient to explain an event? Two objections have been advanced against a positive answer. The first denies the claim of necessity and sufficiency, the second the thesis of sufficiency only. In taking up these challenges we provide a clearing for the paradigmatic explanation of technology.

It has been said on behalf of historians that they usually explain the events of history without recourse to laws.[2] But it seems that, where defenders of the autonomy of historical explanation agree that a certain event is given and that we want to know why it happened, they cannot sketch a satisfactory answer without an appeal to laws of some sort. Thus the way in which this controversy is formulated always leaves the impression that historical explanation is at bottom but a species or variant of scientific explanation, and in this context the idiosyncracy of historical and the limits of scientific explanation never come into view.

The objections that have been raised against the sufficiency of the deductive-nomological model of explanation are more fruitful. Hempel himself has noted that a scientific explanation provides an answer to an (explanation seeking) why-question but not to a request for an explanation of a thing or concrete event. There is no scientific reply to the demand: Explain the northern lights to me. But there are answers to such questions as: Why do the northern lights pulsate? Why do they show red and green colors? A why-question selects an aspect from a concrete thing or event that is sufficiently precise to be subsumable under laws.[3] But even when the explanandum has the required sentential form, it can be subsumed under very different laws because indefinitely many causal lines intersect at the place where an event is located in the nomological network, and so the event instantiates and is subsumable under many laws. There is usually a common understanding regarding the aspect of the explanandum which is of concern and should be explained. When a particular subsumption does not accord with one's understanding, one may doubt the sufficiency of the deductive-nomological model of explanation.[4] Hempel makes the point that a subsumptive explanation shows that an event was to be expected and that in this sense it "enables us to *understand why* the phenomenon occurred."[5] But it is clear that when an explanation disregards that aspect of the event that is of concern to me, it fails to satisfy my need to understand. Hence a satisfactory account of explanation must raise and answer the question of the relevance of the factors to which an explanandum is related.[6] One can try to highlight the explanatory concern by resolving the ambiguity of an explanandum through emphasis in, additions to, or redescriptions of the explanandum.[7] Say I see a hawk sitting on a fence post that I know to be four feet high.[8] The hawk seems to be looking at a squirrel on the ground, three feet from the base of the post. After the hawk and the squirrel have disappeared, a friend of mine, who also has been observing the scene, measures the distance from the top of the fence post to the spot where the squirrel sat and asks: Why was the hawk sitting five feet away from the squirrel? The question is ambiguous in at least two ways. If my friend is concerned with the geometrical relations of the situation, I will answer by subsuming the initially given distances under the Pythagorean theorem and deduce the distance from hawk to squirrel. On the other hand, if my friend is concerned to know why the hawk did not take after the squirrel, I will resort to laws of animal behavior which explain under what conditions a predator is inhibited from pursuing its prey.

Can we say that once an explanatory concern is stated unambiguously its subsumption under the relevant laws by way of special conditions is sufficient to explain the event in question?[9] One could simply agree to define the matter in this way. But if one also agrees that explanation begets understanding and that understanding always admits of explication by explanation, then the narrow definition of explanation just contemplated leaves much of our understanding inexplicable. There are a number of gaps in our understanding of what it means to explain something, and they open up around scientific explanation itself. To begin, we must remember that a scientific explanation normally gets underway only when the scientific laws are given. Even in the case where the laws are discovered in an attempt to solve a problem, the discovery itself, though it is part of an explanation, is not thereby explained. We have no general explanation of how scientific laws are discovered. This is not for lack of attention. Historians and philosophers of science have devoted much ingenuity and diligence to the study of how new scientific laws and theories arise. But what understanding we have of these matters is not derived from deductive-nomological explanations. More particularly, rationalist or inductivist explanations of the emergence of scientific laws which at least emulate the rigor of deductive-nomological explanations have proven quite inadequate. It is worth remarking that the philosophers of science who remind the general historians that their successful explanations are of the deductive-nomological cast do not attempt to cast their own explanations of the history of science in that mold. Another gap is found on the opposite side of scientific explanations. An explanation gets underway only when it is clear what problem is worthy and in need of explanation. But again we have no general explanation of how problems get stated.[10] A closer look at the first gap will lead us to a better understanding of the second.

The problem of the rise and succession of laws and theories in the history of science has many aspects. An important thread in this history and its discussions emerges when we consider that there is apparently no rule whose application leads to progress. This appears from a study of the details and circumstances of any scientific breakthrough. The lack of a rule is equally well demonstrated by the failure of those allegedly possessing such a rule to achieve genuine and consistent progress. Scientific progress seems to be unpredictable in any strict sense, and that is to say, unexplainable.

Yet if we speak of progress in the succession of scientific discoveries, there must be a pattern in this development, and it must be one from weaker to stronger stages. These two findings are not really incompatible. Scientific advances may well be inexplicable and incomprehensible when we look at the future. The hitherto unthought is as of now unthinkable. But that is a psychological limit. Looking at the past, after a great thinker has thought through what seemed unthinkable, the advance will exhibit theoretical ties to the past that are clear to all experts.[11] Progress up to the present is theoretically and hence psychologically perspicuous. Progress in the future is psychologically veiled and hence theoretically opaque.

Thomas Kuhn whose thought on these matters has become well-known and influential has never denied that scientific research makes progress. He has certainly denied that progress is steady and by accumulation. However there is an issue on which Kuhn seems divided, and it is a truly controversial and interesting one. It regards the question of how radical the discontinuities in scientific progress are.[12] We seem to face a dilemma. On the one hand, if the periods ushered in by new scientific theories or paradigms are radically different from their predecessors, they are incomparable or incommensurable with them. We would then have change but not progress.[13] It is the immersion in the details of history that makes us hesitate to belittle and reduce the differences among eras to degrees of crudity and ignorance. One is tempted to posit not just psychological or epistemological differences but differences in the nature of reality, i.e., ontological differences.[14] On the other hand, we cannot deny that in the development of science theories supersede one another in attaining ever greater explanatory power.[15] As noted before, however, the power has not expanded to cover its own history and character.

The result of the history of scientific progress does not explain itself in the deductive-nomological sense in which we have taken "explanation" so far. But the history does exhibit a pattern which can be pointed out. Let us concentrate on one feature of this pattern and point it out very tentatively and briefly. The early scientific theories of the Western world had both world-articulating and world-explaining significance. To articulate something, i.e., to outline and highlight the crucial features of something is also a kind of explanation. It is the kind of explanation that *can* satisfy the request for an explanation of a concrete thing or event. I will call it *deictic* explanation to distinguish it from deductive-nomological or subsumptive explanation. Aristotle's theories were explanatory in both senses. His physics and astronomy contained laws that permitted deductive-nomological or subsumptive explanations.[16] But these laws were moored in the singular structure of the cosmos articulated and pointed out in Aristotle's theory or vision of the world. The articulated world order of Aristotelian physics and astronomy is more or less of one piece with the world of Aristotelian metaphysics, ethics, and all his other disciplines. In this world order, everything had its place and rank. The movements or changes of things could be predicted on the basis of laws which reflected the privileged dimensions of the world and the rank of things. The Aristotelian laws were of limited explanatory power in that each held only for a small class of phenomena (e.g., for sublunar horizontal motion), in that they yielded only rough or relative predictions, and in that they were inconsistent with one another.

The progress of science is marked by improvements in the scope, precision, and consistency of the laws. In thus gaining greater explanatory power in the deductive-nomological sense, the laws lost their power of world articulation. Einstein's theories of relativity no longer reflect or point up a singular world.

They do have deictic power in the sense of delimiting a set of possible worlds and ruling out certain impossible worlds.[17] We can observe a similar pattern in the development from alchemy by way of chemistry to nuclear physics. Alchemy reflected in its laws a definite world of a limited number of stuffs and transformative forces and processes. Nuclear physics, being a microtheory, allows for an indefinite number of molar worlds.

This pattern in the progress of science has no a priori character. It is an empirical fact that the world can be explained in the powerful scientific theories that we now have. The pace of the discoveries of these theories is a matter of historical fact. But given these two facts, it was inevitable that the deictic power of the sciences waned and all but vanished. This is not a failure of science. Nor is it the case that the *deictic* achievement of the earlier sciences was unquestionable or unique. *Art* has always been the supreme deictic discipline. Art in turn has sometimes been one with philosophy, religion, and politics; at other times these disciplines have complemented or competed with one another as disciplines of deictic explanation.

No marshaling of evidence and no elaborating of arguments are required to support the statement that the traditional deictic explanations have lost their force. Artists, prophets, and philosophers are not among the people who are consulted by government when a crisis is to be met or a course of action is to be charted. Politics itself provides the arena of today's most common and consequential discourse, to be sure; but it is less clear whether politics also sets the tone and standards for public discussions and decisions. One must at least consider the possibility that technology has robbed politics of its sovereignty and substance. If, on the other hand, laws of modern science do not by themselves bring out the crucial and remarkable features of the modern world and so fail to provide the orientation needed for political action, it appears that there is a gap of explanation and insight opening up between the apodeictic explanations of the sciences and the deictic explanations of our heritage. Perhaps this lacuna can be filled by the paradeictic or paradigmatic explanation of technology. But before I act on this possibility in Part 2, we must consider more concretely and in detail the connections between science and technology. In particular, we must take account of the contentions, contrary to the suggestion above, that the scientific enterprise in conjunction with technology or with technology as its consequence has in fact begotten a new kind of order by which we are destined to live.

7   Science and Technology

Let us begin with this framework and hypothesis for the explanation of modern technology. We may think of modern science as having rendered the world perspicuous by setting it within the matrix of scientific laws. In this matrix it appears as one possible world. It might, within the same matrix, be differently arranged. Or in other words, any definite state or event in the world can be subsumed by way of its initial conditions under scientific laws. And any such state or event might have been prevented or modified if the conditions had been different. Thus, the change of conditions in accordance with scientific laws yields great transformative power. Modern science lets the world appear as actual in a realm of possible worlds. Modern technology reflects a determination to act transformatively on these possibilities.[1]

Neither science nor technology, however, has a theory of what is worthy and in need of explanation or transformation. Given an explanandum or transformandum, they will explain and transform the problematic phenomenon; neither has a principled way of problem *stating*. To be sure, science has authentic access to the problems that arise within a research program.[2] But these are not the problems whose solutions constitute the technological transformation of the world. Technology in its turn, merely as the determination to transform, faces an indefinite number of transformative possibilities and cannot provide principled guidance to problems.

But before we ask what guidance or pattern there is to the technological transformation of reality, we must consider the influence of modern science on modern technology, the latter tentatively defined as the typical way in which one in the modern era takes up with reality. Consider the following illustration. Wine is an ancient drink and has had an important place and rank in the human world. Like many other things, wine began to be analyzed in terms of modern science with the rise of that science, and the research of the nineteenth century led to a first culmination of this development, a sketch of which was given in Chapter 5. But research has continued, of course. Finer and finer details in the production and the composition of wine are being understood. The process from the vine to the bottle is, in light of the laws of physics and chemistry, seen as a finely detailed stream of physicochemical events. Similarly wine, the product, is visible as a complex substance of organic and inorganic chemicals. Some of the phases or features in the traditional process are laborious and time consuming, some are harmful, others inessential. And similarly with wine. Some substances in the traditional product are not palatable, some threaten its stability, others that are desirable are often in short supply. How should we act on such insight? The answer is not difficult when there is a mortal danger to the vine or a persistent problem of wine spoiling. But where should we draw the line in interfering with the traditional process and product?[3] To take an extreme possibility, once the chemical composition of traditional wine is fully understood, it becomes possible to produce a substance much like it that is not derived from grapes but in another, more efficient way. Is it just sentimentality that prohibits one from calling the new substance wine also? Is such a prohibition any more consistent than if we refused to call something a table unless it were made of wood?

Given the very limited common knowledge of science, it is clear that there cannot be on the part of the public either an explicit knowledge of the fine structure of things or any grounded knowledge of just how these things may be technologically modified, replaced, or supplemented. It seems, however, that there is a general and implicit understanding of the scientific perspicuity and technological malleability of our world. The public takes in stride scientific breakthroughs and technological innovations because they occur within a horizon of general familiarity. We might venture to say that with all the scientific illiteracy there is a public understanding of the sciences as a principled or lawful illumination of reality which opens up new possibilities for dealing with the world. To be sure, that understanding rests on a narrow base. All of us know at least bits and pieces of science. But most of us are only peripherally in touch with the body of scientific theories and with the social organization that undergirds it. But tenuous as the connections may be, as long as there are no inconsistencies or severe disruptions, the public seems to have a sufficient warrant for its correct if vague understanding of science.

Though it is true that science in revealing the lawful fine structure of reality provides new insight and possibilities, one may easily take a second and unwarranted step by inferring that modern science has thereby ushered in a new world view. This inference is greeted by some with triumph and by others with distress. Little is known about the public view in precisely this regard, but the distinction is well worked out as regards the scholarly and literary community.[4] The pursuit of this problem allows us, at any rate, to come to a conclusion about the relation of modern science and technology.

What about the thesis that the scientific enterprise embodies a substantive way of taking up with the world, positively or negatively? Historically, the positive case can be made by showing that science was a liberating event, a breaking of the fetters of superstition, ignorance, and dogmatism.[5] These forces science replaced with rationality, honesty, and a public and inquisitive attitude.[6] A more straightforward argument holds that an inspection of the scientific enterprise reveals that the practitioners of science are held to singularly stringent and august criteria of achievement.[7] Finally, an application to the problem of technology is made when it is held that the deplorable chaos of the contemporary world results from our failure to carry the scientific enterprise to its conclusion by explaining and shaping human behavior according to the best available scientific knowledge.[8]

The first of these three arguments is the strongest because it can point to the very real clashes of scientists with traditional world views. In light of our earlier remarks on the progress of science, it must be admitted that, as the scientific theories advance, they more and more withdraw their endorsement of established world views. If a totalitarian power demands such an endorsement, withdrawal is often both undertaken and acknowledged as a revolution.

But it is one thing no longer to fulfill a task and quite another to fulfill a task in a new way. Scientific progress can at most be *liberation from;* it can never constitute or provide the thing that it is a *liberation for.*

More specifically, when scientific endorsement is withdrawn from a world view, the latter is required to abandon in light of that withdrawal those of its elements that hitherto provided or implied deductive-nomological explanations, those elements, i.e., from which, together with particular conditions, empirically testable predictions could be derived. For the withdrawal of endorsement in scientific progress is not a wanton shift of allegiance but the reflection of the discovery of new and more powerful laws and new explanations that are thereby possible. But it is a mistake to think that a world view must shrink to nothing after it has given up its scientific elements. The Aristotelian hierarchy of being need not be given up with Aristotelian mechanics and dynamics. Accordingly, Einstein's relativity theory has no counterpart or counterargument to the Aristotelian hierarchy. To be sure, withdrawal of scientific endorsement forces a world view back to its deictic resources. If these were slim or unwholesome to begin with, this will now become apparent, and the world view may collapse. Conversely, the more purely and fully a world view is by its nature articulated in a deictic manner, the less it is affected by scientific progress. That is true of poetry and art in general. The more complex world views of politics and religion, however, are required not only to expel their outdated scientific elements but also to rearticulate themselves in light of new scientific laws. Both enterprises are laborious and encourage conservatism. But it is pointless to call for a substantive controversy between science and theology as Paul Feyerabend does.[9] That call will be frustrated not necessarily by the meekness of theology but inevitably by the fact that modern science cannot embody a substantive world view of a scientifically authenticated sort.

We can leave it undecided whether the scientific enterprise as a sociological or psychological phenomenon is singularly edifying or pernicious, whether it would lead us to happiness or ruin.[10] In neither case would the guidance originate from the center of the enterprise, i.e., from the body of the established laws and theories of science. But the rise of science as a power without guidance for the world may have substantive consequences in its own right, and technology may be foremost among them. A world whose articulation disintegrates may as such display definite and consequential traits. This is roughly the thesis of Hans Jonas.[11] More particularly, he holds that modern science has not only withdrawn its support of established world views but promoted their dissolution and the establishment of an alternative vision. The world's cosmic architecture is denied and replaced by the infinite manifold of one homogeneous substrate. Manipulation and novelty are integral parts of this promotion, and it has technology as an inevitable if not immediate consequence. Technology ceaselessly transforms the world along abstract and artificial lines.

This is a considerable argument, and it can be complemented by pointing up the close sociological and disciplinary ties between science and technology.[12] It is important to consider, as Paul Durbin has done, the empirical facts and consequences of this association.[13] Still, it is possible, as Joseph Agassi and Mario Bunge have shown, to distinguish in a principled manner the scientific from the technological procedure.[14] In particular, the scientific methodology is shown to be detached from the common criteria of success as one would expect from a discipline not committed to the establishment of a particular world view.

The distinction between science and technology is also eminently desirable for a critique of technology. Jonas's thesis is so strong because he does not derive technology primarily from science as a sociological phenomenon, i.e., from the habits and characteristics of the scientific community. Rather he derives it from the core of science, from the nature of the scientific laws and theories and of the explanations they make possible. But this strength is also a weakness by is consequences. Current science at its core is true; true in the sense that its theories give us the best representation of the general structure of reality. The truth a realist claims for science can be denied from an instrumentalist position; but the latter is plausible only as long as it avoids precision. The instrumentalist cannot, as we have seen, draw a definite line between everyday knowledge which has access to supposedly real states of affairs and scientific knowledge which, it is claimed, merely deals with convenient and useful formalisms. Yet if we accept the realist view of science and admit that what our current scientific theories and explanations say of the world is true, then we must also admit that technology, if it is the necessary consequence or companion of science, is equally true. Putting it more discursively, technology on that view is a mode of taking up with the world, which is entirely and necessarily in accord with the true nature of the world. One can then deplore the truth of science and technology. But one can criticize technology only in violating the truth.

As we have seen, however, a proper appraisal of the core of science and of the methodology immediately surrounding and serving that core does not warrant an inference from science to technology. That inference does not fail a priori, but it certainly does in fact. A concise and consistent formulation of Jonas's principal thesis fails to agree with crucial features of the technological world. The thesis holds that modern science renders the world homogeneous, infinite, devoid of an encompassing structure and goal. If these processes and their results are not just necessary for technology but sufficient, then technology is nothing but the reduction of the world to unbounded, unstructured homogeneity. Any thesis can be saved by modification, and the present thesis holds if the presence and effects of technology are restricted appropriately. But it is clear from Jonas's discussion of the Industrial Revolution, of mechanics, chemistry, electricity, and electronics that he does not accept the drastic restriction of the significance of technology which the consistency of the thesis would require.[15]

But if technology harbors formative forces that cannot be delineated through recourse to modern science, how can they be delineated? Surely the modern world does not in any plain and indisputable sense tend toward greater homogeneity and loss of structure. On the contrary, where technology is most advanced, the world is most radically and tightly restructured. We can conclude then that the sciences reveal in a principled manner the general structure of reality and that the resulting insight is known to provide great transformative power. Scientific knowledge is a necessary condition of modern technology; it is not, however, sufficient. The question remains of how technology acts on the transformative possibilities provided by science, and the description of the character of technology is a task in its own right. In Part 2 we will try to discover and explicate the basic pattern of technology and determine how and with what consequences we have transformed our world according to that pattern.

PART 2

The Character
of Technology

Part 2 of this study deals with the character of technology. I have said all along that our conflicting and confusing experiences of technology can be clarified if we are able to recognize an underlying pattern in technology. And such a recognition should in turn help us to act constructively on our deeper aspirations. The constructive task is to be taken up in Part 3. In this part we must work out the technological pattern or paradigm. I begin with an introductory chapter which brings the character of our time into broad relief by viewing technology from the standpoint of the beginning of the modern era where the promise of technology was first formulated.

This is followed by a group of four chapters (Chaps. 9–12) whose purpose is to describe and articulate the paradigm of technology. The stages of this enterprise are the following. I begin by considering clear instances of the technological pattern, namely, technological devices; I point up the distinctive features of such devices and highlight them against a pretechnological background. What distinguishes a device is its sharp internal division into a machinery and a commodity procured by that machinery. Next, to give a first indication of the power of the technological paradigm, I turn to one of its global manifestations, namely, the assembly of commodities that constitutes the world of consumption and the prominent foreground of technology. I then articulate the systematic standing of the technological pattern or the device paradigm, first by comparing the latter with competing modes of analysis and then by examining the status of paradigmatic explanation explicitly.

Given a reasonably firm and clear understanding of the decisive pattern of technology, we can raise the question of how we have come to terms with technology socially and politically. This is the task of Chapters 13–16. Again I begin with an introductory chapter in which I consider the problem of orientation in a general way and then discuss two well-known but misdirected attempts at orienting ourselves in regard to technology; the first of these is "raising the value question," and the second the Marxist analysis of Western democracy. I then turn to the political and social understanding that today is dominant in this country, namely, to the liberal democratic view of society

33

and politics. My concern here is to show that the technological culture is the largely unspoken but pivotal issue of liberal democracy. Without modern technology, the liberal program of freedom, equality, and self-realization is unrealizable. But with a technological specification of liberal democracy, the ideal of the liberally just society, where the question of the good life is to remain open, has been surrendered to the establishment of a society that is good in a definite and dubious sense. In Chapter 14 I try to advance this claim through a discussion of some of the eminent renditions of the liberal democratic view. I then try to show that the tensions and contradictions of liberal theory can be resolved if we envision the device paradigm explicitly. And in Chapter 15 I suggest that such a vision is in accord with the concrete circumstances of life and with what empirical data there are on this issue. In Chapter 16, the last of these four, I give a summary description of technological politics in which I propose that politics today has become the metadevice of the technological society; and I attempt to show that this view accounts well for two problems that trouble liberal theorists deeply, political apathy and social injustice.

The two groups of chapters that outline the pattern of technology (Chaps. 9–12) and examine its social and political setting (Chaps. 13–16) provide a fairly balanced and comprehensive view of the character of technology, but a view that lacks depth as well. This I try to remedy through a discussion of labor (Chap. 17) and of leisure (Chap. 18). My reasons for this move are two. First, it seems to me that technology is most consequential in the inconspicuous dailiness of life. And second, the labor-leisure distinction has a privileged tie to the character of technology; it represents the split of the technological device into machinery and commodity writ large. The transition to the reform of technology in Part 3 is conveniently made by investigating the stability of the rule of technology. Such an examination draws the previous findings together and begins to ask what openings for a reform we can count on.

8   The Promise of Technology

The concern of the present study is modern technology. We have tentatively and formally defined technology as the characteristic way in which we today take up with the world. This approach to reality, I have said repeatedly, is guided by a basic pattern. By this I mean that the pattern of technology is fundamental to the shape that the world has assumed over the last three or so centuries. But to speak of a deeply ingrained pattern is also to say that the pattern may be difficult or perhaps impossible to see. It reigns as common sense, as the obvious way of doing things which requires no discussion and, more important, is not accessible to discussion. It is understood in the sense of being taken for granted. It is only when a pattern of procedure or a paradigm, in Kuhn's term, begins to fail and be questioned and perhaps challenged by a new procedure that the paradigm emerges as such.[1] Precisely when we assume that there is a definite and well-entrenched mode to our dealings with the world, we must also reckon with the possibility that we may be unable to bring it to the surface.

To lift this concealment it may be well to step outside of the rule of the dominant pattern and to return to the period where the pattern was first articulated. This is to go back to the founding event of the modern era, to the Enlightenment and to its first beginnings in the early seventeenth century. In this way we can hope to obtain a first and unrestricted, though also un-focused, view of the character of technology. The Enlightenment is known to us primarily as an intellectual and cultural revolution, a breaking of the fetters of religious superstition and ancient dogma. The Enlightenment was the original liberation movement of our time. It is generally accepted that it had reverberations beyond the realm of culture and the intellect, but these are almost exclusively seen in the political area, especially in the rise of the liberal democracies of the West. Technology is sometimes, in an aside, mentioned as an offspring of the Enlightenment, yet its significance is thought to be inconsiderable. It is taken as an essentially uninteresting if powerful tool, neutral in its relation to cultural values and subservient to political goals. In fact, however, technology has become the decisive current in the stream of modern history. But how could it be so concealed and so consequential at once? It is the promise of technology that has both fueled and disguised the gigantic transformative endeavors that have given our time its character.

The promise of technology was first formulated at the very beginning of the Enlightenment. It was not at the center of attention but rather put forward as the obvious practical corollary of intellectual and cultural liberation. Thus both Bacon and Descartes saw themselves as initiators of a new era in which human reason was to attain self-determination.[2] Reason would exercise its power in part by wresting from nature its secrets through scientific investigation. The resulting knowledge would in turn increase the power of reason and allow it to be asserted in the material realm. ". . . I am laboring," Bacon wrote, "to lay the foundation, not of any sect or doctrine, but of human utility and power."[3] And Descartes, speaking of his insights in physics, said:

> . . . they have satisfied me that it is possible to reach knowledge that will be of much utility in this life; and instead of the spec-ulative philosophy now taught in the schools we can find a prac-tical one, by which, knowing the nature and behavior of fire, water, air, stars, the heavens, and all the other bodies which surround us, as well as we now understand the different skills of our workers, we can employ these entities for all the purposes for which they are suited, and so make ourselves masters and possessors of nature.[4]

The main goal of these programs seems to be the domination of nature.[5] But we must be more precise. The desire to dominate does not just spring from a lust of power, from sheer human imperialism. It is from the start connected with the aim of liberating humanity from disease, hunger, and toil, and of enriching life with learning, art, and athletics. Descartes says further of his project just quoted: "This would not only be desirable in bringing about the invention of an infinity of devices to enable us to enjoy the fruits of agriculture and all the wealth of the earth without labor, but even more so in conserving health, the principle good and the basis of all other goods in this life."[6] And in Tommaso Campanella's *City of the Sun* of 1623, new machines and more efficient labor lead to a greatly enriched life where leisure is spent in "learning joyously, in debating, in reading, in reciting, in writing, in walking, in exercising the mind and body and with play."[7] Bacon's *New Atlantis* represents the most influential picture of the liberated and enriched life in a society based on science and technology. These visions preceded reality by more than a century.

In fact the properly scientific grounding of technology did not begin until the middle of the nineteenth century. Until then, the scientific spirit was technologically fruitful in hybrid and approximate forms, in boldness of ex-perimentation, in care of observation, and in the joys of discovery and ac-complishment. When in the second half of the eighteenth century the Industrial Revolution began to employ new machines and more efficient methods of production, it at first increased the common toil and misery.[8] But gradually in the nineteenth century and even more dramatically in the twentieth century, the citizens of the advanced industrial countries began to reap the fruits of the new order. The splendor of the promise of technology appears bright to this very day when we remember how recently misery and deprivation have been shaping human life, especially in the newly settled West of this country. In the older cemeteries of Montana one can find tombstones from the early part of this century that record the deaths of siblings two, three, or four years

old who died within a few winter weeks, weakened from poor food and shelter
and taken away by a contagious disease. Granville Stuart speaks eloquently
of how he and his brother "were famished for something to read" in their
camp on Gold Creek in Western Montana in the Winter of 1860.[9] They heard
of a trunk of books in the Bitterroot Valley. ". . . we started for those books,"
Stuart wrote, "a hundred and fifty miles away, without a house, or anybody
on the route, and with three big dangerous rivers to cross. . . ."[10] They
spent half of all the money they had on five books. " . . . but then we had
the blessed books," Stuart says, "which we packed carefully in our blankets,
and joyfully started on our return ride of a hundred and fifty miles. Many
were the happy hours we spent reading those books. . . . "[11]

The argument that the conquest of nature has liberated us from toil and
misery is strong, and it covers, of course, many more aspects of life than
have become apparent so far. Eugene Ferguson gives a more detailed view
of the matter.

> Relief became possible from the drudgery of threshing wheat,
> digging dirt, carrying water, breaking rocks, sawing wood, wash-
> ing clothes, and, indoors, spinning and weaving and sewing; many
> of the laborious tasks of living were being made easier by the
> middle of the 19th century. Relief from toil does not necessarily
> mean a better higher life; nevertheless, any attempt to get at the
> meaning of American technology must give a prominent place to
> machines that have lifted burdens from the shoulders of millions
> of individual human beings.[12]

The liberating and disburdening character of certain phases and forms of
technology is obvious and significant. Ferguson is a little more guarded but
still confident as regards the enrichment that comes from technology. He says:

> The democratic ideal of American technology shone brightly, too,
> as countless low-priced pictures, books, lamps, rugs, chairs,
> cookstoves, and musical instruments served to lift hearts and
> reduce boredom and despair. The mail-order catalogs that ap-
> peared at the end of the 19th century epitomize the democratization
> of the amenities that has marked the rise of American technology.
> Rail, if you will, at the decline of taste; but look first at the real
> alternatives of bare walls, dirt floors, and minds untouched by
> the imaginative works of writers, poets, painters, and sculptors.[13]

The promise of technology is being reiterated and reformulated in countless
ways. It dominates implicitly the one truly national debate that we have every
four years during the presidential campaigns. Occasionally the promise is
made explicit, and a *locus classicus* of such explicitness is found in the April
13, 1976, issue of the *Wall Street Journal* where United States Steel in a full-
page advertisement asked "a prominent American to speak out." The invi-

tation was issued to Jerome B. Wiesner, then president of the Massachusetts Institute of Technology. His statement begins with this paragraph:

> More than any nation in the world, the United States has the opportunity to lead mankind toward a life of greater fulfillment. This opportunity is based on benefits from our continuing advances in science and technology. It is significant that people everywhere look to the United States to provide the science and technology which they need as they, too, seek to improve their condition.[14]

These remarks are typical not only in asserting a tight connection between a life of fulfillment and technology but also in their implication that the mature technology in an advanced industrial country is identical or continuous with the liberating technology needed to improve one's condition, presumably one of illiteracy, starvation, and disease. But while Wiesner's high seriousness is appropriate to the liberation from such misery, it becomes questionable, if not macabre, when we consider the language of liberation and enrichment that daily addresses us in advertisements such as these:

> Learning languages is not easy. It takes books, classes, cassettes, and hard work. Now, however, you have a choice. You can communicate in a foreign country without speaking the language, or you can learn the language more easily thanks to a new electronic miracle.[15]

> Now you can have some of the world's best dishes. Without leaving home. Without waiting. Without cooking.[16]

> There is now a new, fun way to jog. The new IS&A Computer is a solid-state system that lets you jog in place in the comfort of your own home. . . . In just one week you'll notice the difference, feel great, have greater endurance, and you won't tire as easily.[17]

The promises that are made here regarding liberation from toil and the advancement of literacy, eating, and health seem to be the direct descendants of the promises that one would want to make to the starving people in the Third World. But beneath that semblance is a radical shift in the character of the promise of technology. That shift must lead one to doubt the soundness of the promise.

Wiesner acknowledges such difficulties. His statement continues:

> Yet the survival of our own abundant society is being doubted by many thoughtful people who share a powerful concern, a reasonable apprehension about the impact of technology.[18]

But such doubt can spring from very different concerns. One may be concerned whether technology can hope to be successful on its own terms, whether liberation in one place will not impose new burdens in another. This is Wiesner's concern when he says: ''In this enormously complex world, each

large-scale technological advance has costs, side effects often unantici-
pated.''[19] One may further doubt whether technology can make good its
promise in a socially just way, nationally and internationally, and Wiesner
alludes to this problem when he speaks of "the more equitable and humane
society which we all seek.''[20] But there can also be a much more radical doubt
about the promise of technology. One may ask not just whether the promise
can be kept but whether it is worth keeping, whether the promise is not
altogether misconceived, too vaguely given at first and harmfully disoriented
where technology is most advanced.

We return here to the peculiar way in which the promise of technology
guides and veils the shaping of the modern world. The promise presents the
character of the technological enterprise in broad and ambiguous outline, i.e.,
as the general procurement of liberty and prosperity in the principled and
effective manner that is derived from modern science. Thus it keeps our
aspirations present and out of focus at the same time. The general obtuseness
is not due primarily to the program of technology but arises from its execution.
And at least part of the reason why the implementation of the promise of
technology has become so clouded lies in the character of its development.
As the preceding discussions and illustrations have suggested, the initial
genuine feats of liberation appear to be continuous with the procurement of
frivolous comfort. Thus the history of modern technology takes an ironical
turn. We can shed light on the force and the consequences of the irony of
technology by first delineating the pattern of technology more sharply and by
showing then how the pattern has informed our understanding of the world
and the world itself. This is the task of the following chapters.

But first I want to consider briefly one plausible way in which one might
hope to advance a clear understanding of technology. This is to raise the
historical question and to ask: What is the origin (the promise of) technology?
Where and how did it first arise? What were the various stages of articulation?
We have given some fragmentary answers in this chapter with regard to the
beginning of the modern era, and a few more details will be filled in when
we turn to the relation of liberal democratic and Marxist theories to technology.
But for two reasons these questions must remain essentially unanswered. The
first is the enormity of the task, forbidding even if restricted to the philosophical dimension.[21] The second appears from a brief glance at the most
ambitious attempt to do justice to the philosophical-historical task. Martin
Heidegger has interpreted the history of the Occident as the rise of metaphysics
which culminates in technology.[22] He has tried to show how the profound
vision of the world that the pre-Socratic thinkers had articulated came to be
restricted to the foreground of things and projects in the philosophy of Plato
and Aristotle. The ground on which everything rests and the light in which
everything appears moved into oblivion. Heidegger traces this movement
through the stages of thought that were advanced by Descartes, Leibniz, Kant,
Hegel, and Nietzsche. In Nietzsche's will to power Heidegger sees the final

and extreme attempt on the part of Western humanity to establish itself absolutely, i.e., independent of any ground or illumination that would be other and greater than human existence. Modern technology, then, is just the enactment of the final stage of metaphysics as it is prefigured in Nietzsche.

Heidegger's project is beset with external problems. His view of the history of Western thought has been challenged from many sides. But there are equally severe problems at the center of Heidegger's thought that are unresolved. Heidegger does not tire of warning us not to think of technology as a human fabrication. The attempt to overpower everything is said to be the response to a destiny. When Heidegger talks this way, he seems to be an extreme proponent of what in Chapter 2 was called the substantive view of technology. That view of his position, however, Heidegger also calls into question by emphasizing that humans are not helpless victims but more like partners in the issue of their destiny. It now appears as though either Heidegger's position is inconsistent or our common views of freedom and determinism are unequal to the explication of Heidegger's thought. The problems that arise here, I believe, are not due to a quirk in Heidegger's approach but will occupy anyone who philosophically investigates the origin of technology and is not concerned merely to chronicle the factual stages of technological development but wants to find out how at bottom human existence is engaged in this development and how this engagement is worked out in the history of philosophy.

To come to the final point, it is not simply that these questions are enormously demanding. They have a way of diverting the attention and energy of the philosophy of technology from the task at hand: the problem of attaining a careful and resourceful vision of the crucial features and dimensions of our world and of our place in it. A philosophical inquiry of the origin and development of technology is to set the stage for this task, but setting the stage becomes so difficult and controversial a project that the curtain never gets raised. I do not want to dismiss the historical task. But I think that to get on with the systematic contemporary problem we can fruitfully bracket the historical dimension.[23] To bracket is not to erase. We can with frequent backward glances analyze the character of today's technological world. Then it becomes a question in its own right of how this analysis is to be related to the history of technology. At any rate, what needs to be done is to carry out the analysis carefully and in detail.

9   The Device Paradigm

We must now provide an explicit account of the pattern or paradigm of technology. I begin with two clear cases and analyze them in an intuitive way to bring out the major features of the paradigm. And I attempt to raise those features into sharper relief against the sketch of a pretechnological setting and through the consideration of objections that may be advanced against the distinctiveness of the pattern.

Technology, as we have seen, promises to bring the forces of nature and culture under control, to liberate us from misery and toil, and to enrich our lives. To speak of technology making promises suggests a substantive view of technology and is misleading. But the parlance is convenient and can always be reconstructed to mean that implied in the technological mode of taking up with the world there is a promise that this approach to reality will, by way of the domination of nature, yield liberation and enrichment. Who issues the promise to whom is a question of political responsibility; and who the beneficiaries of the promise are is a question of social justice. These questions are taken up in later chapters. What we must answer first is the question of how the promise of liberty and prosperity was specified and given a definite pattern of implementation.

As a first step let us note that the notions of liberation and enrichment are joined in that of availability. Goods that are available to us enrich our lives and, if they are technologically available, they do so without imposing burdens on us. Something is available in this sense if it has been rendered instantaneous, ubiquitous, safe, and easy.[1] Warmth, e.g., is now available. We get a first glimpse of the distinctiveness of availability when we remind ourselves that warmth was not available, e.g., in Montana a hundred years ago. It was not instantaneous because in the morning a fire first had to be built in the stove or the fireplace. And before it could be built, trees had to be felled, logs had to be sawed and split, the wood had to be hauled and stacked. Warmth was not ubiquitous because some rooms remained unheated, and none was heated evenly. The coaches and sleighs were not heated, nor were the boardwalks or all of the shops and stores. It was not entirely safe because one could get burned or set the house on fire. It was not easy because work, some skills, and attention were constantly required to build and sustain a fire.

Such observations, however, are not sufficient to establish the distinctiveness of availability. In the common view, technological progress is seen as a more or less gradual and straightforward succession of lesser by better implements.[2] The wood-burning stove yields to the coal-fired central plant with heat distribution by convection, which in turn gives way to a plant fueled by natural gas and heating through forced air, and so on.[3] To bring the distinctiveness of availability into relief we must turn to the distinction between things and devices. A thing, in the sense in which I want to use the word here, is inseparable from its context, namely, its world, and from our commerce with the thing and its world, namely, engagement. The experience of a thing is always and also a bodily and social engagement with the thing's world. In calling forth a manifold engagement, a thing necessarily provides more than one commodity. Thus a stove used to furnish more than mere warmth. It was a *focus*, a hearth, a place that gathered the work and leisure of a family and gave the house a center. Its coldness marked the morning, and the spreading of its warmth the beginning of the day. It assigned to the different family members tasks that defined their place in the household. The mother built the fire, the children kept the firebox filled, and the father cut the firewood. It provided for the entire family a regular and bodily engagement with the rhythm of the seasons that was woven together of the threat of cold and the solace of warmth, the smell of wood smoke, the exertion of sawing and of carrying, the teaching of skills, and the fidelity to daily tasks. These features of physical engagement and of family relations are only first indications of the full dimensions of a thing's world. Physical engagement is not simply physical contact but the experience of the world through the manifold sensibility of the body. That sensibility is sharpened and strengthened in skill. Skill is intensive and refined world engagement. Skill, in turn, is bound up with social engagement. It molds the person and gives the person character.[4] Limitations of skill confine any one person's primary engagement with the world to a small area. With the other areas one is mediately engaged through one's acquaintance with the characteristic demeanor and habits of the practitioners of the other skills. That acquaintance is importantly enriched through one's use of their products and the observation of their working. Work again is only one example of the social context that sustains and comes to be focused in a thing. If we broaden our focus to include other practices, we can see similar social contexts in entertainment, in meals, in the celebration of the great events of birth, marriage, and death. And in these wider horizons of social engagement we can see how the cultural and natural dimensions of the world open up.

We have now sketched a background against which we can outline a specific notion of the device. We have seen that a thing such as a fireplace provides warmth, but it inevitably provides those many other elements that compose the world of the fireplace. We are inclined to think of these additional elements as burdensome, and they were undoubtedly often so experienced. A device such as a central heating plant procures mere warmth and disburdens us of all other elements. These are taken over by the machinery of the device. The machinery makes no demands on our skill, strength, or attention, and it is less demanding the less it makes its presence felt. In the progress of technology, the machinery of a device has therefore a tendency to become concealed or to shrink. Of all the physical properties of a device, those alone are crucial and prominent which constitute the commodity that the device procures. Informally speaking, the commodity of a device is "what a device is there for." In the case of a central heating plant it is warmth, with a telephone it is communication, a car provides transportation, frozen food makes up a meal, a stereo set furnishes music. "Commodity" for the time being is to be taken flexibly. The emphasis lies on the commodious way in which devices make goods and services available. There are at first unavoidable ambiguities in the notion of the device and the commodity; they can gradually be resolved through substantive analyses and methodological reflections.[5] Tentatively, then, those aspects or properties of a device that provide the answer to "What is the device for?" constitute its commodity, and they remain relatively fixed. The other properties are changeable and are changed, normally on the basis of scientific insight and engineering ingenuity, to make the commodity still more available. Hence every device has functional equivalents, and equivalent devices may be physically and structurally very dissimilar from one another.

The development of television provides an illustration of these points. The bulky machinery of the first sets was obtrusive in relation to the commodity it procured, namely, the moving two-dimensional picture which appeared in fuzzy black and white on a screen with the size and shape of a bull's-eye. Gradually the screens became larger, more rectangular; the picture became sharper and eventually colored. The sets became relatively smaller and less conspicuous in their machinery. And this development continues and has its limit in match-box-sized sets which provide arbitrarily large and most finely grained moving and colored pictures. The example also shows how radical changes in the machinery amounted to continuous improvements of the function as tubes gave way to transistors and these yielded to silicon chips. Cables and satellites were introduced as communication links. Pictures could be had in recorded rather than transmitted form, and recordings can be had on tapes or discs. These considerations in turn show how the technical development of a device increases availability. Increasingly, video programs can be seen nearly everywhere—in bars, cars, in every room of a home. Every conceivable film can be had. A program broadcast at an inconvenient time can be recorded and played later. The constraints of time and place are more and more dissolved. It is an instructive exercise to see how in the implements that surround us daily the machinery becomes less conspicuous, the function more prominent, how radical technical changes in the machinery are but degrees of advancement in the commodity, and how the availability of the commodities increases all the while.

The distinction in the device between its machinery and its function is a specific instance of the means-ends distinction. In agreement with the general distinction, the machinery or the means is subservient to and validated by the function or the end. The technological distinction of means and ends differs from the general notion in two respects. In the general case, it is very questionable how clearly and radically means and ends can be distinguished without doing violence to the phenomena.[6] In the case of the technological device, however, the machinery can be changed radically without threat to the identity and familiarity of the function of the device. No one is confused when one is invited to replace one's watch, powered by a spring, regulated by a balance wheel, displaying time with a dial and pointers, with a watch that is powered electrically, is regulated by a quartz crystal, and displays time digitally. This concomitance of radical variability of means and relative stability of ends is the first distinguishing feature. The second, closely tied to the first, is the concealment and unfamiliarity of the means and the simultaneous prominence and availability of the ends.[7]

The concealment of the machinery and the disburdening character of the device go hand in hand. If the machinery were forcefully present, it would eo ipso make claims on our faculties. If claims are felt to be onerous and are therefore removed, then so is the machinery. A commodity is truly available when it can be enjoyed as a mere end, unencumbered by means. It must be noted that the disburdenment resting on a feudal household is ever incomplete. The lord and the lady must always reckon with the moods, the insubordination, and the frailty of the servants.[8] The device provides social disburdenment, i.e., anonymity. The absence of the master-servant relation is of course only one instance of social anonymity. The starkness of social anonymity in the technological universe can be gauged only against a picture of the social relations in a world of things. Such a picture will also show that social anonymity necessarily shades off into one of nature, culture, and history.

Since the transformative power of technology is very uneven chronologically, settings that approached the character of a world of things still prevailed at the beginning of this century. Here it pays to look closely, to see in one case and in detail how nature and culture were interwoven and how this texture was rent by the advance of technology and overtaken by anonymity. The case I want to consider is that of a wheelwright's shop just prior to its dissolution. A moving account has been given by George Sturt, the last in a succession of wheelwrights.

Since the web of relations is so tight and manifold, it is difficult to present it in an abstract and summary way. But let us begin with those aspects in which the relation of humans to nature is singled out. The experience of cultivating the land is still alive at this time in England, and Sturt speaks repeatedly of "the age-old effort of colonizing England."[9] But he does not understand colonizing as the domination of nature, i.e., as conquering and subduing, but as an adaption of people to the land, and he paraphrases it as the "age-long effort of Englishmen to get themselves close and ever closer into England."[10] As people adjust to the land, the land discloses itself to the people. There is "a close relationship between the tree-clad country-side and the English who dwelt there." Sturt speaks of "the affection and the reverence bred of this."[11] But it is impossible to abstract a relationship in this pretechnological setting that obtains merely between human beings and nature. What takes the wheelwright into "sunny woodland solitudes," "into winter woods or along leafless hedgerows," and "across wet water-meadows in February" is the search for timber.[12] But "timber was far from being a prey, a helpless victim, to a machine," Sturt says, and continues: "Rather it would lend its subtle virtues to the man who knew how to humor it: with him, as with an understanding friend, it would co-operate."[13] This is a relationship not of domination but of mastery. If the wheelwright, Sturt says elsewhere, "was really master of his timber, if he knew what he had already got in stock and also what was likely to be wanted in years to come, he kept a watch always for timber with special curve, suitable for hames, or shaft-braces, or waggon-heads, or hounds, or tailboard rails, or whatever else the tree-shape might suggest.''[14] Such respectful working with nature is not just as close to nature as conservation; it opens up dimensions that remain otherwise closed. ''Under the plane (it is little used now),'' Sturt says, ''or under the axe (if it is all but obsolete) timber disclosed qualities hardly to be found otherwise.''[15] And elsewhere he says:

> With the wedges cleaving down between the clinging fibres—as he let out the wood-scent, listened to the tearing splitting sounds—the workman found his way into a part of our environment—felt the laws of woodland vitality—not otherwise visited or suspected.[16]

But again the intimacy of the wheelwright with nature did not stop with the materials but embraced his entire world by way of the needs of his customers. Sturt puts it this way:

> And so we got curiously intimate with the peculiar needs of the neighbourhood. In farm-waggon or dung-cart, barley-roller, plough, water-barrel or what not, the dimensions we chose, the curves we followed (and almost every piece of timber was curved) were imposed upon us by the nature of the soil in this or that farm, the gradient of this or that hill, the temper of this or that customer or his choice perhaps in horseflesh.[17]

And similarly he says in another place:

> The field, the farm-yard, the roads and hills, the stress of weather, the strength and shape of horses, the lifting power of men, all were factors which had determined in the old villages how the farm tackle must be made, of what timber and shape and of what dimensions, often to the sixteenth of an inch.[18]

This web of relations had, finally, its social aspects. It contained different guilds or groups, but no classes, i.e., divisions of people whose political and especially economic interests were opposed to one another.[19] The different groups had their character from their work and their relation to nature. In his search for timber, the wheelwright found not only trees but also ''country men of a shy type, good to meet.''[20] And back at his shop he was met by the carters, ''a whole country-side of strong and good-tempered Englishmen. With the timber and the horses they seemed to bring the lonely woodlands, the far-off roads into the little town.''[21] The social network was sustained by fidelity, by wagons that were built to last a lifetime and that were carefully repaired when they had broken down.[22] Prices were charged by tradition and not by calculation of costs and profits.[23] The tie between employer and em-

ployed was one of "kindly feeling" as Sturt puts it, a relation of resourcefulness and trust.[24]

Sturt's account is remarkable not only for its portrayal of the strength and
character of a pretechnological world of things. It is also painfully aware of
the rise of technology and the destruction of the pretechnological setting. This
process too becomes visible at the reference points of nature, materials, and
social relations. Accelerated by the demands of the First World War, a "sort
of greedy prostitution desecrated the ancient woods. . . . I resented it," Sturt
says, "resented seeing the fair timber callously felled at the wrong time of
year, cut too soon, not 'seasoned' at all."[25] The conquest of nature is not
confined to the treatment of the forests but moves into the wheelwright's shop
too, replacing skill with mechanical power which can "drive, with relentless
unintelligence, through every resistance."[26] As said before, domination is not
an end in itself but serves to secure more radically the products of labor.
Thus, as Sturt points out, "work was growing less interesting to the workman,
although far more sure in its results."[27] And domination provides more income
for the purchase of commodities, but at the same time it disengages the worker
from the world. This is Sturt's experience in the following passage:

> Of course wages are higher—many a workman to-day receives a
> larger income than I was able to get as "profit" when I was an
> employer. But no higher wage, no income, will buy for men that
> satisfaction which of old—until machinery made drudges of
> them—streamed into their muscles all day long from close contact
> with iron, timber, clay, wind and wave, horse-strength.[28]

These transformations finally touched the social relations as well. "'The
Men,'" Sturt says of his employees, "though still my friends, as I fancied,
became machine 'hands.'"[29] The loss of skill went hand in hand with the
loss of rustic village life, and the change in the living situation upset the old
social relations. Sturt, speaking of the changes in the life of one wheelwright
in particular, says:

> I was not in touch, through him, with the quiet dignified country
> life of England and I was more of a capitalist. Each of us had
> slipped a little nearer to the ignominious class division of these
> present times—I to the employer's side, he to the disregarded
> workman's.[30]

Sturt had an uncanny sense for the transformative power that changed the
face of his world. He recognized its concealment, the semblance, i.e., as
though technology were only a more efficient way of doing what had been
done throughout the ages.[31] And he recognized its radical novelty, the fact
that technology upsets the tradition from the ground up. The technological
changes forced him to introduce modern machines and take in a partner who
could supervise the new ways of working. "Neither my partner nor myself,"

he says in retrospect, "realised at all that a new world (newer than ever America was to the Pilgrim Fathers) had begun even then to form all around us."[32] This returns us to the difficulty, discussed in Chapter 8, of bringing the distinctive features of this "new world" into relief. As was argued above, these features become visible when we learn to see how the presence of things is replaced with the availability of commodities and how availability is procured through devices. Devices, that was the claim, dissolve the coherent and engaging character of the pretechnological world of things. In a device, the relatedness of the world is replaced by a machinery, but the machinery is concealed, and the commodities, which are made available by a device, are enjoyed without the encumbrance of or the engagement with a context.

But this analysis of the distinctiveness of the device is still deficient, and the deficiency can be brought into relief through two objections. Is not, one may ask, the concealment of the machinery and the lack of engagement with our world due to widespread scientific, economic, and technical illiteracy?[33] And quite apart from one's level of education, is not everyone in his or her work directly and explicitly engaged with the machinery of devices?

We can approach the first point through one of its companion phenomena, people's alleged unwillingness and inability to maintain and repair technological devices.[34] How well-founded is this allegation? One way in which commodities are made available is that of making them discardable. It is not just unnecessary but impossible to maintain and repair paper napkins, cans, Bic ball points or any of the other one-way or one-time devices. Another way to availability is that of making products carefree. Stainless steel tableware requires no polishing, plastic dishes need not be handled carefully. In other cases maintenance and repair become impossible because of the sophistication of the product. Microcomputers are becoming increasingly common and influential as devices that free us of the tasks of allocation, record keeping, and control. The theories and technical processes that underlie the production of microcircuits are too complicated and too much in flux to be known in detail by more than a handful of people. And the microcircuits themselves are realized at a functional level so minute and dense that it does not permit the intrusions necessary for repairs even if structure and functions are fully understood.[35] Finally, microcomputers are being used more and more widely because they are becoming "friendly," i.e., easy to operate and understand.[36] But such "friendliness" is just the mark of how wide the gap has become between the function accessible to everyone and the machinery known by nearly no one. And not only lay people are confined to the side of ignorance of this gap, but so are many, perhaps most, of the professional programmers.[37]

Still, education in engineering and in the natural and social sciences would make much of the machinery, i.e., of the context, of technological devices, perspicuous. But even if such education were to become more common, the context of functions and commodities would remain different from the world of things for two reasons. First, the presence of that context would remain entirely cerebral since it increasingly resists, as we have seen, appropriation through care, repair, the exercise of skill, and bodily engagement. Second, the context would remain anonymous in the senses indicated above. The machinery of a device does not of itself disclose the skill and character of the inventor and producer; it does not reveal a region and its particular orientation within nature and culture. In sum, the machinery of devices, unlike the context of things, is either entirely occluded or only cerebrally and anonymously present. It is in this sense necessarily unfamiliar.

The function of the device, on the other hand, and the commodity it provides are available and enjoyed in consumption. The peculiar presence of the end of the device is made possible by means of the device and its concealment. Everyone understands that the former rests on the latter, and everyone understands as well that the enjoyment of ends requires some kind of attention to the means. Only in magic are ends literally independent of means. The inevitable explicit concern with the machinery takes place in labor. But labor does not in general lift the veil of unfamiliarity from the machinery of devices. The labor process is itself transformed according to the paradigm of the device. This is a thesis that will be worked out in Chapter 17.

10   The Foreground of Technology

In the preceding chapter we have obtained a more sharply outlined picture of the device paradigm. But the picture is partial and limited as well. It has shown us how the pattern is instantiated here and there and in detail. What about the global effect of the paradigm? That question has several aspects. Of these I first want to consider the way in which the employment of technological devices has resulted in an ensemble of commodities. This is a privileged dimension of the universe of technology. Commodities and their consumption constitute the professed goal of the technological enterprise. I use the term ''foreground'' to point up this peculiar side of technology and also to pinpoint a systematic difficulty that besets any attempt to offer a clear view of normal technological reality. The foreground of technology normally comes closest to the fore under such headings as leisure, consumption, or the standard of living. Though these topics constitute the spoken or unspoken concern of most of our public debates, they fail to keep the foreground of our lives in focus. The discussions inevitably drift into the political and economic background. There are confident and forceful public discussions on armament and national security, but very little is said publicly about the kind of life that we typically lead within the horizon of security. Great attention and respect are paid in the business sections of newspapers to the people who direct transportation systems and chemical concerns. But these papers rarely raise the question whether or why so many people should so often want to move from here to there or what kind of world is finally composed by all the plastics, drugs, and chemicals. There are some scholarly descriptions and critiques of the technological foreground of our lives, but we will be in a better position to appraise them after we have delineated that foreground in terms of the device paradigm.

The device paradigm does not just help us somehow to discover the foreground; the very formulation of the paradigm amounts to a sharp delineation of the foreground from the background, of the commodity a device procures from the machinery on which the function of a device rests. How commodities coalesce into a distinctive foreground I want to show in two steps. First I want to illustrate more clearly how pervasively and subtly the device paradigm has been at work in dividing traditional things into commodities and machineries. Then I take up the question of the way the foreground comes to our attention purely and fully.

The distinction between machinery and commodity is most easily made in regard to technological machines. But things of nature and culture and social relations too are being transformed according to the pattern of the device. Wine can serve as an example. In this instance, the division between machinery and commodity is to be found not only between the implements that are used to produce wine and the product, namely, wine. There is rather a fissure running through wine itself. It is turned into a device with a machinery and a commodity. Let us follow some observations that have been made by Judson Gooding.[1] Putting his points in terms of the device paradigm, we can say that the machinery of wine consists in its chemical constituents, and the function of this machinery is seen as procuring a commodity, an aggregate of certain tastes and colors. The taste is to be pleasantly grapey, smooth, light, fruity, and soft. In visual appearance the wine should be clean, clear, limpid, and free of sediments. This is what technologically transformed wine provides. It also provides it much more assuredly than did traditional wine, i.e., with less risk of unpleasant and pleasant surprises. Further, it is more commodious in that is is less fatiguing to drink and more easily afforded. Even its foreign name is made easy to pronounce. As wine becomes a device, the commodity it procures becomes severed from its context, or, speaking more precisely, the world that is opened up in wine as a thing is closed off when it becomes machinery and commodity. Technological wine no longer bespeaks the peculiar weather of the year in which it grew since technology is at pains to provide assured, i.e., uniform, quality. It no longer speaks of a particular place since it is a blend of raw materials from different places. All this holds not only of the common American wines but also of the middle-range quality wines imported from France of which Gooding speaks. It is their development from which the illustrations above are drawn.

The example of wine also allows us to see that the emergence of a technological foreground is, in relation to science, a development in its own right. Modern science, to be sure, is a necessary factor in the advancement of technology. The illustration of the paradigm in terms of television, given earlier, makes the role of science quite plain, too plain in fact. Without important advances in the scientific understanding of electronics in general and of semiconductors in particular, the progress of television would have been impossible. The obvious necessity of scientific insight may, however, conceal the insufficiency of science for the advancement of the device paradigm. In the case of wine, too, technological transformation requires scientific insight into the effects of chemical substances and physical processes on the taste and visual appearance of wine. But it is not as though there were a division with science and the technological foreground on the one side, and the nostalgia for "the majestic, more solid wines that were long considered the kings of the cellar" on the other.[2] For we can tell scientifically what distinguishes a majestic and solid wine from a light and fruity one; we know which of the 170-odd constituents of traditional wine have been lost, just how they got lost, and how constituents, thought to be desirable in technological wine, were increased or introduced. Scientific insight renders phenomena perspicuous and opens up possibilities. But a pattern of procedure is required to act on that insight and to take advantage of the possibilities; the device paradigm constitutes the pattern.

Toward the end of his observations, Gooding raises "the key philosophical question of whether the public's taste has changed and has forced winemakers to change with it, or whether winemaking has changed and forced wine drinkers to follow."[3] Such a question, as argued in Chapter 9, will open up philosophical insights if it is taken as a request for the determination not so much of the origin of this development as of the nature of the change at issue. What must be noted first then is that the development that rightly troubles Gooding is not a change of taste from one thing to another but the switch from a taste for things to one for commodities. One can taste or experience mere warmth only when, through a central heating plant, warmth has been stripped of its pretechnological interwovenness with culture, nature, and community and has been secured merely, i.e., as a commodity. In leisure and consumption, the origin and context of commodities is taken over and concealed in the technological machinery. Commodities are available individually, and we take them up without invoking or enacting a context. The change of taste that Gooding notes is the emergence of the characteristic way in which one moves in the foreground of technology. Gooding himself registers this wider implication. "For better or for worse," he says, "the changes in the world of wine seem to coincide strikingly with changes in the way people live, and in their tastes." He finds three major features in these changes: mobility, standardization, and "a general shift toward lightness."[4] These are clearly traits of a commerce with reality where the rootedness in the depth of things, i.e., in the irreplaceable context of time and place, has been dissolved.

But before we consider more fully the question how citizens in the technological society appropriate the characteristic foreground of their lives, we must ask how and where that foreground comes most clearly into view. Cartoons at times act as a divining rod in alerting us to phenomena that are close to the surface though not yet generally and readily visible. There is a cartoon where a middle-aged woman stands in front of a chest of frozen dinners in a supermarket, holding up two packages, looking a little puzzled; and she says to her husband:

> For the big day, Harv, which do you want? The traditional American Christmas turkey dinner with mashed potatoes, giblet gravy, oyster dressing, cranberry sauce and tiny green peas or the old English Christmas goose dinner with chestnut stuffing, boiled potatoes, brussels sprout and plum pudding?[5]

Harvey looks skeptical and a bit morose. The world of bountiful harvests, careful preparations, and festive meals has become a faint and ironical echo. Mabel is asking Harvey whether on December 25th he would rather consume this aggregate of commodities or that. To consume is to use up an isolated entity without preparation, resonance, and consequence.[6] What half dawns on Mabel and Harvey is the equivocation in calling the content of an aluminum package a "traditional American Christmas turkey dinner." The content, even when warmed and served, is a sharply reduced aspect of the once full-bodied affair.

To engage us, the vision of a cartoon must remain within hailing distance of reality. If the scene of the cartoon above were in color and took up an entire page, if Mabel were young, slim, and pretty, and her speech just a little more cheerful, no further changes would be needed for a standard promotion of technological food. There is in fact an advertisement headlined: "We've just brought a world of good eating a lot closer." That world consists of

> Beef Chop Suey with Rice
> Swedish Meatballs in Gravy with Parsley Noodles
> Linguini with Clam Sauce
> Chicken Paprikash with Egg Noodles
> Chicken Cacciatore with Spaghetti
> Beef Teriyaki with Rice and Vegetables.[7]

It is presented in color on two full pages, each dish shown on a distinctive plate and table or tablecloth, suggesting the richness and variety of this "world of good eating." But this world of course has no depth and context. We are not invited to enter rural Sweden or teeming Shanghai. These dishes are made available to us "in speedy cooking pouches, so they're ready after just 15 minutes in boiling water."

It is no accident that one is led to advertising in delineating the foreground of technology. In advertising, the foreground comes most sharply and prominently into focus. It receives equal time, space, and attention with the political and economic discussions of the background of technology. There is an impartial alternation of news, commentary, and advertisement in the communications media. Daniel J. Boorstin recognizes its central role in a technological society. He puts it this way:

> If we consider democracy not just as a political system, but as a set of institutions which do aim to make everything available to everybody, it would not be an overstatement to describe advertising as the characteristic rhetoric of democracy.[8]

The availability of commodities comes to the fore in advertising. But the relation between availability and advertising requires further analysis. It is certain that advertising serves limited utilitarian purposes such as supplying information and increasing sales. But this is a partial explanation of the phenomenon since the informative content of advertisements is low and the competitive struggle in advertising should lead to a standoff.[9] Thus it has been argued that advertising has a broader and more fundamental function in a technological society. One argument is to the effect that advertising as a whole generates the required demand for consumer goods. Required by whom? For Stuart Ewen it is profit-seeking capitalism at the stage of mass production. To perpetuate its reign, so Ewen argues implicitly but clearly, the capitalist class needs consumers, and it consciously sets out to reeducate the often unwilling working class toward consumptive habits.[10] For John Kenneth Galbraith the class at the leading edge of the transformation of society is larger and more complex, comprising business executives, engineers, research scientists, and others, collectively called "the technostructure." The technostructure is at pains to secure its position nationally and globally, and the management of demand by advertising is a vital part of this enterprise.[11] The legitimation of technology is the topic of a later chapter. By way of anticipation, let me say that Galbraith seems nearer to the mark than Ewen. But we must get closer yet. The consumer culture, at bottom, is not the effect of advertising at all. Universal consumption of commodities is the fulfillment of the promise of technology. Consumption by all was anticipated as soon as that promise was formulated. It was clearly announced in the middle of the nineteenth century. The tie that Boorstin sees between democracy and consumption has deep historical roots.[12]

Advertising does not create the consumer culture but regulates it. And it does more than that. It brings it to the fore and makes it palpable. Boorstin calls advertisement a rhetoric. That term carries connotations of superficiality. Rhetorical language contrasts with the discourse of inquiry, explanation, and justification. Thus rhetoric is a fitting vocable. The commodities of technology have surface character. They are in fact mere and opaque surfaces which permit no insight into their substructure, i.e., their machinery. Advertising remains true to this dimension and refrains by and large from breaking into the technologial background and from presenting analyses and arguments which presuppose and manifest expertise. Stephen Kline and William Leiss have very nearly captured the peculiar ontological status of commodities as it emerges in advertising. They say:

> . . . with the increasing implicitness and ambiguity in advertising imagery, the commodity seems to become a "projective field" in which human states of feeling achievable in consumption are fluidly superimposed upon the non-human, physical-sensory aspects of the commodity. Stretching the metaphor for a moment, the mask of the fetishized commodity, having incorporated the abstract qualities of promised human satisfaction, has more recently still become mirrorlike, reflecting back the vague and distorted images of well-being to be achieved in consumption.[13]

In two regards the account needs to be taken further. First, commodities do not merely seem to be projective fields, wearing mirrorlike masks; they are nothing but opaque surfaces, i.e., narrowly defined aspects of what used to be things of depth. Therefore the picture of commodities, as presented in advertising, heightens rather than distorts their character. Accordingly, the devices on which the commodities rest do not just allow us to take them as commodity bearers; they force us to take them as such and thereby conceal themselves, leaving us with the commodities. It is not the case that a stereo set may be interpreted as a music generator but could also be taken as an embodiment of Japanese virtues or as a display of delicately contaminated silicates. Of the indefinitely many "non-human, physical-sensory aspects" that stereo equipment displays, a very narrow and well-defined set counts as the commodity, namely, the sounds that it emits. Kline and Leiss point out that stereo sets belong to a small class of commodities where some background information is still included in advertisements.[14] And correspondingly, there is some background awareness in the operation of stereo equipment. But even here that awareness is rudimentary and trails off quickly. In sum, what makes something a commodity is not interpretation or projection (a psychological matter) but its structure and construction (an ontological matter). To be sure, the production and use of devices in turn rest on an agreement and understanding about the dominant way of taking up with reality. Thus the ontological matter may have a social foundation. But even granting that, devices, commodities, and their characteristics are so firmly and implicitly understood that the daily commerce with commodities requires nothing like a case-by-case interpretation or projection of feelings.

In spite of the firmness of this understanding, Kline and Leiss are correct, I believe, in sensing an ambiguity and fluidity in our dealings with commodities.[15] This brings us to the second point of clarification. A term is ambiguous, as remarked before, if it conveys a plurality of senses. Every term is ambiguous in isolation, but normally ambiguity is resolved in context. This linguistic point can be generalized. A sound, a patch of color, a taste in one's mouth mean something in the context of one's world. If that background is distorted or impoverished, the meaning of something becomes open to question. In a setting where all I see is a patch of blue, I cannot tell what it means. Is it a piece of sky, a velvet curtain, a bit of deep water, or a projection on a screen? In the case of a commodity, as we have seen, the background is by design taken over and hidden by the machinery of a device. Kline and Leiss allude to this state of affairs. They call it "the obfuscation not only of the social labour 'hidden' in the product, but of the material resources as well."[16] Commodities are contextless in their various ways and thus ambiguous. But this ambiguity is, within the framework of technology, a positive trait. It is a mark of the freely disposable character of commodities, of the absence of commitments a context would exact, and of the possibility of combining commodities with few restraints. The ambiguity and fluidity are contained within a common understanding of technology and are therefore well handled by the consumer. Elsewhere Leiss had talked of "the individuals who search for the satisfaction of their needs in the jungle of commodities."[17] But what evidence is there that people are seriously and manifestly disoriented or lost in the consumer culture?

Kline and Leiss point out that advertisements place commodities in settings that have typical formats.[18] These settings are not contexts in the traditional sense but collages of different commodities. A typical example is the automobile advertisement that presents "the man who does everything." Leaning on his car in front of his garage, he is surrounded by a skateboard, hang glider, surfboard, waterski, motorboat, snow skis, dirt bikes, bicycles, snowmobile, backpack, and all the implements required for a suburban lawn.[19] In such pictures, the foreground of technology is stylized in vague allusions to traditional stations of life, e.g., that of the country squire. There are others such as the man of the world, the caring housewife, the *jeunesse dorrée*, the rugged Westerner. Alvin Toffler, in his breathless way, has outlined the great variety of life-styles that are being assembled.[20] The scaffold from which these life-styles are suspended is part tradition and part technology. Many of the assemblages of commodities are still arranged and located by tradition. The cities are in the places that pretechnological people had found favorable. Suburban homes mimic villas, mansions, or ranches. But the traditional settings are affected by what may be called the structures or the middle ground of technology which serve the storage and transportation of commodities. Thus there arise supermarkets, high-rise buildings, expressway systems, and airports. The skeleton of the middle ground in many cases displaces traditional settings and assigns new places to the foreground.

In the interplay of tradition and technology, the latter now has the upper hand. Tradition is being reduced in part to machinery where it provides the substructure for the overlay of commodities and consumption. So it is with the traditional family and with historical downtown centers that are converted into shopping and amusement malls. In part, tradition is used as a resource, i.e., as raw material that lends some of its shapes, colors, and tasks to commodities equivocally called by a traditional name. "Grande Marque Red Bordeaux" and "Chicken Paprikash with Egg Noodles" are examples.[21] But since the absorption of the traditional culture by technology has not been total, we are bound to our world by some traditional ties and not merely by those of consumption. Moreover, many people move daily into and out of the background of technology in labor, administration, and research. Our relations to the technological universe are complex. In contrast, the universe of advertising is entirely one of commodities and consumption. It distills the foreground of technology ideally and thus presents the technical and distinctive side of our age. In this way it has superseded art as the archetypical presentation of what the epoch is about. In advertising, the promise of technology is presented both purely and concretely and hence most attractively. Problems and threats enter only as a background to set off the blessings of technology.[22] Thus we find ourselves archetypically defined in advertisements. They provide a stabilizing and orienting force in the complexity of the still-developing technological society.

This brings us to the final point in the discussion of the foreground of technology. It concerns the ways in which we are coming to terms with the universe of commodities. How evident and certain does the meaning of the foreground appear to us? If there is a deep-seated ambiguity, it regards not the multiplicity of senses within the foreground of technology but the sense of the foreground itself. Ambiguity is mirrored and recognizable in ambivalence. And there are two major ways in which we are ambivalent about the foreground of technology. The first concerns the question: How far can we push the attenuation of our experiences?[23] Or to explicate the problem: How thin and disembodied, i.e., superficial, can commodities become before the tie is ruptured that connects them with the things from which they are derived and from which their significance continues to draw nourishment? Simulated environments and experiences have received much attention, but most of it is focused on technical feasibility and economic efficiency.[24] There is great and often implicit confidence about a central and defensible equivalence of real and simulated experiences. The more striking illustrations are drawn from experimental and future settings, and the extreme case is the experience that is induced by direct manipulation of the brain. It is extreme because here the commodity has reached its ultimate attenuation; it is no longer even a physical aspect of a thing or event, however thin and partial. It is equivalent to the thing only in its effect on the brain. What is outwardly present is the machinery of the stimulation device only; the commodity has become one with the brain. But it seems that at the point of greatest outward dissimilarity between the thing and the device, there is also the possibility of a perfect match of the effects of thing and device. It is merely a matter of scientific and technical sophistication, so it seems, to produce by electronic stimulation, for instance, an experience of the wilderness which has all the intensity and nuances of the real experience.

I believe that the structure of the brain is so minutely organized that direct stimulation, i.e., stimulation that bypasses the sense organs, will of necessity be crude and hence global and relatively inarticulate and disorganized. This is of course an empirical matter. What is philosophically remarkable and evident even now is that there is a widespread and easy acceptance of equivalence between commodities and things even where the experiential differences are palpable. People who have traveled through Glacier Park in an air-conditioned motor home, listening to soft background music and having a cup of coffee, would probably answer affirmatively and without qualification when asked if they knew the park, had been in the park, or had been through the park. Such people have not felt the wind of the mountains, have not smelled the pines, have not heard the red-tailed hawk, have not sensed the slopes in their legs and lungs, have not experienced the cycle of day and night in the wilderness. The experience has not been richer than one gained from a well-made film viewed in suburban Chicago.

There are countless other cases that show how far we have gone in settling for and in the foreground. But precisely when we consider cases of the greatest ease with the foreground, we are also reminded of a growing uneasiness with it and a corresponding desire to recover things in their depth. These reactions appear under such headings as voluntary simplicity, back to basics, self-care in health, running, neoconservatism, arts and crafts, and others. They will require more attention later on. The point here is to note them as evidence of one kind of ambivalence that is felt about the foreground of technology. Another kind is manifest in our estimation of the foreground relative to its background. Although the consumption of commodities is the avowed end of technology, there is something playful and slightly disreputable about life in the foreground. The playboy and the housewife spend their entire lives in the foreground, and neither is highly respected. The typical figures of technology that we look up to are engaged in the background of technology, in research, business, or politics. It seems that we are more confident of our means than of our ends.

11   Devices, Means, and Machines

We now have an intuitive grasp of the pattern of technology and of its distinctive features. We have examined clear and concrete instances of the paradigm, and we have considered one aspect of its global effect and some of the social issues bound up with that aspect. But before we pursue these broader concerns, it is desirable to give the intuitive and descriptive account of the technological pattern a measure of systematic firmness and clarity. This is the task of the present chapter and of Chapter 12, and these two will bring the explicit account of the pattern of technology to a first conclusion. I begin the task of systematic explication by considering in this chapter what competing approaches to the paradigmatic analysis of technology there are. In the next chapter I examine the methodology of paradigmatic explanation directly.

First then we should look at alternative models and perspectives that have been employed in attempts to clarify the common hopes and misgivings regarding the technological transformation of our world. The most common symbol of the powers and perils of technology has been the machine, and the most common critique of technology alleges an unhappy imbalance of technological means and ends.

Modern technology begins with the introduction of the steam engine in mines, factories, and for transportation. Early capitalism had developed organizational technologies, financial devices, division of labor, and mass production. Inventors had begun to automate water-driven milling systems. But there were inherent limits to the strength of draft animals and human beings, and to the location and availability of wind and water power. Ingenious machines had existed since Antiquity. But it was only when steam engines came on the scene as prime movers that machines became a striking and tangible power of transformation and the symbol of a new age.[1] Among the steam-driven machines, it was the locomotive on the railroad that had the strongest effect in changing the face of the land. There was awe at the speed, power, and range of the locomotive. It was welcomed as the great servant whose labors would fulfill the promise of technology.[2] It was also feared and detested because of its ugliness and its omnivorous irreverence. Thus the machine served as a focal point of the ambivalence with which the new age was greeted.[3] In the nineteenth century the terms "machinery" and "mechanism" were employed much in the same way in which we now use "technology" to characterize the modern era.

The controversy about the status of the machine from the start revolved about the means-ends distinction. Very early the critics of the machine made their point by saying that the machine had emancipated itself from the position of a servant or means to that of a master or an end. More than a century ago, Emerson put it in these lines:

Things are in the saddle,
And ride mankind.
There are two laws discrete,
Not reconciled,—
Law for man, and law for thing;
The last builds town and fleet,
But it runs wild,
And doth the man unking.[4]

Though the machine lost its preeminence as the symbol of the new age toward the middle of this century, the question of means and ends has persisted as a pivot of the critique of technology.

The first question is whether the means-ends distinction applies at all to modern production and consumption. Hannah Arendt thinks of ends as those human achievements that are firm and enduring and provide humans a secure and common dwelling place.[5] Works of art establish such a place, and the great words and deeds of political action fill it with lasting significance. To the stability of work and action there is opposed labor, the production of the necessities of life that are consumed without an enduring accomplishment. In modern technology, the production and consumption of labor grows cancerously and all but devours work and action. Although labor has escaped from privacy and attained social prominence, it has not gained stability. The question whether *within* the life of production and consumption comfort has on balance increased must be subordinated, Arendt argues, to the realization that the world of machines has begun to destroy the world of genuine ends and is unable "to offer mortals a dwelling place more permanent and more stable than themselves."[6] Arendt tries to support this central thesis through more detailed observations on machines and means. The work of *homo faber,* the artisan, is guided by an end that engages the worker and guides and organizes the ensemble of tools and materials.[7] In the case of the machine, on the other side, especially in its advanced and automated state, there is no play between means and ends. The machine is designed to yield one product, and the necessity of production also encompasses humans and forces them into its productive rhythm. Thus Arendt uses the means-ends distinction to illuminate the difference between the world of modern labor or technology on the one side, and the world of traditional work and action on the other; the fluidity and instability of the one, the firmness and security of the other. The question arises here whether the distinction as Arendt works it really serves her purpose well and whether it would not have been more fitting to an analysis of features within technology. Arendt's answer, particularly to the second part of the question, is emphatically negative:

Within the life process itself, of which laboring remains an integral part and which it never transcends, it is idle to ask questions that presuppose the category of means and end, such as whether men

live and consume in order to have strength to labor or whether
they labor in order to have the means of consumption.[8]

But surely this is said from an abstract and distant viewpoint. The testimony
of laborers clearly shows that most consider labor a necessary evil, a mere
means, and that "the means of consumption" is the end of their labor. As
will be urged in Chapter 17, it is the reduction of work to a mere means that
has led to its degradation, and it is a certain understanding of the means-ends
distinction that sanctions that degradation. Much is to be learned from Arendt's
analysis of the vulgar and disorienting aspects of technology as a system
devoted primarily to production and consumption. But I am not sure that
Arendt's notion of labor reveals them unambiguously. Technology shows its
force most disturbingly as it dissolves the tradition of cooking and the celebration of family meals, both ferial and festal. The helpful distinctions here
are not between fluidity and stability, labor and work, since both technology
and the culture of the table fall on the side of fluidity and labor in Arendt's
scheme. The first appropriate distinction is rather between disburdenment and
engagement, the disburdenment procured through convenience foods and the
engagement provided in the culture of the table; and that distinction requires
elaboration in terms of the peculiar means-ends distinction the device paradigm
embodies.

In fact most critics of the machine and technology have employed the
distinction of means from ends within and to the object of their concern.
Thomas Carlyle was among the first to use the notion of machinery for a
comprehensive critique of his time of which he says in 1829:

> It is the Age of Machinery, in every outward and inward sense
> of that word; the age which, with its whole undivided might,
> forwards, teaches and practices the great art of adapting means
> to ends.[9]

Timothy Walker who replied to Carlyle in a "Defense of Mechanical Philosophy" found it hard to see anything objectionable in the adaptation of
means to ends. "What would the writer have us do?" Walker asks. "Pursue
ends without regard to means?"[10] Carlyle's answer is implicit at best. His
statement about the Age of Machinery quoted above continues this way:
"Nothing is now done directly, or by hand; all is by rule and calculated
contrivance."[11] Elsewhere he says: "Everything has its cunningly devised
implements, its pre-established apparatus; it is not done by hand, but by
machinery."[12] The suggestion in such remarks is not that once having chosen
ends we should be indifferent about means but that we do violence to things
and events when we divide them into means and ends. The rule of instrumentality, in Langdon Winner's expression, allows us to take possession of
things and to overpower them.[13] But in the process we extinguish the life of
things and lose touch with them. Carlyle distinguishes from the mechanical
approach to things, the dynamical which considers "the primary, unmodified

forces and energies of man, the mysterious springs of Love, and Fear, and
Wonder, of Enthusiasm, Poetry, Religion, all of which have a truly vital and
infinite character. . . . ''[14]

Carlyle's essay is important because it conveys a sense of the new technological approach to reality; Carlyle is relentless in showing its all-pervasive
character:

> We may trace this tendency in all the great manifestations of our
> time; in its intellectual aspect, the studies it most favors and its
> manner of conducting them; in its practical aspects, its politics,
> arts, religion, morals; in the whole sources, and throughout the
> whole currents, of its spiritual, no less than its material activity.[15]

The new approach is already so well entrenched, however, that it resists
Carlyle's attempts at an incisive critique. Where Carlyle describes its pattern
concretely, Walker, the defender of mechanism, finds unintended praise.[16]
Where Carlyle attacks machinery, Walker is mildly puzzled and able to dismiss
the attacks as mysticism.

More recently, arguments have been developed that might give Carlyle's
intuitions sharper contours. They too depart from the means-ends distinction
and begin with the general claim that our technological means have somehow
outrun our ends.[17] Laurence Tribe approaches this phenomenon through a
critique of policy analysis, the predominant mode of appraising technological
problems.[18] He argues that such appraisals reduce in fact, if not necessarily,
the fullness of things to relatively few quantitative criteria.[19] Winner puts the
point more strongly. The available techniques of measurement, he says, often
determine what gets to be measured.[20] This is a case of what he calls "*reverse
adaptation*—the adjustment of human ends to match the character of the
available means.''[21] But in this form, Tribe's first point seems to conflict with
his second, which says that policy analysis fixes our attention on end states
thus suppressing the process of implementation through which we define
ourselves as much as through the choice of end results.[22]

Although policy analysis fixes its gaze on final values, it has no way to
judge or justify them. They enter the process of assessment as brute givens.
What is analyzed and evaluated are various strategies of implementation. But
even in the area of its professed and admitted competence, in the attention
to means, policy analysis is haunted by its inability to comprehend ends.
Tribe points out that certain technologies such as genetic engineering and
electronic stimulation of the brain, "although pursued largely as means, have
the effect of significantly altering the ends,—and indeed the basic character—
of the individuals and the communities that choose them.''[23] In response to
these predicaments, Tribe calls for "constitutive rationality,'' i.e., a kind of
principled discourse through which we can constitute our values rationally
and publicly.[24] Tribe stresses the tentative character of this proposal.[25] But it
can be furthered only, it seems to me, if we first analyze more incisively the

character of technological instrumentality to which constitutive rationality is to respond.

To begin with that task, we must recognize that the reduction of the fullness of phenomena in technological measurement and assessment is no more alarming than the common attenuation of the depth of things to commodious surfaces, and the former cannot be challenged without a challenge to the latter. One who has accepted television as a definition of entertainment will likely agree that a rise in income constitutes an improvement of life. Social scientists who are proponents of quantitative analysis will concede that it is impossible to measure everything. But as long as the reductive tendency that is intrinsic to the technological procurement of commodities remains unchallenged and to the extent that sociologists know themselves to be in procedural and substantive agreement with the technological paradigm, they will be undisturbed.

That paradigm also sanctions commodities and their consumption as ends. So sanctioned they are beyond dispute. There may be disagreement about what commodity should get preference. But such disputes are resolvable within the framework of technology. As the work of the Food and Drug Administration and other government agencies shows, these matters are not without principle and significance. But their investigation will not reach "the sources of the vague unease" of which Tribe speaks.[26] He says correctly that our discontent is independent of *how* certain exotic technologies are used. The mere fact *that* they are used makes us uneasy. But we should not, with Tribe, restrict this profound if hidden transformative significance "to the overall movement of technology, and to certain critical technologies, rather than to most day-to-day incremental changes—which may be quite properly regarded as essentially instrumental."[27] It is the pervasive transformation of things into devices that is changing our commerce with reality from engagement to the disengagement of consumption and labor. Only if we envision and challenge this inclusive pattern can we, in agreement with Tribe's demand, discern how we redefine ourselves in the process of implementing the values of technology. The character of technological implementation can be ignored by policy analysis as long as the device paradigm determines its general outline and provided there is, in accordance with the paradigm, an acceptance of the way in which we reshape our dealings with reality and so ourselves. Concentration can then be restricted to the determination of the course of action that will best render commodities available.

Tribe's writings are evidence that the common agreement on the paradigm of technology is being infected with uneasiness. But doubts about the paradigm will always be deflected and perhaps coopted if they are directed toward these ends or those means of technology. The entire and distinctive means-ends structure of technology must be grasped and exposed. Winner's notion of reverse adaptation implies that in technology means sometimes determine ends and thus people become enslaved by their servant. But what is gathered under the heading of reverse adaptation belongs into three different categories.

Certain such imbalances are due to common human traits such as egotism, laziness, and apprehension which, when strongly exemplified by bureaucrats in large organizations, seem to put the cart before the horse. But the problems that so arise are intelligible and in principle manageable within the framework of technology. Disclosure of information, sunset laws, efficiency considerations—all are tools of technology to diagnose and remedy ills of technology. A second and more significant imbalance of means and ends stems from the diffidence about the significance of the ends of technology, i.e., commodities and consumption. There is a deep-seated suspicion, as suggested in Chapter 10, that a life of consumption is not an end worthy of human beings. But the reign of the technological paradigm as a whole is in such instances so powerful that a reorientation is possible only within it. Fulfillment is then sought and often found not in leisure and consumption but in labor and the procurement of commodities. The disappointment with the ends yields to a fascination with the means. Finally and most profoundly there is a sense of impoverishment and impotence in technology which expresses itself as the experience of an insensitivity and impersonality of the technological machinery to the desire for self-determination.[28] The instruments have arrogated the definitions of ends. Winner puts it this way:

> Abstract general ends—health, safety, comfort, nutrition, shelter, mobility, happiness, and so forth—become highly instrument-specific. The desire to move about becomes the desire to possess an automobile; the need to communicate becomes the necessity of having telephone service; the need to eat becomes a need for a refrigerator, stove, and convenient supermarket.[29]

But as Walker reminded Carlyle, ends are always tied to means. The sense of powerlessness that Winner discusses comes into focus only when more attention is paid to the peculiarity of the technological tie between means and ends. In technology, the ends emasculate humans more subtly and consequentially than the means. Commodities allow no engagement and atrophy the fullness of our capacities. This they would do even if they could be entirely severed from their supporting machinery. To be sure, the machinery of devices resists engagement too, not just in consumption, when it is inaccessible, but also in labor, as we will see in more detail later. In paraphrasing Ellul, Winner remarks:

> The original ends have atrophied; society has accepted the power of technique in all areas of life; social decisions are now based upon the validity of instrumental modes of evaluation; the ends are restricted to suit the requirements of techniques of performance and of measurement.[30]

But what are the original ends? If they are understood as vaguely as the blessings of which the promise of technology speaks, then the rise of technological instrumentality is their unobjectionable if ironical companion. If the original ends are the engaging forces that used to center and sustain life in a pretechnological setting, their atrophy was destined with the rise of the device paradigm no matter how pliant that device might ever have seemed. Thus to do justice to the experience of debility in the face of technology, its entire means-ends context must be addressed.

This same point holds when Winner raises the question of responsibility relative to technological systems. "One finds that it is sometimes very difficult," he says, "to locate praise or blame for events that occur within massive aggregates of men and machinery."[31] Again there are cases of traditional modesty or cowardice that appear in a new technological guise. But one must recognize that responsibility within technology is narrowly circumscribed, and the call for radical responsibility is misplaced if the recipient of the call is expected to exercise responsibility individually and within the system. We think of executives of large firms and of nationally prominent politicians as powerful. But their range of options is very constrained. Their power is contingent on their adherence to the technological paradigm. They can exercise power only in maintaining and advancing the availability of commodities. If one were to become dissatisfied with this paradigm and decided to steer matters in a different direction, one could call a press conference, speak one's mind, and that would be the end of one's power and the last we will hear of that person. It is not the case that people in technology hide in the maze of means and refuse responsibility for the ends. As long as technology as a whole is generally sanctioned, there is no need or possibility to adopt responsibility for this or that part of technology. People do accept, as a rule, responsibility for technology as a whole. What form this assumption of responsibility takes is a further concern, and so is the question of what openings there are today for taking responsibility in a radical and critical way. It must also be said that, although the question of responsibility can be decisively raised only about and not within technology, there are important matters of responsibility within technology which pertain, e.g., to the safety of products or the efficiency and honesty of service. But being located within the paradigm, these problems are fairly clear and tractable.

Machinery is a means, of course, and it is a mere means. But the import of that mereness is often overlooked both by the critics and the defenders of technology. Since machinery is merely a means, so the proponent of technology reasons, it will serve whatever ends and not constrain our choice of ends. If there is a problem of technology, it is remedied by considerations that concentrate on the clarification and selection of our ends. But as argued in Chapter 9, this view overlooks the fact that the rise of mere means is a revolutionary event and transforms from the ground up what now can count as an end. The critics of technology, as we have seen, sense that the very means-ends distinction in technology is problematic. But this crucial intuition is often misexpressed and confused when it is held that the solution of the problem consists in reducing the machinery to its supposedly proper sphere of being a mere means. This move, if made consistently, misleads the initial discontent and insight. Machinery as a mere means is paradigmatically embodied in the technological device, and a device typically procures commodities and calls forth the life of consumption and disengagement which troubles the more radical critics of technology. The semblance of the innocence of means in technology has a corollary in the equally misleading semblance as though there could be independent or guiding ends or final values for technology. As already suggested, the technological paradigm gives a radically new meaning to goals, values, or ends. If this is overlooked, an examination of technology by way of "raising the value question" will almost always be ensnared within the framework of technology and fail to be radical. This problem will be worked out in Chapter 13.

There is a view of technology, however, which seems to be a radical alternative to the critical and affirmative schools sketched just now and to the paradigmatic characterization as well. It presents machinery as an end as well as a means. Though Walker in the main defends machinery as a means, he also alludes to it as an embodiment of harmony, regularity, and beauty, and in this sense the universe itself is in essence machinery.[32] Quite generally in the middle of the nineteenth century, the machine became a symbol of a new age.[33] But the general praise was as little focused as Carlyle's criticism. In the first half of this century, however, the machine was characterized as the embodiment of a new moral and aesthetic order whose steward was the engineer.[34] Le Corbusier (Charles Édouard Jeanneret-Gris) set off the new aesthetics against the old.

> The Engineer's Aesthetic and Architecture are two things that march together and follow one from the other: the one being now at its full height, the other in an unhappy state of retrogression.

> The Engineer, inspired by the law of Economy and governed by mathematical calculation, puts us in accord with universal law. He achieves harmony.[35]

> Our engineers are healthy and virile, active and useful, balanced and happy in their work. Our architects are disillusioned and unemployed, boastful or peevish.[36]

Le Corbusier at length discusses ocean liners, airplanes, and automobiles as paradigms of this new order. It seems plausible to see in the International Style of which Le Corbusier was a founding father, in its rigor, purity, and resourcefulness, a consistent reflection of the engineer's order. But there are also indications in Le Corbusier's theoretical work of a flaw in this order. By and large, Le Corbusier does not downgrade architecture in principle. Engineering is more properly a challenge to architecture than a final goal. Moreover, when today we look at Le Corbusier's exemplars of the new order in the relentless and iconoclastic spirit that Le Corbusier himself promotes, we recognize these ancient ships, cars, and planes as awkward, inconsistent, poorly thought out, naive, and touching at best. They are already antiques as we say, some not only in construction and execution but in their very conception. The order of engineering constantly surpasses and degrades its creation.

If one is inclined to grant the creations of the International Style an adequacy and beauty that has weathered the decades, this eminence is not due to engineering ingenuity. One may indeed claim that the International Style has not only failed to advance or enrich the engineering order but has thoroughly misunderstood it. Buckminster Fuller has so argued and said:

> The "International Style" . . . demonstrated fashion-inoculation without necessity of knowledge of the scientific fundamentals of structural mechanics and chemistry.
>
> The International Style "simplification" then was but superficial. It peeled off yesterday's exterior embellishment and put on instead formalised novelties of quasi-simplicity, permitted by the same hidden structural elements of modern alloys that had permitted the discarded *Beaux-Arts* garmentation. It was still a European garmentation. The new International Stylist hung "stark motif walls" of vast super-meticulous brick assemblage, which had no tensile cohesiveness within its own bonds, but was, in fact, locked within hidden steel frames supported by steel *without visible means of support*. In many such illusory ways did the "International Style" gain dramatic sensory impingment on society as does a trickman gain the attention of children.[37]

In response, Fuller designed his Dymaxion houses, one of which in 1929 was conceived as "of light metals and plastics, planned radially around a core of mechanical services."[38]

> The house is suspended from a central mast, using the superior tensile strength of steel; it is hexagonal, that is, its members are triangulated because of the stability of this form. . . .
>
> It can be assembled from its parts in twenty-four hours, as well as be carried through the air en bloc. It is designed for a specific longevity and it is to be then turned in for an improved model. Thus it involves the minimum of commitment to site, fixity, and tradition.[39]

Again one may find honesty, rigor, beauty, and resourcefulness exemplified in this design. A model is in fact on exhibit in the Museum of Modern Art in New York. It has become a museum piece in more senses than one. It now merely marks a course of which a still later stage is represented by Reyner Banham's and Francois Dallegret's *Un-house* (1965). It is "the ultimate in throwaway living where all the products including clothing are dispensed with and the artifacts—such as they are—come through the electric media under an inflatable dome. . . . the standard of living package plus inflatable dome push mobility and transience towards their extreme limit.''[40]

What has happened to the engineer's order? The engineer reduces a problem to its essential functions and realizes the latter in the most efficient way possible. Such isolating of functions seems to be a purifying, liberating, and rational affair. It eliminates the ballast of tradition, site, commitment, and fixity. But ends cannot be kept firm when means are relativized, nor can problems remain articulate when their context is erased. Ends and problems so treated are attenuated to commodities until they almost disappear and there is nearly nothing.

A final challenge to the clarifying force of the device paradigm comes from reflections of David P. Billington. We can connect them with the preceding issues by paying attention to the fact that the instability of the machine and hence its inability to serve as an end and focus of orientation for technology becomes so dramatically apparent in architecture when we look at utopian proposals where the spirit of technology can take its course without regard to economic and political circumstances. One might say however that the merely utopian character of the architectural examples is not an accident and that it is a fundamental mistake to think of a house as ''a machine for living.''[41] Billington urges a distinction between structures and machines. He says:

> Structures and machines are related by contrast. Structures are roads, bridges, terminals, dams, harbors, waterworks, power plants, office towers, and public housing blocks, whereas machines are cars, trains, trucks, turbines, ships, pumps, motors, television sets, computers, and window air conditioners.[42]

Billington contends that both the theory and the practice of technology are preoccupied with machines. Thus we get a distorted view of technology. A fuller and adequate view would allow us, Billington holds, to restore technology to its place as a servant of society.[43] Billington's contention, if taken as an analysis of technology, constitutes a decisive objection to the present enterprise. Billington describes the machine in terms closely akin to those of the device paradigm. Machines, he says, are transient; they quickly become obsolete due to progress in science, research, and development. They are environmentally independent or ubiquitous, as we would say. They encourage restlessness. Structures, on the other hand, are permanent and designed for a particular site. They foster repose and patience. If machines and structures are equally part of technology, then a characterization of technology in terms of the device, given its kinship to machines, would yield a one-sided and misleading picture.

How is a metropolitan office tower related to the device paradigm? It is clearly an imposing structure, and if thought of as machinery it certainly has nothing of the concealed and shrinking character that can be seen in the development of a dentist's chair, for instance. Though skyscrapers are permanent, massive, and ostentatious and thus very much unlike the machinery of other devices, they exhibit important traits of the paradigm. A high-rise building, though imposing, is still not accessible either to one's understanding or to one's engagement. Fuller's critique of the International Style, that it conceals rather than reveals the functions of the building, holds of architecture to this day, with a few determined exceptions to the rule such as the Centre Pompidou in Paris.[44] The appropriation of space through visual and bodily engagement is out of the question in the case of a skyscraper. It makes space available in an abstract three-dimensional grid into which one inserts oneself through an equally abstract transportation system. As always, there are echoes of pretechnological experiences in these devices. Thus a higher location in a high-rise is better and more prestigious as though, being up there, one had mastered a mountain or were lord over those below. But in fact one has no real sense of position or location; one is not oriented to those around one in the other apartments or offices, and one is not related to a center because skyscrapers, as a rule, have none.[45] For one's spatial orientation, a high-rise apartment may as well be suspended in a vicinity of empty space. Compared with the articulation of internal space in a medieval church, that of a skyscraper is normally very primitive indeed. This, of course, is due to the uses for which an office or apartment tower is built; it is to make space available in small and often variable units. But this is to say that architecture in the traditional sense asserts itself with difficulty at best against the reign of the device paradigm. Contrary to Billington's implication, the spatial indifference that is found within an office tower holds true also of the building as a whole relative to its setting. Robert Socolow has put the point this way:

> The downtown office building of the 1960s already stands as a metaphor for the whole society's desire for independence from the natural setting: temperature, humidity, air exchange, and lighting are all controlled mechanically, independent of season, wind speed, or whether one is on the north or south side of the building. Neither materials nor design change as the location is moved in latitude by thousands of miles. (In physicists' jargon, the building is invariant under ninety-degree rotations, displacements in space, and translations in time.)[46]

Thus we find the environmental independence that Billington thought distinctive of machines in certain structures as well. We find it there, as Socolow suggests, because the desire for disburdenment which is the corollary of such independence is a deeply ingrained trait of society. But the reading of Billington's position that has been given so far is not complete and balanced. Billington's distinction has the force more of a proposal than of a description. Billington himself notes that the undesirable features of the machine are at times also found in structures. Still structures, he argues, provide a clearer opening for attempts to reorient technology. That is a crucial and helpful point, and it will occupy us more closely in Chapter 25.

We have seen in this chapter that the peculiar means-ends division found in the technological device can be discerned in seemingly conflicting contentions about the significance of machines, means, and ends in technology. But it has been said in Chapter 3 that in the analysis of a concrete phenomenon one formal pattern can never conclusively be made to prevail over another merely by its formal properties. The application of a paradigm finally depends on a substantive concern, and it stands or falls with that concern. Before we develop and apply the device paradigm further, we must pay more attention to the nature and foundation of paradigmatic explanation.

12   Paradigmatic Explanation

To some scholars methodological matters seem sterile, others regard them as decisive. Some are impatient with the endless refinement of tools which forever seems to prevent them from getting on with their work while others abhor the waste of effort and the unhappy confusions they foresee unless one clarifies first how one is to proceed. Both views presuppose that method and subject matter can be addressed separately; I want to argue that this is not so. To talk about one is to discuss the other. It is a matter of pedagogy which is to be taken up. But if one insists on the distinction and wants to know whether the following reflections spring from a methodological or substantive concern, the answer is emphatically that we are ultimately concerned about substantive issues; it is out of a concern to do them justice in dubious times that we must turn to matters of method. This is also the major reason for taking up the question of method when the matter at hand requires it rather than dealing with methods at the start and once and for all. Though such an arrangement would be more orderly, it might suggest that, once principles and procedures are worked out, the fundamental problems are solved and little can go wrong from then on. This position, as will be explained in Part 3, is contrary to the orientation of the present essay. But from the subordination of method to substantive concerns, it does not follow that we can set aside the issue of procedures. To recall earlier remarks, the concern with antecedent and controlling conditions is powerful today. And it is precisely when we want to be equal to substantive concerns that we must do our best to connect them well and fruitfully with established ways of thinking.

Let us begin with a summary of what we have learned about methods of argument and explanation in Part 1. The physical sciences today provide the standard of explanation. As a body of laws and theories they give the most general and precise description of the world. By subsuming particular events under these laws we explicate the lawfulness or intelligibility of those events. But the physical sciences fail to provide a theory in the sense of a steady and orienting view of our world. The laws of science circumscribe a possibility space which allows for many actualizations. We must introduce limits or constraints into the possibility space to obtain a view of the actual world. David Layzer puts the matter this way:

> Laws and constraints are complementary aspects of the physicist's description of nature. Laws describe the regularities underlying phenomena; they are few in number and each applies over a wide domain. Constraints serve to select from the set of all events governed by a given law the particular phenomenon of interest. The laws define what is possible, the constraints what is actual or relevant. The constraints can take the form of initial conditions, boundary conditions or symmetry conditions.[1]

The sciences as a body of laws and theories have no criteria of relevance or selection; so they are necessary but not sufficient to provide a view of our world. But how significant is that insufficiency? Layzer illustrates his point by showing how Newton's laws must be constrained to give a picture of the solar system. Is not the ascertaining of these special conditions a straightforward scientific matter also? The conditions after all are given, they are data; there is nothing arbitrary or mysterious about them. We must remember, however, that to speak of the solar system is to single out for consideration a very small part of the universe and a very large setting in relation to our everyday world. The problem of selecting constraints is not that the givenness or objectivity of conditions is in doubt but that there is a disorienting overabundance of given conditions. It is the microcharacter of most physical theories that has revealed the infinitely intricate structure of things and dissolved the contours that gave prescientific worlds a surveyable coherence and determinacy. But there is no hope of charting all the details of the world that we know to obtain at the physicochemical level. Even if we restrict the compass of inquiry to a matter of great interest such as the human brain and to a tiny speck within it, a complete description remains out of reach. "It is no use," F. H. C. Crick says, "asking for the impossible, such as, say, the exact wiring diagram of a cubic millimeter of brain tissue and the way all its neurons are firing."[2]

But research and explanations at many levels are in fact undertaken all the time. How then is the selection of constraints being accomplished? At the frontiers of physicochemical research, matters of relevance and problem selection are intrinsic to the search for new laws. At higher levels of complexity as in mineralogy and biology it is an empirical fact that things fall into natural kinds with general properties and predictable patterns of behavior. It is at the level of human beings and human society that complexity becomes forbidding.

Even crude and molar features of social behavior such as the rate of inflation or the outcome of elections defy precise explanations and predictions. Humans are composed of physical particles arranged in particular ways which instantiate and constrain the laws of natural science, and human beings are part of nature and exhibit the regularities of a natural kind. But resting on this orderly basis, there is a complexity in and between humans that allows no precise and penetrating summaries. Mainstream social science in this country has vigorously and vainly sought to discover laws of human society that would approximate in rigor and comprehensiveness those of the physical and biological sciences.[3]

We have come to identify science with the search for empirical laws and regularities. Given the intimate tie between lawfulness, intelligibility, and reality, there is no special or hidden motive in the scientific approach to the world. To do science is to be equal to the character of reality in the intensive and perspicuous way which sets human beings apart from other creatures. I want to insist on a realist view of science and on the nobility of scientific knowledge for its own sake that goes along with realism. At the same time we must recognize that the search for laws can be motivated by a desire for control. The question of motivation is moot where the search is fruitful and successful. But when the search is pressed, as it has been in much social science, against substantial and continuous evidence of failure, one may infer that the concern is not with laws but with control. The search for laws in the social sciences often takes the form of the pursuit of lawlike connections between independent and dependent variables. If such connections are found, the phenomenon that is captured in the dependent variable may be controlled through the selection of an appropriate value for the independent variable. A phenomenon so captured becomes available, and the laws or functions of social science are the devices that procure it. The significance of what is so made available is thought to be antecedently given. Social scientists would not deny the need of given ends and goals, but they take them to be unproblematic or inscrutable. Their concern is with the machinery of laws that takes account of the given as inputs and outputs, as raw materials and commodities. There is a technological bias in the social sciences whenever they search for once-and-for-all devices of explanation and control. The claim to generality has different forms and degrees. The concern may be with the a priori, timeless, cross-cultural, transcendental, invariant, or universal. There is no a priori reason why such approaches must fail; they do so in fact and in light of the given complexity of human society. The resulting theories fail either straightforward in being falsified or more subtly in being vague, vacuous, or uninterestingly narrow. There is only one way in which they can succeed, i.e., when they capture a phenomenon in the sense of making it captive, of confining and reducing it. If mental well-being is defined as a kind of euphoria induced by direct stimulation of the brain, then we may well be able to devise a function of contentment. If the work world is taken over and streamlined by a state apparatus, we can design regulations to control employment and productivity. The success of such social theories will depend on the extent to which we accept an equivalence of the reduced and the original phenomenon. The discussion in Chapter 10 has suggested that tolerance for such equations is already remarkable. But in the social sphere our allegiance to the full-bodied original phenomena is still strong enough to let social theories of lawlike aspirations suffer shipwreck.

The lawfulness of reality gives the world its steady and intelligible character. The firmness and accessibility of the world are reinforced where the laws of nature are instantiated in typical and recurring ways as in the species of plants and animals and in the cycle of the seasons. The world is remarkable or significant because the conditions or givens that instantiate the laws are heterogeneous, articulated in distinct and eminent ways. Significance is heightened when distinct conditions are unique and therefore not predictable as a phase in a recurring pattern or subsumable merely as a specimen of a kind. That conditions must be considered if we are to obtain explanations is granted by every scientist. But the conditions are not accidentally called *initial* or *boundary* conditions. The explanandum is in the shadow of the explanans, and we would not speak of the explanandum as the wholeness of the *final* or *central* conditions.

The emphasis in the social sciences on laws and regularities is of a piece with the stress on the first members of the following pairs:

is—ought
fact—value
theoretical—practical
description—prescription
analysis—advocacy
empirical—normative

Some kind of significance of the second members is granted by the social scientist; but what those terms stand for is either disregarded or attempts are made to extend the realm of the first members to encompass that of the latter. Those attempts take the form of efforts to capture values and norms as variables. But we can say that as a matter of fact norms and values have, due to their complexity, eluded the snares of functional devices. It seems to me that we can do justice to norms and values only if we turn our attention from laws to conditions as given in their own right. This suggestion may sound like strange counsel, issuing from scientific realism. But really it converges with the prephilosophical and prescientific experience of unique and decisive things and practices, of persons, works of art, prophecies, political deeds, and more humble ones such as the exercise of a craft, the celebration of a meal, of birth, of marriage, and of death.

If to explain is to provide understanding, then, as suggested in Chapter 6, there must be in addition to the kind of explanation that subsumes under laws another kind of explanation that traces and brings into relief the significance of a thing or event in its uniqueness. Subsumptive explanations are apodeictic. This vocable designates both the deductive nature of such explanations, the fact that one deduces the explanandum as a conclusion from laws and conditions, and the cogent force of such explanations. If the premises are accepted, the conclusion cannot be refused. Explanations, on the other hand, which do not derive what is to be explained from laws and conditions but simply point up something in its significance, we have called deictic. These two kinds of explanation take one another for granted. Something that I set out to explain apodeictically must have come to my attention as significant, as worthy or in need of explicit subsumption under laws. The significance of the explanandum has been or is capable of being established through a deictic explanation. Conversely, when I trace the significance of something and point it up, I presuppose that the thing as it is given embodies the lawfulness of reality and that the various strands of this lawfulness could be explicated through apodeictic explanations.

We can now restate earlier points by saying that the natural sciences have an apodeictic orientation and that the social sciences, inasmuch as they model themselves after the natural ones, exhibit the same inclination. That tendency shows itself in the stress on the first members of the dichotomies listed above. The complexity of the explananda, however, with which the social sciences have to deal, resists apodeictic explanations. One might now conclude that this predicament requires the social sciences to turn to deictic explanations, i.e., to endeavors that are designed to exhibit and clarify the phenomena of the social sphere. But as we have used the term, deictic explanations are more specific. A deictic explanation articulates a thing or event in its uniqueness. "Articulation" has an appropriate ambiguity for our purposes. To articulate is both to establish a unique thing or event as does the artist or the prophet and to disclose or reenact it as does the teacher or the celebrant. The distinctive feature of a deictic explanation is not its method but its subject, something unique and concrete that is at the center of attention and of its world, a holy place, for instance, that focuses and orients the world about it. The notion of deictic explanation must seem impossibly ambiguous until one sets one's methodological bias aside and grants the primacy of the subject matter. But precisely when that is allowed, it appears that there is today no subject matter for the social sciences that would call for deictic explanations. The traditional focal things and events of religion, art, and daily practice have lost their commanding places in our world, the firmness of their contours, and their orienting force. We have seen brief illustrations of this in the preceding discussions of the hearth, of the festive meal, of wine, of the work world. And the general thesis of the eclipse of religion and art in our world is too widely accepted to require detailed substantiation here. Nor have the traditional focuses yielded to new ones. We have seen in the preceding chapter that the attempt to advance a machine or a structure as the embodiment of the new age has not been convincing. The interstate highway system in this country is surely a monumental and farflung structure in Billington's sense. But hardly anyone would argue that through its construction and use we place ourselves in our world just as did the Medievals in theirs when they built and prayed in cathedrals.

From all this one might conclude that our world is decaying to a state of featureless indifference because the authorities from which one would naturally expect articulation and orientation fail to provide them. But what we in fact witness about us is not the rise of homogeneity, the leveling down of all structures, but the most radical and forceful reshaping of the globe ever. Something is going on that needs to be illuminated and understood. Yet as we have seen, it will not be captured in the modes of explanation that are proper to the sciences and to the great focal powers of the past, i.e., through apodeictic or deictic explanations. But there is a third possibility of explaining, one where we try to comprehend the character of reality by discovering its predominant pattern. A pattern is more concrete and specific than a law and yet more general and abstract than a unique focal thing. To illuminate reality by disclosing its pattern is a quasi-deictic explanation. Let us call it paradeictic or paradigmatic explanation.

One cannot talk about paradigms today without talking about the work of Thomas Kuhn.[4] I hope it clears the air when I acknowledge my debt to Kuhn but disclaim any attempt to have his sanction. The difficulties and ambiguities in Kuhn's use of the term are legendary.[5] They make it advisable to be as clear and modest as possible in one's claims for paradigms. It is not merely a play on words to say that deictic and paradeictic explanations fail to be apodeictic, that they cannot exact assent in the manner of scientific explanations. The force of deictic explanations will occupy us in Chapter 21. As regards paradigmatic explanations, the first question is of course what counts as a pattern and how a pattern is established.

We use patterns straightforwardly in everyday life to appropriate our world. We use them to recognize things and to shape things to our purposes. To identify a bald eagle we look for a large hawk with a white head and tail and a flat-winged glide. To tell a mule deer from a whitetail deer we look for large ears, a white, ropelike, black-tipped tail, and for equally branching antlers if it is a buck. A pattern in this sense is the configuration of characteristic features we keep in mind as a guide to order and sort out the manifold appearances of the world. In similar ways we look for patterns in electrocardiograms and seismograms to ascertain the cardiac condition of a person or the geological structure of a valley. We impose rather than discover a pattern when we use a template to mount a ski binding or a pattern to cut the material for a dress. A pattern, then, is an array of crucial features, abstract and simple enough to serve as a handy device, concrete and detailed enough to pick out a certain kind of object effectively.

These unproblematic and pretheoretical uses of patterns help us to grasp in a tentative way what a paradigm is. Problems arise, however, when the use of paradigms is extended beyond the realm of common agreements and

purposes in an effort to settle deeply controversial issues. To gain access to
these problems we must, to begin with, remember that it is convenient to use
"paradigm" both for a more or less abstract pattern and for a more or less
concrete and clear phenomenon which exhibits the pattern in question particularly well. Let us begin the problematic discussion with a seemingly
straightforward and innocent use of paradigms. To prove the existence of a
certain kind of thing, say material objects, one may produce a clear instance
or paradigm of the kind in question, pointing to chairs or tables. But to one
who doubts or denies the existence of material objects a chair is not evidence
for one side of the dispute but the very thing whose status is in question. As
Anne C. Minas points out, paradigm case arguments are question begging or
circular.[6] If one does not already command or concede the notion of a material
object, nothing can serve as an instance. What is vexing about paradigmatic
explanation is the semblance of concreteness, of incontrovertible evidence.
When we point to a paradigm in the sense of a clear example, it is usually
granted that there is something to which we point. But what can always be
and often is disputed in theoretical discussions is the claim that this something
exhibits the pattern or instantiates the notion that is in question. Paradigms
seem primitive or undemonstrable. You see them or you do not. But this stark
all-or-nothing standing of paradigms is characteristic only of metaphysical
discussions where the dispute concerns abstract notions or involves attempts
to dislodge a skeptical objection. In the disputes of social science, patterns
are more extended. They have a number of components and features and are
therefore more open to discursive arguments. Moreover, paradigms in the
sense of eminent and clear cases are usually granted. It is conceded that this
is an example of a game, that of a bargaining situation, and similarly for a
functional system, a free market, or a class struggle.[7] A first set of difficulties
arises when the pattern is spelled out explicitly and generally. The formulation
must be general enough to have applicability beyond its initial examples and
succinct enough so that it does not vacuously apply to all possible cases or,
worse, lead to inconsistent findings. Assuming that a paradigm has met the
criteria of consistency and precision, problems arise next when it is in fact
applied. Through a convergence of unusual factors I may have encountered
what seems like a clear instance of telekinesis and telepathy. I may then devise
a telekinetic and telepathic paradigm of communication. If the paradigm is
precise at all, however, it will fail to apply generally. Yet paradigms in the
social sphere seldom fail clearly because what they are applied to, society,
is so multifarious that there is always some positive evidence and enough
complexity to disqualify negative evidence as likely due to disturbing and
misleading factors of which we are ignorant. The more plausible and better
known paradigms of social science all are matched by social reality to the
extent where they can be said to meet the criterion of applicability.

Paradigms in social science can be taken as the characteristic ways in which
theorists see reality. A paradigm in this sense is an entity in the world of

science or theory and at one remove from social reality. The paradigm in this sense characterizes a group of scholars and their work and possibly little else. But for subscribers to a paradigm, social reality itself exhibits the features of the paradigm. The paradigm has taught them what to look for, and they see nothing else. In fact they may deny that they are beholden to any guiding pattern; they simply report, so they say, what is the case. But allegiance to a paradigm does not require that one be blind to it. One may be conscious of it and also claim a privileged appropriateness for it. Finally, it is possible that one professes allegiance to one paradigm, say social Darwinism, but is held by others to propagate quite another, say racism. We can restate an earlier point along these lines. The professed paradigm of many mainstream social scientists in this country is a set of laws that would rival the laws of natural science in precision and predictive power. Why has this paradigm in spite of its clear if not conclusive failures of precision or applicability not been abandoned? We may conjecture that the work of its adherents is sustained by another, implicit paradigm, that of getting social reality under technological control. But how would one substantiate such a charge? One who is committed to the paradigm of the technological device will obviously see it dominate everything, other paradigms and their proponents included.

Social paradigms, then, exhibit in a more diffuse way the circularity and lack of demonstrability that we have found in metaphysical paradigms. This mootness may be concealed because it is often thought that, in order to establish a paradigm as disclosing a society's essential features, it is sufficient to show that the paradigm is consistent, precise, and applies to the social realm. But given the complexity of society, there are indefinitely many patterns that can be highlighted, and by the criteria of consistency, precision, and applicability alone we cannot decide which are essential. Another factor that conceals the circularity of social paradigms is the semblance of one paradigm's victory over another. One may claim superior precision or applicability for one's paradigm or try to show that one's paradigm comprises all others and constitutes their underlying pattern. But such victories are empty or dubious. I can delineate precise patterns of heat exchange and show that all societies are heat exchange systems. I can argue that whatever is called bargaining, allocation of resources, or political action is at bottom nothing but a mode of exchanging heat. But is it so essentially?[8]

None of these skeptical considerations contests the claim that contemporary reality is neither indifferently homogeneous nor structured around unique and abiding focal things and practices. Social reality seems to be patterned. Theories of society with all their diversity are best understood as attempts to discover the dominant pattern.[9] This persistent and widespread search is reasonably understood as a response to something that in fact exists. One must rest one's case somewhere; that should cause no embarrassment as long as the final move is not made in a facile or premature manner. If there is no way of reaching forever behind the givenness of reality and *if* reality is given in a pattern, then it would likewise be impossible to get back of the paradigm in which the pattern becomes explicit. And any attempt to get beneath the paradigm by grounding it in some way would then fail and find the paradigm circular and undemonstrable. A paradigm as a theoretical entity will prevail, however, if enough people acknowledge its efficacy in clarifying their vision; and the paradigm will sharpen their perception if what it teaches people to see is admittedly what they essentially do and what essentially moves them. That a paradigm provides essential clarification can be taken in different ways. When the pattern of my world and my commerce with it come clearly into view, I may rejoice in the discovery and be encouraged in my endeavors; on the other hand I may be dismayed to find that my best interests are imperiled and that I have been an accomplice in their jeopardy; or, finally, I may be divided in my allegiance and feel challenged to resolve my predicament. It is only in the first kind of discovery that a paradigm is ontologically and epistemologically not only unsurpassable but also dominant. In the second case, the paradigm as a pattern or tendency in reality vies with other forces of equal or greater significance; epistemologically, the paradigm becomes a device to delineate and restrain developments on behalf of things that truly matter.

It is obvious that the device paradigm that has been delineated on these pages is designed to locate the crucial force that more and more detaches us from the persons, things, and practices that used to engage and grace us in their own right. One talks about the latter in deictic discourse. Paradeictic explanation, when it comes to the device paradigm, is tied to deictic explanation. But the converse is true also. Assuming the prevalence of the device paradigm, deictic discourse and explanation cannot simply be nostalgic but must rethink and reopen the grounds of engagement. This is a matter for the third part of this book.

In conclusion of this chapter it may be well to summarize the features of the device paradigm. From what has been said so far, it is clear that such a presentation will not be a cogent demonstration. It provides pointers and reminders. It delineates a pattern from various sides. One can, first of all, take the historical approach and sketch the pattern by presenting the closer historical background from and against which it emerges. It first comes into relief when past and present are seen as times of toil, poverty, and suffering and when at the same moment a new natural science emerges from which great transformative power can be derived. On the basis of this power, a promise of liberation, enrichment, and of conquering the scourges of humanity is issued. The promise leads to the irony of technology when liberation by way of disburdenment yields to disengagement, enrichment by way of diversion is overtaken by distraction, and conquest makes way first to domination and then to loneliness.[10] One can, second, proceed paradigmatically or illustratively and provide a paradigm, in the sense of a clear example, which illustrates this development and its result; one can, for instance, trace the development that leads from a fireplace to a central heating plant, from a horse-drawn wagon to an automobile, or from a pretechnological meal to a T.V. dinner.

Third, one can explicate paradeictically or abstractly the pattern that is embodied in clear examples. Central heating plants, cars, and T.V. dinners are technological devices that have the function of procuring or making available a commodity such as warmth, transportation, or food. A commodity is available when it is at our disposal without burdening us in any way, i.e., when it is commodiously present, instantaneously, ubiquitously, safely, and easily. Availability in this sense requires that the machinery of a device be unobtrusive, i.e., concealed, dependable, and foolproof.[11] The ensemble of commodities constitutes the foreground of technology in which we move by way of consumption. The machinery of devices constitutes the background of technology. We take it up in labor by constructing and maintaining the devices of technology. This is the original procurement of devices and thereby of commodities. Derivative procurement takes place when devices are activated in consumption.

Finally, one can provide an ontological account of the paradigm by showing how the device paradigm is serving as an implicit guiding pattern for the transformation of human existence and the world. Things in their depth yield to shallow commodities, and our once profound and manifold engagement with the world is reduced to narrow points of contact in labor and consumption.[12] Here paradigmatic explanation returns to and receives direction from the fundamental concerns which can be illuminated in deictic discourse. In most concrete phenomena of the technological universe, the cut between commodity and machinery, foreground and background can be made in more than one way. What should guide the incisions is our concern to shed light on changes that imperil things, practices, and engaging human relations, and the desire to make room for such phenomena when they are struggling to assert themselves against the dominant pattern of availability. Such a guiding concern is a response to the claim of things in their own right. The real point of the technological paradigm is its critical office. It is exercised through the demonstration that, if we are concerned about the loss of engagement, the device paradigm reveals more clearly than any other just how and to what extent people move away from engagement. If that concern is granted, the demonstration can attain at least a measure of cogency.

The illuminating force of the device paradigm is most striking when it is compared with social and political theories that also advance claims and criticisms about the way in which we take up with our world, how we orient ourselves in it, and about the salient features and problems of society. The following chapters, read by themselves, may seem like the very competition among paradigms that in this chapter was shown to be forever inconclusive. Thus the ultimate substantive concern that has here been adumbrated must be kept in view. That concern, as agreed before, requires more development.

But it must also be noted that the paradigm of availability delineates from without and *ex negativo* a substantive position and can begin to trace its general contours.

13   Technology and the Social Order

The following is the first in a group of four chapters that deal with the relation of technology to society and politics. Any extended discussion of technology has to take up this problem, and, in most discussions of technology, its connection with social and political issues is in fact tackled first and head-on. I have taken a less direct approach. The first part of this study has been a kind of brush clearing to obtain an open view of the problem and pattern of technology. Part 2 has so far been devoted to the articulation of that pattern. We can now turn to the further and deeper question of how we have worked out our relationship to technology and its ruling paradigm. So far I have mainly argued that there is a deeply consequential pattern to our lives of which we are at best fleetingly and uneasily aware. Such an argument implies of course that we should bring this pattern to the surface and to our attention.

In turning to the social and political realm, we enter the foremost arena of public awareness and concern, an arena whose dimensions and rules determine what gets attention and what not. If the rise of technology has been, as I have claimed, the most significant event of the modern period, then the kind of public attention it has received must tell us something important about the quality of our social and political life. That we should judge society and politics in light of technology is indeed the working hypothesis of this part of our essay. But the force of the hypothesis needs qualification. The judgment, first of all, to which it leads is tentative, for so is the procedure by which the verdict is arrived at. Paradigmatic explanation finally needs to be grounded in deictic considerations, and these are not provided until we come to Part 3. Moreover, the common understanding of society and politics has its own weight and dignity. Hence, for the time being, the confrontation of technology and society is as much a test of the present theory of technology as it is of the quality of our common aspirations and accomplishments.

The social and political realm and the theories that try to make sense of it are complicated and contentious. Introducing technology as an object of analysis into that complex does not by itself simplify matters. Therefore, it is advisable to proceed at first in smaller and careful steps. This I want to do in the present chapter, and I propose to take three such steps. To provide a tentative orientation I begin with some brief remarks on what is involved in orienting oneself both today and in a pretechnological setting. I then discuss one current and widely applauded attempt at orientation, that of raising the value question. Finally, I examine a straightforward and frequently if not consistently held view of how and where we are to locate responsibility for the present social order; I am speaking of the Marxist view. These initial considerations prepare the ground for the more insistent inquiries of the following three chapters.

To begin, then, it is widely admitted that there is a problem of orientation in the technologically advanced countries. There is a literature of disorientation that in various ways chronicles and analyzes this loss of direction.[1] What is it to orient oneself? When life was rooted in a particular region, the direction that points to the rising sun sometimes attained a privileged rank. To orient originally meant to erect a church "with the longer axis due east and west, and the chancel or chief altar at the eastern end."[2] It was to take one's bearing *a sole oriente*, from the rising sun. But Copernicus taught us, so it is said, that the sun does not really rise. And space in modern cosmology is isotropic; it has not privileged points, directions, or axes. Science may be a necessary condition of disorientation. But to repeat an earlier point, it is not the task of science, in its central sense as a body of laws and theories, to ascertain the conditions that are prominent and abiding and allow us to be at home in the world. Disorientation is the result, at least approximately, of a certain way in which we take up with reality, and the loss of the traditional points of reference may not be experienced as debilitating at all. A world in which the sun is thought to rise always in the same region may seem stifling and antiquated. That is the tenor of Buckminster Fuller's account of living on "Earth."

> I travel between Southern and Northern hemispheres and around the world so frequently that I no longer have any so-called normal winter and summer, nor normal night and day, for I fly in and out of the shaded or sun-flooded areas of the spinning, orbiting Earth with ever-increased frequency. I wear three watches to tell me what time it is at my "home" office, so that I can call them by long distance telephone. One is set for the time of day in the place to which I am next going, and one is set temporarily for the locality in which I happen to be. I now see Earth realistically as a sphere and think of it as a spaceship.[3]

But usually, the loss of the traditional norms is not considered in these sanguine terms. Many analysts of the technological society are concerned about the progressive erosion of standards. What heightens the sense of crisis enormously is the disagreement among the analyses regarding the source of our troubles and consequently about the appropriate remedies. In discussions where technology is recognized as the title for the character of our times, it is sometimes thought that we can find our bearings in relation to technology by raising the question of values.[4] But such a procedure may only strengthen and conceal the reign of what we seek to question. To see this, let us follow Kurt Baier and distinguish between the value possessed by things and the values held by people.[5] "The value of something," Baier says, " . . . is a certain sort of property of it."[6] More precisely, it "is the thing's capacity to confer a benefit on someone, to make a favorable difference to his life."[7] We can see here that the discourse of values does not recognize things in their entire depth, where nearly every discernible property is significant and an essential tie to the world of the thing. Such discourse rather presupposes the means-ends distinction that comes into its own in the machinery and function of the device. Accordingly, Baier defines values held by people as the "*tendencies* of people to devote their resources (time, energy, money [the means of all means]) to the attainment of certain ends."[8] The relative stability of ends and the radical variability of means that again comes to fruition in the device is likewise congenial to value talk and stressed by W. Norris Clarke: "The essential principle of education involved here [i.e., in the endeavor to control technological progress], it seems to me, is a shift of emphasis from means to ends, from teaching customs or *ways* of doing things—so quickly obsolete or irrelevant today—to teaching basic values or *goals* to be aimed at steadily through the flux of changing ways and means."[9] The affinity of the discourse of values with the paradigm of availability is palpable when Baier talks about ways of assessing the value of things:

> A book, a lecture course, an invention, a suggestion has greater value than another if it satisfies more fully than the other thing the listed desiderata; if it is generally easier to satisfy the conditions under which it can or will play its characteristic causal role (being available for reading, attending, etc.); if it more reliably brings about or is a greater help in bringing about certain intended changes in the lives of people, or brings them about in more lives, or in a larger proportion of lives to be improved; and if the changes brought about constitute a greater improvement.[10]

No matter how the question of values is raised and settled, the pattern of technology itself is never in question. Technology comes into play as the indispensable and unequaled procurement of the means that allow us to realize our preferred values.

One can, of course, extend value talk to encompass the discourse of focal things by defining the values of objects and subjects in such a way that the values are satisfied or instantiated only by things. But value talk then becomes awkward and misleading. One cannot hope to guard focal things and the engagement with them by saying that some values are hard and measurable and others soft, fragile, and elusive.[11] Rather there are certain goals that are consonant with the paradigm of technology, and these appear to be hard and measurable in value talk. Some of these values pertain to the means or machinery of technology, to employment, resources, or productivity. Though these are instrumental values, one can appeal to them as guides or ends in political controversies because the ends proper that they serve are understood and granted by almost everyone. Those final values are commodities. Since they are procurable, they are also quantifiable, i.e., hard. Commodities, in comparison with focal things, are highly reduced entities and abstract in the sense that within the overall framework of technology they are free of local and historical ties. Thus they are sharply defined and easily measured. Focal things, on the other hand, engage us in so many and subtle ways that no quantification can capture them. As with social phenomena, it is not the case that things are imbued with mysterious unquantifiable properties. Rather their significance is composed of so many, if not all, of their physically ascertainable properties that an explicit quantitative account must always impoverish them greatly. We can count the number of fast food outlets, the hamburgers sold, the times a family eats out.[12] And such a measurement of eating understood as consumption can with some additional data capture its commodity. But how can we begin to measure a family meal, thoughtfully prepared and celebrated at home? Again we can measure highway miles; we can count cars per population and scenic resting places. But how does one determine and quantify the essential dimensions of a hike in the wilderness? When there is a conflict in public policy between the engagement with focal things and the procurement of availability, value talk conforms to the abstract and narrowly defined character of commodities. But when value talk is about things, it falters, and the object of discourse slips from our grasp. Discourse that is appropriate to things must in its crucial occurrences abandon the means-ends distinction. It must be open to and guided by the fullness of the focal thing in its world, and it can communicate the thing only through testimony and appeal.

The nature of principled discourse of focal things requires an investigation of its own. Here I only want to set if off against value talk and expose the futility of value talk for the radical analysis of our relation to technology. In spite of its shortcomings one should, as a matter of prudence and pedagogy, encourage discussions that raise the value question. Without this familiar if inadequate approach, a fundamental analysis of technology remains forbidding. Moreover, values will remain indispensable as ways of summarizing, recollecting, and preparing for our experiences with things. It is the fundamental status of values that must be rejected.

Normally the value question is raised within the paradigm of availability. Technology in our sense is the unspoken and invisible framework of discussion of values, and such discourse, taken at face value, engenders the illusion as though people's orientation comes to the fore in their choice of values. But the implication that the existence and power of the framework of technology trivializes the choice of values since it occurs within the framework and leaves the latter unquestioned would be challenged by Marxist critics. In their view, the essential choices that most people make are directed not by some concealed and consequential pattern but by other people who, at least in the Western democracies, constitute a small and definite minority class. The opposing view which sees technology as the major social force has to be established in its own right. But that complex task can be clarified if we first consider an influential alternative to that view. For the Marxists, then, it is the capitalists who currently determine the shape and direction of social developments. The Marxist thesis is advanced in different degrees of sophistication. In its crudest form it has become part of the standard political idiom, and its origin is scarcely recognizable. But it shares its crucial flaw with its learned siblings, and it has led to much confusion in political debates. The crude thesis is occasioned by overt stresses in the economies of liberal democracies. The notions of the class struggle and of exploitation are then employed to locate the blame for the economic problems. The class division is made in terms of "the consumer" and "the big corporations." Exploitation is defined as the maximizing of profits by the corporations at the expense of the consumer. An example of the kind of charge that is made in these terms is the contention that "the gasoline prices are rising so fast because the oil corporations are ripping off the consumer; they are only interested in their profits." Editorial writers, senators, the person in the street, and academics level accusations of this sort, and there is always broad if uncertain approval. The lack of firm and consequential assent is due to the suspicion that the charge depends for its force on untenable interpretations of "corporation" and "profit." Corporations can be bearers of blame in this broad social sense only if they are identifiable with a definite set of persons whose interests are clearly opposed to those of the rest of the population. Accordingly, profits are objectionable if they constitute a surplus that is diverted to purposes that are contrary to the common will or good. But we know how tightly and manifoldly corporations are tied to society by way of their stockholders, managers, and employees, and we also know that most of the profits are channeled back into the economy to sustain and expand the productive machinery.

To define the central point of the Marxist critique more sharply, we can narrow the scope of its critical concern in three moves. First of all, the Marxists share with almost anyone who sees cause for criticism the view that the present social order fails to serve people's best interests. Second, they agree with democratic theory that people's interests are decisively served by a fair assignment of rights, power, income, and wealth. And finally, like liberal democratic theorists, they would find little fault with the articulation of civil rights in statutes and the Constitution. Marxists see the decisive shortcoming of our society in the extreme and unjust concentration of power and wealth. The holders and beneficiaries of that power and wealth constitute the ruling class. To substantiate the Marxist claim one must, to begin with, identify this class. Its identification is sometimes made with surprising vagueness, even when a clear identification is crucial to an argument. Stuart Ewen suggests in his book, *Captains of Consciousness,* that there is a group of people who, in order to secure the power of capitalism, have systematically been shaping popular attitudes toward consumption. He names advertising theorists and writers who made such shaping their business. But who gave them a mandate to do so? Ewen refers to "mass industrial capitalism," "modern industry," "business," "a profit-seeking mass productive machinery," or "expanding capitalism."[13] Attempts have been made, however, to isolate sociologically a determinate ruling elite. G. William Domhoff's endeavors provide an example of the insuperable difficulties that such an enterprise faces. If a ruling class is concretely defined according to wealth and criteria of class cohesion and consciousness, it turns out to be too small (a few hundredths of a percent) and is found to occupy too few offices to be able to rule something so large and complex as today's United States.[14] Domhoff's strategy is to appeal to this core group when he argues for the determinacy and cohesiveness of the governing class. But he allows for an indeterminate fringe of business executives, scientists, scholars, and politicians who are connected to the core by institutional bonds of various sorts. And when he argues for the governing power of the elite he refers to its periphery.

It is true of course that the center of the higher circles enjoys a disproportionate amount of wealth and political power. But what is it to enjoy wealth? Merely to have one's name on countless stock and bond certificates means nothing. Wealth is enjoyed through the exercise of power or through consumption. Power, based on wealth, can be direct, the power, for instance, that a majority stockholder has in controlling a corporate board of directors and thereby the direction of the corporation. But John Kenneth Galbraith and others have argued that the control of big business is in the hands of an elite of experts who own a negligible portion of the corporations they direct.[15] Or wealth bestows power indirectly by giving readier access to political office. Granted that the rich are disproportionately well represented in politics, the decisive question is whether they exercise their power against the wishes of the people. They have, to be sure, succeeded in preserving the privileges of the rich. But as was just suggested, those privileges are in the main either vacuous or exercised in consonance with popular goals.[16] What sets the rich truly apart is the enjoyment of wealth through personal consumption. They are the ones who have the yachts, Picassos, and castles in Spain. Such extravagance raises ethical questions. But if the wealth, so consumed, were to be distributed over the entire population, the general benefit would be small.[17] In that sense the consumption by the wealthy is economically insignificant. It is certainly not the sole or major sink of corporate profits in this country.[18]

Writers of Marxist orientation have made significant contributions to the social critique of Western democracies. Marcuse has analyzed the stealthy reduction of the universe of political discourse and action.[19] Baran and Sweezy have exposed the inability of Western economies to deal rationally with their productivity and to engender a life of dignity for all. Braverman has furnished a penetrating account of the degradation of work.[20] But the real thrust of these endeavors is inevitably deflected because they finally rest their case on the assumption that there is a definite exploiting capitalist class. It is not just that the critical insights depart from and return to an erroneous factual claim; the primal and final error tends to infect and blur the intermediate insights themselves. If blame for the problems of the technological society is in the end attributed to the selfish interests of a determinate class, then the therapy that naturally follows from this diagnosis will prescribe an excision of those interests and little more. It is only a short step from saying that the capitalists are principally at fault to concluding that not much else is wrong. A fortiori nothing is really wrong with technology except that it has been abused by the capitalists. Marcuse's *One-Dimensional Man* provides a telling example of a Marxist analysis that wavers between the substantive and instrumental view of technology, between seeing in technology a historical project that "shapes the entire universe of discourse and action, intellectual and material culture," and seeing technology as technics that "as a universe of instrumentalities, may increase the weakness as well as the power of man."[21]

On the Marxist analysis, the reform of the technological society in the Western democracies should be simple. It requires only that the power and privileges of a vanishingly small minority be canceled and technology be redirected toward the common good. The means for such reform are clearly in place. People can read and write, communicate, speak and assemble freely. There is universal franchise, secret ballot, and election of the legislature or the executive. Faced with these possibilities, Marxists must resort to a massive exculpation of the people to save their case. They must explain popular passivity by reference to the power of advertisement, the threat of unemployment and police brutality, the promise of a high standard of living, the subversion of the mass media, and other more subtle modifications of the climate of opinion and action. But if all these factors were tools of domination, one should also discover evidence of resistance in regard to each if not revolt.[22] When Marcuse, Baran, and Sweezy contemplate the lack of such evidence, they are moved to pessimism about the possibility of reform or revolution.[23] But they are unwilling to conclude that there must be a kind of consonance between the character of social reality and people's aspiration. What makes this difficult to come into view for a Marxist analysis is the emphasis on power relations among classes. To have introduced this consideration into economic and social analysis was one of Marx's great contributions.[24] But in time it diverted attention from the study of the concrete and inconspicuous material environment in which people come to terms with their lives. In spite of the illuminating details in the critique of popular culture that Marcuse particularly has provided, in the general and concluding view of Marxist critiques modern culture appears in a superficial and summary way. And accordingly, the positive goal of the good life that Marcuse, for example, advances is in accord with the dubious promise of technology.[25]

Clearly, I have not done justice to the range and subtlety of much of Marxist work. My concern has been roughly to attend to the Marxist claim regarding the social center of gravity and responsibility. My argument that Marxists misplace that center and that an analysis of technology allows us to locate it more appropriately is ironical, given that no nineteenth century critic of the emerging technological society paid closer and more persistent attention to the concrete features of that society than Marx. But his fascination with power and his Hegelian determination to foretell the future made many of his followers feel bound to vindicate rather than develop his position.

The liberal democratic view, on the other hand, has always maintained a certain aloofness from the grimy details of production and the dubious circumstances of consumption. Yet it has become deeply implicated in the development of modern technology. It is impossible to grasp the power and extent of modern technology without understanding liberal democratic theory. That theory is a force even in places where modern technology has a conservative or socialist cast. I am unable here to develop this suggestion. Instead I turn to the examination of liberal democracy to throw light on the ways in which technology has come to rule our lives. And as noted earlier, taking up technology in this framework is to consider it in terms that are most widely shared and taken most seriously.

14   Technology and Democracy

Political discourse today constitutes the forum in which we transact our most important business. Thus in discussing the political circumstances of technology we take an important step toward understanding the rule of technology. In this chapter I am primarily concerned with the theoretical dimensions of politics. Political theory, however, should not be taken as an abstract and inconsequential comment on political reality. Rather the concepts and concerns of theory have practical significance in reflecting and informing our political aspirations. To be sure, the common aspirations are modified and deflected in many ways, and hence the practical outcome of political action is, as we will see in the remaining chapters of Part 2, quite at variance with political theory.

Still, it is helpful to begin with theory. In the modern era it has been given its dominant features by the liberal democratic tradition, "liberal" taken in

a broad sense which will become clear in what follows. The decisive theoretical traits are conveniently introduced through a brief historical sketch. It
will show that the liberal democratic vision of society is guided by a distinctive
convergence of the notions of liberty, equality, and self-realization. This
cluster of concepts seems to be in happy consonance with the instrumental
conception of technology.

After that brief exposition, I turn to a critical examination of how valid
and viable liberal democratic theory is in the concrete circumstances of modern
technology. I begin by asking how well the liberal democratic enterprise has
fared by its overt and professed norm of equality. Seeing its failure on that
score, we must probe more deeply and question the very consistency of the
core cluster of concepts: liberty, equality, and self-realization. It turns out
that these norms can be realized jointly only according to the pattern of
technology. This becomes clear when one asks not merely whether opportunities in a liberal democratic society are equal and just but what kind of
opportunity they represent. Yet the implementation of the liberal program
yields a semblance of success only because the technological specification of
democracy, when examined radically, is seen to constitute a definite vision
of the good life and so answers a question that liberal theorists are at pains
to leave open. This pivotal problem, however, is not confronted in liberal
theory and remains an unspoken and deeply perplexing issue. Even in cases
where modern technology becomes an explicit problem, the failure to grasp
it incisively veils the social significance of technology.

Beginning then with the historical sketch, let me repeat that the strand of
the intricate network of democratic theory that is most pertinent to an understanding of technology is one that is part of the liberal tradition and has
been made prominent by John Stuart Mill, who in turn found its best articulation in Wilhelm von Humboldt's writings. It serves as a motto for Mill's
On Liberty and says:

> The grand, leading principle, towards which every argument un-
> folded in these pages directly converges, is the absolute and es-
> sential importance of human development in its richest diversity.[1]

This principle, as Mill recognized, came out of German Idealism and was
inspired by classical notions of human culture.[2] Humboldt might have been
thinking of Goethe as a representative of this ideal, a man who was a lyric,
epic, and dramatic poet, a literary critic, stage director, painter, natural scientist, and state official. And Humboldt himself in his manifold talents and
accomplishments contributed to the rich diversity of which he speaks.[3] Though
the cultural conditions of human development have changed radically in the
nearly two hundred years since Humboldt developed his liberal democratic
theory, his principle is still thought to be crucial to liberal democracy presently
and for the future. According to Macpherson, a liberal democracy is "a society
striving to ensure that all its members are equally free to realize their capa-

bilities."[4] That principle competes with a commitment of liberal democracies to "a capitalist market society."[5] And Macpherson suggests "that the continuance of anything that can be properly called liberal democracy depends on a downgrading of the market assumptions and an upgrading of the equal right to self-development."[6] In Macpherson's view, the unsolved problem of liberal democracy is its relationship to the class division that is entailed by capitalism. Liberal democratic theorists began, so he argues, by sanctioning the established classes at the expense of equality. Then they thought class division to be a merely accidental obstacle to liberal democracy. In the early twentieth century, they believed that classes had made way to a pluralism of interests. Finally, around the middle of this century, they recognized the rule of an elite which was periodically elected and approved by the people at large.

Ronald Dworkin, to the contrary, has argued that a free market system least prejudges the opportunities that are offered to people in pursuit of their self-development and that it allocates opportunities most efficiently. Admittedly, the market leads to inequalities, but these can be curbed through taxation and transfer payments.[7] Macpherson and Dworkin agree, however, that a moral principle is central to a truly liberal democracy. "Mill's model of democracy is a moral model," Macpherson says. Its moral significance lies in its concern to foster equal "chances of the improvement of mankind."[8] As suggested above, there were exemplars of a fully developed human being when Humboldt first formulated the principle, and so there was an understanding of the direction in which one had to move if humankind was to be improved. But little argument is needed to maintain that Goethe and Humboldt no longer constitute widely agreed upon models for the improvement of humanity. Does it make sense to urge a social and political commitment to the ideal of people "acting as exerters and enjoyers of the exertion and development of their own capacities" when it is quite unclear what the direction of such development should be?[9] Dworkin gives an emphatically affirmative answer and argues that it is in fact distinctive of liberalism that it subscribes to a theory of equality which

> supposes that political decisions must be, so far as possible, independent of any particular conception of the good life, or of what gives value to life. Since the citizens of a society differ in their conceptions, the government does not treat them as equals if it prefers one conception to another, either because the officials believe that one is intrinsically superior, or one is held by the more numerous or more powerful group.[10]

For Dworkin, this position does not betray a retreat from moral issues but is itself the "constitutive political morality" of liberalism.[11] "Its constitutive morality," he says, "provides that human beings must be treated as equals by their government, not because there is no right and wrong in political morality but because that is what is right.''[12] To arrogate the determination of the good life for others is to practice paternalism.[13]

Dworkin's formulation of the liberal democratic position is attractive because it seems to provide a principled and moral foundation for the apparently arbitrary way in which ends are formulated and selected in technology. The unexamined multiplicity of ends reprehended in prior chapters now seems to be the result of a commitment to a more fundamental ethical principle, equal respect for all citizens, and to the consequent endeavor to prejudge citizens' preferences as little as possible. Dworkin's position also sanctions the inclination of the social sciences toward empirical laws and their reserve concerning norms or values as discussed in Chapter 12. Laws, it was urged in the same chapter, circumscribe a possibility space that allows for infinitely many actualizations. Similarly, if the social sciences restrict themselves to the analysis and description of social structures and functions and refrain from advocacy and prescription, they appear to respect the notion of equality Dworkin finds basic to liberalism. Finally, it is clear that the universe of political discourse in this country is delimited by Dworkin's principle of liberalism. This is well illustrated by the national debates that are engendered every four years by the presidential elections. Those debates are entirely devoted to the question of how the means toward the good life can be secured and improved. They deal with the problems of how our lives can be made more secure, internally and internationally, how economic growth can be promoted, how access to opportunities can be broadened. The question of what the good life itself is never comes to the surface.

Dworkin suggests in effect that an instrumental notion of liberalism as a social order is the appropriate way to secure a substantive notion of liberty and equality. He thus belongs to an old tradition of political theory where the machinery of the state is devised so as to prevent the abuse of power and to a somewhat younger tradition that is concerned to make political institutions pliable to citizens' self-determination. But there is a strand in the fabric of political and especially democratic theory that we have ignored so far and that provides a crucial link between democracy and technology. It is the utopian tradition that was not concerned to fit democratic principles onto a class-divided society but proposed a new kind of society without classes where everyone would lead a free and rich life.[14] Macpherson, I am sure, is correct in his claim that the *liberal* democratic tradition became dominant in the early nineteenth century precisely because it abandoned the *utopian* democratic ideal of a truly egalitarian society.[15] But although there were henceforth no successful attempts to realize the utopian ideal in the political practices of the Western democracies, the ideal lived on in the promise of technology that was discussed in Chapter 8. It was said there that the promise of technology has become a commonplace. As such it has deeply informed our conception of democracy. Daniel Boorstin in fact suggests an equation of the promise of technology with the concept of democracy. He asks us to ''consider democracy not just as a political system, but as a set of institutions which do aim to make everything available to everybody."[16] He speaks of "our high-technology, well-to-do democratic society, which aims to get everything to everybody."[17] And most explicitly he says:

> "Democracy," according to political scientists, usually describes a form of government by the people, either directly or through their elected representatives. But I prefer to describe a democratic society as one which is governed by a spirit of equality and dominated by the desire to equalize, to give everything to everybody.[18]

Summarizing this brief historical account, we can say that the concepts of freedom, equality, and self-development are joined and developed in different constellations and with varying emphasis and that this conjunction of concepts has a close affinity to modern technology. Let me now state these connections more explicitly and abstractly. To begin, it seems obvious that the notions of liberty and equality are root concepts of democracy. The latter is unthinkable without the former. But what role does self-realization play in democratic theory? We must remember that liberty and equality are basic political norms but certainly not clear ones. Liberty is easily defined in a negative way, as the absence of constraints; correspondingly, liberation is most obviously an enterprise of breaking fetters and throwing off burdens. The Enlightenment was in large part just such a liberation movement. But liberation cannot simply be the razing of all established or traditional structures. There comes a point where the foundations of any kind of social existence are threatened and liberty turns into chaos. Now the ideal of self-realization comes into play as providing limits and a center for freedom. This ideal enjoins us to clear away what stands in the path of self-realization and to procure what is needed to achieve the ideal.

Self-realization similarly helps to specify and stabilize equality. Given that there are ineradicable differences among human beings, in what respect are we equal? And to what does equality entitle each of us? The norm of self-realization suggests that we are all equal in being capable of developing our common and various talents and that we have a right to the opportunities for such development. Self-realization constitutes a uniquely congenial specification of freedom and equality as they were understood in the Enlightenment because it appears to be a standard that puts the slightest constraints on the rebellious spirit of that movement and yet promises to provide enough guidance to steer society past social catastrophe. Finally, this vision of society appears to be practically feasible through modern technology, the latter understood instrumentally. In this view, technology provides powerful and effective means without constraining the individual's choice of the good life.

Having the crucial points of liberal democratic theory before us and seeing how it commonly appears to be joined to technology, we must now ask how well this vision accords with the obvious and the more hidden features of contemporary reality. It is clear, as has already appeared from the historical sketch, that the liberal democratic vision of equality has not asserted itself in practice. In the work world of this country, for instance, opportunities are sharply predetermined by one's sex, race, and above all by the social stratum into which one has been born.[19] The popular imagination is fond of illustrations that seem to show that this is the land of opportunity and upward mobility. And tales of the self-made man are no doubt used as instruments of social stability. They are thought to explain and justify the social order. This phenomenon belongs to the question of social justice and will concern us in detail later. At any rate, the common misunderstanding in regard to the opportunities a liberal democracy provides in the work world does not concern the nature of equal opportunity itself but rather the gap between the ideal and reality. It is therefore an error which is remedied when we are ready to face the facts of inequality. This is increasingly the case. But to act on the recognition of the inequality of work turns out to be extremely difficult for the body politic.

If in our society a principle of selection and limitation governs the distribution of work opportunities, then the principle indirectly determines social and material opportunities as well. The resulting inequalities are an embarrassment to liberal democracies. But again that means that in principle at least the conceptual resources of liberal democratic theory are adequate for the analysis and remedy of these problems. It is far different when we try to grasp *the nature* of the opportunities that have in fact been provided by the liberal democracies. It is undeniable that in respect to health, comfort, mobility, and access to culture the gap between the most and the least privileged is narrower in liberal democracies than in many other societies. And technology is surely the decisive factor in the narrowing of this gap. This achievement has been celebrated many times.[20] To be sure, none of the Western democracies has achieved the equality that liberal proponents like Macpherson, Dworkin, or John Rawls require. But each of these societies has a broad middle class where roughly equal opportunities obtain. Since these areas of equality are surrounded by unjustifiable extremes of poverty and affluence, they fail, of course, to represent embodiments of justice. They do, however, afford an illustration of what today's life among equal opportunities would be like. We may take them therefore as hypothetical cases of a liberal democracy, successfully realized in a technological setting. And it is just such possible success that turns out to be profoundly questionable when one asks what kind of opportunity is equally provided here.

Probing the nature of these opportunities takes us to a deeper level of democratic reality and analysis. At this level we no longer examine society by the standards of liberal democratic theory but in light of the pattern of technology. One should not, however, think of this deepening of the critique as subjecting the democratic program to an extraneous standard. Rather, the consideration of technology in this context exposes a profound, if not fatal, flaw in the liberal democratic structure. We can approach the salient point in a conventional way by distinguishing in sequence three visions of society, each appearing to be a necessary condition for the subsequent one. Let us call the first the constitutional or formally just society where equal liberties for all citizens are anchored in the constitution and in the civil and criminal legislation which specifies the constitution. This country very nearly realizes the vision of the constitutional society. But formal justice is compatible with substantive inequality. I may have the right to do nearly everything and yet the economic and cultural means to do next to nothing. This is one reason why liberal democratic theorists press for a second vision of society, that of a fair or substantively just society. They recognize that justice is as much a matter of economic arrangements and legislation as of civil rights and liberties.

But most political philosophers have a still brighter vision of society; for it is possible that typical life in a constitutional and just society is indolent, shallow, and distracted. What we finally want is a good society. The primary liberal democratic commitment is to a (substantively) just society. Liberal democrats merely hope for a good society; they believe that it is neither necessary nor possible to advance the good society politically; one can only let it happen. It is not possible to give it any political realization because that would be a violation of equal respect for all citizens. It is not necessary because we can in building the just society restrict our arrangements to the opportunities for the good life without prejudice to the individual conceptions of the good. I want to argue that just as the constitutional definition of society remains incomplete and corruptible without a statement of substantive justice, so the just society remains incomplete and is easily dispirited without a fairly explicit and definite vision of the good life. The last point can also be put this way: justice and culture are inevitably and strongly continuous with one and another.

Right now I want to show that justice, to the extent that it exists in Western democracies, is of a piece with technological culture. An alternative to this continuity is proposed in Part 3. We can begin this part of the analysis by connecting the distinctions just made with the notion of opportunity in the following way. A constitutional society furnishes formal or vacuous equality of opportunity. A just society secures fair or substantive equality of opportunity. Whether we have a good society depends on *the kind of opportunities* that the society provides for its citizens. And this last question is inevitably answered in some definite way. Moreover, the answer is always and already given in the ways in which we have set up formal and fair equality of opportunity. Thus in the liberal democratic and technologically advanced countries it is not so much the degree of equality and the range that distinguish their opportunities; it is the nature of the opportunities that sets them apart. Opportunities in a pretechnological society were to be grasped and acted out as a destiny. More precisely, one opportunity among others, however few, was to be taken up and lived out in a lifelong commitment; and all other opportunities ceased to be open and to exist. In a liberal democracy, on the other hand, any one opportunity is realized in a context of opportunities that remain open, and therefore an opportunity never turns into a destiny but merely into a state one is free to leave for the sake of one of the many opportunities that have remained open. Ronald Dworkin's principle of restraint is taken to the extreme point where in political decisions even the expectation of a commitment to a destiny would be arrogant. Ironically, Gerald Dworkin allows interference by authorities, i.e., paternalism, in the choice that persons make only when that interference is needed to

> preserve the liberty of the person to make future choices. This gives us a principle—a very narrow one—by which to justify some paternalistic interferences. Paternalism is justified only to preserve a wider range of freedom for the individual in question.[21]

Dworkin has in mind interference with "decisions which are far-reaching, potentially dangerous and irreversible," or "which are made under extreme psychological and sociological pressures," or those that entail "dangers which are either not sufficiently understood or appreciated correctly by the persons involved."[22] But Gerald Dworkin's principle is really a guide for the shaping of society, and it is so in the broad sense in which the principle is formulated at the end of the quotation above. But how, concretely, do we act on this principle? It is clear that things that are to be taken up and relinquished easily must be free of contextual ties. If taking something up is to enter into strong and manifold bonds, then to abandon that thing is to suffer the trauma of the disruption of those ties and of injury to one's faculties. But when the supporting structure of daily life assumes the character of a machinery that is concealed and separated from the commodities it procures and when these become isolated and mobile, then it becomes possible to style and restyle one's life by assembling and disassembling commodities. Life becomes positively ambiguous as we saw in the discussion of the foreground of technology.

Liberal democracy is enacted as technology. It does not leave the question of the good life open but answers it along technological lines. The question of life cannot be left open, either individually or socially. In living together, in doing this rather than that, we inevitably make decisions and give our lives a direction. Both the initial promise of technology and the modern democratic theories were profoundly ambiguous. The promise of technology ironically attained precision and force as it was acted out. Technology developed into a definite style of life. The theories of democracy remained vague, in some cases studiously so, about the character of life that they mean to promote. They were therefore overtaken by technology which they could not rival in energy and determinacy.

How technology has patterned our life both in its concrete details and its broader compass will be covered further in the remaining chapters of Part 2. The answers will carry more force if we can develop them against a fuller understanding of the curiously veiled position that technology has in liberal democratic discourse. One might say that the theory of liberal democarcy both needs and fears modern technology. It needs technology because the latter promises to furnish the neutral opportunities necessary to establish a just society and to leave the question of the good life open. It fears technology because technology may in fact deliver more than it had promised, namely, a definite version of the good society and, more important yet, one which is "good" in a dubious sense. The pivot of this predicament in liberal theory, however, is not the phenomenon of technology itself but the question of whether we can establish a just society without a commitment to a good society in a strong sense. This indirection of liberal discourse may bespeak the fear, mentioned above; but as likely or more so, it may have deep historical roots and stem from the original cast of the Enlightenment which, as noted earlier, was conceived as an intellectual and cultural event and only incidentally as a practical one.

Now to give the conjecture just proposed a measure of substance, let us look first at some liberal democratic policies that illustrate the salient point, and then at the ways in which that point has exercised such liberal proponents as Ronald Dworkin, Rawls, and Macpherson. The policies in question come out of the democratic commitment to liberation. In this endeavor, liberal democratic policy is often unwittingly and perhaps inevitably the accomplice in the dissolution of the traditions used to encourage a vigorous realization of freedom. To make divorces, abortions, and entry into the labor market easy, to strike down residency requirements, and to protect pornography is of course to withdraw formal social support from the traditional family, from the reverence for emerging human life, from rooted communal living, and from the view that there are privileged and sacred ways of expressing love. To be sure, when such traditional goods are in jeopardy they cannot be secured by civil and criminal law. The law can conform to matters of ultimate concern or morality only when there is something like unanimity. There are probably more shared views on morality in this country than we realize.[23] But to make a controversial moral point prevail through the law as conservatives intend to is to compromise the point. The discourse that can do justice to such matters is deictic. It can never exact assent apodeictically though it can work toward consensus in a principled way. If one skips this task and reaches for the cogency of the law or the Constitution, one suggests in effect that the point in question lacks genuine authority.[24] Here lies the kernel of truth in Ronald Dworkin's version and advocacy of liberalism. The political forum cannot deal with matters of ultimate significance straightforwardly through political decisions. The forum must be kept open. But openness is not emptiness.

Conservatives are correct, I believe, in their attempt to draw matters of ultimate concern into the universe of political discourse. But, as suggested, they tend to short-circuit the discursive transaction of such problems. What is worse, as a rule they are inconsistent in their policies. The traditional good they seek to secure through civil and criminal legislation they undermine through economic legislation. It is through the latter that democracies are given substance, and in this regard conservatives and liberals alike have fallen prey to the irony of technology. Both are committed to a policy of economic growth in excess of the increase in population. Though they differ in the ways in which they want to distribute the fruits of economic growth, both factions understand such growth as an increase in productivity which yields more consumer goods. Improved productivity, as we shall see, entails the degradation of work, and greater consumption leads to more distraction. Thus in an advanced industrial country, a policy of economic growth promotes mindless labor and mindless leisure. The resulting climate is not hospitable to the traditional values of the conservatives. This is the predicament of the conservatives. Nor is such a climate favorable to "human development in its richest diversity." It produces a wealth of different commodities. But underneath this superficial variety, there is a rigid and narrow pattern in which people take up with the world. This is the liberal predicament.

These considerations suggest illustrations of the point that, when we promote a just society along liberal democratic lines, we also advance the technological society and its specific and dubious notion of the good life. But it seems impossible for liberal democratic theorists to acknowledge the essential continuity between the just and the good society and to rethink both justice and goodness in light of this affinity. Thus Ronald Dworkin, who has given such a precise account of the presently dominant version of liberalism, defends this version against all objections save one: "that it denies to political society its highest function and ultimate justification, which is that society must help its members to achieve what is in fact good."[25] Dworkin acknowledges the force of the objection but believes that on this issue "reasonable and moral men will disagree."[26] In this remark there lies at least a suggestion that the value neutrality that supposedly is required by the underlying "constitutive political morality" of liberalism infects and dissolves its fundament. Dworkin admits that the fundament has one objectionable feature: it occludes public discourse about the good life. It does so by design at the level of "political decisions." It need not do so, even by liberal standards, at the fundamental level where the constitutive political morality of liberalism is articulated. The subject of political morality is after all eo ipso within the discourse about the good life. But such fundamental discourse, so Dworkin suggests, will remain inconclusive by the standards of reason and morality, and hence the liberal political morality is really no more fundamental and constitutive than the value neutrality which follows from it at the level of political decisions. Dworkin believes that, at any rate, the problems that are "fundamental for political theory" are to be raised "in moral philosophy and in the philosophy of mind."[27] I would agree that as long as fundamental problems are so located their discussion will remain inconclusive.[28] If the fundament of the social order can be discovered, it will be through the examination not of minds and morals but of the concrete and typical ways in which people take up with their world.

Dworkin sees clearly that moral neutrality is too weak a foundation for a just society.[29] On the other hand, an insightful and articulate moral commitment to equality is too strong to yield a merely just society and will involve us in the question of what a good society is. Dworkin can keep that question at bay only through vagueness. It besets his appeal to the principle that we owe all persons equal respect. The appeal is forceful when it expresses a concern for people who are deprived and neglected in an obvious way.[30] Here the call for equal respect is consonant with the liberating promise of technology. I agree with Dworkin that this call badly needs to be heard in this country and that this necessity is an indictment of our policies. On the other hand, of all the fellow citizens to whom he wants us to extend equal respect, most are not in a situation of need but in one of distracting and debilitating affluence. These are the people who have been overtaken by the irony of technology. What does it mean to treat someone so situated with respect? Must it not mean that respect takes the form of distress and of a concern to invite these people to consider their deeper and fuller aspirations? But this is the question the liberal school is unwilling to face. Respect must decay to indifference. Dworkin avoids this conclusion through his vague and distant view of the technological society. From that viewpoint it may appear as though our central social concern ought to be the extension and completion of the truly liberating phase of technology. But technology in many respects has passed this stage. When Dworkin counters moral neutrality explicitly by volunteering a liberal commitment to the good society, vagueness settles on the features of such a society or, when concrete features of a cultural sort are envisioned, their effects are kept bland and uncontroversial.[31]

The problem of the good life is irrepressible once the question of justice is fully opened up, and we can see how this problem comes to the fore at various levels and in different contexts. But might it not be possible to draw a principled and appropriate line between justice and goodness if we see this task clearly and approach it with both rigor and circumspection? This is one of the challenges John Rawls tries to meet in his celebrated theory of justice.[32] The line can be drawn in Rawls's terms if we can specify a fair arrangement of the primary social goods which does not favor a particular notion of the good life. The primary social goods are rights and liberties, powers and opportunities, income and wealth, and self-respect. Evidently some conception of goodness is at work here. Rawls acknowledges this but also believes that the goodness here invoked is general and uncontroversial, "thin" as he says.[33] That view has been challenged from many sides.[34] The major vehicle of these challenges is the counterexample. One takes a hypothetical kind of a legitimately good life and shows that Rawls's just society fails to be neutral toward that sort of life. I think these charges are in general both devastating and indecisive. They are devastating in the sense that Rawls's argument has strongly formal, even deductive, pretensions.[35] And if one can show that Rawls's premises yield the wrong conclusions, that demonstration should signal the defeat of Rawls's endeavor. But in addition to its formal guise, Rawls's theory has a richness of insight and of contemporary relevance which allows it to survive formal defeats. Consequently, more helpful light falls on Rawls's enterprise when we confront it, not with hypothetical and formally sketched counterexamples, but with the situation that exists, i.e., with the technological society and its distinctive pattern. This I want to do critically here and more constructively in various chapters of Part 3, and in either instance I hope I will be forgiven for using a great book as a mere foil.

We may begin by asking how Rawls responds to the charge that his theory of justice is unfair to certain conceptions of the good life. He could raise the generality of his theory and designate justice as pertaining to those "things which it is supposed a rational man wants whatever else he wants."[36] But one might rightly wonder what such things would be or even whether there can be such things. The reply is that these things consist of the primary social goods. One could still be puzzled as to the nature of primary social goods, and Rawls would then present the standard list given above. Can one now in good conscience profess to have a concept of the subject of justice which is sufficiently specific and clear to serve as a framework for the choice of principles of justice? As Rawls notes, liberties and rights are more easily defined than social and economic arrangements.[37] But what if one persists in wanting to know, e.g., what the opportunities are that Rawls wants to be secured in a just and equal manner?[38] Rawls answers this question implicitly at best and in roughly two ways.[39] Opportunities in one sense are universally shared social or economic structures so basic as not to prejudge the question of the good life. In another sense, opportunities consist in the availability of such a variety of ways of life that no reasonable variant is precluded. But both senses, I want to argue, are conceived technologically or they are incoherent.

First we must recognize that the question of whether there can be largely value-neutral opportunities does not admit of a helpful general answer since it is just generality which occludes the decisive issues. Turning then to opportunities in the sense of basic structures, we may think of these among others as the economic infrastructure, the systems of transportation, utilities, and communication. Consider a system of roads and highways or a telephone and television network and assume them to be equally available to all. Surely they do not tell people when or where to travel, whom to call, or what to watch. On the other hand, a mountain valley that has been split by a road is no longer a place for solitary hiking. A perfect telephone system would suffocate the art of correspondence. And television at the least discourages municipal theaters and symphonies. We can see here the outlines of the technological pattern. Basic social and economic structures can be indifferent only as to the choice of commodities; but they are far from neutral as to the choice of engagement with things versus consumption of commodities.[40]

Rawls might reply that the social arrangements are more or less just as long as anyone is free and able to hike someplace, write letters, or stage plays with like-minded people. If there is sufficient opportunity for a variety of life-styles, there cannot be a complaint of injustice. And we can in fact, so it seems, have voluntary associations for engagement with things within the liberally just society. But as Rawls himself recognizes, "The social system shapes the desires and aspirations of its members; it determines in large part the kind of persons they want to be as well as the kind of persons they are."[41] Still, let us assume that groups of people have a clear view of the present technological structure of society and a strong commitment to various kinds of engagement with things. Let them act on their convictions by forming voluntary associations as Rawls suggests.[42] Clearly, however, the deeper the commitment and the more determined the action, the more radically such an association will want to transform its immediate social and even physical setting. Failure to do so would amount to complicity with a kind of life that the association rejects. To the degree of their decisiveness these groups will attenuate the bonds with the larger community and so the subject of justice. At the limit we would have various societies where once there was one, and each would have wedded justice to a definite vision of the good life. To be sure, between technological homogeneity and sectarian fragmentation there is a just and fruitful middle ground. Much is to be learned from Rawls in locating it. But it cannot be found without the recognition that justice is strongly interwoven with goodness.

Yet even when technology is explicitly envisaged as a social problem and in its connection with democracy, technology has a tendency to deflect a searching examination. Before we turn to the concrete circumstances of this elusiveness, we should take note of its theoretical reflections. They can be seen in the considerations of Macpherson and of Jürgen Habermas.

Macpherson takes a much more critical view of present liberal democracy and therefore penetrates more nearly the veil that conceals the technological specification of democracy. His call for a participatory democracy implicitly aims at the disengagement that technology has imported into democracy. And he is closer to the mark yet in formulating as the first prerequisite for the emergence of participation "a change of people's consciousness (or unconsciousness), from seeing themselves and acting as essentially consumers to seeing themselves and acting as exerters and enjoyers of the exertion and development of their own capacities."[43] "The other prerequisite," he says, "is a great reduction of the present social and economic inequality. . . ."[44] But when he looks about for factors that may fulfill the prerequisites and advance participatory democracy, he finds them in people's dissatisfaction with what economists would call the externalities of technology, the deterioration of the environment, the depletion of resources, unemployment, urban decay, the inability to manage economic growth.[45] These are shortcomings by the technological standards themselves. They are failures of procurement and availability and so within the framework of technology. We will see in subsequent chapters that these problems are solvable within technology and, if solved, would only strengthen the rule of technology. Preliminary evidence that Macpherson's factors of discontent are challenges within and not to the ruling paradigm can be seen in the fact that these problems are fully at the center and attention of public discourse.

Macpherson's positive sketch proposes to revive participatory democracy along formal lines, through new forms of gathering, organizing, debating, voting, delegating, and so forth. But if the substance of the good life remains technologically or even ambiguously defined, reform will be impossible or inconsequential.[46] The direction of school systems in this country is often quite participatory in form. But when one considers voter turnout, composition of school boards, and the role of experts, one will find that the school system is not much more politically vibrant and vigorous than the telephone system. The substance of the good life must be taken into consideration if radical political reform is to become a live option. To illustrate the difficulty of inaugurating a principled discussion of the good life, let me in conclusion of this chapter turn to some of Jürgen Habermas's reflections on technology and the good life.

Habermas recognizes that the questions of ethics in regard to the social order are not controversial but eliminated and repressed.[47] This state of affairs, he contends, can best be explained through the distinction of work and interaction. The distinction also is said to help us understand the fundamental change in temperament that distinguishes our time from all others and that the classical sociologists have tried to capture in various pairs of contrasting terms.[48] "By 'work' or *purposive-rational action*," Habermas says, "I understand either instrumental action or rational choice or their conjunction."[49] Interaction, on the other hand, is defined as *"communicative action,* symbolic interaction. It is governed by binding *consensual norms,* which define reciprocal expectations about behavior and which must be understood and recognized by at least two acting subjects."[50] In traditional societies, interaction is superior to work and keeps the productive activities of work within bounds.[51] In the bourgeois revolution, work emancipated itself from interaction. Economic productivity expanded and was legitimated by the market ideology, i.e., the principle of fair exchange. Since work is purposive-rational action, the expansion of work at the expense of interaction is well called rationalization. It proceeds from below by transforming traditional structures such as labor, trade, and transportation. It proceeds from above when the traditional world views are criticized by the standards of purposive rationality. This critique attempts to unmask traditions as ideologies and thereby hides and makes inaccessible its own ideological character.[52] It allies itself with the modern sciences not only because they provide a model of rational critique but because their methodology "reflects the transcendental viewpoint of possible technological control."[53] This orientation has issued in "the scientization of technology" the explanation and promotion of technological processes on a scientific basis.[54] The drive toward total rationalization Habermas calls the technocratic intention which finally establishes itself as the technocratic consciousness.[55] This domination can be broken and a genuine discussion "about the goals of life activity and conduct" can be initiated only if the conditions for the ideal speech situation can be approximated.[56] "Communicative competence" is Habermas's term for the set of those conditions that includes unrestrained discussion, significant rapport despite the inviolable distance between the partners of communication, and full complementarity of expectations, including exclusion of unilaterally constraining norms.[57]

Let us begin our critical remarks with a consideration of communicative competence and work our way back from there. Richard J. Bernstein has pointed out that one may take the outline of communicative competence as a set of conditions necessary for any communication. But in that case the move from necessity to sufficiency of conditions can bring us to all kinds of actual communication, deceptive, self-deceptive, or distorted. And so communicative competence has little guiding force.[58] If, on the other hand, we think of communicative competence as an ideal of communication that, when approximated, guarantees the establishment of discursively redeemed, unconstrained consensual norms, the ideal is abstract and pale to the point of impotence.[59] One seed of this dilemma lies in the distinction between work and interaction, which is reminiscent of Hannah Arendt's between labor and action and suffers from similar deficiencies.[60] To posit *"subsystems of purposive-rational action,"* i.e., relatively autonomous elements of work within the normative framework of interaction, is to read the notion of mere means, which is typical of modern technology, back into pretechnological settings.[61] To be sure, traditional cultures had focal things and practices where norms were eminently embodied and enacted.[62] Accordingly there were prosaic and utilitarian matters peripheral to the focal ones. But what an immersion in the concrete details of a traditional setting impresses on one is the close texture of means and ends, of the ferial and the festal, of productive and social relations. An adumbration of such a fabric was given in Chapter 9.

It is the failure to examine incisively the radically novel means-character of modern technology that flaws Habermas's investigations and proposals. He senses the idiosyncrasy of rationalization, i.e., of the emancipation of work from interaction, but he provides no sufficiently radical analysis. This appears by the way when Habermas discusses rationalization from below, i.e., the subordination of traditional structures to standards of work. These structures include labor, trade, transportation, and institutions of private law. But if it is true that in traditional settings there were always and already subsystems of work, the structures just mentioned must have been examples. And if labor or trade, for instance, already constituted subsystems of purposive-rational action, there was no need to subordinate them "to conditions of instrumental or strategic rationality."[63] Rationalization from below would have been unnecessary and impossible as a fundamental and noteworthy restructuring. But we know that traditional labor and trade were indeed thoroughly transformed in the course of technology. Habermas is right that something like rationalization from below took place. But his notion of work and its distinction from interaction are unable to capture precisely the nature of this change.

Habermas's lack of incisiveness is more notable in the central points of his diagnosis and therapy. In light of Habermas's distinction, the course of modern technology is marked by the escape of instrumental and strategic rationality from the guidance of norms. Why do not means without ends run wild and end in disaster? According to Habermas the inclination of emancipated work toward fatal crises is checked by state intervention in social and economic affairs, and this leads to a repoliticizing of the institutional framework of society.[64] But the corrective measures, Habermas contends, do not spring from a positive vision of the good society; they rather constitute "reactive crisis avoidance," i.e., a series of ad hoc measures which patch up ever new and unexpected cracks in the system.[65] But in whose interest is it to keep the system intact? Habermas recognizes it is impossible in an advanced technological society to delimit a class in the strict sense that has a dominant position based on the exploitation of other classes.[66] Yet he claims that latent class antagonisms persist.[67] And his continued use of the term "capitalism" suggests that there remains a class of capitalists. The notion of the techno*cratic* consciousness implies the same thing. There must be a class of people who do the *kratéin,* the dominating, in or through technology.

Habermas thus stakes out a position precariously poised between the more orthodox Marxist positions we touched on in Chapter 13 and the realization that underlying the standard distinctions of both the Marxists and the liberal democratic theorists there is an elastic structure or pattern which bestows coherence on the shifting and occasionally disparate surface features in the economics and politics of technologically advanced democracies, a structure, moreover, that shields and removes itself from public scrutiny. And occasionally Habermas seems to imply that this basic structure commands the consent of all. The eclipse of interaction by work, he says, "is paralleled subjectively by the disappearance of the difference between purposive-rational action and interaction from the consciousness not only of the sciences of man, but of men themselves. The concealment of this difference proves the ideological power of the technocratic consciousness."[68] But even here we find a telling ambiguity. Is "the consciousness of men" the technocratic consciousness itself, or is it in its obtuseness the consequence of domination by a class of technocrats?

The resolution of this ambiguity would require an explication of the underlying structure or pattern of the technological democracies. As said before, however, Habermas is deflected from these tasks by his uncritical notion of work, understood essentially as instrumental action. This finally makes his proposals converge with those of the liberal democratic positions. Technology is in the end and after all acceptable as rationalization if it is taken as a mere tool and subordinated to a higher kind of rationalization, namely, the institution of communicative competence.[69] But the latter is merely the iteration of tool procurement at a more sublime level, very much like Macpherson's reform proposal.[70] Accordingly, Habermas fills the gap as regards the end to which those means are to be put with the conjuncion of the liberal democratic maxim of equal self-realization and the technological promise of liberation and enrichment.[71] To be sure, there is the more systematic claim that communicative competence will of itself give rise to genuine consensual norms for the good life. But given the experiences that we all have had with "unrestrained discussions," that claim would be altogether unconvincing without the background of the promises of technology and democracy.[72]

It appears then that we can make room for the discussion of the good life only if we have before us the pattern of technology and the peculiar way in which, under the semblance of a mere tool, it preforms our discourse and agenda. Having seen the complex and various ways in which the technological paradigm informs our dominant theories of the social order, we must now attend to the concrete and empirical circumstances of the rule of technology.

15 The Rule of Technology

The question this chapter poses is how people have in fact worked out their relationship to technology. Concrete and detailed answers have been given in the chapters that introduced the device paradigm and the foreground of life that is distilled by the pattern of technology. Although such investigations are indispensable to opening up new perspectives, they have an unavoidable appearance of anecdote and conjecture. For this reason, and also to get beyond the diffractions that the pattern of technology undergoes in the prevailing social theory and discourse, we must consider what empirical findings there are on this point. As suggested before, however, the data of the social sciences are not by themselves helpful. They are precise and ambiguous at the same time. We may think of them as objective points on the social map which are compatible with many, though not all, encompassing outlines of the character of society. In trying to sketch this fuller picture we must allow ourselves to be guided by intuition and firsthand experience. The attempt to obviate the need for such guidance by assembling a sufficient number of data points would be futile. Social reality is too rich and complex to be captured in this way.

Before we turn to the empirical findings, we must therefore construct a linkage between the intuitive and theoretical considerations developed so far and the results of polls and questionnaires on people's attitude toward technology. A helpful link to this end is the question of responsibility. Is there a clearing in which people can take responsibility for technology? Do they have occasions and forums of choice? And with what degree of awareness do they decide? When one attempts to answer these questions, one has to establish, so it appears from the preceding chapters, a position that escapes the obscurity of the substantive view of technology and overcomes the superficiality of the instrumentalist view. The inadequacy of the substantive and instrumental views becomes apparent in the unsatisfactory and sometimes inconsistent answers that they provide to the question of responsibility. Langdon Winner has put the issue succinctly:

> On the one hand we encounter the idea that technological devel-
> opment goes forward virtually of its own inertia, resists any lim-
> itation, and has the character of a self-propelling, self-sustaining,
> ineluctable flow. On the other hand are arguments to the effect
> that human beings have full, conscious choice in the matter and
> that they are responsible for choices made at each step in the
> sequence of change. The irony is that both points of view are
> entertained simultaneously with little awareness of the contradic-
> tion such beliefs contain. There is even a certain pride taken in
> embracing both positions within a single ideology of technological
> change.[1]

Different concepts of technology naturally suggest different notions of free-dom and responsibility. The substantive concept implies determinism, the instrumental concept agrees with libertarianism. One might be tempted to approach the question of the rule of technology from the side of freedom and determinism, to ascertain the ethical and metaphysical groundwork on which to erect a theory of technology. But a glance at the literature shows that one cannot fall back on a universally accepted answer to this question, and none can be worked out here. Enough indications, however, have been given in earlier chapters to afford orientation vis-à-vis freedom and determinism. The natural sciences reveal reality to be thoroughly lawful. Within the boundaries of lawfulness, things and events stand out in unique ways which can be scientifically acknowledged and explicated but not (without regress) predicted or warranted. To stand out in such ways is to be significant. Human beings stand out in a privileged way because they are both significant and capable of significance, i.e., they can grasp significance and make it prevail more fully. This capacity for significance is where human freedom should be located and grounded. Again, we cannot expound here how such a notion of freedom is related to traditional notions.[2] But we can point out how this view informs and advances the present inquiry. It is guided by a definite significance, or, as it was expressed on earlier occasions, by a substantive concern. This is a very general answer, given that "significance" is nothing but the highest generic term for things and practices that stand out in their own right. What specifically are those things and practices? A less general answer was given when it was said that the present critique of technology is moved by a concern for those things and practices that used to and still can engage and grace us in their own right and which are now threatened by technology. One must go further in the description of those things and practices, and we will do so in Part 3.

Regarding the rule of technology, the foregoing remarks already imply the decisive question; and it can be put explicitly this way: How are people positioned between their engagement with things and the approach to reality which is patterned by technology? This question is answered, first, by delineating the scope of action and the occasions of decision where people work out their position in relation to engagement and technology. And, second, the answer requires reflection on the kind of awareness with which people work out their lives.

Turning first to the question of the leeway that people have in working out their technological existence, there is a scope of action about technology in that there are even today pretechnological and metatechnological practices of engagement. This scope of action in which people exercise their responsibility becomes concrete in an occasion of decision. The chief obstacle in delimiting such occasions stems from the fact that technology is seldom offered as a choice, i.e., as a way of life that we are asked to prefer over others, but is promoted as a basis for choices. It is so advanced in political or properly technological terms. Ronald Dworkin has provided the political formulation, and in light of it a decision against technology or, more accurately, against technologically specified democracy is one against freedom simply and for prejudice, paternalism, or totalitarianism. The properly technological version is given as the promise of liberation and enrichment, and to refuse the promise would be to choose confinement, misery, and poverty. The point can be made differently. Enlightened and confident proponents of technology do not meet their critics with antagonism and reproof but with sympathy and resourcefulness. They will invite the dissenters to explain what they find deficient or lacking in the present scheme of things, and the technologists will agree with their adversaries that these things should and someday will be made available. The procurement of availability seems to deflect and co-opt all criticism. Or in terms of the previous considerations, technology has the tendency to disappear from the occasion of decision by insinuating itself as the basis of the occasion. When modern men and women today make their decisions as voters or consumers, technology, as a rule, has provided the fundaments of their choices.

But lest we lapse into the substantive view of technology, we must persist in the search for points of genuine choice. And again our concept of technology tells us where to look. Genuine choices occur when one is called upon to decide between engagement and disengagement. Such decisions are made in the realm of leisure and consumption, but often they are too close and inconspicuous to become visible in the usual categories of social science. A genuine choice is made when a family decides to eat out more often. The practice of preparing a traditional meal, of setting the table, of saying grace, of conversing and eating thoughtfully is partly surrendered to the machinery of a fast-food chain and partly lost. The meal has been impoverished to ordering and consuming standardized foods. When one moves from city to city in pursuit of professional advancement, the possibility of a rooted kind of life is cut off just as the means for the consumption of freely disposable commodities are increased. When parents decide to give their child a stereo set and receiver instead of a flute and instruction, they help to inundate the child with sounds and fail to encourage fully embodied and disciplined engagement with music. Whenever something is replaced rather than repaired, a piece of history, something that bespeaks and sustains the continuity of life, is then surrendered to the garbage heap; and an opportunity to mark and affirm the stages of life is lost.

People do have choices here. It is to take a condescending view if one excuses families who surrender and betray their traditions by saying that advertisements told them to eat out more often and to refurbish their home according to the dictates of the Sears catalogue. Of course, people no longer have a choice between horses and motorcars or between shoemakers and shoestores. And the residents of a valley may have no choice whether it will continue to be farmed or will be dammed. But it is possible to delimit in people's lives occasions where in the absence of economic or legal pressures they confront an issue that turns on engagement versus distraction. And through such decisions they confirm or protest the rule of technology.

With what kind of consciousness are such decisions made? To answer this question we must develop and illustrate reflections that were proposed in Chapter 12. When a social paradigm is deeply entrenched, it not only informs most human practices but it also patterns the organizations, institutions, the daily implements, the structures of civilization, and even the ways in which nature and culture are arranged and accessible. All of reality is patterned after the paradigm, and in this sense we can say that the paradigm has acquired an ontological dimension. When applied to technology, this is not to explain the paradigm's origin but to highlight the extent and intensity of its rule. When the pattern is so firmly established, it also tends to become invisible. There are fewer and fewer contrasts against which it is set off; and meeting us in objective correlatives, it attains an objective and impersonal force. To move within the realm of devices and commodities is then entirely normal, and to exchange the engagement with things for the consumption of commodities is to extend the range of normalcy. This relation to technology is neither one of domination by technology nor one of conscious direction of technology. It is perhaps best called one of implication in technology. Living in an advanced industrial country, one is always and already implicated in technology and so profoundly and extensively that one's involvement normally remains implicit. The rule of technology is not the reign of a substantive force people would bear with resentment or resistance. Rather technology is the rule today in constituting the inconspicuous pattern by which we normally orient ourselves.[3]

But whenever the turn from a thing to a commodity or from engagement to diversion is taken, the paradigm by contrast comes into view at least partially, and an occasion of decision opens up. It is of course an empirical question how aware people are of these occasions. An answer by question-naires is impossible because the pattern of technology is too implicit and complex to be available as a framework for yes-or-no answers, rankings, or even multiple choices among statements. There is empirical evidence that bears on the question, but it is necessarily ambiguous. Still it is not without significance. Some of the ambiguity can be resolved if we first answer the question ourselves as citizens and eyewitnesses of the technological society. We have ourselves taken the step from engagement to diversion; we have had occasion to see others take it and to talk to them about it. What moves one to take the step, so firsthand experience tends to show, is the persistent glamour of the promise of technology; the relief that one looks forward to in having the burden of preparing another meal lifted from one's shoulders; the hope of a richer engagement with the world on the basis of greater affluence; the desire to provide one's child with the fullest and easiest means of development; the impatience with things that require constant care and frequent repair; and the wish to affirm one's existence through the acquisition of property that commands respect. But these sentiments are tinged, especially in retrospect, with feelings of loss, sorrow, and of betrayal, both in the sense that one has betrayed a thing or a tradition to which one owes an essential debt, and in the sense that one has been betrayed in one's aspirations. Implication in technology then receives an admixture of uneasiness which results in what may be called complicity.[4]

Such reflections afford a framework for the consideration of empirical findings. There are three surveys on people's attitudes toward technology that I want to consider. To begin with, it is fair to claim, I believe, that the concept of technology that guides those investigations is a prereflective version of the paradigm that is being worked out here. Two of the surveys ask for agreement or disagreement to the statements "People (today) have become too dependent on machines," "Technology has made life too complicated," and "It would be nice if we would stop building so many machines (factories) and go back to nature."[5] Clearly technology is seen here as something more than a neutral instrument and yet not as a force in its own right. It is understood as the comprehensive and dominant way in which reality is being shaped today. The explicit definition in one of the surveys shows an obvious kinship with our notion of technology. It defines technology as "the activity which leads to the widespread availability of products based predominantly on . . . scientific knowledge."[6] The surveys agree that there is "considerable ambivalence" in people's attitude toward technology, that "the public applies a rather wide range of sometimes contradictory values to its evaluation of technology."[7] On balance the attitude seems favorable. People do not want to go back to nature. On the other hand, such a suggestion reveals the weakness of an unreflective notion of technology and of interviews which, without probing and prompting, elicit answers that are definite in form and inconclusive in content. Is a return to nature the decisive countermove to technology once technology is more thoroughly examined? What is it that people do not want to return to? Caves? Campfires? Hunting and gathering? They do believe that the quality of life is better in the country than in the city and that we have become too dependent on machines. But they do not find that life in the technological society is too complicated.[8] They appreciate the comforts of present technology.[9] But it appears from other investigations that a general increase in technological comforts, i.e., a rise in the standard of living, does not lead to greater satisfaction or happiness.[10] People's implicit denial that the progress of technology has increased their mental and spiritual well-being is accentuated by their occasional denial that technology has increased their material well-being, a denial clearly at odds with the facts.[11] Apparently people cannot let go of the promise of technology and continue to be vitally concerned with a high and rising standard of living.[12] They look forward to higher standards of pleasure, comfort, convenience, security, and leisure.[13] This trust or hope in technology is particularly strong among the poor and less educated, although these people know that in the past their hope and trust have not been fulfilled.[14]

It appears then that the popular attitude toward technology as it appears in surveys is compatible with the relation to technology that has been explicated above as one of implication or complicity, and the inevitable ambiguities of survey findings can be resolved accordingly though other resolutions are no doubt possible. There are also empirical investigations in greater depth that bear on our understanding of the ways in which people have worked out their relation to technology.[15] The results are striking, particularly when their research interest and conceptual framework are not aligned with those of our present concern. An example can be found in Sennett and Cobb's study of *The Hidden Injuries of Class,* and the phenomenon in question is the move from the ethnic neighborhoods of Boston to the suburbs.[16] In the old neighborhoods people live in extended families which provide an engaging social context. But engagement can be experienced as a burden. "What appear as sustaining bonds at one time," the authors say, "may appear as oppressive chains at another."[17] They show in a number of cases how the departure from extended family and tradition is taken as a liberating move: "It can be said that an American dream of freedom, of alone-ness, has seized hold of these once-isolated people—and left them dissatisfied."[18] The American dream of freedom is a version of the promise of technology. The progress of technology makes a single-family house in the suburbs attainable for at least some workers, and it provides the mobility such residence requires. It liberates a young couple from the "oppressive closeness" of their parents. But when people so disengage themselves, they also become lonely. Similarly, this holds for people who try to escape from the restrictions of a rural setting. Sennett and Cobb report from studies of such migrants: "They came to Los Angeles to work in order to be free, on their own; and they feel lonely."[19]

16   Political Engagement and Social Justice

This is the last of the four chapters dealing with the social and political setting of technology. It begins by summarizing and highlighting the character of technological politics and then attempts to secure further if not final conviction for it by showing that it can explain what remain scandals and puzzles to traditional liberal theories: political apathy and the persistence of social injustice. Speaking summarily, then, we can say that technology undergirds our political and social system. The system therefore comfortably survives crises that would be grave threats to it were it capitalist or democratic in the usual senses of these terms. This country has had riots in the big cities, lost a war, had a president resign in disgrace, had inflation approach 20 percent and unemployment rise above 10 percent, and sees its energy basis erode. But the common pace of life has hardly been affected. Political action, when it faces a crisis, finds its orientation in the device paradigm. Politics has become the metadevice of the technological society. Wherever subsystems of technology clash or founder, there is a call for political action to procure ease and safety for the system as a whole. Habermas is correct in seeing that government has become strangely meliorative and remedial.[1] It is the agency of last resort and yet barren of positive guidance. This becomes intelligible, however, when we recognize the government as the ultimate servant of technology.

Often the government solves a crisis by creating a government agency that becomes a device for the procurement of a definite social benefit. The citizen participates in the solution of such a crisis as the beneficiary of the social commodity and as the supporter of the governmental machinery. But this relation to the machinery is narrowed to the payment of taxes. Otherwise the machinery has its paradigmatic inaccessibility. The citizens normally do not understand it; and if they did, engagement would still be impossible. There

are islands and overlays of social engagement in bureaucracies; there is occasional cordiality, friendship, and grace; and though all this is important in
making life for the workers in a bureaucracy and for the recipients of the
benefits more bearable, the commodities are finally allocated mechanically.
In fact, the intrusion of humane and personal considerations into the central
mechanics of a government agency would invite corruption.

Government proper, particularly in its legislative and executive branches,
has not entirely taken on the form of a device. Technology constitutes the
pattern that is distinctive of our age, but it impresses itself on matters that
have a deeply traditional cast and force. It also proceeds on various fronts
and at different rates. This gives rise to stresses and crises which, as Habermas
has remarked, have the unforeseeable and uncontrollable character of natural
catastrophes.[2] They are beyond technological control, however, only in their
origin. Once they have come into view, they are interpreted as burdens of
which we can free ourselves by assigning them to appropriate machineries.

This common and unchallenged framework has an orienting and stabilizing
force. It affords a measure of patience and confidence and tolerance for the
changes that typically result from technological solutions: increasing disburdenment and the procurement of narrow commodities in place of the complex
engagement with things. If there is impatience, it is typically not with the
framework within which problems arise and solutions are attempted but with
delays or inefficiencies in the procurement of commodities. The overall economic stability has certainly grown with the progress of technology.[3] It is a
reflection of that increase in stability that the tolerance for disturbances has
decreased.

As the machinery of government becomes more sophisticated and powerful,
disturbances change from unforeseeable crises to deviations from a standard
state which are anticipated in their range if not their details and met through
homeostatic adjustments. Society then becomes a nearly closed system. Aldous Huxley's *Brave New World* is the exemplar of such a society, and
Manfred Stanley has provided a theoretical outline of it under the heading of
"the libertarian technicist society."[4] It appears clearly from Stanley's sketch
that when government becomes a perfect technological device, political disengagement becomes complete as well. Though there is a discernible tendency
in this direction, government as of now is still an open system.

It is open in two very different senses. From the technological point of
view it is negatively open, open in the sense of being incomplete. From the
standpoint of a critique of technology, it is positively open, i.e., it affords an
institutional forum of discourse and action where the citizens could preserve
and make room for engagement. Members of the technological society are
largely impotent vis-à-vis corporations and government agencies when they
are called upon to act as consumers and taxpayers. But as citizens they have
a scope of action that is undeniably wide and genuine. Again it is to take a
condescending view of people's energy and judgment to blame the politicians,

the lobbies, and the media for civic apathy. Complacency bespeaks a general acceptance of the technological society. Acceptance, of course, ranges from quiet resentment to chauvinist affirmation.[5] The positive opening within technology, at any rate, lies fallow for the most part. This is clearest in regard to the electoral process where the openness of the social order is most evidently institutionalized. There is some indication that voters in recent years have become more consistent in their decisions.[6] But the general political awareness is still deplorably low, and participation in voting has generally been declining since the Second World War. In 1976, only 54 percent of those eligible to vote cast a ballot in the presidential election.[7] This is often seen as a failure of technology since it is, supposedly, the poor and uneducated who typically do not vote; and it is seen as a failure of democracy because, so it is said, many are alienated from the political process due to its overpowering size, remoteness, and corruption. But Arthur Hadley has found that the largest single group of nonvoters consists of people who are apathetic out of contentment.[8] And while the people who vote represent little more than half of those who are eligible to vote, the people who participate in the shaping of the political issues and in the selection and promotion of the candidates to be voted on constitute only a quarter to a third of the eligible voters.[9] Finally when we look at the character of the political activity that does take place in the electoral realm, we must recognize, as was remarked before, that it engenders no searching debates of the good life and the common good and hence no radical decisions and actions. Beyond the common implication in the technological order there is little sense of civic responsibility. Voters and interest groups typically look at a candidate as a potential supplier of a commodity that is only obtainable politically. And candidates see themselves in large measure as brokers of various and often conflicting interests whose strength is measured by the size of their voting constituency.

I want to stress again that electoral politics still presents the most open forum for collective reform. This would become apparent and decisive if actions taken on the private occasions of decision which were discussed in the last chapter were to gather momentum and lead to the insight that one soon exhausts the private bounds of engagement and that broader and deeper engagement requires that we make room for it collectively, i.e., politically. These prospects will concern us in Part 3. Meanwhile there is a collective scope of action already articulated within the democratic and technological social order. It is bounded on the one side by the promise of liberal democracy which was to secure equal opportunities of self-realization for all. As we have seen in Chapter 14, following Macpherson, the democratic vision had to contend with class divisions and became dominant only when it entered into an uneasily evolving compromise with class divisions. Thus the collective scope of action is on the other side delimited by continuing and obvious inequalities. The technological promise of liberation, enrichment, and conquest has an obvious kinship with the promise of democracy. And Boorstin and others have conflated the two. But it was also argued that the developments of the two promises were quite dissimilar. The promise of technology was acted out and developed into a definite style of life which ironically evacuated the ideals of freedom, wealth, and mastery. The promise of democracy was technologically specified, but even in this version it has not been kept. Availability is not equal for all; some people's life is clearly more commodious than that of others. This requires explanation since the democratic call of equality for all still has force and is to this day the battle cry of reforms.[10] But why have reforms not been more successful when the formal elements of liberal democracy are certainly at hand and when technology, quite apart from having specified the notions of equality and self-development, has provided powerful means of information and communication that should aid the cause of the less privileged?

As Boorstin's position and the distribution of wealth in technologically advanced socialist countries show, technology is not by its nature socially unjust. It may in fact have a weak tendency toward equality. The obvious inequalities in this country (and in all Western democracies) derive from historical circumstances. This illustrates once more both that technology is not the sole structuring force of contemporary reality and that it decisively transforms almost all traditional forces. To see this we must look more closely at the shape of inequality.

It is generally recognized that a satisfactory treatment of the question of equality requires an antecedent understanding of whether, generically speaking, all persons are in fact equal and if so in what respect, given that there are obvious ineradicable differences among humans. Assume that this question has been answered along Kantian lines. We are all equal because each of us belongs to the realm of morality as a member and as a sovereign. Each of us regards himself or herself and everybody else as an end in herself or himself.[11] The question then arises what we, acting socially, owe one another as equals. How, in the arrangement of our lives, is respect for equality to be made manifest? Different answers are conceivable. We might be concerned to secure equality of education, or of political power, of moral excellence, aesthetic sensibility, of skill and responsibility in the work world, or in other ways. But it is clear that in general we have no such concerns. Substantive equality is measured solely by wealth and income. It is controversial whether wealth or income is a better measure of equality and inequality.[12] Wealth seems to bestow power. But as suggested in Chapter 13, wealth does not provide power that could be used against the paradigm of technology and the common allegiance that it commands. Within the paradigm, there is a range of options, but it is narrowly circumscribed. Personal income yields no directive power at all over against technology. There is controversy also as to the way in which income should be measured.[13] But whether it is measured this way or that, the unchallenged significance of income is that it in turn is the measure of what is technologically available to a person. It determines how many commodities are at one's disposal. Income is a measure of equality that is consonant with technology, and so it has become the standard of living in a technological society.[14] It is again an indication that technology is so deeply entrenched that there is controversy whether, by the standard of income (or wealth), justice or prudence require equality.[15] But there is no challenge to the standard itself.

What is the shape of inequality in this country, measured by income? There are two crucial features. First, there is a sharp difference between the incomes of the richest and poorest families. In 1970, the lowest fifth made 5.5 percent of total family income, the highest fifth made 41.6 percent.[16] In 1978, the bottom 8.2 percent of all families made under $5,000 annually whereas the top 3.6 percent made $50,000 and over. Second, between these extremes, there is a fairly linear slope of inequality. As one goes up in $5,000 increments of annual family incomes for 1978, one picks out roughly 16 percent of the families with each step up to the increment from $25,000 to $50,000, which corresponds to the largest group of families with 24.3 percent.[17]

The origin of inequality lies in the ranks of late Medieval Europe. These developed into the class divisions of the early modern period which in turn were smoothed into the present wage differences and contours.[18] The latter have considerable stability, but they no longer divide families into clearly delimited classes. The blurring of income differences is strengthened through the increasing number of families where two moderate incomes, one from the husband and one from the wife, may lift the family into the top quarter of family incomes.[19]

Given that liberal democracy has provided a notion of equality and has advocated it, and given that the machinery of government to implement that notion is available, why is inequality so generally accepted?[20] It is clear that it is resented by the poorest families. They are excluded from the blessings of technology, and for them the promise of liberation and enrichment has retained some of its early and genuine appeal. But there is a broad middle class, clearly poorer than the really rich, that could muster the political power to enforce greater equality but fails to do so. There are several ready answers which in the end prove unsatisfactory. (1) Inequality mirrors merit. The rich have worked for what they have. But this would require that everyone have the same opportunities at the start, which is not the case.[21] (2) Inequality is necessary for the common good. Differences in reward constitute incentives for the kind of hard and creative work that raises everyone's wealth. But it does not appear that steps toward greater equality diminish initiative.[22] (3) Inequality has become immaterial. The majority of people have crossed the threshold of abundance, and it is pointless to be concerned with degrees of abundance. But there is in fact no evidence that the absolute level of affluence determines people's degree of happiness and that a general rise in the standard of living leads to greater happiness. On the contrary, people measure their happiness according to the rank they occupy within the income structure of a reference group, the most encompassing of which is their country.[23] And people remain vitally interested in a rising standard of living. (4) People are ignorant about the facts and functions of inequality. They accept a degree of inequality because they accept theses (1) and (2) above in support of it, not knowing the weaknesses of these positions. And they believe that the government is committed to equality and working to achieve it through taxes and transfer payments. They do not sufficiently realize that the equalizing force of taxes is nullified through loopholes.[24] But this is not convincing. Inequality is an obvious and persistent phenomenon in this country. If equality were a vital concern to a majority of people, they would insist on obtaining appropriate information, and today's information and communication technology makes that an entirely feasible task.

  The present inequality, then, must have a different rationale, and, again, the question is not how it arose but why it persists, and, more precisely, how technology has put its stamp on it. I believe that inequality favors the advancement and stability of the reign of technology. The unequal levels of availability represent a synchronic display of the stages of affluence that many people can hope to pass through. What the middle class has today the lower class will have tomorrow, while the middle class aspires to what the rich have now.[25] The goals of tomorrow do not consist of vague conceptions and promises; they are realized and lived by those above my standing in the economic order. We all identify our lot and aspirations with those above us. Thus, the pervasive relative deprivation fuels the motor of technological advancement. The aspirations of the people are to some extent fulfilled. I do attain eventually what my wealthier neighbors have today but not until they are wealthier yet. The rising tide lifts all ships, but it does not equalize them in size. Social justice, understood as an equal level of affluence, will not be advanced merely by technological progress. A slowing or decline of general affluence, on the other hand, increases injustice. The scale of income provides a principle of selecting those who will pay for economic declines. In letting the poor and powerless suffer primarily, the allegiance of the more prosperous to the status quo can be secured. And since the slope of inequality is continuous and fairly linear, the boundary of the favored can be shifted without creating or revealing clearly demarcated social classes.[26] Class formation is also prevented by the upward orientation of most people and by their refusal to make common cause with those below them against those above them. I believe that it is this shifting and blurred outline of social injustice that profoundly discourages so many of the poor and less educated from participation in politics and gives rise to the limited politically active and attentive public. And, of course, quite a few of the people at the middle and upper levels of wealth and education feel disburdened from genuine citizenship because they are certain of the stability of the political framework and content with the benefits they derive from it.

It seems then that technology in itself is socially indifferent though not inconsequential. There is some tendency, as remarked before, to let the scope of availability expand and to let more and more people have its benefits. But the paradigm of availability becomes socially active only where it is threatened by social unrest. In such instances measures are taken to transform the negatively engaging social relations into commodities, i.e., into mutual services that are safely and easily available. The development of labor relations illustrates this pattern. On the other hand, as long as human misery borders on the universe of technological affluence without disturbing it, misery is callously neglected.

The peculiar conjunction of technology and inequality that we find in the industrially advanced Western democracies results in an equilibrium that can be maintained only as long as technology advances. The less affluent must be able to catch up with the more affluent at least diachronically; they must be able to attain tomorrow what their wealthier neighbors have today. If the general standard of living comes to be arrested for the indefinite future, inequality will become stationary and more manifest and will require a new solution. At the moment, it is clear, the tendency is to maintain the dynamic balance of technology and inequality by maintaining technological progress through a rearrangement of energy resources. We will consider the prospects of this tendency in Chapter 19.

As long as the tendency remains largely unquestioned, politics will remain without substance.[27] It will not be the realm where the crucial dimensions of our common life will be considered or altered. These are always and already determined by technology. Politics is merely the metadevice of the technological order. This is not all there is to politics. Traditional notions of service, leadership, and civic responsibility still move some people to political action which goes beyond technology. But the technological cast of politics constitutes its presently central features. Politics in this sense is well understood by people and used when they face an otherwise unsolvable problem. But a device, once designed and in use, does not engage or even permit engagement. The calls for participatory democracy which are oblivious to the substance of politics and merely recommend new forms of transaction are pointless and will remain inconsequential. One may as well call for participation in pocket calculators. A calculator not only disburdens one of the intricacies of computation, it resists efforts at engagement. It is beyond our care, maintenance, and radical intervention. One can, of course, study its history and construction. And one may find new and more frequent uses for it. But the first course of action is entirely cerebral and inconsequential, and the second is entirely playful if it goes beyond the genuine requirements of technological life. And so it is with politics within a technological society.

17   Work and Labor

We have now outlined the character of technology historically and systematically, in detailed examples and in its wider social compass, theoretically and with regard to empirical data. We have so obtained a picture of the technological pattern which has a measure of coherence and balance. But if it is true that the paradigm of the technological device has shaped the modern world pervasively and incisively, then the possibilities of tracing the pattern of technology in our world are endless. If we want to give the present account of technology more depth, what phenomena should we take up for investigation? There are spectacular or obviously disturbing cases of the rule of technology that one might consider, such as medicine, the military, art, space exploration, artificial intelligence, or starvation in the Third World. I will have to leave them aside for two reasons. First, these problems are so complex that simply to lay out the significant features and data would take us beyond the limits of this volume. Second, I believe that the working of technology is more telling and consequential in the inconspicuous everyday world of an advanced industrial country such as ours.

It is in this everyday world that we work up and firm up the attitudes and procedures that bring about or at least sanction irrational expenditures for military armaments, the need for space spectaculars, and callous disregard of global poverty. The particular phenomena that I want to examine are labor and leisure. These too are, of course, difficult and ramified topics. But we all know them as participants and observers. Thus everyone can test, illustrate, and substantiate points that are sketched schematically. And obviously, it cannot be my concern to treat labor and leisure from every angle but to exhibit in them how technology has led to a radical transformation of the human condition. Finally, as indicated in Chapters 9 and 10, there is a privileged tie between the device paradigm and labor and leisure. The sharp division in our lives between labor and leisure is a unique feature of modern existence.[1] It is my thesis that this division reflects the split between machinery and commodity in the pattern of technology. Leisure consists in the unencumbered enjoyment of commodities whereas labor is devoted to the construction and maintenance of the machinery that procures the commodities. Labor is a mere means for the end of leisure. Let me elaborate, then, the instrumental character and the fate of technological work in this chapter. Technological leisure will be examined in the next chapter.

Roughly speaking, the reduction of work in technology to a mere means has resulted in the degradation of most work to what I usually will call labor.[2] A critique of work in modern technology is inevitably seen against the background of pretechnological work. The latter is thought to provide the alternative and so informs one's view of technological labor significantly. But there are two sharply differing views of work in a pretechnological setting. One is the idyllic view which appreciates the artisan's and peasant's work for its natural pace, its variety and skill, its social richness, its connection with the rhythms of celebration and of the seasons.[3] In Chapter 9, following Sturt, I sketched this kind of work world as a foil for the device paradigm. Sturt mourned the passing of this world although his appreciation of it contained the realization of what he called "the sordidness of business," the periodic lack of warmth, light, and free time, the awareness of occasional fatigue and boredom.[4] Still, the joy and pride of workmanship are evident and dominant in Sturt's account. "But the joyous work of artisans or peasants is probably a myth," replies William Form, a representative of the harsh view of pretechnological work who has a correspondingly positive view of technological labor. "Most townspeople," he says further, "were not craftsmen and much of the work even of craftsmen was dull and routine. The work of peasants was drudgery."[5] Not all pretechnological work was either this or that. Nor is there a real question of our literally and entirely going back to pretechnological work in any form. But the issue is significant because it is clear that in at least some pretechnological settings work was fulfilling and ennobling, that it oriented the workers in nature, culture, and society and allowed them, as workers, full and bodily participation in these dimensions. Technology has given us enormous power, and it is a legitimate question whether we, as citizens of the technological society, are able or willing to employ that power on behalf of good work. There is a question whether we are confident enough of the quality of typically technological labor to measure it against good pretechnological work which was typical at least within certain cultures. To answer these questions, we must first outline the character of technological work.

The division of work is a well-known feature of the technological setting. What is less obvious is the twofold division of work in technology. The first kind is the celebrated division of labor with which Adam Smith begins *The Wealth of Nations*.[6] It must be distinguished from the specialization of work which is as old as human culture and practiced in the very pretechnological work world that some of us admire. Nor is the division of a work process into steps and the frequent repetition of just one step characteristic of modern industrial labor. A tinsmith who is about to make a great number of funnels would not complete one after another, each from start to finish, but would first do all the drawing on sheet metal, then all the cutting, and so on, and would make specialized devices which the economy of scale would permit and reward. The typically modern division of labor, on the other hand, divides one process into many simple parts and assigns the performance of each to a single worker.[7] The monotonous and endless repetition of one small task is typical of much of modern labor and gives it its stupefying and draining character.

There is another division of work essentially connected to the first and quite familiar once we acknowledge it; but its crucial consequences are officially ignored. One aspect of the division can be captured by the distinction between dividing work and divided labor. More broadly, it can be delimited by distinguishing between work at the leading edge and in the wake of technology. Work at the leading edge of technology is devoted to expanding and securing the device pattern in order to provide more numerous, more refined, and new kinds of commodities for consumption. Commodities are more fully available if the supporting machinery is less obtrusive, i.e., more concealed and reliable. Commodities are more numerous if the machinery is more productive. The ground level of the technological machinery is industry which produces goods and services. This basic machinery too shows a tendency toward shrinkage and concealment. But the emphasis from the start has been on reliability and productivity. Both ends are served by the division of labor. Divided labor, however, must be preceded by the work of dividing. This was first accomplished by the individual entrepreneurs and inventors of the early industrial era and then taken over and perfected by the highly trained elite of research and development scientists and engineers, and of experts in law, finance, marketing—in short, by the group of people that Galbraith has called the "technostructure."[8]

Work at the leading edge of technology is dividing for historical reasons. Technology did not enter an empty stage but a world that was filled with work and celebration, with hardship and joy. Human life is always full at any one time, and innovations can take place only by displacing some tradition. Thus, technology had to displace and destroy the traditional crafts. As pointed out in Chapter 11, a crucial accelerator in this development was the invention of the steam engine which provided a prime mover that was free of the limits of time, place, and vigor and encouraged the building of large and complex machines. These machines were not only more productive than humans but also more reliable since they liberated production from the uncertainties and burdens of training and tradition, from the risks of individual judgments, and from the varying moods of the workers. The total liberation from these human liabilities is accomplished through automation. The latter was the implicit and sometimes the explicit goal of technological production from the first.[9] The goal is only now coming within reach on a broad scale for two reasons. One is the original lack of scientific knowledge and engineering expertise, the other the pull of the tradition where production had always been the work of humans who used tools, so that it was difficult to envisage the development of tools to the point where the users of the tools became largely dispensable. It was possible, however, to bring the human element closer to machine-like productivity and reliability through the division of work. Divided labor is more productive, and Adam Smith thought it was so because it favored dexterity, saved time, and led to the invention and improvement of machines.[10] But this is to take a limited and misleading view. Divided labor favors dexterity only if we understand by the latter the ability to execute a simple motion quickly and reliably. If by dexterity we mean the manifold and trained ability of bodily timing, strength, and responsiveness, then the division of labor is the elimination of dexterity. And though the observations of people who performed divided labor might have led, as Smith has it, to certain improvements in machines, the goals of the division of labor, namely, reliability and productivity, are primarily embodied in machines, not in their operators, and primarily derive from their designers, not their users. As Marx saw much more clearly, the division of labor fits labor to the machine, not the other way around.[11] This tendency finds its first culmination in the time and motion studies of Taylor and Gilbreth.[12] The productive process, and human work in particular, was regarded as a force of nature that had to be conquered and rendered available like warmth, nutrition, or health. Thus it is the saving of time and the joining to machines that makes divided labor more productive.

The division of labor makes work more reliable because the simplicity of divided labor eliminates the need of skill, thus enlarging the labor pool and making workers more freely substitutable for one another. It also makes it possible to tie human operation to the speed of a machine or an assembly line, thus to pace work and to guarantee a certain output per time unit. To take a traditional practice such as baking bread and to divide it into steps that were sufficiently simple so that most could be turned over to large machines was a difficult, challenging, and rewarding task. Giedion has painted a vivid picture of this enterprise, of the seemingly insuperable barriers, of many dead ends, and of the final success. And he has given similar accounts of the mechanization of agriculture and of butchering.[13] Boorstin has traced the corresponding developments for the procurement of clothing, milk, fruit, vegetables, transportation, and security.[14] The latter case is instructive because here the device paradigm does not split an ensemble of things and practices into tangible machines and commodities. Rather a network of pretechnological social relations is displaced by an organizational machinery which yields a financial commodity.[15] In a pretechnological setting, security in the face of catastrophes is had from the goodwill and charity of parents, siblings, or neighbors. But such security was sometimes unreliable and always burdensome to giver and receiver. Insurance technology first reduces security to the guarantee of a cash payment, then decomposes the resourcefulness and precariousness of society by mathematical means, and finally institutes a financial and legal machinery to insure the collection and distribution of money. The machinery of this device, especially at first, was not primarily a physical entity but a network of computations, contracts, and services. But it had from the start the concealed, inaccessible, and disburdening character of technological machinery. Accordingly, the commodity, though it was a regrettable necessity more than a final consumption good, represented commodiously available security, support that did not require asking, imposing, or begging but could be claimed through a call to the insurance agent.

The procurement of security is an instructive case also because it lies halfway between the division of work and the general division of life which is characteristic of technology. Except for charitable organizations, security from the vicissitudes of life was not the task of a certain class of people but a mutual responsibility of all. The insurance industry led to divided labor within itself and without, i.e., relative to social agencies and programs. But it did not divide the work of a certain guild. Rather it split off and took over a task from each of us and freed and impoverished us all at once. Thus the procurement of security stands midway between the division of the work world and the division of the domestic world with its typical combination of liberation and impoverishment. It is telling that both Giedion and Boorstin move without break or signal from the description of the one kind of division to that of the other. This suggests that the division of work is part of a larger pattern of division, i.e., of the device.[16]

The heroes of the division of work, such men as Cyrus H. McCormick, Gustavus F. Swift, Philip D. Armour, Gail Borden, George W. Pullman, and Elizur Wright, were the ones who actually built the technological society.[17] They knew that they were at the leading edge of a new era. They were masters of a difficult enterprise, they loved their work, and they worked feverishly.[18] The pride that they took in their work was justified by the liberating and enriching effects of early modern technology. But as I have suggested before, liberation has gradually given way to disengagement, and distraction has displaced enrichment. These are, however, primarily phenomena in the foreground of technology, in the area of leisure and consumption; and more will have to be said on this theme in the following chapter. Work at the leading edge of technology has led to equally profound transformations in the background of technology to which we attend in labor. Leading work is of course itself part of the background, and it occupies the best part. It is most skilled, most interesting, most humane, most highly regarded and remunerated. The last features are the more remarkable as the leading work inevitably leaves in its wake a wasteland of divided and stultifying labor. Wherever there is a traditional area of skillful work, it is disassembled, reconstructed, largely turned over to machines, and artisans are replaced by unskilled laborers. This process leads to a continuing contraction of expertise and a corresponding expansion of unskilled labor.[19]

Such a development should cause deep embarrassment to powerful democratic societies. Work in the Western world, at least since Roman times, is regarded as a crucial tie between human beings and their world. In this country, hard work is still regarded as that activity that most surely bestows dignity.[20] At the same time work is being more and more degraded and disliked. How can the significance of this development remain hidden from public view? The first factor in this concealment is the misguided view of technological liberation that we have first met in Chapter 8. As the quotation from Ferguson stresses there, technology unquestionably eliminates or meliorates dangerous, injurious, and back-breaking work though, unquestionably also, we do not go as far in this direction as we might. But here too we ignore the irony of technology and fail to distinguish genuine liberation from disengagement. Ferguson considers carrying water an insufferable drudgery.[21] This is so only if we look at a pretechnological practice from a technological point of view where carrying water is seen as a mere means of obtaining water. On that condition, a water utility and plumbing system is of course vastly superior. But as Boorstin reminds us, Rebecca, going to the well, not only found water there but also companionship, news of the village, and her fiancé. These strands of her life were woven into a fabric technology has divided and privatized into commodities.[22] This is not to say that the construction of modern water supplies could or should have been resisted.[23] But this and the other examples of Ferguson's show how, guided by the technological view of labor as a mere means, we exaggerate the liberating character of the transformation of work and thus cover up the concomitant cultural and social losses. We pretend that liberation is only possible at the price of the degradation of work. Thus we sanction that degradation even where the preservation or restoration of work would not lead to unacceptable dangers or hardships.

A second factor that hides the degradation of work from the common view is the belief that the commerce with sophistication must itself be sophisticated. The machines of technological labor are of course much more complicated and embody much more science and engineering than the tools of pretechnological work. Hence the general piety that "the changing conditions of industrial and office work require an increasingly 'better-trained,' 'better-educated,' and thus 'upgraded' working population."[24] More specifically, it is assumed that anyone who tends a machine is (at least) semiskilled.[25] Craftsmen continue to be considered skilled though the perfection of machine tools has led to the dispersal and deterioration of the original skills. Not surprisingly, farm workers and housewives who command exacting but partially or primarily pretechnological skills are considered unskilled.[26]

Third and finally, we assume that the increasing length of average education reflects rising requirements of training for typical technological work. But this summary view fails to inquire whether education in this country, for instance, is also of increasing quality; nor, if that were the case, does it ask whether typical labor allows for the exercise of greater knowledge and training. The answer to both questions is probably negative. To avoid the consequent embarrassment of finding that much of our education is irrelevant to labor, length of education has been put to new purposes which are really foreign to its nature. Since desirable work is scarce, education is used as an obstacle course which is lengthened as such work becomes scarcer.[27] Educational requirements are used as a device to screen applicants.[28] And finally, educational credentials serve to solidify the privileges of professions and the stratification of society.[29]

Though trenchant critiques of the degradation of work and the evisceration of education have been put forward, we continue to conceal these phenomena from ourselves, and so do many experts. An example is provided by Eli

Ginzberg and George J. Vojta, who advance the thesis "that human capital, defined as the 'skill, dexterity and knowledge' of the population, has become the critical input that determines the rate of growth of the economy and the well-being of the population."[30] They ignore the fact that it is not the skill of the population but of a small and shrinking elite of experts that determines the course of technological progress. Ginzberg and Vojta take length of education as "a measure of improvement in human resources," ignoring the question of the quality and relevance of extended education.[31] They exhibit the usual disdain for pretechnological skills when they say: "The upgrading of the labor force is also evidenced by the disappearance of 800,000 private-household jobs and a 2.5-million decline in farm employment."[32] Perhaps some of these workers became computer keypunch operators and so will be working with the most sophisticated kind of machinery modern technology has produced. But keypunch operation in fact needs few skills; it is boring and stultifying.[33]

To show how the degradation of work is concealed is not quite to answer the question of why we allow such concealments. There was in fact a period when the destruction of the work world and its traditional practices was vividly felt and resisted by the workers.[34] It took a long, arduous, and sometimes violent process to discipline people from pretechnological work to divided labor, and the directors of this forcible development were the early entrepreneurs and capitalists. This suggests of course that the degradation of work is not the consequence of technology but the machination of an exploiting class. It should follow from that thesis that divided labor will not be found in industrialized societies that expressly combat the exploitation of workers. We know, however, that work in Russia is as divided as it is here. Braverman excuses this development as due to unfortunate historical circumstances, the need of Russia to obtain large and quick productivity gains and to arm herself against aggression.[35] That is special pleading; and it is impossible to construct a general argument to the effect that industrial socialism would be free of alienated labor.[36] To be sure, one can define alienated labor as "system-related," as stemming from the fact that the means of production are not owned and controlled by the workers themselves.[37] But if it is true of corporate capitalism, as suggested in Chapter 13, that ownership is largely impotent as regards the course of technology and that the latter is determined according to a definite pattern by a technical elite, then the same should hold for a technologically advanced socialist society. The latter may be more concerned to meliorate working conditions. But that concern is possible and growing in the Western democracies too as we shall shortly see.

Meanwhile it remains to be explained how it was possible to enforce the work discipline of divided labor against initially overt resistance and why the concomitant degradation of work came to be concealed. The answers are to be found, I believe, in the deepening entrenchment of the device paradigm, in both its mechanical and commodious aspects. From the start of the Industrial

Revolution, as mentioned in Chapter 8, the promise of liberation and enrichment through technological devices accompanied and sought to justify the disruptions and miseries of industrialization. The advocacy of a new work discipline was the reverse side of that promise. Increased production of commodities was possible only on the basis of reliable and efficient machinery, and since the latter was impossible without human components, human work had to become reliable and efficient, i.e., regulated, as well. Thus "the habit of regular and continuous industry" was essential to the new age.[38] It was advocated not just by capitalist entrepreneurs but also by preachers, moralists, educators, and town officials.[39] And the moral complexion of these exhortations is plausible given that the goal of technological liberation was directed toward very real hunger, disease, and illiteracy. Thus the consistency and the increasing successes of the technological program eventually won over the workers and transformed their implication on the labor side of technology into the relation that in Chapter 15 was described as complicity.[40] Just as the broad middle class, being committed to technological progress, tolerates social injustice since it has become a motor and stabilizer of that progress, so it tolerated degraded work since at least until now it has been the necessary condition and counterpart of consumption. And indeed, the tie of degraded labor to technology has been more intimate and hence more disquieting than the tie of social injustice to technology. That may be the reason why the degradation of labor has been more hidden than social injustice. The unions always complain of the latter but rarely of the former.

To what extent the workers are aware of the degradation of work is a controversial question. In fact the controversy is radical to the point where in one view the lack of awareness of degradation is taken to be evidence that divided labor is not in fact inferior to any pretechnological work.[41] The variety of the workers' responses when asked about the quality of their work surely depends on the way in which the questions are framed.[42] One may assume that inquiries of a global kind receive more favorable replies. Workers who are asked to judge labor as part of their total situation and entire life will naturally hesitate to pass negative judgment on what is basic to their existence and, as a single activity, commands most of their time. On the other hand, if one is asked to judge one's work on specific days or when one is invited to reflect on one's work informally and at length, it appears that divided labor causes dissatisfaction and resentment.[43]

If labor is largely resented because it has been degraded, we face, as said before, a deeply unsatisfactory situation in this country because what is being degraded is also held out as the one activity that most surely gains a person the approval and admiration of society. To be "a working woman" or "a working man" is to have dignity. To be unemployed, willingly or not, is to arouse suspicion and scorn as a rule and amusement and envy at best. But is this fault, that runs through most people's lives, inevitable? Technology progresses, and two developments promise to reshape labor conditions funda-

mentally. One is the reorganization of labor relations and assignments so as
to win the cooperation, loyalty, and enthusiasm of the workers. The other is
the automation of much labor on the basis of the microelectronic revolution.
Great claims are made for both. The restructuring of working arrangements
is seen as "a turn of Copernican significance."[44] Of the import of the microelectronic developments it is said that "the human race is now poised on
the brink of a new industrial revolution that will at least equal, if not far
exceed, the first Industrial Revolution in its impact on mankind."[45] The more
specific outlines of these phenomena have a familiar ring, however; but at
least they promise finally to realize the brightest ambitions of the modern era.
Christoph Lauterburg contends that the salient point of the new work world
is "a new image of man." But it is in fact the venerable vision of liberal
democratic theory, based on the experience, as Lauterburg has it,

> that every human being possesses an incredible potential for in-
> tellectual and personal growth and development; that every human
> being wants to exhaust that potential; that on the other hand, he
> is in a position to do so only if he lives in an environment which
> truly challenges him and offers him appropriate opportunities to
> learn and to develop.[46]

The effect on the work force of the microelectronic revolution in production
is to be one of liberation; for "robot applications to date," so *Business Week*
tells us, "have relieved people of work that is hazardous, dirty, or monotonous:
loading stamping presses, spraying paint in confined areas, and in making
the same spot welds day in and day out."[47]

But here also the traditional rhetoric is an overlay on the ironical subversion
of its promises. The tendency of the productive machinery in technology is
unaffected or strengthened by the supposed revolutions. It tends toward greater
reliability and productivity. The apparent humanizing of the working conditions, inspired in part by Japan's example, is gaining wider acceptance in the
West entirely in response to the deteriorating reliability and productivity of
the labor force. It turns out as a matter of fact that the human component of
the productive process gets poorly integrated if it is treated in terms of exchangeable and mechanical parts. Hence humans are given job security and
a measure of initiative and responsibility in exchange for more reliable and
productive performance. One can only welcome such improvements of the
working conditions. But one must also recognize that they are constrained by
immovable boundaries and rest on precarious foundations. Thus two of the
three nonhierarchical work arrangements, that Lauterburg considers exem-
plary because the workers are free to divide responsibilities and are encouraged
to devise and implement innovations, are centered around highly automated
production processes that go on around the clock.[48] The inhuman and unal-
terable restraint of work at ungodly and socially harmful times does not seem
to bother Lauterburg. And he seems to be unaware of the fact that the range

of innovations that the workers can propose is closely hemmed in by their lack of expertise in engineering, chemistry, computer science, and so forth, by the availability of capital, by marketing considerations and other factors that are and must be centrally determined. The framework of reforms is constrained by the intricacy of the productive machinery in the widest sense, which has been built up over 200 years, is still growing in size and intricacy, and therefore needs central planning if it is not to fly apart.[49] Intricacy in its microelectronic version greatly advances productivity but in turn requires the powerful insights of modern logic, mathematics, physics, and chemistry. It leads to devices that are physically so dense and complex in structure that they are beyond direct intervention or modification by anyone. Thus crucial and growing parts of the technological machinery are becoming intellectually and physically ever more remote from the common person's competence. The circle of expertise is suffering a final contraction and centralization. These aspects of technological organization cannot be changed through a rearrangement of responsibilities unless the machinery of production is disassembled, simplified, and decentralized. That would be the end of high technology as we know it. Its size and intricacy are presently beyond reform because they are entailed by the common commitment to a high and rising standard of living.

If reliability and productivity are basic to technological production, then even what limited humanization of the work place is possible remains no more secure than the consonance of humanization with the basis of production. Given a choice between a worker to whom a long-time commitment and a measure of discretion must be granted and a worker who can "work three shifts a day," as *Time* has it, and who "takes no coffee breaks, does not call in sick on Mondays, does not become bored, does not take vacations or qualify for pensions," the latter will be preferred by the goals of technological production that *Business Week* in this context characterizes as "improved productivity, faultless performance, and lower labor costs."[50] The latter worker, however, turns out to be a robot. The ineradicable imperfections of human labor are overcome by dispensing with human labor. The degradation of work ends with the elimination of work.

How much work will be eliminated? Some experts estimate that up to 75 percent of today's factory work force could be displaced.[51] Not only tedious, unpleasant, and harmful work will be taken over by automation but more and more skilled occupations as well, including those in the service sector whose growth Ginzberg and Vojta thought to provide the basis for the population's increased well-being.[52] What is the reaction of organized labor? The unions, *Business Week* tells us, "recognize that technological progress is essential."[53] And one union official is quoted as saying: "We don't like the idea of losing jobs, but it's part of life."[54] It is part of life in a setting where technological progress is essential, i.e., where the growing consumption of commodities is the avowed goal of society. In such a setting even organized labor sees itself primarily as a consumer and is content to speak as a consumer even when faced with the possibility of the loss of much work. The gains in the consumption of commodities justify and indeed necessitate the workers' growing and finally total disengagement from the productive machinery.

The widespread elimination of work can come to pass in several ways. Though the productivity gains that arise from automation may maintain or raise the general affluence, those who are employed will receive a greater share of it. Employment will be a privilege, and unemployment will conform to the gradient of present poverty and powerlessness.[55] Once unemployment begins to spread into the broad middle class, innovations will become necessary. They could take one of three forms: (1) The development of respectable and enjoyable forms of unemployment. (2) Making work and creating employment which are essentially idle. (3) The redistribution of available labor through the shortening of labor time per person. But a more profound and principled reform is possible also; we will consider it in Part 3.

18   Leisure, Excellence, and Happiness

The counterpart to labor is leisure. The latter constitutes the foreground and the avowed end of technology. But we are uncertain of this end and reluctant to evaluate it. How can we hope to judge technological leisure incisively and fairly? I begin the investigations of this chapter by sketching a traditional concept of excellence which still commands, I believe, wide if implicit approval. When we examine our leisure by this standard intuitively and with the aid of the social sciences, we find its value to be low. But should we not judge technology by its own rather than traditional criteria? One way of doing this is to see how people's professed happiness is related to the progress of technology and the rise in the standard of living. It turns out that avowed happiness appears to decline as technological affluence rises.

This is a distressing and perhaps surprising result since the promise of technology can well be taken as one of happiness; and for at least two centuries we have taken incredibly massive and radical measures to fulfill the promise. But there must be something in the implementation of the technological program that is deeply flawed and unsatisfactory. This central deficiency has both troubled and eluded social theorists, as I try to show in a discussion of work by Tibor Scitovsky and Fred Hirsch. I then propose an alternative explanation which is guided by the pattern of technology. I begin by giving a fuller account of how, following the device paradigm, we have progressively divided and decomposed the fabric of our lives. This is particularly evident when we consider how technology has step by step stripped the household of substance and dignity. The resulting emptiness is to be filled with consumption, especially the consumption of those central commodities which constitute the foremost and final aspect of technology. Among them television programs have a privileged place. Seeing how television both enthralls and disappoints people, we may have here a clear view of what flaws technology at the center.

Working out the arguments in support of these points we must, to begin with, remember that it is the area of leisure and consumption where technology now must rest its case. Few proponents of technology will deny that we have exploited and damaged the environment and that most technological labor as such fails to give the worker pride and satisfaction. But they will defend these negative aspects by pointing to the fruits of technology. These, according to the promise of technology, are of two kinds. Technological liberation has procured negative benefits; the goods and services, in other words, that have freed us from hunger, disease, illiteracy, and discomforts in general. But these benefits have been secure for many decades. Ivan Illich has in fact argued that the healing and helping agencies of technology are now doing more harm than good.[1] Cancer, of course, remains to be conquered. Elsewhere, however, it is doubtful whether the advances in medical research, technology, and expenditures are yielding a reasonable advancement of health.[2] Thus if we are committed to the further sophistication and expansion of the technological machinery of the industrially advanced countries, it can only be for the sake of more numerous, varied, and refined consumption goods, to be enjoyed in leisure. But it is not just that the promise of enrichment provides a continuing rationale for the promotion of technology. There is, I believe, an underlying apprehension that technology has failed so far to make our lives positively rich and that it is not a matter of continuing the enrichment through technology but of first ushering it in. The fear that the positive and shining goal of technology has after two centuries of gigantic efforts remained distant and may even slip from sight lends a note of urgency if not panic to the pronouncements of those who urge that we continue to promote technology.

This becomes apparent in the fervor with which the promise of technological enrichment is reiterated in view of the microelectronic revolution. According to James Albus of the National Bureau of Standards: "The robot revolution will free human beings from the pressures of urbanization and allow them to choose their own life-styles from a much wider variety of possibilities." Similarly British Agriculture Minister Peter Walker: "Uniquely in history we have the circumstances in which we can create Athens without the slaves." And finally Isaac Asimov: "Robots will leave to human beings the tasks that are intrinsically human, such as sports, entertainment, scientific research."[3] These assurances implicitly dismiss like promises that have been made for 350 years, presumably because the latter really have not been fulfilled. There is a tacit admission of failure also in the common refusal to defend the value of typical technological culture. Detailed and searching critiques of leisure and consumption have been given, of course; and they bear telling titles such as *The Decline of Pleasure, The Harried Leisure Class,* and *The Joyless Economy.*[4] But the normal reaction to such indictments is not a reasoned reply to the effect that typical life in a technological society is after all one of profound pleasures, vigorous enjoyment, and refined taste. One rather tends to rise to a point of order, reminding the critics that such matters are not up for discussion in a liberal democratic society and that to insist on such discussion is to betray elitism, paternalism, arrogance, or authoritarianism. We have seen in Chapter 14 how liberal democratic theory specifically shelters technology from public examination.

The question on what grounds one can legitimately attempt to reopen a common conversation about the good life will occupy us in Part 3. A satisfactory answer will have to give an account not only of the appropriate procedure and kind of discourse but of the standards as well by which we can judge the worth of our lives. Here I will simply assume that there is in fact a sound way of approaching the problem. As regards the criteria of excellence, it is a matter not of proposals but of reminders. I believe that there still is a vaguely understood and agreed upon notion of excellence. It is embodied in the kind of life we would have liked to lead if only the world had not been mean and oppressive and we had been endowed with greater strength, more talent, and a richer education. Having failed to attain this kind of life, we often wish our children might, and we may even try to steer them toward that goal. This ideal, as suggested in Chapter 14, was in fact one of the animating forces of liberal democratic theory whose secret hope it was that under the benign conditions of liberal democracy everyone would naturally realize the ideal. Substantively speaking, we can detail this notion of excellence by turning to its roots which come from the Classical and Judeo-Christian tradition. From the former it has inherited three features: (1) The excellent person is a world citizen who understands the structure and coherence of the universe in its scientific and historical dimensions.[5] (2) The excellent person is gallant as well as good and intelligent and seeks physical valor as well as intellectual refinement.[6] (3) The excellent person is accomplished in music and versed in the arts.[7] To the virtues of world citizenship, gallantry, and musicianship the Judeo-Christian tradition has added (4) the virtue of charity according to which real strength lies not in material force or cunning but in the power to give and to forgive, to help and to heal.[8] These kinds of excellence were periodically revived and reshaped by such movements as chivalry, humanism, and the Renaissance.[9]

In the history of the West, the first three virtues were proper to an elite, of course. But at least since the early modern period they have had popular analogues. To world citizenship there corresponds an interest and expertise in government and politics, exercised in frequent and extended discussion and in participation wherever possible.[10] Gallantry has its counterpart in bodily strength and skill which were displayed in one's work. Musicianship found expression in singing and dancing and in telling stories. But the elevated notion of excellence is more commensurable with a technological culture than the popular. The latter was too interwoven with the fabric of pretechnological life to be separable from it and transferable to technological conditions. The excellence of high culture, on the other hand, was already set in a context of free time and leisure which is now in a partial version arising for all as the counterpart to labor. And it was, after all, the ambition of democratic technology to procure for all what used to be the privilege of the few.

We can measure the worth of typical technological leisure by the traditional standard of excellence in two complementary ways. We can ask what degree of excellence people have in fact achieved; and we can ask how much of their free time people devote to the pursuit of excellence. In correspondence to the traditional virtues, the first question divides into these more concrete queries: (1) How well educated and literate are people? How well do they understand the scientific structure of the world? How active and informed is their participation in politics? (2) What typically is the condition of people's physical vigor and skill? (3) How well acquainted are people with the arts and how proficient are they in making music and in other artistic practices? (4) How compassionate are people privately and as citizens? How devoted are they to helping others who suffer deprivation and hardships? How conciliatory are they toward their opponents and enemies? We have already touched on fragments of answers to these questions in earlier chapters. We have noted in Chapter 4 that people's command of science is weak. In Chapter 15 we saw that people's participation in politics is minimal. People tolerate grave social injustice as shown in Chapter 16. These distressing indications agree with a mass of formal evidence that has become common knowledge and with our direct, personal intuitions and experiences. Functional illiteracy is spreading. Scores of national tests, measuring scholastic proficiencies, are declining. Voter turnout continues to fall. Obesity is a national problem. The television programs that critics like the least are being watched the most. Foreign aid as a share of the federal budget and the gross national product has been decreasing for a generation. The gap between the rich and poor countries and between the rich and poor within this country is widening. There is a strident tone to politics within this country and one of increasing belligerence to our foreign policy.

Some of these findings could be made more precise through reference to data gathered by the social sciences. Let me instead take up the task of quantitative confirmation by turning to the second of the complementary questions of excellence, the one which asks: How much time do people typically devote to the pursuit of excellence? The time in question is of course free or leisure time, i.e., time that is not needed for sleeping, working, domestic and personal maintenance, or travel. The remaining free time, however, is not the ultimate fundament for an appraisal of the pursuit of excellence. The amount of free time is in turn based on decisions about how we want to shape our lives, and it is the progress of technology that has confronted us with the necessity to decide. When the productivity of labor rises through technological innovations, we can take the gains in the form of greater affluence or in the form of more free time; we can work less at the same level of prosperity or increase prosperity at the same level of work. The nominal workweek has decreased from roughly seventy hours in 1850 to about forty hours in 1960.[11] But to this decrease we must add, according to Sebastian de Grazia, the free time gained through vacation and earlier retirement, and we must subtract the time lost through moonlighting, commuting, and work around the house, especially the increase in work around the house due to the fact that both spouses work outside the home. De Grazia finds that these factors diminish the gain of free time to eight and a half, rather than thirty, hours per week from 1850 to 1960.[12] In relation to the rise in the standard of living, the decline of labor time is small. Average real family income has more than doubled from 1950 to 1973.[13] Recent subsistence levels are probably 50 percent higher than the comfort level at the beginning of the century, and today's comfort level may be three times as high as that of seventy years ago.[14] And during the period of the most dramatic rise in the standard of living, i.e., since the Second World War, the length of the actual average workweek has not shrunk at all.[15] From all this it is clear that we in this country, at least in our corporate roles as union members, managers, voters, and politicians, have consistently decided to enjoy the blessings of technology in the form of more commodities rather than more leisure.

But there is still a substantial amount of free time, on the average roughly four hours per weekday, six hours on Saturdays, and eight hours on Sundays.[16] How much of this time is spent in the pursuit of excellence? The categories of social research reflect the four traditional virtues but weakly. Activities such as reading the newspaper or engaging in conversations can advance one's world citizenship, but they may also be done merely for diversion. Some of the categories, however, are more central to the traditional kinds of excellence and may provide benchmarks. World citizenship surely benefits from attending programs in political or union training to which on the average less than a minute per day is devoted. (The same measure of spending time is used in what follows.) Less than half a minute is spent on attending special lectures, less than a minute on scientific reading, and about five minutes on reading books (of whatever sort). Gallantry is served through active sports, which take up six minutes, and through outdoor activities, such as hiking, on which two minutes are spent. Musicianship is most directly making music to which one minute is given. Artwork takes less than half a minute, as do visits to museums. Half a minute is devoted to theater performances and concerts. Records are played for one minute. An indication of charity is volunteer work on which between one and two minutes are spent.[17] These are of course rough, global, and partial measures, global since they are not differentiated by sex, age, or education, and partial since they reflect the responses of a particular sample at a particular time. But they conform so well to other studies and findings and to our own considered experiences that their import is unmistakable.[18] However much we as a society may admire excellence, we are certainly not devoted to its pursuit. All the activities which have been taken as suggesting a dedication to excellence constitute when taken together less than a quarter of the time spent on watching television.[19]

To these distressing findings one might make two replies. The first says that the citizens of the technological society are certainly no more indolent and ignorant than those of pretechnological times. But to say this is to eviscerate the promise of technology. Champions of technology take great pride in the radical novelty and power of technology. Bertrand de Jouvenel's remarks are typical.

> We live in an Age of Opportunity. Our modern civilization is far superior to any other in terms of power, and thereby we enjoy undreamed of possibilities to foster the good life not for a tiny minority, as in earlier societies, but for the multitude. This is a wonderful privilege; nonsensical therefore is the attitude of those who regret not having lived at some former epoch: no matter that their personal circumstances might have been better, their means of improving the circumstances of their fellowmen would have been slighter. It is right to rejoice in the greatness of these means: it is proper to feel responsible for their personal and optional [optimal?] use.[20]

It is obvious that this glorying in technology is restricted to the machinery of technology, to "Technology as a Means" according to the title of de Jouvenel's essay. The ends are left open but are assumed to be grand. The essay ends with the suggestion that the processes of technological innovation are "to procure a life rich in amenities and conducive to the flowering of human personalities."[21] Though the technological means-ends structure is radically novel, it retains the traditional subservience of the means to the ends; and that subordination is in fact sharper and more extreme in technology than in the tradition. Hence to disavow ambition regarding the ends, i.e., leisure, is to compromise the greatness of the means, i.e., of the technological machinery; more, it is to put into doubt the sense of the gigantic technological enterprise where it goes beyond its strictly liberating functions.

Another reply to the bleak picture of leisure that we have seen is to reject the traditional standards of excellence as inappropriate to a technological culture. They were, one might say, useful as traditional signposts, but eventually technological culture must be allowed to take its own course. It was useful at first to speak of automobiles in the customary framework as horseless carriages. But in due course we have come to recognize cars as novel devices in their own right. The force of this reply lies in the insight that technology has in fact a character of its own that calls for a commensurate analysis. This

I have attempted to provide in terms of the device paradigm, and the salient part for an appraisal of leisure is the commodity whose mode of presence is availability which in turn has the aspects of instantaneity, ubiquity, safety, and ease. Technology succeeds on its own terms when a greater number and variety of commodities become available and when availability is more and more refined. Success of this sort is surely and abundantly evident. But it is achieved very nearly by definition rather than by measurement against an agreed upon standard. Technology could of course and may in the future fail to meet increasingly its goal of procuring commodities. But precisely if it succeeds, there is a legitimate question whether the procurement and consumption of commodities provide happiness. It is helpful to frame the question this way because it appeals to a standard which in regard to technology is well positioned between independence and affinity. It is one to which technology has submitted from the start. The promise of technology was really one of happiness though that was not always explicit.[22] But it has been close to the surface throughout as it is today in advertisement, the characteristic rhetoric of technology.[23] Happiness, though prominent in the pursuits of this country, is of course an ambiguous term.[24] One sense that had much currency in the early years of the nation was that of pastoral contentment. Jefferson was its great proponent. But he failed to see how technology began to undermine and disrupt the rural basis of such happiness and to transform the notion of happiness itself.[25] How radical and successful that transformation has been is difficult to establish. It is a straightforward enterprise, on the other hand, to find out how happy the citizen of the technological society typically professes to be, and one can relate these findings to the progress of technology and to less technological settings. One finds that during the twenty-five years after the Second World War, while the standard of living more than doubled, professed happiness declined rather steadily and significantly, and one finds that people in the technologically advanced countries are no happier than those in less-developed ones.[26] This shows clearly that in technological societies happiness is not simply thought to be higher consumption. But the research also shows, as was seen from a different angle in Chapter 15, that people are not willing to let go of advanced technology. What kind of happiness does technology procure then? And why do people remain both enthralled and unsatisfied by it?

To answer, one must act on the suspicion that there is something in the character of technological goods that accounts for the divided and unhappy reaction of consumers. But that something is difficult to grasp and typically ignored by social scientists. Tibor Scitovsky's book on *The Joyless Economy* is instructive both for its determination to shed light on consumer dissatisfaction and in illustrating the danger of being deflected from the crucial difficulty. The implicit but definite background against which Scitovsky outlines the failings of technological culture is a life of traditional excellence that he finds more nearly exemplified in Europe than in the United States.

Scitovsky's account is rich in illuminating observations. But he does not trust his judgment and taste enough to let them speak for themselves. He feels the need for cogent guidance to gain entry into the realm of cultural criticism, and he believes to have found this guide in behavioral psychology. The crucial doctrine he adopts from this discipline is the point that pleasure and comfort are incompatible in the following sense.[27] Comfort is the feeling of well-being that derives from an optimally high and steady level of arousal of positive stimulation whereas pleasure arises from an upward change of the arousal level. Since there is a best or highest level of pleasure that constitutes comfort, one cannot indefinitely obtain pleasure by rising from comfort to more comfort. When the optimal level of arousal and stimulation is surpassed, the result is pain and discomfort. Hence pleasure can only be had at the price of discomfort. Scitovsky finds that American technological culture favors comfort; and that accounts for the dullness and shoddiness of our leisure possessions and practices. The tendency toward comfort, in turn, Scitovsky traces to our Puritan heritage, to our disdain of pleasure and our preference of work over play and of production over consumption.[28]

He finds no fault with the technological machinery as such and accepts the typical technological means of leisure but thinks they should be put to better ends. "The objection, therefore," he says, "to unskilled and effortless pastimes such as television, driving, and shopping is not that the stimulus they provide is inherently inferior, which it is not, but that it is limited in quantity and so provides only a limited quantity of enjoyment."[29] The quantity of stimulation and enjoyment can be increased if more variety and novelty are given to the content whatever its form or channel.[30] Scitovsky often urges engagement, education, and skill as necessary for genuine pleasure, a view that is consistent with his commitment to traditional excellence.[31] But these urgings are irrelevant and outdated if pleasure is thought to be sufficiently defined as a rise in the arousal level stemming from varying and novel stimulation. The problem is that behavioral psychology generally, and Scitovsky in particular, have modeled the stimulus-response relation on the device paradigm where the stimulus and its channel are mere means, to be judged only by their capacity for transmitting novelty and, in a world of scarcity, by their cost efficiency.[32] By these standards there can be no objection to the attenuation of things to mere commodities which has its extreme conclusion in drugs or direct stimulation of the brain. This, surely, is the most cost-effective stimulation, and it seems merely a matter of technical ingenuity to procure abundant variety and novelty. But when commodities have reached the final stage of reduction and refinement, leisure outwardly will no longer be distinguishable from sleep or unconsciousness. A person devoted to such leisure could hardly be more different from the person of that traditional excellence that Scitovsky rightly cherishes.

An alternative critique of technological goods is provided by Fred Hirsch. Many of his substantive points are touched upon by Scitovsky also. Hirsch, however, does not resort to an alien discipline to ground his argument but centers his critique in economic analysis itself, albeit in the philosophically sensitive and historically circumspect style of the great economic pioneers. To train Hirsch's insights on the problem at hand, one may call his critique a "types-of-goods-analysis." There are three sorts of goods that people desire or need for their well-being. (1) Commercial goods are the standard goods and services that can be produced by private firms, priced, purchased individually, and measured in the aggregate by the gross national product (GNP). (2) Positional goods owe their value to a high rank in a hierarchy, not to their intrinsic or absolute properties. A Ph.D. is now a positional good in the hierarchy of education and credentials, but it would cease to be that if half of all high school graduates were to obtain Ph.D.'s. (3) Public and social goods can only be owned in common and must be acquired and maintained at public expense or cannot be bought at all. Examples are clean air, open spaces, civility, and mutual trust. Hirsch argues that the technologically advanced economies excel at producing commercial goods but are unable to provide the others and, worse, imperil and erode those goods. The general rise in productivity and affluence allows people to buy more and more goods, among them goods that at first are valued as positional but cease to be positional when large numbers of people possess them. Not only did cars and single family homes lose their glamour when they had become common; the spread of these goods has led to definite harms and inconveniences such as crowding, pollution, waste of energy, loss of public transportation and open space. Not only are people frustrated in their pursuit of positional goods; they end up in a worse position than they occupied when they set out on their pursuit. As regards public and social goods, the private corporations that dominate the economy are unable to provide them and therefore transform them into commodities and so draw them into the realm of commercial production. Public playgrounds are replaced by private sports facilities; condominiums with private guards are substituted for secure communities. Hirsch contends that the detrimental effects of commercialization and of commodity fetishism (as he defines it) have until recently been checked by an unacknowledged but powerful social morality which held capitalists and workers to standards of truth, trust, acceptance, restraint, and obligation.[33] This moral legacy is now being depleted, and, unless we learn to restore it, we have hard times ahead of us.

Apart from the conclusion, Hirsch's arguments seem to be well-founded and trenchant to me. They are much richer in their connections and implications than can appear from the sketch above. And yet the analysis remains limited and, due to that limitation, makes technological production and consumption appear too precarious. The analysis thus overstates the need for reform that arises from within technology and in that sense exaggerates the reform potential that is intrinsic to technology. This last point will be taken up in Part 3. Here I am concerned to enlarge Hirsch's critique of technological consumption and leisure.

The question is how well Hirsch's types-of-goods analysis explains the failure of general happiness to rise with the standard of living. Hirsch takes up the question explicitly and points out that people who rank high on the income scale profess to be happier than those lower on the scale.[34] Happiness, then, is a positional good or the consequence of positional goods and in either case cannot be increased through a general rise of the standard of living. Lifting a ladder does not change the relations of the rungs. But not only does an increase in the GNP, so Hirsch argues further, conceal the inevitable constancy of rank happiness; it also overstates the value of the absolute gains that everyone obtains at his or her level. The futile mass competition for positional goods leads to commodities that provide no net gain but simply serve to offset negative effects of that competition. Thus when millions buy single family homes, private residences become so distant from social institutions that two cars and expensive and extensive driving become necessary. The affluence of a spacious house and lot and of two cars, then, provides no better life than a more modest dwelling close to downtown. We must therefore distinguish, as regards commodities or commercial goods, between final consumption goods and defensive goods or regrettable necessities. The GNP counts all commercial goods indifferently.[35]

It is surely true that the frustration in positional competition and the negative side effects of that competition lead to unhappiness. But how deep is the dissatisfaction? Is it deep enough to bring into doubt the very soundness of commodity production and consumption? Is it a source of fundamental instability as the tenor of Hirsch's book suggests? Dissatisfaction, if properly channeled, can promote growth and stability. And that seems to be the case in modern technology. To see this we must first realize that rank happiness and rank dissatisfaction presuppose a social homogeneity that sets technological societies apart from their late medieval and early modern predecessors.[36] There was no way in which a medieval peasant could have become a bishop or duke. But common people today can become millionaires if they are lucky in the lottery or invent a simple, efficient, and patentable spray nozzle. People in the lower reaches of a technological society are not opposed to those above them; they do not find what the privileged have and do alien or detestable. Poor and rich are largely members of the same culture; it is just that the poor desire a more extensive and expensive version of their present state. As the janitor who won in the lottery said: "I have eaten bread all my life; now I want cake." This accounts for the common upward orientation which, as suggested in Chapter 16, is a stabilizing factor in Western technological societies. The goal of upward orientation is of course the highest standard of living, the consumption of the most numerous, varied, and refined commodities; and the exclusion of skill and training from consumption makes the rise to a high station possible and easy as regards obligations. It is not quite so simple, of course. There are still niceties of taste and tradition and friction, so we hear, between new and old money. But hired expertise can deal with most of these problems.

Still, dissatisfaction will remain productive only if it bears some fruit for those who are dissatisfied. In the Western democracies, the fruits of technology are reaped by the broad middle class in the arrangement of diachronic equality which was outlined in Chapter 14. Those lower on the ladder of affluence will have tomorrow what those above them have today. A stagnant or receding economy is of course fatal to that arrangement. Such a fatality can result when technology runs up against physical limits to growth. But here, as generally, Hirsch believes that the social limits, though more concealed as yet, are really more forbidding. Even if production procures for the middle class tomorrow everything that the rich have today, it would not be the same for the middle class. Not only has the novelty worn off when a commodity reaches the lower ranks; some luxurious commodities such as cars have become necessities on arrival among middle- and lower-income families, and the sheer numbers needed to furnish the lower ranks with a commodity lead to congestion and pollution.[37] These are certainly serious impediments to diachronic equality. But technology has mitigating tendencies as well. The transformation of things into devices and the progress of devices exhibits a shrinking of the machinery and an attenuation of commodities so that demands on space and resources diminish. This tendency is clearest in the development of electronics which now is at the leading edge of technological progress. In this area also the introduction and production of devices and commodities require a mass market so that broader segments of the population have the benefit of newly minted devices. To be sure the spatially and physically massive procurement of commodities that one sees in second homes, recreational vehicles, and tourism will have to be slowed due to physical and social limits. But there is much waste in past practices that can now be mined. One must also remember that congestion is not always avoided and thought to be an evil.[38] Especially in leisure, people often seek congestion. Sheer numbers of people seem to create an impression of importance and excitement.

The decay of social and public goods is not a net loss within the device paradigm. Mutual trust and interdependence, for instance, provide a sense of warmth and acceptance, but they are burdensome too as we have seen in Chapter 17 when we considered the emergence of insurance. Public and social goods are never as strictly available as commodities. But it is not really their public and social character that makes them uncertain. Some of the goods whose deterioration and demise Hirsch rightly laments are really no more public or social than some goods that are now flourishing vigorously. When 85 million people watch an event such as the Super Bowl, it would be hard to deny that they are enjoying a public and social good. What makes that spectacle so successful is the intricate and efficient machinery which guarantees a pleasurably consumable commodity.[39] What makes educational systems and public parks relatively precarious is the lack of such a machinery. The goods whose welfare concerns Hirsch are distinguished by their relatively pretechnological character. Hirsch uses as one illustration of the commercialization and privatization effect which erodes the "public and social" goods a phenomenon that has always had eminently private character, namely, sex.[40] Commercialization and privatization, in short, disburden people from responsibility for the maintenance of certain goods and free them from the dependence on other people, from their varying moods and strengths, and from the demands that they will make at unforeseen or inopportune times. Such gains may be thought to outweigh the losses of pretechnological social comity and public amenity.

But Hirsch's master argument has a generality not met by pointing out that commercialization (the device paradigm in our terminology) has successfully and with some net benefit taken over pretechnological areas. Hirsch's argument contends that when we attempt to define certain goods, such as education or military achievement that used to be understood and secured in a social morality, strictly as commercial goods (as commodities) and thus try to dispense with the social morality, the commercial good may turn out to be a faint and useless or even harmful fragment of the real thing. No attempt to remedy incomplete instructions with another set of regulations can be finally successful. If anything the regulatory hierarchy will collapse under its own weight. For commercialization to be successful locally it requires a global morality which orients, directs, and rights the commercial system as a whole. I agree that not every device will reliably procure the intended commodity; far less can the totality of devices at any time be expected by itself to attain or maintain a balanced and benign state. Some undergirding human understanding is needed. But it need not be moral in the sublime or demanding sense of that word. It is probably sufficient when people have that implicit grasp of the distinctive pattern of their world and of their approach to it which tells them that the consumption of commodities requires them to do their part in the construction and maintenance of the supporting machinery.[41] Technology has its unloved laborious side. But as suggested in Chapters 15 and 17, people's understanding of technology and their allegiance to it are sufficiently strong to sustain the technological society. Without affection but with enough acceptance we obey traffic laws, put in the hours at work, and pay our taxes. Superficially, the loss of the pretechnological social fabric can lead to the decline of sociability and friendliness which Hirsch and Scitovsky note.[42] But it can lead as well to the smooth and affable handling of people by receptionists, executives, and party goers which totally baffles and misleads one from a relatively pretechnological setting. What distinguishes technological life is not surliness but its division into surfaces, rough or pleasant, and concealed, inaccessible substructures. Perhaps it is this divided character of our lives that leaves us unhappy.

To pursue that suggestion we must recollect and elaborate the ways in which we have divided our lives according to the device paradigm. And again the realm of analysis should be the one where the benefits of the device were to be finally enjoyed, i.e., the realm of leisure. By the device paradigm the texture of pretechnological life was divided in two directions. Our emphasis has been on what may be called the horizontal division. It occurs when the full significance of a thing is reduced to one function which is then secured as a commodity on the basis of some machinery. Thus in Chapter 9 we considered the fireplace whose function came to be seen solely as one of producing warmth, a function then taken over by more and more efficient and hidden machinery, so that finally the consumer faces a pure commodity that rests on an implicitly understood but specifically impenetrable machinery. When such an incision is made in a phenomenon that is woven into the larger fabric of life, it is inevitably severed from neighboring phenomena as well, from the commerce with nature, the organization of the home, the relations of the family members one to the other. In the same chapter we looked at the ways in which technology unraveled the context of a pretechnological work world. In Chapter 17 we saw how familial and neighborly trust and charity are taken to procure security in the face of unexpected adversity; and once this function was severed from its context, it could be taken over by the device of an insurance industry. The tissue of family life might have healed of course and become whole again. In fact, however, the progress of technology has led to more and more separation of functions, i.e., to vertical cuts in the web of pretechnological culture. This has finally resulted in the availability of largely free-floating commodities which are assembled into fashionable styles of life as was pointed out in Chapter 10.

The primary context of pretechnological life that suffered decomposition function by function was the household. The common view that such a household consisted of an extended family and constituted an economically self-sufficient unit is in error, but only by degrees.[43] Though father and mother were normally the only adults in a premodern household, there were also young servants or helpers, apprentices, and sometimes journeymen; and relatives who could be counted on for help were always close by. The village, the typical wider setting of premodern life, was a kind of extended family in its own way. It is also true that towns and even villages had butchers, bakers, blacksmiths, and so forth who disburdened households from producing all of their goods. But many economic activities remained centered in the household, and the husband's work was equally so, or it was at least within the family's proximity and experience. A family nourished, educated, trained, and entertained its children in a tradition that was alive in the parents' competence and represented to the children in the parents. Thus the parents commanded rightful authority, which made possible that unity of discipline and love whose decay Christopher Lasch has analyzed.[44] The first and most traumatic disruption of the pretechnological household was the transformation of work into a mere means of production whose outward manifestation was the establishment of factories, the urbanization and proletarianization of people, and the consequent destruction of village life. Technology, as remarked in Chapter 8, touched most people's life first in its brute laborious and mechanical aspect. For a while in the nineteenth century the family became a refuge and counterforce to the disruptive and cruel reality at large. But it is the *family* that is the "haven in a heartless world." The family is less than the household, and the continued attenuation of our social substance became apparent as scholarly and common concern was narrowed from the family to marriage and finally to companionship.[45]

As the technological machinery became established and productive, the surrender of household functions to technology took on the pleasant appearance of liberation and enrichment. The housewife was to be freed of the burdens of baking, putting up food, sewing, hauling water, and tending the fire. Other burdens such as washing and cleaning were lightened. The husband, though the frequently authoritarian head of the family, exercised power on the basis of extrinsic attributes, the paycheck and physical force. The family, severed from the work world, was no longer a place where he could prove and enact genuine competence and resourcefulness. The family more and more became a mere setting for consumption, and since consumption makes no demands of skill and discipline, there was less and less of substance to which the parents needed or were even able to initiate their children. This created, if not a vacuum, at least a great deal of emptiness in the family with which we are trying to cope to this day.

The attempts at coping have numerous and intricate aspects of which two are helpful for our concerns. The first is the belief that for every problem there is technological expertise which can take over the burden of solution. Thus a host of professions sprang up to tell parents how to feed, clothe, and treat their children. Much of this work was mystification and trivialization since there was nothing of substance within the family that required the aid of "the helping professions."[46] The problem was not that the advancement of technology burdened the family with new tasks to which the parents were unequal; rather the tasks that once gave the family weight and structure and the parents genuine power were one by one taken over by the machinery of technology. There are of course real strains and overt crises in the modern family for which social work is eminently desirable.[47] These difficulties arise from the uneven conquest of the family by technology. Technology has undermined the authority of the parents but not entirely disburdened them of nurturing and educating their children. When parents act as if they were largely freed of responsibility for their children, neglect or abuse are the results. The typical middle-class family, however, continues to function well at the level of health and comfort and yet is disfranchised from the shaping and maintenance of the world.[48] The consequent sense of impotence is only heightened when professionals make parents believe that their confusion, resulting from the loss of world appropriation, is an indication of parental incompetence.

The other aspect of the family's fate that brings out the dubious character of leisurely consumption is the predicament of the housewife in the progress of technology. In one sense her power increased in the middle and late nineteenth century. The husband, as was said, became more and more of a privileged guest in his house since the world of his work and competence lay outside. The housewife, on the other hand, continued to perform or supervise tasks in the house that were vital for the welfare of the family. Moreover, the home that she managed and presided over constituted a realm of order and serenity, comparing favorably with the often ugly and disruptive developments of maturing modern technology. But when in the twentieth century the household was reduced to a terminal for commodities, male chauvinism and the requirements of technology conspired to reduce the housewife to a manager of consumption.[49] The vacuity of consumption was covered up by unreasonable demands of fastidiousness, styled up to a new ethos of wifely and motherly duty by advertisers whom Ruth Schwartz Cowan aptly calls the "ideologues" of the 1920s.[50]

Yet even today home and family retain through the work of the housewife comparatively many pretechnological features of stability, tradition, warmth, and engagement. They are deeply appreciated by husbands and children. But they stand outside the ruling paradigm and fail to have its sanction.[51] We enjoy profoundly a meal that has been carefully prepared, invokes a family tradition, and responds to our personal tastes and foibles. But such a meal is a tenuous weapon in a struggle between husband and wife since one can always heat a frozen dinner or go out to eat. And so the housewife has the worst of two worlds. As the stewardess of pretechnological practices her position is weak; as a citizen of the technological society her position is infected with doubt, if not contempt, since she is largely confined to the realm of technological ends, to the side of commodity and consumption of which we are anything but proud and confident. We like to rest our case in the penultimate area of means, on the side of machinery where husbands have their place as laborers; and the seriousness of their contribution is indicated by the paycheck. As stewards of the means of technology they are given the decisive power of the means to all means, namely money.

This profound inequity explains the bitterness with which Lillian Breslow Rubin, for instance, speaks of "the deadening and deadly quality of the task of the housewife."[52] It explains the confusion of many housewives as to what society expects of them.[53] And finally it explains the prima facie curious move into the labor market on the part of those housewives who do not have to work to be financially secure. A housewife who takes a job as a secretary or saleswoman exchanges a position where she can largely organize her own work, has a good amount of free time, is able to acquire and exercise many skills, works for people whom she knows intimately and loves well for a position with little skill, no responsibility, and much regimentation. But the latter position has the sanction and respect of the ruling paradigm, and the former does not.[54]

The varied evidence, so far presented in this chapter, suggests that the consumption of commodities appears flawed at the center when we measure it against standards of excellence and undertake it to attain happiness. This evidence must now be capped by a closer and descriptive look at the experience and pleasure of consumption. Consumption, defined generally as the uptake of commodities, occurs in the background of technology as well as in its foreground. The machinery of labor not only procures commodities for final consumption; it is itself designed, produced, and maintained by forces that have commodity character. Computers provide drafting power, stamp mills procure crushing power, backhoes furnish digging and excavating power; and these various forces have the instantaneity, ease, and, ideally, the safety of commodities. The loss of skill, initiative, and responsibility that follows upon the spread of productive commodities was discussed in the preceding chapter. But as a rule we have used commodity in a narrower sense which is clearest in the case of final consumption.

Between productive and final commodities are, as we have seen, inter mediate ones, called defensive products, regrettable necessities, or negative benefits.[55] These are goods that displace discomforts and harms, as warmth replaces cold, health supersedes illness, insurance takes the place of precariousness. The harms may be natural conditions, but they can also be, as Hirsch points out, unintended side effects of technology. And as Hirsch also shows, a device that procures a luxury in one setting provides a mere necessity in another. The first introduction of these intermediate commodities undoubtedly provided great relief, pleasure, and a burst of happiness, less so where the benefits were indeterminate in space and time, as with vaccination and insurance, and dramatically so on such definite occasions as the arrival of electricity or the early and first purchase of a car. These were archetypal moments of technological liberation of which we can capture echoes today when electricity has been restored after a breakdown, when the phone is finally installed in a new house, or when at last we have our car back after a lengthy repair. In the period of deprivation, our world is dark and confined. Our dignity and freedom seem threatened when we must laboriously attend to tasks that are normally a matter of course. However, it is also a common experience of people whose technological liberty and mobility were curtailed by heavy snow or the loss of electricity that life assumed a calmer pace and more vivid colors. Still, the return to technological normalcy is greeted with relief and as a surge of power and freedom. This is also the experience of people who move from the North to the Sun Belt. There seems to be an accrual of dignity when one is freed from the "wicked labor" of having to dress when one wants to venture outside, of having to prepare the car for winter and still see it break down, of having to battle snow and frost. The move to the Sun Belt is a technological advance.

But as remarked before, the great defensive devices that protect us from hunger, cold, disease, darkness, confinement, and exertion have been in place for at least a generation now; they constitute the inconspicuous periphery of normalcy that we take for granted, especially so since most of us have been born into this setting. Technology now mimics the great breakthroughs of the past, assuring us that it is an imposition to have to open a garage door, walk behind a lawn mower, or wait twenty minutes for a frozen dinner to be ready. Being given riding lawn mowers, garage door openers, and microwave ovens, we feel for a moment the power of wielding the magic wand. The remembrance of strain and impatience, of relative powerlessness, yields to a sentiment of ease and competence. We seem to move with the effortlessness of youth, with the vigor of an athlete, with the quickness of the great chef. But it is an entirely parasitic feeling that feeds off the disappearance of toil; it is not animated by the full-bodied exercise of skill, gained through discipline and renewed through intimate commerce with the world. On the contrary, our contact with reality has been attenuated to the pushing of buttons and the turning of handles. The results are guaranteed by a machinery that is not of our design and often beyond our understanding. Hence the feelings of liberation and enrichment quickly fade; the new devices lose their glamour and meld into the inconspicuous periphery of normalcy; boredom replaces exhilaration. As long as we remain enthralled by the promise of technology, we will try to discover remaining burdens and seek and welcome devices that will disburden us. But there are barriers to this pursuit. Extensively, regarding time and space, the social and physical limits to growth make it impossible for nearly everyone to have second homes in the mountains and third ones by the sea or to vacation in Greece this year and in Italy the next. Intensively, regarding the daily and domestic sphere, disburdenment leads to more and more frivolity and clutter and to a worsening balance between means and ends where a sophisticated machinery is required to procure a commodity which is as quickly attained by a simple mechanical tool. Electric pencil sharpeners and can openers, automatic bathwater dispensers and doors that open on voice command are examples.[56] To be sure, we have not reached the extensive and intensive limits of liberation and enrichment. Given our infatuation with technology there will be continued movement toward those limits in spite of the diminishing returns.

But it is clear that, if technological boredom is to be kept at bay, there must be a kind of enrichment which is unlimited. It is available under the heading of entertainment and comes in the shape of commodities that we ingest, that we eat, see, or hear. These constitute the final and central commodities and the foremost foreground of technology. The procurement of such commodities, of food, shows, and music, is largely free of social and physical limits. Since entertaining commodities are essentially private, greatly attenuated in their physical bulk, and consumed entirely, leaving hardly a residue, crowding is not a problem. Since there are obvious limits to the time and capacity of an individual's consumption, entertainment respects rather than attacks physical boundaries.[57] Interest is maintained not through the extension of the consumption activity but through the novelty and diversity of the entertaining commodities. To be sure, there must be a source that yields ever new and different dishes, stories, and melodies. It is comprised of tradition and culture, news, and staged events. The first segment constitutes a nearly inexhaustible and partially self-augmenting store of events, plots, stories, and settings. History can be mined for television specials and series. Nature can be portrayed to terrify or amuse us. Ethnic dishes can be discovered and packaged. And what was once entertaining can be rediscovered or revived. Seasons in the opera or in football exploit the tradition not only in what they procure but also in the sequence and rhythm of presentation which mimic the cycle of the seasons and the trajectory of epic or epochal events.[58]

A more finite resource of entertainment consists of the social, moral, and sexual taboos. The unmentionable is said, the strictly private is exhibited, and the forbidden is done. In a pretechnological setting such taboos were compounds of economic and moral restraints. They had to be observed not only to respect divinity and guard a notion of human dignity but also to guard against the collapse of the social order and its economic basis. But when the substructure of a society is transformed according to the device paradigm, social morality can shrink to the acceptance of the paradigm, the willingness to labor and to respect the demands of the technological machinery; and private morality is conflated with the liberty to consume whatever commodities are procured by the machinery. The traditional taboos become available as an exploitable resource since they are not needed for the new order and can be mined with impunity.[59] This is perhaps the worst case analysis since, as Hirsch contends, an undergirding social morality of the traditional sort may remain necessary for the functioning of a technological society. But there is at least a tendency toward the worst case; and, whether we will reach its extreme stage or not, there are independent reasons why the exploitation of taboos must eventually run its course. The contravention of taboos is entertaining only to the extent that there are residues of traditional morality which are pleasantly irritated when the taboos are violated. As these moral sensibilities fade, the "immoral" first becomes bizarre, then ridiculous, and finally boring.

It is an empirical question whether the exploitation of taboos is innocuous. The effect that television has on children is a focus of this concern.[60] Considering the available evidence, one is struck, I believe, by how relatively slight the indoctrination effect of television is. The truly striking influence that television has on our lives is by way of its displacement effect, by its tendency to prevent an idyllic childhood and a vigorous adolescence, to suffocate conversation, reduce common meals, supersede reading, to crowd out games, walks, and social occasions.[61] And this irresistible displacement effect rests in turn on the incredible attractiveness that television possesses and which has rightly, I believe, been likened to addictiveness. The force of television surely derives from a convergence of factors, many of which we have already touched upon. Inasmuch as television is a window on the world, it appears to be the most radical breach in the pretechnological wall of confinement and ignorance. It seems to be an exemplar of liberation and enrichment, and parents often intentionally expose and habituate their children to television, guided by the promise of technology.[62] To surrender one's children to an alien force of education and information is a tendency that runs parallel with the diminishment of authority that parents suffer.[63] And both tendencies are reinforced by the technological desire to be disburdened of an annoying task (which child rearing sometimes is) by a dependable machinery that television provides with unequaled perfection; neither naps, books, toys, nor babysitters can pacify a child as steadily and reliably as television.

Thus as children most of us become accustomed to television. But that is possible and can continue into adulthood only because of the central attraction of television. There may be physiological components to its addictiveness. What must be said from the standpoint of technology is that television is eminently in tune with the device paradigm. It is first of all perfectly available as an institution or in its form. It requires no commitment in dress, transportation, or manners. It is equally available in its content. This is favored, though not required, by its form and in harmony with the ruling paradigm. Commodities are designed not to make demands.[64] Exertion is given in labor and has no place in leisure, and due to the typically draining character of technological labor, little energy is left for leisure anyway. Technological leisure, Irving Howe said in 1948, just before the age of television, "must provide relief from work monotony without making the return to work too unbearable; it must provide amusement without insight and pleasure without disturbance. . . . "[65] More positively, television remains the purest, i.e., the clearest and most attenuated, presentation of the promise of technology. It appears to free us from the fetters of time, space, and ignorance and to lay before us the riches of the world in their most glamorous form. In light of this cosmopolitan brilliance, all local and personal accomplishments must seem crude and homely.[66] But not only are large portions and dimensions of the world procured for commodious viewing and so implicitly given commodity character. There is also the explicit and elaborate celebration of the most advanced and paradigmatic foreground of technology which, as shown in Chapter 10, is presented in advertisements. This exhibition of individual commodities is complemented by a more implicit and contextual presentation of commodities in the typically glamorous technological settings of the programs dealing with contemporary matters.[67] So seen, television is not so much the result of unfortunate developments in the media industry as it is the inevitable completion of technological culture.

If television is in fact so typical of technological culture and of consumption, the common attitude toward it may explain why technological leisure keeps us both enthralled and unhappy. We know from the work of television critics and from the responses of our friends and from our own that there is little pride in the quality of television programs and less in the habit of extensive viewing. The television viewer's implication in technology typically takes the form of complicity as defined in Chapter 15. We feel uneasiness about our passivity and guilt and sorrow at the loss of our traditions or alternatives.[68] There is a realization that we are letting great things and practices drift into oblivion and that television fails to respond to our best aspirations and fails to engage the fullness of our powers. These impressions generally agree with more systematic findings that show that television is "not rated particularly highly as a general way of spending time, and in fact was evaluated below average compared to other free-time activities."[69] More engaging activities such as "being with friends, helping others, religion, and reading," sports and games (by men), and cooking (by women) are thought to be more satisfying than television viewing.[70]

At times an occasion of decision in the sense of Chapter 15 arises for a family regarding television. The breakdown of the set, the unavailability of a channel, or some sort of experimental situation breaks the habit of viewing.[71] In such a situation almost all families experience a restoration of vigor and depth. They recall with fondness and a wistful pride life without television. But when the externally induced break comes to an end, a decision must be made from within the normal framework of orientation. Some people give up television for good or succeed in curtailing it in a principled way (and some do so without an inducement from without). Most people, however, return to regular and extensive television watching.[72] Refusing television is normally too much and not enough. Within the framework of the device paradigm, giving up television is excessively demanding. Television embodies too vividly the dream of which we cannot let go. It provides a center for our leisure and an authority for the appreciation of commodities. It is also a palliative that cloaks the vacuity and relaxes the tensions of the technological condition. So it is normally not enough to reject or constrain television. One must recognize and reform the larger pattern if one is to reform its center. Thus we are led to the question of the reform of technology. That question can be raised more helpfully if we first ask how stable the framework is that needs to be changed.

19   The Stability of Technology

Some critics believe that an intrinsic instability of technology will force a reform. I begin this last chapter of Part 2 with a discussion of the kinds of instabilities that have been discovered in technology. But I find none of them fatal to the survival or affluence of the technological societies. Technology has the conceptual resources and thus the physical and social ones as well to deal with its crises. What is required to that end is the extension of the technological paradigm to the global scale where the earth itself is seen and treated as a device, namely, as a spaceship. If that technological totalitarianism comes to pass, life will take on an essentially secure, trite, and predictable cast.

But even if my arguments were to convince the critics of technology, they would not satisfy its proponents. The latter would insist that the future of technology is open in an exciting and creative sense. They would point to the marvels and possibilities opened up by the microelectronic revolution. In conclusion of Part 2 I examine both popular and scholarly support for this thesis. It appears, however, that the impact of microelectronics on our lives will be entirely contained within the paradigm of technology.

The trait in the character of technology that concerns us finally, then, is its stability. The lack of stability is frequently a target of the critics of technology. The charges extend from suggestions that the course of technology is precarious to assertions that technology is headed for self-destruction. And the claims of instability vary again as regards the flaw in technology which is seen as the pivot of infirmity. A recurring criticism holds that technology suffers from a profound moral or spiritual defect.[1] Technology dehumanizes and alienates us, it is said.[2] The consequent moral decay is of course compatible with the outward stability of technology, and that seems to diminish the significance of the spiritual failure. As suggested in the preceding chapter, when the economic and social penalty of indulging in a vice is removed by technology or turned into a benefit, morality becomes a resource that is available and exploitable for entertainment. To urge a straightforward adherence to pretechnological morality as E. F. Schumacher does so earnestly must then appear quaint and ineffective, much as we may admire the moralist. The vices of greed and envy against which Schumacher speaks so often are indistinguishable within a technological setting from the hard-driving and competitive spirit that is widely considered a positive force in the advancement of technology.[3] This is not to deny morality but to urge that it must be fundamentally rethought in the technological era. The inappropriate vision of the spiritual criticism of technology is heightened or exposed by the substantive sense of technology it often employs. The liabilities of that concept are then easily taken advantage of by the proponent of technology.[4]

I believe that most critics of the moral defects of technology sense the weakness of their approach and therefore reach for criticisms of technology which cannot so easily be dismissed and which allege that technology, because it is spiritually defective or in addition to its being so, is overtly unstable or self-destructive.[5] Whether the allegations of the tangible defects of technology stem from a deeper concern or not, they must be considered in their own right. The variety of these claims can be ordered by distinguishing the flaws to which they point. The central flaw might be structural, psychological, or physical. Hirsch's analysis, considered in the preceding chapter, can be taken to assert that commercialization and the futile competition for positional goods are intrinsic and expanding features of advanced industrial production and consumption and, though not themselves immoral, lead through their expansion to the erosion of the indispensable moral basis of the technological society. Staffan B. Linder argues that gains in productivity due to technological advances make labor time more valuable, and the latter in turn raises the value of leisure time. To make the best use of the valuable but inevitably limited leisure time we cram more and more devices, commodities, and consumption into the sphere of leisure, a move that increased production enables us to make. The result is a life that becomes more and more hectic, tense, and unhappy.[6] A purely structural flaw of technology would be one that would imperil technology even if humans possessed infinitely robust psyches and the physical environment were infinitely resourceful. But technology is usually said to exhibit structural deficiencies relative to human frailty and ecological limitations. Still, it makes sense to distinguish these flaws since they are often emphasized separately. For Schumacher it is a matter of simple inspection that technology is not only morally objectionable but leads to psychological stresses which threaten to tear the fabric of society.[7]

Finally, it is a familiar warning that the progress of technology is about to exhaust the capacity of the planet, both as a source of energy and raw materials and as a sink for wastes. At times that technological tendency, particularly in conjunction with other flaws, is thought to be nearly irreversible and quite possibly lethal.[8] Even if a cataclysmic catastrophe can be avoided, the physical limits to growth, so it is said and so it appears, will bring to an end the period of technological growth and affluence that began with the Industrial Revolution; and that of course comes to saying that technology itself as a unique form of life will come to an end.[9] When this conclusion is reached by writers such as Schumacher, Illich, and Warren Johnson, who also express the gravest reservations about the spiritual soundness of technology, there is an unmistakable note of satisfaction in their claim that technology is finally a self-destructive or at least self-limiting phenomenon.[10] These authors are gravely pessimistic about the physical and psychological sustainability of technology; but they are simultaneously optimistic that this spiritually pernicious force will run itself into the ground. This may be called the unwarranted pessimism of the optimists. Closer inspection shows, I believe, that technology at its center is sufficiently resourceful to cope with its supposed flaws.

Technology in the paradigmatic sense has the conceptual resources to deal with its crises, and it therefore obtains the material resources as a matter of course, at least in the long run. In light of the device pattern, the dissatisfaction with the spiritual quality of technology is one with the end of technology. But the end of technology is composed of radically novel objects and activities, of commodities and consumption. The latter must be analyzed and understood before they can be criticized. Criticism is necessary, as I have urged in the chapter above. A critique, however, that immediately applies traditional standard to entities without precedent will unavoidably be deflected from its goal, i.e., from the end to the means. And indeed, the consequent critique of the structural, mental, and material flaws of technology is in the main one of the technological machinery. In Chapter 18, I have suggested how within the framework of the device paradigm one will likely counter and overcome Hirsch's apprehensions regarding the structure of production and consumption. The mental stresses of a technological culture which Schumacher sees coming to the surface in "symptoms such as crime, drug addiction, vandalism, mental breakdown, rebellion, and so forth," are either not typical of or not fatal to the central and advanced technological societies, the Scandinavian or Western European countries or white middle-class America.[11] Advanced technology inflicts severe injuries only on people and peoples who live at its periphery, and it remains indifferent to these harms, as said in Chapter 16, unless they become harmful to the central regions of technology.

It is less easy to suggest that technology has the conceptual tools to deal with the physical limits to its growth since the evidence for the voraciousness and blindness of technology is so massive.[12] The relationship of technology to the natural environment will concern us again in Chapter 22; let me here simply outline the technological solution to the environmental crisis. To uncover it we must remember that the promise of technology is one of liberation from burdens and constraints in the principled, i.e., forceful and reliable approach that is based on scientific insight. To act on the promise is to construct a technological machinery which has a tendency not only toward instantaneity and ubiquity of procurement but toward ease and safety as well. It is undisputed that in this way technology has established areas of security as regards health, shelter, warmth, clothing, and food. But these successes sprang, we might say, from local concerns and efforts which responded to challenges that were confronted here and there and separately. But now that the device paradigm through its local applications is beginning to envelop the globe and indeed is reaching into outer space, a global application of the device pattern becomes necessary. And, we might ruefully say on behalf of the proponent of technology, we have been slow in so extending the pattern. In the final extension of the paradigm, the globe itself must be seen and treated as one technological device. This has already informally been done when the earth is taken as a spaceship. Occasionally this concept is explicitly used to urge an extension of the technological paradigm as in the following remarks of R. Buckminster Fuller's:

> One of the interesting things to me about our spaceship is that it
> is a mechanical vehicle, just as is an automobile. If you own an
> automobile, you realize that you must put oil and gas into it, and

you must put water in the radiator and take care of the car as a whole. You know that you're either going to have to keep your machine in good order or it's going to be in trouble and fail to function. We have not been seeing our Spaceship Earth as an integrally-designed machine which to be persistently successful must be comprehended and serviced in total.[13]

Christopher D. Stone has noted the force with which the term "spaceship earth" has "captured the popular imagination."[14] He believes this to be the hopeful sign of a rising planetary consciousness and respect, a change of consciousness that Laurence H. Tribe similarly believes to have been advanced by the vision from outer space of "the earth as a dramatically finite and surprisingly delicate blue-green globe."[15] Respect of the earth of course shades off easily into enlightened self-interest. When a global perspective is more than a hope and is articulated as a framework for analysis and proposals as in the report of the Club of Rome, it is evident at once that the device paradigm delimits the dimensions of concern. The apprehensions regard the fuel supply and the carrying capacity of spaceship earth for humans, not the level of respect for all forms of life that mother earth has brought forth. The study of *The Limits to Growth* explicitly urges the extension of our concerns to "a global perspective."[16] Such a perspective is concerned with human population, resources, industrial production, and pollution. It formalizes global developments in terms of feedback systems and urges the attainment of an equilibrium through a negative feedback system whose obvious illustration is a technological device, a heating system with a thermostat.[17]

Thus the device paradigm provides the conceptual framework that makes it possible to deal technologically with the physical limits to growth, and it provides the rhetoric to make the technological solutions widely understandable and acceptable. It is able to exact a measure of restraint and patience from the broad middle class of the advanced industrial countries on whose loyalty it depends. Or, to avoid the appearance of a substantive view of technology, the class of people who have both embraced and most benefited from technology are able to maintain their allegiance to technology in the face of severe physical constraints by extending to the global scale the pattern of technology with which they are locally and intimately familiar. Within little more than a decade a seemingly total obliviousness to limits of growth and resources has given way to a high level of ecological consciousness in politics and the mass media. Such a rapid and relatively smooth change would have been impossible if it had required the establishment of a new paradigm rather than the extension of an existing one. To be sure, there is still much inertia and wrongheadedness in the reigning environmental policies. But the global ecological situation is more promising socially and physically than most critics had dared to hope a decade ago.

Environmental stability under the rule of technology requires us then to take a global and long-term view, and within that perspective the machinery of technology needs to be modified. This much is understood by everyone. But the technical details, since they pertain to the machinery, are typically and mostly hidden by ignorance and indolence from the citizen of the technological society. Indolence conceals the fact that the powerless both within and especially outside the advanced industrial countries are carrying the main burden of reform through poverty, disease, famine, and death. Regarding the more strictly technical, i.e., physical, aspects of adapting the technological machinery to physical scarcity, there are still hopes that a technological breakthrough of some sort will disburden us from all constraints and once more open up an era of limitless growth. But it is becoming clear that stability and eventually moderate growth are being achieved incrementally through engineering ingenuity applied in a thousand and one places and by exploiting wasteful practices, past and present.[18]

If the rule of the technological paradigm remains unchallenged, we can predict a global future that tends toward a physically homeostatic equilibrium, first for the technologically developed nations and then, after long and bitter misery, for all people on earth. Culturally there will be an appearance of growth and progress since within the physical limits there will be scientific discoveries and technological innovations which will allow for the refinement, variation, and dissemination of devices and commodities. And the latter can be varied nearly ad infinitum by resorting to the resource of traditional culture as pointed out in the preceding chapter.

To a proponent of technology this prognosis will appear positive but not positive enough: positive because it acknowledges the stability of technology, not positive enough because it takes a negative view of the creative and revolutionary potential of technology. Is not that view, the proponent will say, due to a lack of information or a failure of imagination? Are we not poised at the threshold of another technological revolution, namely, the microelectronic revolution? A look at that phenomenon will help to test and illustrate once more what has been said about the stability of technology and about its character generally; and such a consideration will provide a fitting conclusion to this part of the philosophy of technology.

How serious are we to take the microelectronic revolution? It is of epochal significance; so at least we are told in cover stories of *Newsweek* and *Time* and by representatives of science and industry.[19] According to the National Academy of Sciences, "the modern era of electronics has ushered in a second industrial revolution. . . . Its impact on society could be even greater than that of the original industrial revolution."[20] And *Newsweek* tells us that as "the industry likes to picture the future, the new technology offers potential solutions to humanity's most intractable problems—the allocation of energy resources, food enough for all and the worldwide improvement of health care, to name just a few."[21] To these pronouncements we should add those quoted in Chapters 17 and 18 which predicted that robots and automation would lead to a radical improvement of the work world and of the quality of life.

Are the developments in this field truly of revolutionary significance? To answer, let us consider a digital watch and compare it with a spring-driven one. The latter kind of clock was first built in the early sixteenth century. Thus it was thoroughly familiar a century later to men such as Bacon and Descartes. In the late seventeenth century, Newton provided the scientific insight that provided a precise and general explanation of its workings. There have been many refinements in the construction of mechanical watches within the following three centuries, but they would all be readily intelligible to a Bacon, Descartes, or Newton. But what would they say when shown a digital watch? Even if we gave them hundreds of watches to dissect and examine, their inner workings would remain impenetrable to them. To understand a digital watch at the level at which they comprehended mechanical ones, they would have to recapitulate 300 years of revolutionary science or do graduate studies in modern logic, mathematics, physics, chemistry, and engineering. When it comes to the structure and working, i.e., the machinery, of a digital watch, it is surely no exaggeration to say that it is separated by a revolutionary gap from the machinery of the spring-driven watches that were current only ten years ago.

But in another sense the digital watch is not revolutionary at all. This becomes apparent when we ask how difficult it would be to teach someone like Newton not how to comprehend but how to use a digital watch. And it is clear that it would take only a few minutes.[22] In fact it is easier than teaching someone how to read the dial and hands of a traditional watch. Thus what a digital watch procures, namely, time indication, is familiar and accessible. Of course it procures it much more commodiously, i.e., in digits, with more precision, more variety, greater completeness, and with less bulk, without the need to wind it up, to turn it past 31 November, or to take account of leap years. But such a gain has a negligible effect on the quality of our lives.

Still, could it not be that the productivity gains in the machinery of technology will, as an earlier quotation has suggested, bring about a world where food is universally adequate, diseases conquered, and literacy accomplished everywhere? And could it not also be that the enrichment with more advanced commodities, each of which is locally negligible, will have a profoundly new global effect? As regards the first possibility, the belief that rising affluence in the industrial countries will bring relief to the Third World rests on the assumption that our failure to help the starving peoples overcome famine is due to presently insufficient wealth on our part. But this is doubtful at best. In 1950 the standard of living in this country was incomparably higher than that in the developing countries. By 1973 average real family income had more than doubled.[23] During the same time foreign aid as a share of the federal budget has declined by a factor greater than 5 and now hovers between 1 and 2 percent.[24] Effective foreign aid is difficult to achieve. But clearly our determination to achieve it has not grown as a function of rising affluence. There is of course a possibility, as mentioned above, that high technology will by its own dynamics come to pervade the entire world and so extinguish famine and disease. But it would do so slowly and over the graves of millions who have died of hunger and illness.

What about the possibility that the unprecedented character and the eventually all-pervasive presence of microelectronic devices will profoundly change the quality of our lives, including our leisure? This clearly is the implication in the lead paragraph of the *Newsweek* article on microelectronics. It says:

> A revolution is under way. Most Americans are already well aware of the gee-whiz gadgetry that is emerging, in rapidly accelerating bursts, from the world's high-technology laboratories. But most of us perceive only dimly how pervasive and profound the changes of the next twenty years will be. We are at the dawn of the era of the smart machine—an "information age" that will change forever the way an entire nation works, plays, travels and even thinks. Just as the industrial revolution dramatically expanded the strength of man's muscles and the reach of his hand, so the smart-machine revolution will magnify the power of his brain.[25]

Such pronouncements, however, are simply promissory notes that yield little insight into the flavor and texture of the new microelectronic world. But here too *Newsweek* has intrepidly pressed ahead and given us a glimpse of the microelectronic everyday. It is the preamble to the article where a microelectronic citizen speaks to us as follows:

> Welcome! Always glad to show someone from the early '80s around the place. The biggest change, of course, is the smart machines—they're all around us. No need to be alarmed, they're very friendly. Can't imagine how you lived without them. The telephone, dear old thing, is giving a steady busy signal to a bill collector I'm avoiding. Unless he starts calling from a new number my phone doesn't know, he'll never get through. TURN OFF! Excuse me for shouting—almost forgot the bedroom television was on. Let's see, anything else before we go? The oven already knows the menu for tonight and the kitchen robot will mix us a mean Martini. Guess we're ready. Oh, no, you won't need a key. We'll just program the lock to recognize your voice and let you in whenever you want.[26]

The sketch is short of course and may seem shallow and glib. But in its essentials it is like the more studied scenarios in the *New York Times* or like the sweeping and breathless account one finds in Toffler's *The Third Wave*.[27] What does the picture tell us? Let us look at the individual features. (1) The smart machines will be "friendly," i.e., easy to use. (2) We will consider them indispensable. (3) They will allow us to do the following: (*a*) We will be able to be evasive or rude on the telephone by way of electronics rather than through our children or personally. (*b*) We will be able to turn off appliances at a distance so saving ourselves the trouble of having to traverse entire rooms. (*c*) We will be disburdened from having to plan our menus and from having to mix drinks for guests with our own hands. (*d*) We will be spared the possibility of losing the house key or of having it stolen.

It is clear that the further technological liberation from the duress of daily life is only leading to more disengagement from skilled and bodily commerce with reality. Perhaps the account above fails to do justice to the riches of information, entertainment, and games that the new electronics will present us with. But these too will be consumed, i.e., they will not make demands of commitment, discipline, or skill.[28] They will be more diverting due to greater variety and closer fit with our individual tastes. Since they will fail to center and illuminate our lives, however, their diversion will more and more lead to distraction, the scattering of our attention and the atrophy of our capacities. It is already apparent that the new video technology is not used by people as the crucial aid that finally allows them to develop into the historians, critics, musicians, sculptors, or athletes that they have always wanted to be. Rather the main consequence of this technological development appears to be the spread of pornography.[29]

The distinction between machinery and commodity in the pattern of the technological device is important to the recognition that in one crucial regard the microelectronic revolution is eminently traditional and predictable. But the distinction must be properly drawn. There is both a split and a necessary connection between machinery and commodity; a split in the way in which we as consumers are familiar and in touch with the commodity on the one side, and ignorant and incompetent with regard to the particulars of the machinery on the other side; a necessary connection because it is possible only on the basis of discrete and prohibitively complex machineries to enjoy totally unencumbered and supremely refined commodities. If the distinction is not made in this way, the import of the microelectronic revolution will remain cloudy, and there is then a temptation to see once more, if not the effulgence, at least a few rays of the promise of technology behind those clouds. To illustrate this point let me turn to remarks of Daniel Bell. I want to consider these also to meet the charge that my appraisal of the microelectronic revolution has picked an easy target, the pronouncements of overly enthusiastic or popular authors, and has failed to take note of the kind of scholarly , circumspect, and qualified investigations Bell has put forward.

Already in his book on *The Coming of Post-Industrial Society,* Bell has drawn a distinction between social structure and culture which in important regards parallels that between machinery and commodity. The realm of the social structure consists of the economy, technology (in his narrower sense), and occupational structure and is governed by the principles of functional rationality and efficiency. The realm of culture is that of the symbolic expression of meanings, the expressive ways in which we conceive of ourselves, treat one another, deal with nature, and consider matters of ultimate concern. These two realms or forces follow their own principles and rhythms.[30] In the nineteenth century, culture was consonant with the modern social structure. A spirit of devotion to hard work, frugality, and sobriety pervaded advanced industrial capitalism. But that spirit, through its success in promoting mass production and consumption, made possible its own suffocation and was superseded by a spirit of hedonism which now constitutes a challenge to the survival of the liberal democracies.

It is obvious from my remarks on the rule of technology in Chapter 15 and on Hirsch in Chapter 18 what in general my reservations are on Bell's view. Here I am concerned to show how his lack of incisiveness veils the bearing that the microelectronic revolution has on society. It must be stressed that when Bell considers this subject, he looks almost exclusively at the effect of microelectronic devices on the social or technoeconomic structure, not on culture—about which he has serious reservations. But the social structure is after all in the service of culture whose dominance Bell stresses elsewhere, and inevitably cultural concerns are implied or surface at crucial junctures.[31] When he calls the computer the "thing" in which postindustrial society comes to be symbolized, the significance of that society comes to rest on the machinery side of the technological device, and the dubious but decisive character of the commodity side is thereby obscured.[32] That obscurity is deepened when Bell (following Fritz Machlup and Marc Porat) lumps together under the heading of information final commodities as well as machineries, i.e., television programs, music, and games as well as banking transactions and records, scientific papers, marketing services, and the like.[33] The failure to distinguish here allows an uncritical transfer of the astounding and admirable features in the development of the machinery to the entire technological condition.

Although Bell mentions hedonism in an aside and is properly skeptical of educational advances by way of electronics, the common optimism that flows from a consideration of technological machinery to cover all of technology rises to the surface.[34] Bell speaks of

> a rapidly increasing population, more literate and more educated, living in a vastly enlarged world that is now tied together, almost in real time, by cable, telephone and international satellite, whose inhabitants are made aware of each other by the vivid pictorial imagery of television, and that has at its disposal large data banks of computerized information.[35]

He sees "the entire nation (if not large parts of the world)" becoming psychologically (not geographically) urbanized, adopting "a highly interactive, heavily mobile, culturally and politically attentive mode" of life.[36] Finally he suggests, if uncertainly, that information and theoretical knowledge, procured electronically, represent "turning points in modern history."[37] And he concludes his study with the traditional promise of technology:

> But the nature of modern technology frees location from resource site and opens the way to alternative modes of achieving individuality and variety within a vastly increased output of goods. This is the promise—the fateful question is whether that promise will be realized.[38]

I have tried to show that we have enough evidence to see that the promise cannot be fulfilled when we straightforwardly accept the setting to which Bell alludes. The technological setting, patterned after the device paradigm, so I have argued, is profoundly connected with the way in which we conduct our lives. I have also urged that the results of the rule of the technological paradigm are distressing in a significant and even decisive respect. If there is a way of recovering the promise of technology, it must be one of disentangling the promise from the dominant way in which we have taken up with the world for two centuries now. It must be a way of finding counterforces to technology that are guided by a clear and incisive view of technology and will therefore not be deflected or co-opted by technology. At the same time such counterforces must be able to respect the legitimacy of the promise and to guard the indispensable and admirable accomplishments of technology. To delineate these counterforces is the task of the third part of this study.

PART 3

The Reform
of Technology

Focal things and practices can empower us to propose and perhaps to enact a reform of technology. These things and practices are therefore at the center of Part 3 which leads up to the focal concerns and then derives measures of reform from them. The first step is to connect the concern to reform with the openings for reform that have appeared in Part 2. This is the task of Chapter 20. Its major point is that a fruitful reform of technology must be one *of* the device paradigm and cannot allow itself to be confined *within* the framework of technology. And to undertake a consequential reform, one must find an appropriate kind of discourse. It must be a speaking that avoids the liabilities of those moral arguments and attempts at social reform that are patterned by technology. Instead it must be guided by a matter of final concern. Chapter 21 considers these difficulties and seeks to explain the proper discourse of reform, namely, deictic discourse, whose necessity has been stressed throughout this study.

Deictic discourse is about something that addresses us in its own right and constitutes a center by which we can orient ourselves. On this continent, nature in its pristine state is the clearest and most eminent instance of such a thing. In Chapter 22 I try to show how the wilderness has inspired deictic discourse and how, when we speak about the wilderness appropriately, we can say that it constitutes a focal concern and a fruitful counterforce to technology. In Chapter 23 I go on to develop the notion of a focal thing more generally in an effort to point out that focal concerns can prosper in the daily context of technology. But they can do so only if we grant them an assured place through a focal practice. I take running and the culture of the table as instances of such a practice. In Chapter 24 I pause to consider difficulties with focal concerns and alternatives to them. Having disposed of these problems more or less, I proceed to spell out concrete measures of reform for the personal and private realm, for the tradition of excellence, and for the family.

The final and most recalcitrant problem for a reform of technology out of a focal concern is the question whether we can extend the reform constructively to the national community. This is the problem of Chapter 25. The key difficulty is to recognize that such an extension can only come to pass through a philosophically informed restructuring of the economy. More precisely, it is a matter of recognizing and developing tendencies that are assuming shape even now. They announce themselves in the distinctions between the standard of living and the quality of life, between the centralized and highly automated industry on the one side and the local, labor-intensive economy on the other. The philosophy of technology allows us to see these and related issues in a principled and hopeful way. Such a hopeful vision can be joined with the initial hope of the promise of technology. It helps us to see how the early hopes can be clarified and recovered. Those are the reflections of Chapter 26, and they bring the present essay to its conclusion.

20   The Possibilities of Reform

In turning from the analysis of technology to proposals of reform, we must first establish a fruitful connection between these two parts of our essay. We must draw on the insights gained from the examination of technology without acting as though with the examination in hand the reform were a matter of course. Accordingly the first chapter of the third part begins by surveying those points of Part 2 where we have come upon the problem of reform. Among the possibilities for reform that do emerge, the most promising is the suggestion that a signal and orienting event or practice might arise from within technology and answer our misgivings about technology in an intrinsically technological manner. Finding this promise unwarranted at least for now, we can clarify the task at hand by distinguishing reforms *within* the paradigm of technology from reforms *of* the paradigm. The distinction is tested and elaborated against further reform proposals, among them the program of appropriate technology.

To begin then, it is not difficult to obtain agreement that some kind of reform of technology is to be wished for. Problems and pains are too widespread and obvious to permit complacency. But just as there is much confusion and inconsistency about the character of technology, so there is about the direction of reform. Hence if there is anything to the analysis of the preceding two parts of this study, it must prove itself in principled and appropriate suggestions of reform. Yet, as said before, it would be misleading to speak of the prior parts as the foundations on which a reform proposal can now be erected as though an understanding of the problem and character of technology would entail the basic outline of a reform. It is the other way around. What concerns or distresses one about technology is its tendency to destroy or displace things and practices that grace and orient our lives. It is the concern for these focal things and practices that sharpens one's vision for the momentous features of technology. So talk about the reform of technology is really the completion and justification of the analysis of technology. Of course the relationship between the critique of technology and one's ultimate concerns is reciprocal. We are at times diffident or even unaware of our profoundest commitments and more alive to what strikes us as detrimental and degrading in our lives. Following up these injurious tendencies and explicating them can then help us to obtain a clearer and more confident view of what truly and positively matters to us. Still, though the relationship is reciprocal, it remains anchored on the side of our substantive and positive concerns.

Another way of stating the problem of reforming technology is this: The reform proposal must correspond to an analysis of technology that is incisive and principled. If it answers to a superficial analysis, it may well be feasible, but it will remain inconsequential too. If the reform proposal responds to profound misgivings which, however, have not been explicated in a systematic analysis of technology, the suggestions may be ambitious, but they will have no purchase on the deeply entrenched rule of technology and be easily dismissed as utopian. To find a course away from superficiality and utopianism one requires both radicality and circumspection. To serve the latter it may be well to recall the places where we had come upon the reform of technology while analyzing its character. The most persistent and common reform tendency consists naturally in a return, knowing or not, to the founding promise of technology, in a reiteration of the prospect of liberty and prosperity on the basis of advancing scientific insight and of continuing engineering ingenuity. Throughout Part 2 and particularly in Chapters 18 and 19, we have seen both how strongly we still cling to the promise and its restatements and how ironically and inexorably the promise has been and likely will be subverted as long as the pattern of its implementation remains implicit and unchallenged.

It remains so, as appeared in Chapter 13, when we cast our misgivings about technology in the form of "raising the value question." Since in the common view technology is seen as an assembly of mere means and since values are taken as general standards of preference that are to be realized in whatever is the most efficient way, values are in preestablished harmony with technology. The superficial variety of ends that the technological machinery procures engenders the illusion that fundamental decisions are to be made in the technological realm of ends and that a debate on values is the road to those decisions. And though it is not unimportant which technological ends are chosen, they remain commodities one and all. Thus the value debate typically leaves the debilitating division of our lives into mindless labor and distracting consumption unexamined and intact.

Macpherson and Habermas, as seen in Chapter 14, are disturbed by the character of the technological machinery in the broad sense and by the kind of life it fosters. But the instrumental conception of technology survives their misgivings and scrutiny and serves as the pivot of their reform proposals. The latter call for greater equity and efficiency of the machinery and for more participation by the people in its direction. Yet without a trenchant analysis of that machinery and of its bias, people's allegiance to it cannot be judged. And if it is true, as argued in Chapters 15 and 16, that technology together with its inequities commands as of now the uneasy loyalty of the people, calls for social justice will be ineffective, and proposals for a different kind of government are idle.

In Chapter 11 we did come upon an attempt to grasp the idiosyncrasy of the technological approach to reality and an endeavor to discover in it the basis of a new order. It was the counsel of functionalism to define and realize the functions of the things about us by the principles of science and engineering, and it was the conviction of functionalism that a world so designed would be one of formal beauty, of vigor and honesty. But that program failed to realize the instability of the concept "function." Since the function of something, a house or a chair, was thought to be something other and less than the traditional thing in the fullness of its features, how was the function to be fixed? The theorists of functionalism did not see that the reduction of things to commodities that had been going on for more than a century constituted a deeply ingrained answer to this question, and, since they too had implicitly accepted the answer, they overlooked the crucial significance of the question. So functionalism came to be submerged in the mainstream of technology.

And yet perhaps we should not so quickly give up on the initial concern of functionalism, i.e., on the endeavor to find a new order at the heart of technology. Technology, even in a vague, general, and pretheoretical sense, and whether conjoined with science or not, surely stands for what is typical of our time. It is natural and honorable to want to discover greatness in the character of one's time and to claim that greatness as one's own. Let us consider two such efforts. The first can be taken as the affirmation of a point that was rejected in Chapter 12. There I said that the technological era, unlike Classical Greece or the Middle Ages, had not brought forth focal things or events, temples or cathedrals, processions or celebrations in which the significance and coherence of life had come to be focused. Perhaps we have not looked far enough. What about the physically, scientifically, and technically imposing objects and enterprises of our time? R. R. Wilson in an essay on "The Humanness of Physics" tells us: "When Ernest Lawrence built his cyclotrons with a dedicated passion he was not that different from Suger, also with a dedicated passion, building the cathedral of St. Denis."[1] Wilson has the applause of the editors of the anthology in which his essay appeared: "One has but to see the Central Laboratory of Fermilab rising cathedral-like from the plains of Illinois to see the aptness of Wilson's comparison of accelerator builders to the cathedral builders of the thirteenth century."[2] The first launching of the space shuttle provided another occasion for attempts to discover epochal meaning at the center of technology. One writer saw a secular test in the launch: "A people are testing themselves in relation to their heritage. . . . A people are testing their resolve to reach beyond the ordinary and thereby, if history repeats, magnify the human spirit."[3] Others saw in the shuttle "a space-age Taj Mahal that leapt into the sky on twin pillars of impossibly bright yellow and blue flame." They praised the astronauts' heroism and "their willingness to trust their lives to an untested craft, a faith in technology and sheer scale that many Americans wish they could recapture."[4]

The medieval cathedral was a focal point of its time because it embodied the unified vision of the world that the Medievals had attained from different traditions and through many trials.[5] Though the cathedrals were built on and represented intricate theoretical principles that were incomprehensible to lay people, the crucial points of those principles were open to all: the beginning, middle, and end of the history of salvation; the hierarchical order of reality that culminated in divine majesty; and the place one occupied in history and hierarchy. The cathedrals were accessible to all in the practices of construction, extending over many generations, and then in the practices of celebration. Though a simple person would not have a sophisticated understanding of the cathedral as a model of the cosmos and as the embodiment of the City of God, that person's grasp of its meaning and participation in its presence could still be profound and direct.

The validity of the vision of the world in the high Middle Ages is a question in its own right. I am here concerned to stress some of its formal features: comprehensiveness, unity, accessibility, and enactment. Such features (or their instantiation) are merely necessary conditions for the greatness and validity of a world view and of the focal things and practices in which it comes to be present. But they are conditions that are clearly not met by the accelerator and the space shuttle. What do these objects tell us about the beginning and end of all things? About the order of society and the universe? How can they be comprehended in a profound if unsophisticated manner by ordinary pople, and how can such people participate in them firsthand? We may find positive answers to these questions by treating technological objects as symptoms of a certain order; they do certainly not constitute comprehensive and eloquent embodiments of that order. They fail to gather our world and to radiate its central meaning into ordinary life. Are the astronauts truly heroes whose faith in technology we should emulate? "Behind the astronauts," Ronald Weber answers, "we recognize armies of skilled technicians, and the astronauts themselves seem as interchangeable as the parts of their machines."[6]

The claims for the presence of meaning at the heart of technology that we have considered are just suggestions, undeveloped and untested. But there is also a thoughtful and extended argument to the same effect. It is Robert Pirsig's *Zen and the Art of Motorcycle Maintenance*.[7] The book is not a straightforward philosophical treatise. It has a complex literary structure; it exhibits ingenious pedagogy; it contains striking and profound observations; and the philosophical views that it advances are not always consistent with one another (a virtue, perhaps, in a book of this kind). Still, there is a clear and central thesis. It is conveyed in the title which recalls Eugen Herrigel's *Zen in the Art of Archery*.[8] The latter book is an account of how Herrigel came to attain enlightenment and peace through the practice and discipline of archery to which he was initiated by a Zen master. Accordingly Pirsig suggests that peace of mind can be found in the midst of technology by carefully attending to a technological object such as a motorcycle. The suggestion is made explicit in the great promise of the book: "The Buddha, the Godhead, resides quite as comfortably in the circuits of a digital computer or the gears of a cycle transmission as he does at the top of a mountain or in the petals of a flower."[9] What makes the pronouncement so attractive is its promise of reconciling nostalgia and technology. It tells us that we can find a world of peace and serenity and be at home not just in God's pristine and vanishing creation but in the midst of our own creations which surround us daily.

To attain harmony with technology, so Pirsig tells us, we must take up the practice of maintaining and caring for the technological objects about us. This instruction responds in a positive way to the disengagement and disfranchisement that beset typical technological culture. It tells us to penetrate the commodious surfaces of technology, to reassert our mastery over the machinery of technology, and so to become full members of the city of technology. To the counsel of engagement there corresponds an analysis of disengagement. Pirsig sees it in three forms. The first stems from the envelopment in technological devices such as automobiles or planes which insulate us from the character of the land, the rhythm of the day, and the expanses of plains and mountains.[10] Disengagement can, second, stem from ignorance and resentment of technology, from the inability to understand how water faucets and motorcycles work, from incompetence in using or repairing such devices, from the frustration and anger in the face of technological failure, and, finally, from a broader rejection of the forbidding and ugly character of the technological landscape.[11] There is a third kind of disengagement which debilitates the professed experts of technology—motorcycle mechanics, for instance— when they deal with technological devices in a distracted and offhand way, covering up one blunder with another.[12]

How incisive is the diagnosis and how helpful the therapy? Beginning with the third sort of disengagement, we see at once that there is nothing specifically technological about it. Inattention and blundering can blight any human activity. What is new in technology is its endeavor to overpower human frailty either through personnel management techniques or by eliminating the human component altogether. The ignorant and resentful disengagement from technology that is represented in Pirsig's book by John and Sylvia Sutherland is ambivalent. It is not clear whether John and Sylvia want perfect technology, faucets that do not drip, motorcycles that start unfailingly, and pretty factories set in a parklike environment; or whether they want no technology at all. Pirsig's proposal, finally, to counter the disengagment of consumption through the maintenance of technological devices is incomplete and becomes less and less helpful as technology progresses. For, as we have seen in Chapter 9, technology systematically withdraws devices or their machinery from our competence and care by making technological objects maintenance free, discardable, or forbiddingly intricate. When a great number of motorcycle functions are regulated by microelectronic rather than mechanical devices, the thoughtful inspection and tuning of the cycle beside a shady curbstone in Miles City, Montana, will have become a thing of the past.[13] They will be impossible and unnecessary. A call for caring makes sense only within a reform proposal that recognizes and fruitfully counters the technological tendency to disburden and disengage us from the care of things.

Pirsig realizes that there are underlying "systematic patterns of thought" that must be grasped and changed if there is to be a reform of the immediate problems that trouble us.[14] He also recognizes that the underlying patterns of our lives are in the form of a division or a split between surface appearances and underlying forms.[15] But that split is seen too subjectively, generally, and abstractly. It is a split that is not so much embodied in the concrete world about us as it is one of attitude, the romantic attitude that is oriented toward immediate appearances versus the classic attitude that searches for the rational and scientific structure of things. The account of these attitudes is both too strong and too weak, too strong in letting the attitudes pertain to all phenomena whatever, rivers as well as motorcycles, factories as well as piles of sand; too weak in defining the attitudes primarily as ways of seeing rather than shaping so that the shape of things remains largely unquestioned, and what is recommended is little more than a change of vision. Accordingly the counterpoint to this split is not so much the full bodily engagement with things in their own right as a mystic and metaphysical force or principle that Pirsig calls Quality.[16]

It is ironical that a book that is so rich in concrete descriptions and insights takes this central and evasive leap into an autistic kind of metaphysics, a leap that finally drives Phaedrus, the narrator's former and alter ego, insane. But the narrator clings to the hope that he can "get away from intellectual abstractions of an extremely general nature and into some solid, practical, day-to-day information."[17] This descent from metaphysics to the everyday world remains unfruitful. Pirsig believes that the typical predicament that we face today is the collision with clear and well-defined problems for which a standard solution is unavailable, so that we feel stuck.[18] But surely in the context of being stuck technology is more likely to appear as the source of solutions than the source of our vague and profound misgivings. Pirsig's political and social views are correspondingly barren. "The social values are right," he says, "only if the individual values are right. The place to improve the world is in one's own heart and head and hands, and then work outward from there."[19] And, finally, all the narrator's insight into Quality is powerless to help him reach his son Chris. He finally reaches him not through metaphysical acumen but by recognizing Chris as a person in his own right, one who has kept faith with his father through all the latter's trials.[20]

We can capture more precisely what is unsatisfactory in the reform proposals considered so far by distinguishing between reforms *within* the paradigm of technology and reforms *of* the paradigm.[21] Reforms within the pattern or framework of technology are in implicit agreement with the way in which the promise of technology is being worked out according to the device paradigm. Such reforms can be central or piecemeal. Central reform proposals assume that the technological enterprise is basically, though not entirely, well conceived, but they imply or contend that its center has been missed, obscured, or lost; reformers are accordingly concerned to uncover the central force of technology and to let it have its properly beneficial and powerful effect. The restatements of the promise of technology, the program of functionalism, the concern with the value question, the fascination with technological spectacles, the democratization of technology, the global extension of the device paradigm, all these are central attempts at reform that are internal to technology. They all spring, as any reform proposal must, from a dissatisfaction with technology; but when they translate their dissatisfaction into a program of action, they are guided by too shallow a notion of technology; they overestimate or underestimate its character and force and remain inconsequential. Reformers overestimate technology when they believe that at the center of the promise of technology *and* in the implementation of the promise there is a tendency toward something like traditional excellence. But this belief ignores the ironical turn in the realization of the technological promise. Reformers underestimate technology when they take an instrumental view of it and believe that, having no center of its own, it can with little ado be given one from without. This approach ignores the definite and deeply entrenched style of life in which technology issues.

Central reform proposals within technology will always fail when they ignore the idiosyncrasy and momentum of technology. The attempts at finding an inspiring and ennobling force that is intrinsically technological have so far failed in fact. But it would be dogmatic and invidious to deny the possibility of such a discovery altogether. The search for a guiding force of an essentially technological sort becomes objectionable only when it entails the neglect or destruction of great things that are clearly and already present. As I want to show in Chapter 23, the orientation toward vague and distant but supposedly magnificent technological goals indeed tends to settle like a blight on the things of simple splendor that are all about us. The fact that all the central reform programs have so far been without consequence is of course a sign of failure, and the failure may in turn indicate that these proposals are moved by a concern that can be satisfied only through a reform *of* the paradigm of technology. Central proposals would then be ways in which people misspeak themselves when talking about technology. We will consider this possibility more closely in Chapter 22.

Piecemeal reforms within the framework of technology address a particular area of our lives that has not been rendered available, one that is unsafe, severely limited, or inaccessible. Such an area may be large as that of energy resources or small as *tic douloureux;* it may be significant such as prison reform or frivolous such as hair transplants. There is little disagreement *that* the large or significant problems should be solved and those first that are both large and significant. This is simply a matter of continuing and perhaps concluding the genuinely liberating and constructive program of technology. But there are complicating factors that make it difficult to set off salutary technological reforms against frivolous ones and internal from external ones. The line between soundness and frivolity has been blurred in technology. It is no longer clear, for instance, where in orthodontics the line between cosmetics and hygiene is to be drawn or where in the procurement of information enrichment turns into disorientation and stultification. There are problems of justice also. Assuming that frequent meals at fast food outlets are frivolous, should one oppose them, knowing that the burden of homecooked meals would disproportionately fall on women? Or should one try to prevent them from becoming available to the poor, given that the broad middle class freely and universally enjoys this luxury? Finally, there are unquestionably serious problems such as lung cancer and acid rain for which, it would seem, one should try to find a technological fix by all available means. But these problems spring largely from frivolous consumption, and is it not more reasonable to prevent them from arising than to fix them technologically?

The difference between the treatments of a problem can also be stated as a difference of kinds of problems. The prevention of a problem such as water shortages requires social change, the introduction of more parsimonious practices through education, rationing, or pricing. The cure of water shortages requires the procurement of abundant water through a technological device such as desalination. We can take this issue as a social or a technological problem. Alvin M. Weinberg, who has cast the matter in these terms and coined the notion of the technological fix, has also argued that the latter is quick and reliable whereas social change is "a frustrating business"; it is "difficult, time-consuming, and uncertain in the extreme."[22] Hence we should to the largest possible extent convert social into technological problems. The technological fix is of course in the middle of the mainstream of technology. It disburdens people to the point of disengagement, and it conceals its debilitating tendency behind the liberal democratic principle of leaving people's "habits or motivation" unquestioned.[23] Since technology has for two centuries been eminently successful by its paradigmatic standard, there is, as Weinberg stresses, strong historical evidence to support his recommendation for future reliance on technological fixes.[24] But whether continued confidence is warranted is an empirical question. Two future technological fixes of which Weinberg thinks highly are the intrauterine contraceptive device and nuclear power desalination.[25] The IUD is an example of a technological fix that works as much through discrimination as through technology. It puts the real burden of birth control, as is generally the case, on women and particularly exposes them to physical harms and dangers. One might reply on behalf of technology that the IUD is simply a biased and imperfect device and that an equitable and efficient one is desirable and possible. The fact is that none has been devised so far.

Still it is not clear that this is an instance where technology, having disposed of the manageable problems, is running up against an intractable one. But the latter event is more obvious in the second instance of Weinberg's technological fixes of the future. Two of his statements will establish the point.

A large program to develop cheap methods of nuclear desalting has been undertaken by the United States, and I have little doubt that within the next ten to twenty years we shall see huge dual-purpose desalting plants springing up on many parched seacoasts of the world. At first these plants will produce water at municipal prices. But I believe, on the basis of research now in progress at ORNL and elsewhere, water from the sea at a cost acceptable for agriculture—less than ten cents per 1,000 gallons—is eventually in the cards.[26]

In short, the widespread availability of very cheap energy every-where in the world ought to lead to an energy autarky in every country of the world; and eventually to an autarky in the many staples of life that should flow from really cheap energy.[27]

This was written in 1966, and we should now be in the middle of the period when the huge desalting plants were to spring up. But Weinberg's words seem to come from a different era altogether. The nuclear power industry has run up against apparently insuperable physical, economic, and political ob-stacles and has had to halt its expansion at a very early stage of its projected program. The energy problem is of course still with us and, being large and genuine, in need of reform. But the path toward a solution that this country has taken is not "the hard path" in Amory B. Lovins's term, one that pursues high and massive technology to force an abundance of energy.[28] How did this come about? Did we suddenly discover how to bring about social change efficiently? Or was there spontaneous social change in the desired direction? The answer is simpler as we now see. The main cause of change has been a stronger than suspected tie between ecology and economy. Warren Johnson, considering his earlier prognosis of ecological chaos, put it this way:

The mistake, I now see, in this way of thinking was to assume that there was a difference, even a separation, between economics and ecology, and that the economy could go where it pleased uninhibited by ecological constraint until the whole economic order broke down. But the last few years have made it clear that the economy is heavily influenced by ecological factors, especially the onset of scarcity.[29]

Scarcity is of course relative to technology. The one-time scarcity of wood was overcome through the coal industry and the one-time shortage of whale oil through kerosene production. What is novel in our present scarcity and must give pause to the technologist is the resistance of that scarcity to hard technological solutions. What surprised the environmentalist is the relative smoothness with which the industrial countries are adapting to scarcity. The mechanism that is transmitting the ecological pressure on the economy into social change is a homely one, ignored by both technologist and environmentalist but greatly respected of late, namely, the market mechanism of supply and demand.

But pointing out these developments is, so far, simply to give detail to the more general point, made in the previous chapter, that technology has a self-stabilizing tendency. The question here is whether these recent trends embody a principle that distinguishes frivolous from genuine problems and directs us to the solution of the latter. And this question is embedded in the still more important one of whether the present departure from high and hard technology constitutes a reform *of* rather than merely one *within* the framework of technology. To begin with, we can certainly say that to the extent that we are turning away from the traditional expansion of massive technology we are turning to a new kind of technology, even if we have not approached it very closely. E.F. Schumacher has called it "intermediate technology" to situate it between primitive and high technology.[30] In this country it has been promoted under the title of "appropriate technology." The intermediate and appropriate technology movement sprang from the recognition that the transfer of advanced technology to Third World countries was wasteful, disruptive, and harmful to those countries and that technology had to be scaled down to connect beneficially with local circumstance and competence. This recognition naturally led one to question high technology in its original setting as well. The successes that advanced technology has had in transforming the social structure of the industrial countries to its benefit and growth is no proof that it is truly conducive to human well-being. As we have seen in the preceding chapter, the injuries that technology has inflicted on the environment and social welfare in the technological societies is evidence for Schumacher that advanced technology is in itself pernicious. Hence just as the intermediate technology movement developed appropriate counterproposals to high technology intervention in Third World countries, so the movement went from the critique to the reform of advanced technology in its native context.

Many of the reform proposals are indistinguishable from those of enlightened proponents of technology.[31] They emphasize that conservation is our cleanest and readiest energy resource and that conservation can be achieved through reliable, small-scale, and unspectacular measures. They further stress national or personal self-reliance and a regard for the integrity of the environment. This convergence of the critics and proponents of technology is certainly a salubrious development worthy of every good person's support.[32] But were the proponents of appropriate technology to center their position in the intersection with enlightened technology, they would implicitly support the technological style of life. It is clear from their programs that they want to provide an alternative way of life. This becomes apparent at two levels. The higher is defined by their willingness to break with the liberal democratic reticence regarding the good life, to sketch and to call for a kind of excellence that they articulate in terms of traditional standards and virtues. There is Schumacher's well-known triad of health, beauty, and permanence and his reminder of the instructions given in the Sermon of the Mount.[33] But there are also secular versions, centered on two kinds of virtues, social and ontological, one guiding us in our relations with our fellows, the other in our commerce with things; the first rendered as loyalty, cooperation, neighborliness, or selflessness, and the second as austerity, frugality, or simplicity.[34] Occasionally this new way of life is in turn centered in the notion of homecoming, one that received a national if passing voice when in 1972 George McGovern, on accepting the Democratic nomination for president, issued his call: "Come home, America!"[35]

This fairly traditional and abstract notion of excellence is paralleled at a more concrete level in proposals to restructure the tangible world around us. The social virtues are to be promoted by rendering our social settings smaller, more enduring, and endowed with more self-determination. Such settings would allow us to know and acknowledge one another, to join in common enterprises, and to take responsibility for them. The ontological virtues become attainable when the work world provides creative and autonomous occupations.[36]

The reform proposal that is proper to the appropriate technology movement points in the right direction and is capable of fruitful development as I intend to show in the following chapters. But it is also, as I want to argue now, in danger of being deflected from its central aspirations. Its higher standards of excellence remain too vague and conventional; its practical proposals are, as a consequence perhaps, either indistinguishable from or subvertible by mainstream technology. The latter case is illustrated in Ivan Illich's *Tools for Conviviality*. One would expect a book, so entitled, to speak of the *convivium* in which conviviality finds its fundament. In the introduction, Illich shows himself to be aware of the various meanings of conviviality, and he wants us to understand it as "graceful playfulness."[37] But this is a fleeting hint. "Convivial" is explicitly defined *"as a technical term to designate a modern society of responsibly limited tools."*[38] Tools (taken broadly) over which the individual has no control violate conviviality. But telephones, tape recorders, and cameras, for instance, are convivial.[39] At one place Illich defines "ideally convivial" techniques this way:

> Almost anybody can learn to use them, and for his own purpose.
> They use cheap materials. People can take them or leave them as
> they wish. They are not easily controlled by third parties.[40]

To require that tools, whenever possible, meet these conditions seems like a reasonable demand, and they certainly serve Illich well in his slashing attacks on the powers that be. Yet we may lead the disengaged and distracted life that is typical of advanced technology in the midst of conviviality as defined by Illich. The electronic and video marvels that we are being promised meet his definition of conviviality. Illich tries to secure the good life by establishing boundaries that would keep dehumanizing technology outside and allow the good life to flourish within. But such limits are always drawn too narrowly and too broadly at once. Illich, to give another example, would restore a more human scale to our dwelling and traveling by restricting all speeds to that of a bicycle, 15 mph, I suppose.[41] But what if technology gives us human-powered vehicles that allow us to move at 50 mph?[42] Would not conviviality have to accept the present patterns of commuting and population distribution?

Technology will be appropriated, it seems to me, not when it is enclosed in boundaries but when it is related to a center. Schumacher stresses that we can be whole only if we are "truly in touch with the centre."[43] But this center is abstractly conceived. To see and to attain it we must, so Schumacher suggests, accept three "metaphysical ideas": the "Levels of Being" or "Grades of Significance," the existence of problems that contain opposing forces and can only be solved through love, and the validity of the traditional ethical norms as defined by the virtues.[44] The forces around which Johnson proposes to center our lives are more concrete. He speaks warmly of "the authentic pleasures available in our society."

> Some are unique to the affluent society—the education, the books, the good communications, the opportunity to travel, and the extraordinary experiences possible in our fluid, individualistic society. Others are more universal—family, friends, eating, drinking, working, playing in the park, or walking down the avenue. Whatever one's tastes, there are pleasures to be enjoyed and cultivated.[45]

Such a passage, however, inspires as much melancholy as hope. All these things and practices are so easily and unnoticeably subverted by technology. Johnson speaks far more univocally of the good life when he portrays village life.

> The villagers know their small world intimately—its rhythms, its moods, its natural history, and all its human occupants. The peasant works on the land or at a trade that his father and grandfather did before him; roots have not been allowed to wither, or ties to fragment. The beauty to be perceived in the village world is of the changing seasons, the ripening crops, children playing, and a mother nursing her infant. Peasants have not seen the art of all ages, as we have, but their own folk art grew out of their own experience and is an intrinsic part of it. Pervading everything are religious beliefs that give meaning to their lives, from the great events of birth, marriage, and death to the small objects that have been made sacred.[46]

Here surely is an unmistakable counterpart to the technological society. Village life was not invariably so harmonious and benign. It could harbor superstition, oppression, and cruelty.[47] As in the case of work, it is not a matter of trying to establish a universal superiority of the pretechnological world but to challenge the technological society which believes itself to be superior to all prior societies by confronting it with prior human accomplishments that were real and genuine if not all that frequent. Even if the challenge is issued fairly, the question remains, How can the challenge be made fruitful and cast into a proposal of reform? When the proposals of appropriate technology are close to our situation, they are ambiguous and fragile; when they are firm and incorruptible, they seem remote from the complexities and liabilities of the present. How can we give our deepest aspirations a voice that is both unmistakable and helpful?

21   Deictic Discourse

The problem of this chapter is how we can hope to reopen the question of the good life. The liberal tradition believes that this issue has been left open and that the opening has been filled with a rich cultural pluralism. Critics of liberalism acknowledge the openness of our culture but find it to be chaotic and desolate. Both parties fail to see that beneath the appearances and parlances of radical openness there is a definite pattern of institutions and procedures and of life. The recognition of this pattern allows us to clear away the misleading overlays of moral discourse in the technological society and to acknowledge the immunity of technology to traditional moral analysis, an immunity that has confused and misled contemporary attempts at social reform.

Seeing these difficulties clearly, we can hope to speak in a principled and forceful way about the good life when we allow ourselves to be guided by focal things, matters of ultimate concern that are other and greater than ourselves. Such discourse, which I have called deictic throughout, does not strive after cogency since it cannot, nor does it wish to, control its subject matter. But neither is it arbitrary since it is guided by an eminent, publicly accessible, and tangible concern which can be pointed up and explained. The elaboration of deictic speaking, of the attitude it embodies and the force it possesses, its connection with democracy, and its complementary relation to apodeictic and paradeictic explanation—these are the main issues of the present chapter.

In taking up these topics, we must remember that the only serious discourse which commands wide attention today is political. It talks about the preliminaries of the good life with such obstinacy and with so profound a sentiment of its importance and legitimacy that one may well despair of raising the question of what kind of life these preliminaries are to serve and whether they are serving their purpose at all. To bar the government from action in favor of a particular conception of the good life is of course, as stressed in

Chapter 14, the intention of liberal democracy. The liberal democratic theorists did not intend to purge all serious public discourse of a concern with ultimate norms of human conduct. But the result was inevitable. When the only kind of action in which we all join consciously and vigorously is political and if political action must be kept morally neutral or minimal, the universe of serious public discourse will shrink to fit this narrow notion of politics. On the surface at least we are still confident and even proud of the supposed openness and richness that liberalism has bestowed on our lives.

Yet there is in political reflection, if not action, a recognition that the moral vacuity at the center of public life is debilitating. We have touched on Habermas's indictment of this development toward the end of Chapter 14. Roberto Mangabeira Unger uses the term "liberal" to name a system of thought that has become unrivaled in power. At the same time he finds an antinomy in the liberal doctrine between arbitrary desire and objective reason, between subjective values and universal rules, an antinomy that is "fatal to its [the liberal doctrine's] hope of solving the problems of freedom and public order as those problems are defined by the doctrine itself" and "leads to conflicting, irreconcilable, and equally unsatisfactory theories of society."[1] Alasdair MacIntyre similarly observes the arbitrary, interminable, and unsettlable nature of public argument; and though he calls the crucial event that ushered in this chaos by its more traditional name of "Enlightenment," he recognizes that liberalism as defined by Dworkin identifies "a stance characteristic not just of liberalism, but of modernity."[2] Like Unger he sees a conflict between arbitrary individualism and rational organization.[3] Thus to the more conventional view which sees in liberalism or the Enlightenment the liberation from the dogmatism and oppression of the dark Middle Ages there is counterposed the view of the catastrophe of liberalism which overturns the traditional order without being able to institute a new one.

What both views have in common is the belief that the moral situation of the liberal democracies is open, either positively in providing rich opportunities of self-development or negatively in being chaotic. Of these the latter view is more obviously incomplete since it is at odds with the stability and comfort that characterize modern life in its most typical form, in the advanced industrial societies of Scandinavia, Western Europe, and the broad middle class of North America. Manfred Stanley, as noted in Chapter 16, has theoretically illuminated this evident fact by showing that "the heightened technological rationality in public life" is entirely compatible with "the relativistic domain of multiple, aesthetically rich, and morally directed private worlds."[4] The "libertarian technicist society" which would arise from the perfection and coordination of these two realms extends, as Stanley points out, a promise of "social stability."[5] Its scandal would not be political, civil, or social when we take these terms in a structural or functional sense; the scandal would be a moral one in a profound and catholic sense. "A libertarian technicist society," Stanley says, "would presuppose a permanent schizoid dissociation between two kinds of reality.'' It thereby would thwart any of the versions of the "persistent hope for progressive redemption from the present" that we find in the classical social theories of the modern period.[6] And so the positive view of the moral openness of liberal democracies comes to be seen as a forlorn hope also.

But in all this hopelessness there is a sign of hope. Since liberal democracy has not in fact left the question of the good life open we have taken a collective position in our actions, though not in our discourse, regarding the good life. We have worked out a definite and distinctive way of life, as shown in Part 2. But to see clearly what hope there is to reopen a conversation about the good life, we must clear away the misleading present overlays of moral discourse on the moral character of our way of life. For clearly there is discourse in the technological arena of an apparently moral sort. It is of two kinds; the first consists of public disputes. They regard, to begin with, the maintenance and expansion of the technological machinery. As in all human endeavors, we find here incidences of ineptness, negligence, corruption, and the like. To identify and remedy such failures we use morally charged terms such as responsibility, honesty, and integrity. But there is at least a good possibility that the technological society might cohere and function by an understanding and acceptance of the device paradigm alone without the foundation of traditional morality. And indeed controversies about "moral" breakdowns usually come to be conceived as examinations of technical failures and end in attempts to devise mechanisms that will prevent such failures in the future. Further, there are open questions about the most efficient ways of securing resources or delivering the fruits of technology. And there too we invoke morally tinged concepts such as a prudence, dedication, prejudice, and cowardice to promote or discredit a particular technological policy. But again the paradigm of technology itself sets the standards by which such problems are solved, at least in the long run. Then there are struggles about the global and national distribution of the benefits of technology. The goal is clear of course; one seeks a maximum share of commodities. And the determining force is mostly raw power. The picture is complicated by the shifting alliances that the parties enter into and which are often promoted under moral labels. But what makes such an alliance prosper or shatter is its success or failure in procuring commodities.

There is, however, another complication of truly moral character, and that is the influence of the ideals of democracy or religion. There is at times in the name of liberty, equality, justice, or charity an effective political movement of a selfless kind. But the discussions of Chapters 14 and 16 have suggested that the force of these moral movements is uncertain at best in their effects. What is more troubling is the nature of their effect which is to admit more people to the blessings of technology. It is unquestionably urgent to free people from oppression, famine, disease, and illiteracy. To aid them, however, in the destruction of their culture and heritage in exchange for pointless consumption is a dubious sort of help, though surely it would be morally inconsistent to withhold from others what at least for now we prize ourselves. Finally, conservatives at times inject relatively pure moral issues into public debates, issues such as the death penalty, abortion, or pornography. Though these issues have their moments on the public stage and sometimes result in serious and even fatal harm to individuals, they are met with less and less understanding since they are so foreign to the technological temperament, and if the latter retains its vigor or increases it, those moral matters will be more and more emasculated.

These discussions seem to be morally chaotic or inconclusive because either they are not at bottom conducted and settled by moral standards at all or they conclude in an arrangement that, regardless of its partly moral genesis, is no longer animated by moral concerns. MacIntyre's examples of "interminable and unsettlable" moral disagreements are really of this kind.[7] Historical contingency aside, these disputes become intelligible, predictable, and resolvable in accord with the pattern of technology. The great exception is the issue of war and armament. The arms policy of the great powers is technological in its attempt to procure safety through technological devices. But it is notably antitechnological in its disregard for standards of efficiency. A policy of disarmament and of global surveillance to insure it would certainly be more paradigmatic of technology. From where, then, does the irrational escalation of arms and insecurity come? Perhaps the vacuity of typical technological life engenders a craving for brute physical supremacy at the collective level.[8]

At any rate, the moral import of the public disputes that we have considered is superficial. It is also preliminary because, being concerned with the means and machinery of technology, it leaves entirely unquestioned the moral standing of the end of technology, namely, consumption. The moral discourse that pertains to consumption, however, is pivotal to technology because our allegiance to technology revolves around it. This second kind of moral talk within the confines of technology is largely private, as is consumption, and the semblance of moral inconclusiveness takes on a different complexion. Here we often talk as though our actions were guided by that absolute freedom which is beyond all moral obligation and justification and as though this were itself the new morality.[9] To use two examples: say there are tourists who want to shoot an elk from close range inside a fenced game farm. Is that not cruel and lazy? "I say, if they want that head they are entitled to it," the game farmer replies.[10] Say a husband and father in his forties buys a sportscar for himself. Is that not frivolous and immature? "If I can afford it," the man replies, "I don't have to justify it to anybody." But this apparent freedom or arbitrariness is highly structured. It is in one regard merely an ironical and sometimes macabre echo of the liberty and prosperity that technology has promised and procured as the choice among indifferently available commodities. The freedom that we proudly or defiantly flaunt is restricted to the commodity side of our lives, to the inconsequential area of consumption. In another respect, the appeal to sovereign and impenetrable freedom is a ploy to cover up a network of reasons and aspirations which is no less open to insight and judgment than premodern moral situations. Moral examination and evaluation are never conclusive for reasons that will concern us soon. And they attain force only as they respond to concrete cases. Given the mere hints of cases that were provided above, we must conjecture about their ethical texture. But we can reasonably assume that the trophy hunter does not have the time and skill to engage in a real hunt and yet wants to have the prestige and the reminder of wildness that a mounted elk's head promises to procure. In fact the game farmer cited above prefaces his moral pronouncement by saying: "This is a sporting enough hunt for persons who want to finish out their trophy room and are not capable of a strenuous hunt."[11] Similarly the middle-aged man may be dejected, seeing his children leave his care and his work taking a predictable and mediocre course. He may be attempting to recapture a sense of youth, vigor, and adventure; and so he buys a device that promises to embody those attributes and to bestow them on its owner and driver. It is worth noting that there is a kind of discourse where the cover of the appeal to unconditional self-determination is lifted and the concealed motives are spoken out loud. That happens in the rhetoric of advertisement which expresses and approves for us the technological aspirations that we find both attractive and a little dubious. This frankness gives advertisement its forward flavor.[12]

But it is not only the case that moral issues of some sort are in question when appeals to morally unbounded freedom are made. In light of the analyses of Part 2 above, we can see them fitting into a broader pattern. As already indicated, freedom comes here into play, not just negatively as the force that disburdens me from justification but positively too as the ideal of self-development, the fulfillment of my capacities and aspirations, an ideal of freedom in which the promises of technology and liberal democracy are joined. But the pursuit of this freedom is ironically deflected from its goal when self-realization is specified as consumption. It was argued in Chapter 18 that consumption procures a momentary and quickly fading sense of prosperity and power and overall leads to the atrophy of our capacities and the impoverishment of our lives. In Chapters 15 and 18 it was suggested that we have a vanishing or perhaps dawning sense of how tenuous and futile our allegiance to consumption is. This sense, joined with our reluctance to act on it, I have called complicity. I believe that what shows itself in the vacuity or arbitrariness of most private moral discourse is neither ethical pluralism nor ethical chaos but complicity with technology.

A morally trenchant conversation about the good life requires, then, that the pattern of our actions which is disguised and diffracted in the prevailing moral discourse is itself made the moral issue. And the very fact that what we normally do, unlike what we typically say, exhibits a commitment to a definite and pervasive way of acting entitles us to the hope that such a

conversation is possible. Still, there are a number of reasons why that enterprise will be arduous and perilous. The first is that the liberal banishment of
ethical concerns from the sphere of government sprang in part from a plausible,
if not justifiable, response to pernicious historical forces. The first of these
is dogmatism, the insistence on a set of moral principles that have been cut
off from their animating and legitimating source. The second is bigotry, the
unwillingness to allow one's moral position to be tested in light of competing
views or scientific findings. Finally, there is presumption where the holder of
a moral position infers from it a feeling of personal superiority and claims a
privileged voice in the determination of the collective morality. Mischievous
and dictatorial versions of these tendencies are still with us, and it is tempting
to want to extirpate them in the liberal democratic way.

A second problem that one faces in making the technological way of life
a moral issue lies in the fact, alluded to in prior chapters, that the moral
measure of the device paradigm cannot be taken by the traditional moral
standards. This is not to say that the typical technological enterprise is free
of problems of honesty, compassion, or fortitude, nor does it mean that these
problems are not identifiable and evident as culpable by the traditional standards. It is rather that to one who has accepted the technological paradigm
the traditional standards are alien in proportion to that acceptance, and such
a person is unlikely to be dislodged from the allegiance to the paradigm by
an appeal to traditional morality alone. Hence the task is not only one of
moving attention from the superficial and misleading moral talk to the underlying mode of behavior but also one of setting aside a traditional moral
idiom and of discovering one that is appropriate to our deeper concerns.[13]
The final obstacle to proper moral discourse is the most difficult. When it
comes to examination and explanation, science today sets the standard; its
mode of discourse, as seen in Chapters 4 and 5, is distinguished by cogency.
And though the popular command of scientific theory and information is
weak, the cogency of science is accepted and respected. Scientific cogency
which pertains to theoretical propositions has a practical technological ana-
logue in control which pertains to the procurement of commodities. Something
is truly a commodity only when it is present in the assured and accessible
fashion that we have called availability. Moral discourse is not cogent, and
its insights cannot be procured. This is so for good and desirable reasons, as
I hope to show. Commonly, however, we take an impatient and frustrated
view of the lack of moral cogency and control. This leads to the ironical
circumstance where a practice that is based on cogent insight and embodies
a commitment to control is to be questioned by a kind of discourse which is
forever contestable. There is an appearance of arrogance when one attempts
a moral examination of the technological enterprise.

And yet, as suggested in Chapter 18, a certain willingness to measure the
technological culture by the standard of traditional excellence still exists in
our common aspirations. In social thought, there is a clearer effort to determine

a goal beyond our implication in the present as is evident from Stanley's succinct summary, referred to earlier:

> Consider Saint-Simon's ideal of cooperative rationality; John Stuart Mill's desire for the spread of the "higher pleasures" of civilization; Marx's ideal of surmounting the dualist tensions of "individual versus society" and "theory versus practice"; Durkheim's expectation of organic solidarity; Weber's wish for the renewability of charismatic inspiration; or Mannheim's planned freedom. We find in these and other themes of classical social theory persistent hope for progressive redemption from the present.[14]

But how is one to travel the distance from the morally self-sufficient posture of the technological society and its insistence on effective procedures to a transcendent moral standard and social ideal? The common move among modern social theorists is the endeavor to derive strong conclusions from weak assumptions. "Weak" is meant here in the technical sense of minimal, self-evident, or uncontroversial. "Strong" means decisive, orienting, implying a definite order of things. To begin with weak assumptions is to issue an invitation that cannot be well refused. It is to say to the citizens of technology something like: If you accept anything at all, you will surely accept this (the set of weak assumptions). In this way one tries to avoid moral arrogance and to take account of the moral minimalism or vacuity that characterize the technological society. The social theorists then try to avail themselves of the commitment to cogency and control by using effective procedures, i.e., modes of reasoning that approximate logical deduction, to show that a consistent allegiance to the initial assumptions entails an allegiance to a society that is more just, more vigorous, more compassionate, more harmonious than ours is now. Consistency then requires the citizens of technology to accept and even work toward social reform, bringing about the kind of society to which, so it is concluded, they are committed to begin with. Thus John Stuart Mill invites us to pursue nothing but the greatest amount of satisfaction for the greatest number of people, and he assures us that in most cases the pursuit of one's private pleasures will conform to the larger principle.[15] John Rawls invites us, at least in one vein of his complex and admirable book, to assume nothing but the role of a rational, self-interested person among equals.[16] Blaise Pascal issued a similar invitation in the seventeenth century to show that one must accept God's existence; and in the eleventh century Anselm of Canterbury thought one would come to the same conclusion if only one entertained the concept of God.[17] The attempt to begin with little and end with much has a long ancestry. It has become the dominant move of moral discourse in our era because it seems so adequate to the modern temper. But the critics of these various moves have invariably shown that, if one assumes little, one can conclude but little. If a strong conclusion is arrived at, then strong assumptions have joined the argument on its way from the initial assumptions; or the latter turn out, on closer inspection, to have been stronger and hence less easily acceptable than initially thought.

Why, then, should one set out to criticize a way of life that has a tendency toward stability, seems morally self-sufficient, is deeply entrenched and widely accepted, one that is heir to a tradition of moral restraint and embodies a commitment to effective procedures that the critic cannot equal? The critique of technology has two necessary and jointly sufficient conditions. The first is the existence of a concern of ultimate significance that one sees threatened by technology.[18] The second is a profound regard for one's fellows. At least some matters of ultimate concern can be guarded and enjoyed in privacy. Hence a privately viable ultimate concern would allow one to remain reticent if one did not care for others of one's kind. If I am moved by a deep regard for others but have no conception of what should ultimately concern them, again I would have no reason to speak up. But if there is something that I have experienced as greater than myself and of ultimate significance and if the welfare of humankind truly concerns me, then I will want to join the two concerns and act on that joint concern to ensure its welfare. In this chapter I will assume that such a concern is given, and I will try to show how in response to it a fruitful discourse of criticism and reform is possible, a kind of discourse that I have called deictic all along for reasons soon to be given. Not only at first but in the end also one cannot do more than assume such a concern in the sense of accepting it and responding to it. One can never procure or control it or build it up from small and uncontroversial pieces. Still, one should begin with little by way of clearing the ground first and of obliging the justifiable reservations that are likely to meet deictic discourse. If that procedure is helpful, it is also misleading in this sense. It may give the appearance of laying down necessary conditions that determine in advance and ever more closely what can finally count as a matter of ultimate significance and a pivot of reform. Such a procedure is also misleadingly abstract and may suggest that an ultimate concern has essentially ideal and intangible character.[19] Still, this way of proceeding advances by small and familiar steps and is so more likely to reach its goal than one that takes a great leap as it were. The enumeration and elucidation of the features that belong to deictic discourse and its object should be understood then as the anticipation and recollection of real or concrete things that are their own warrant. On such an understanding it will be apparent also that the variety of features is just the unfolding of the one way in which we respond to a matter of final significance.

We can unfold it by attending to the discourse in which an ultimate concern becomes eloquent. Such discourse embodies a kind of attitude, and it has a certain force. The attitude will be one of enthusiasm, sympathy, and tolerance. To be enthusiastic, according to the original sense of the word, is to be filled with the divine. Something is of ultimate concern if it is divine in a catholic sense, if it is greater and more enduring than myself, a source of guidance and solace and of delight. It is from enthusiasm that one draws the courage of speaking to others in a way that finally matters. In this way, enthusiasm leads to sympathy, the concern for the integrity and final well-being of my fellow human beings. In sympathy I want to share the greatness that I have experienced; I want the others to respond as I have responded; and since divinity has addressed and filled me in the fullness and subtlety of my powers, sympathy does not desire allegiance simply but one that comes from the undiminished capacities of the other, i.e., one that confirms the other's integrity. I will therefore reject or accept with reservations someone's allegiance when it engages only some of that person's faculties, and I will forestall an allegiance if its accomplishment would injure a person's capacities. Thus sympathy leads to tolerance. Tolerance springs from the realization that, if violence is used to give deictic discourse compelling force, the method of addressing someone disables that person from grasping fully what I want to say. And my use of compulsion is itself oblivious to the character of the thing on whose behalf I want to speak.[20]

This explains the lack of cogency and control in deictic discourse which was pointed up above. However, deictic discourse is contestable not only because it makes such profound and hence defeasible requirements of its recipient but also because of the richness of its concern. The two sources of contestability are really one. An ultimate concern can so fully engage one's capabilities only because it has so many dimensions. But if I find that a thing engages my powers entirely, I must know that it also may exceed them. Thus I can never possess a matter of ultimate concern; I may fall short of it or even be mistaken about it.[21] Correspondingly I can expect another to speak more appropriately of my ultimate concern or to disclose to me one that is greater. Thus tolerance is the renouncement of violence, the acknowledgment of my fallibility, and the openness to others in matters of ultimate concern. It should be understood, however, that the experience and affirmation of my limitations do not normally take the form of a nagging doubt about the validity of what finally matters to me. They rather bespeak my certainty that the force that centers my life is a living and inexhaustible source of significance. Similarly, though tolerance renounces force in trying to obtain assent, it is not diffident or indifferent about its concern.

We can shed further light on the attitude that deictic discourse embodies by linking it to the concept of democracy. I believe that a revival of democracy requires the restoration of deictic discourse. The most apparent link between the two phenomena is of course tolerance. It signifies the commitment to liberty and equality that is characteristic of democracy. Tolerance, however, when defined as a feature of deictic discourse, points out more clearly in what regard people are equal and for what they are free. They are equals in that they are all capable of ultimate significance, and they must therefore be free to act on behalf of that significance and to withhold assent to another's ultimate concern. Hence if assent to a common concern is to be secured, it must be in the cautious and respectful way that is unique to democratic procedures. The feasibility and enforceability of collective decisions will be discussed in Chapters 22 and 25. Here we must stress a crucial difference between tolerance as presently defined and the commitment to liberty and equality in the technologically specified liberal democracies. Whereas the latter implies that the question of the good life and of fellow feeling must and can be left open, the former springs from the experience of what is finally good in and for life and from the profoundest regard for one's fellows, i.e., tolerance springs from enthusiasm and sympathy. One might reply on behalf of the technological democracies that both liberty and realism require a more radical tolerance, one that allows the other to be left alone entirely if that is desired. Enthusiastic and sympathetic tolerance might be subtly oppressive.[22] And even if it is not, it could well, by dragging admittedly uncontrollable matters into the political debate, lead to debilitating stalemates in the public arena. The rejoinder to the first objection is clear from preceding arguments. Technological democracies have themselves been unable to provide the radical openness that the objector calls for. People today have no real opportunity to become ranchers, weavers, wheelwrights, poets, or musicians. It is increasingly difficult for them to be faithful to a place and to persons. And the technological society often does leave them alone, i.e., isolated or institutionalized, when that is anything but desired. The question of the good life, as said before, cannot be left open. What remains open is not *whether* but *how* we will answer it.

But can deictic discourse avoid confusion and chaos in trying to find an answer? Clearly, the answer will in part depend on what kind of force deictic discourse possesses. Since such discourse is centered around a matter of ultimate concern, we must, to understand the discourse, take that concern as given, and as given in the strong sense of concrete or tangible embodiment. Given that kind of presence, enthusiasm can be vital and tolerance resourceful. Discourse of ultimate concern can draw continued strength from something that is present visibly, forcefully, and in its own right, and it can address others by inviting them to see for themselves. Thus deictic discourse need not cajole, threaten, or overwhelm. The word "deictic" comes from Greek *deiknýnai,* which means to show, to point out, to bring to light, to set before one, and then also to explain and to teach. Speakers of deictic discourse never finally warrant the validity of what they tell but point away from themselves to what finally matters; they speak essentially as witnesses. Enthusiasm gives deictic discourse the force of testimony. Sympathy requires that one testify not simply by setting out in some way what matters but by reaching out to the peculiar condition in which one finds the listener, by inviting the listener to search his or her experiences and aspirations; and so one ensures that the listener is as fully engaged as possible by the concern to be conveyed. Sympathy gives deictic discourse the force of appeal.

The language of ultimate concern has a great variety of forms that can be ordered and considered from many points of view. The two regards that are helpful to our purpose are testimony and appeal. Accordingly, we can distinguish kinds of deictic discourse that are eminently testimonial or appellative. The former kind is poetical, the latter political. Poetry, at least in its traditional form, gathers, guards, and presents something of ultimate significance. How that is possible in words is the great question of poetics. Poetical speech, at any rate, is the purest kind of deictic discourse since it is the most adequate linguistic medium of ultimate significance. It is not always the most effective since it can be demanding of its listeners or require the calm and open setting that is rarely given. Political discourse, on the other hand, at least in its higher forms, forcefully reaches out to its listeners, takes account of their situation, and searches out the strongest existing bonds between the audience and the matter of concern. Thus it is most likely to create conditions of collective assent and the basis of common action. But it does so by referring to the ultimate concern itself in general and common terms.

To appreciate the force of deictic discourse, finally, we must recall earlier remarks on scientific and paradigmatic explanation.[23] Scientific explanation owes its cogency to the rigorous subsumption of a sharply defined event under precise and empirical laws. The force of such an explanation is manifest in the deductive form that it takes. Hence we have called such an explanation "apodeictic." It is limited in scope because in general it cannot disclose to us how it gets underway, i.e., how its laws are discovered and how something emerges as worthy or in need of explanation. But it is just the well-defined scope of these explanations and their perspicuity that force assent and give them cogency. In a scientific explanation it is entirely clear what in general (the laws) and in particular (the conditions) is the case and how the general and particular (the explanans) issue in a definite outcome (the explanandum). I cannot withhold assent and must declare: Yes, this is so. But the assent that is exacted by scientific cogency is as narrow as the explanation. Normally it ties me into the world by so thin or shallow a bond that I am not moved to act. It is only when a scientific explanation comes to be located at the center of a more profound concern that it can serve as a trigger for action." . . . Therefore the sulfuric compounds in the air are dissolving the stone of the cathedral." Given such an explanation we will act to stop the burning of high sulfur fossil fuels in the vicinity of the cathedral. But this is not because it is scientifically self-evident that chemical reactions involving sulfur compounds must be stopped; we may find them desirable in the production of paper. It is so rather because the cathedral is a focus of a tradition that we value and want to guard. Hence we much rather accept the expense of switching to a different fuel than see the cathedral decay. The cathedral as a concrete thing in turn is inexhaustible to scientific explanation. Even one crocket is the intersection of countless causal chains as appears from the questions we can ask about it: How did the limestone come into being? How were tools able to shape it? What are the kinetics of a mallet blow? How does the metal of the chisel interact with the mineral structure of the stone?

What makes the stone appear cream colored? And there are endlessly more questions, each of which can be unraveled into indefinitely many further questions.

Yet cathedrals move us to act. They do so, among other ways, through a kind of discourse that conveys the distinctive and eloquent features of such an edifice. Thus Cardinal Melior's speech moved the citizens of Chartres to undertake the construction of the Gothic cathedral.[24] Their response was not merely declarative but active; to say yes to the cardinal's address was to commit oneself to action. Active assent, of course, does not always issue in epochal enterprises. It has more prosaic variants. When I say, "Yes, this child is drowning," I commit myself to saving it. Extending a point of Wittgenstein's we can say that the criterion of a certain kind of understanding and assent is a certain kind of action.[25] And active assent is determined by the thing or practice to which it is given; they must be of considerable or ultimate concern. Thus when someone fails to act in the face of an ultimate concern, we are entitled to say that the person has failed to comprehend it. Incomprehension can stem from incapacity as in the case of retarded or mentally ill people. It can also be due to the lack of background, the experiences that would sensitize a person to a matter of ultimate concern. But it is not only difficult to obtain active assent, it is also difficult to judge it, and for the same reason. Active assent is given to something that is complex, i.e., rich and profound. Thus even when active assent to it is given, its validity can be judged only as the responsive action unfolds; and, responding to something intricate and extended, such action may exfoliate over years or decades. It takes time to see whether the assent to "Do you love me?" is declarative or active.[26]

Deictic discourse and explanation do not have the cutting edge of paradeictic or paradigmatic explanation either. The latter begins with the delineation of a pattern that can be examined as regards its consistency and precision, and we can then hold the paradigm against the thing to be explained to see if it exhibits the pattern. This allows us to assume the position of a third party which establishes whether there is a match between explanandum and paradigm. But as urged in Chapter 12, the appearance of conclusiveness is misleading since any contestable thing will exhibit many features and instantiate many paradigms. When a paradigm is devised and applied to highlight something decisive in a certain phenomenon, we often allow ourselves to be dazzled by the precision, novelty, and applicability of a paradigm and are so inclined to grant the point in question. But critics only need to catch their breath, outline and employ an alternative paradigm, and so dislodge the first paradigm's claim to unique or privileged illumination. The question then arises as to what ultimately moved us to bring out the features that concern us, and such a question is answered through a deictic explanation.

Deictic discourse is explanatory in a good and common sense of the word. It illuminates what concerns me and, if successful, provides you with an understanding that will move you to act as I have been moved. It is a general, brute, and perhaps unenlightening fact that humans react forcefully to things with which they have contact by way of understanding, and it is similarly a fact that things will be so influential only if they have a certain complexity and extent. These general facts come to life when there is in fact a unique and eloquent thing that addresses us in its own right albeit through someone's testimony. There can be no general argument that establishes the force of deictic explanation. What we can do in general, however, is to make room for it by recognizing that deictic explanation is not only compatible with apodeictic and paradeictic explanations but is complementary to them. The former provides the orientation that the latter normally presuppose and require.[27]

Deictic explanation discloses something to us and elicits active assent; it moves us to act. Thus it teaches us what we ought to do by telling us what is.[28] It fills the gap in the is-ought dichotomy and the others that were listed in Chapter 12. But it remains contestable because it cannot, nor does it want to, control its subject matter or the conditions of its reception Though deictic discourse is contestable, it is principled as well. It has a publicly accessible subject matter that can be considered and examined. It rests its case not by subjective standards but by pointing away from the subject to the thing in question.[29]

Still there is a general method of refusing it which may be mistaken for a refutation. This kind of refusal is itself immune to refutation But it can be exposed, understood, acknowledged, and so deprived of its sting. It takes advantage of the symmetry that necessarily obtains between the knower and the known, between my subjective capacities and what I experience as a matter of significance. Since one with lesser or different capacities will not experience the same significance, the claim is always possible that what I call significance is not the eloquence of something in its own right but an imposition of mine on a neutral or ambiguous state of affairs. More popularly, to "Come and see the great thing that has happened" one can always reply: "*You* think it is great, but is it really?" The rejoinder to this tactic is the reminder that the powerful and largely innate capacities that human beings possess, precisely in being so flexible and rich, impose few selective constraints on what we are in principle able to experience. But though I can make this point locally, pointing out how it obtains in a certain region of experience, I must, in making the point, invoke an unquestioned and unquestionable global context. I cannot in principle fully dissociate myself from myself so that as a third party I can demonstrate the objective adequacy of my experiential capacities to reality as it is in itself. And critics of objective significance can always bring their objection down to this unanswerable level. But unassailable charges should be conceded, not because they are so powerful but because they are inconsequential. The question of ultimate significance, as said before, is not to be answered in general anyway. It comes to a head when something addresses me really, concretely, and finally. When, in responding to such an address, I am met with a skeptical objection, such a counter will test my enthusiasm and sympathy, and such a test should be welcomed with tolerance.

We have come to the problem of deictic discourse being troubled by the character of technology and searching for a voice in which to articulate our misgivings and aspirations. We now have a general and tentative notion of how such speaking might proceed. We must render this notion more concrete and show how it can serve to ground and direct a critique and reform of technology. This we can do by considering the challenge of nature in this country.

22   The Challenge of Nature

Deictic discourse is empowered by a focal concern. On this continent nature in its pristine state is the focal power which is most clearly eloquent in its own right since it has, through definition as it were, escaped the rule of technology. How it came to attain this force is best seen when one briefly considers the conquest of North America by technology. Out of this history, as we will see in the first part of this chapter, has come the endeavor of environmentalists or conservationists to speak on behalf of nature itself, i.e., to grant it presence in deictic discourse. Though these concerns are evident, they still get entangled in the prevailing technological idiom. The solution to this embarrassment, I will argue, is not a flight from technology but the realization that nature in its wildness attains new and positive significance within the technological setting. The concluding part of the present chapter is devoted to the articulation of this view.

Nature constitutes a singular challenge for technology in this country, especially nature in its pristine or wild state. In this latter sense, nature is in an obvious way the counterpart to technology. It is by definition a part of the world that has not been touched by the hand of technology.[1] But though there is a clear distinction between wilderness and technology, it is much less clear why we should prevent technology from crossing the physical counterpart to that distinction and from penetrating the remaining wilderness areas. This question can finally be answered in deictic discourse only. The difficulties that beset such discourse are more visible and resolvable when such speaking is of nature in its wild state. And this is so not only because the subject of deictic discourse is in this case conceptually so well distinguished from technology and its tendency to subvert or suffocate deictic discourse; it is also so for historical reasons, the consideration of which will prove helpful.

In the initial encounter of Western civilization with the North American continent, the lines between technology and nature seemed to be clearly drawn.

People were poised at the edge of a pristine and gigantic continent to conquer the virgin land. In fact, the relation was much more complex and difficult.[2] First of all, the continent was not untouched at all; it was well settled and populated by a culture that Western civilization for the most part did not understand. And so the conquest of the American continent was at the same time the destruction of great cultures and peoples. A second and still less obvious difficulty lies in the fact that the terms of the fight between humans and nature changed dramatically while the battle was in progress. But the nature of the change remained unclear. And this in turn made it hard to see that the conquest of the continent destroyed not only the Native American cultures but also led to the loss of the European culture from which the conquest was launched. One reason for this concealment was the fact that there seemed to be traditional frameworks already in place for meeting the challenges of the continent. North America was seen, wrongly and yet definitely, as an empty continent. In the one framework America appeared as a garden, a pastoral setting of fertility and beauty for the life of simplicity and joy that had long been a dream of European culture.[3] Though Virginia may have answered to the physical characteristics of that dreamscape, other parts of America did not. What decisively damaged the pastoral view of America, however, was the early realization that even where nature contributed its share of peace, order, and beauty, people failed to provide theirs.[4] As Leo Marx has shown, the ideal remains crucial for the way in which Americans try to understand their world and themselves. But the early damage to this ideal made prominent the other traditional framework in which Europeans saw the new continent, a framework that was far more robust and better suited to the task of settling America and able to co-opt if not absorb the other framework. It was the view of America as a wilderness. Roderick Nash, who has chronicled the development of the American attitude toward wilderness, points out that this attitude has strong and deep roots in the Old World. From this mooring nature in its wild state appeared hostile and terrifying, an enemy from whom one had to wrest enclaves of culture. Nature was beautiful only when it had been cultivated and turned into a garden.[5] The premodern attitude toward wilderness is not as relentlessly negative as Nash makes it out to be. More important, it obtained a cutting edge in the New World that it had long lost in the Old. To be sure, there were large wilderness areas in medieval Europe, and the notion of colonization or cultivation was still alive within England at the beginning of this century. But throughout this period there was also a relation to nature where humans had come to terms with nature. The wilderness was seen from within a long and finely developed tradition of commerce and familiarity with nature. There were catastrophes in the human encounter with cultivated nature. But they never entirely erased the experience of the intimacy and bounty of nature. All this was left behind at the threshold of the New World where Western civilization found itself on a continent that was thought of as wild simply and entirely.[6]

The conquest of the American continent by white people is a long and complex story. Our concern is with one feature of this process. It emerged after the first phase of colonization. The first settlements were erected in a struggle with nature that was still fought on pretechnological terms. But, gradually, the forces of colonization gathered momentum, and the assault on the entire continent was launched.[7] It coincided roughly with the Industrial Revolution in America, and it mirrored an ambivalence in the domination of nature. There were certainly romantic and heroic components in the struggle with the wilderness.[8] And there were attempts at settling down in the true sense, making a place one's own and doing justice to the land. But there was also and increasingly the tendency to look at nature merely as raw material that was to be used and abandoned after it was used up.[9] What made the tendency a gigantic transformative force was the systematic development and refinement of this approach. Driving nature to submission was finally not the work of individual adventurous pioneers but the extension and application of an approach to reality that was based on science, developed by engineers, and primarily practiced in factories. To be sure, the challenge of the frontier in turn spurred the development of the American centers of technology.[10]

The conquest of the continent consumed most of the energy of the Americans. Like Frederick Jackson Turner, we are inclined to think of this conquest as completed when the frontier ceased to exist in 1890. But this is to take a merely extensive view of the matter. Civilization's initial grip on the land was often tenuous and hasty. It was through the rise of industrial technology that people took intensive possession of the land. This final subjection of nature and the land was still a pioneer experience in the sense that it had few cultural antecedents and obstacles to contend with. The conquest in its extensive and intensive dimensions generated excitement and provided cohesion and direction for the people.

It therefore escaped the general attention that no lasting ties to the land were being established, that firm traditions of communal living failed to grow up, that no focal points of celebration and orientation were being taken up by the communities, that the sense of responsibility for the land and for one another was weakly developed.[11] European culture seemed outmoded for the task of conquering the continent and so was lost. The restlessness of the conquest suppressed the very need of a new culture along traditional lines. And yet the technological culture of domination and disengagement did not establish itself as the sole and unquestioned approach to nature. As nature changed from an adversary to a resource, the heroic tradition of the initial struggle lost its foundation. North America had begun to understand itself in distinction from Europe as a land of majestic natural forces. What national character it had was shaped by the encounter with those forces. To be sure, the first articulation and parlances of the force of nature came from the Romantic movement in Europe. But they only provided the initial spark.[12] Wilderness is nature in a more primal state than the nature of fields, pastures, and vineyards. Wilderness is older than human memory; its beauty owes nothing to human work; its life is intricate and harmonious beyond human planning.[13] Thus wilderness is a much more provocative challenge to human domination than groves and hedgerows which bespeak a human hand. Nature in Europe is cultivated nature. Wilderness has been a memory for centuries.

Wilderness is a challenge for technology. We can see how deeply ambiguous this sentence is because wilderness can be a challenge *within* the framework of technology and *to* the framework of technology. Technology is geared to meet challenges, to dam rivers, drain swamps, log forests, and mine coal. Wilderness areas, within this framework, appear as the last bastions yet to be taken by technology, the last areas where we should be able to cut, drill, and extract. At the very least these areas should be made available as recreational resources. But wilderness is a challenge also to this entire way of dealing with nature, i.e., to technology itself. In the controversies about the establishment of wilderness areas, the unspoken disagreement is always on how we should understand the challenge of nature, whether we should meet the challenge with domination or with respect.

It seems, of course, as though there is a continuum between domination and respect. The domination of nature, as we saw in Chapter 8, is as old as modern technology since it was the basis of its promise of liberty and prosperity. Surely the attack on nature was at times executed with violence for the sake of violence, and it led to the thoughtless ugliness that turned the Sutherlands in Pirsig's book against technology. Yet the conquest of nature remained tied to the goal of liberating and enriching human existence. Once the heedlessness of the exploitation of the natural resources came to be recognized as a danger to the welfare of technology, the latter's conceptual resources, as urged in Chapter 19, could be drawn upon to bring technology in balance with its physical setting. To act in the technological spirit of scientifically grounded security and stability is to have proper respect for the limits and fragility of the natural environment. It is consistent with that sort of respect to urge the protection and preservation of those parts of nature that are not known to be useful but may turn out to be so in the future. "But when conservationists argue this way," Christopher Stone holds,

> to the exclusion of other arguments or find themselves speaking in terms of "recreational interests" so continuously as to play up to, and reinforce, homocentric perspectives, there is something sad about the spectacle. One feels that the arguments lack even their proponents' convictions. I expect that they want to say something less egotistic and more emphatic but the prevailing and sanctioned modes of explanation in our society are not quite ready for it.[14]

Robert Socolow says similarly:

> The conservationists have separate languages for talking to one another, to politicians, and to their avowed opponents. Except

when they talk to one another (and perhaps even then) they refrain
all too often from articulating what really matters to them.[15]

Clearly the problem of deictic discourse comes to the fore here, a problem
that has been noted by Laurence Tribe and John Rodman as well.[16] What is
most important is the manner of its emergence. It is not a problem here of a
certain sort of speaking in search of suitable subjects or in search of a general
justification of itself. Rather it is the experience of something in its own right,
of nature in its primeval character, that seeks appropriate testimony in our
speaking. If such speaking comes to pass, it breaks the continuity between
the domination and respect of nature. Respect no longer springs from enlightened self-interest but is the recognition of something other in its own
right. As Stone and Socolow point out, the technological universe is not
hospitable to the language of such acknowledgment. Technology constantly
threatens to undermine or crowd out deictic discourse of wilderness. To the
extent that the latter is eloquent at all, it is so not by the grace or familiarity
of its idiom but by the strength of the thing that comes to the fore in it.
Nothing in this country, I believe, possesses similarly universal eloquence.[17]
Hence nothing is as likely to awaken again the exchange of deictic discourse
in the public forum and then the practice of engagment which is the ground
and end of such speaking. Given that in deictic discourse of nature the identity of the subject is evident, we are able to identify certain ways of
speaking about nature as failures of deictic discourse where the mode of
speaking and reasoning becomes, at the last moment, subvertible by technology.

The failures, so one may conjecture, arise from attempts to gain some
distance from the immediacy of nature; they stem from an effort to be disburdened of the need for testimony and appeal and from a desire to refer
instead to some general value.[18] Reference to such a value suggests a justification for one's devotion to nature, and the relative abstractness and generality of the value gives the putative justification an impersonal, objective
air. Thus one might defend wild nature in the name of formal characteristics
such as complexity or diversity and contrast such values with monocultures
in agriculture and ecological impoverishment through the loss of species.[19]
But one would then have to welcome the transformation of desert lands into
subdivisions since by any measure of complexity the latter surpass the former.
More radically, one can question the value of complexity itself. Duane Elgin,
clearly an advocate of the integrity of nature, tends to mention complexity
in conjunction with clutter and urges us to reduce both in our lives.[20] Do
more substantive values such as beauty, stability, and integrity afford a justification for the defense of nature and perhaps even criteria for deciding what
parts and tendencies in nature should be favored?[21] The traditional notion of
beauty has so suffered from the corrosive effects of the Enlightenment and
technology that it is surely too tattered and torn to provide guidance. Rather

than assuming that nature can be judged and defended in the name of beauty, one should hope to learn again what beauty is from the splendor of pristine nature. Stability and integrity, on the other hand, if formalized into a concept of homeostasis, are so flexible as to permit the justification of anything and everything.[22]

I am sure that defenders of nature, when faced with such objections, would not simply cling to their values and abandon nature, conceding that the indefensible should not be defended. Surely they would reply that the objections spring from a misunderstanding, that complexity is meant to be a natural richness, that beauty lies in the harmony of an untouched landscape, etc. There might accordingly be attempts to render the guiding values more precise so that they will be immune to counterexamples or trivialization. But that is simply to move the general and abstract characterizations of nature closer to the immediate and grounding experience of wilderness. As long as an explicit distance is maintained, however, between one's characterization and one's experience of nature, the former will remain vulnerable to a kind of subversion that the advocates of nature are unable to avert from their explicit position. Discourse of nature can hope finally to be successful only if it abandons the conceptual outposts and bulwarks and allows nature to speak directly and fully in one's words. What will come to pass in such a speaking? It may tell us this:

> I recall mornings, at the crack of dawn, on the Gualala River when we would walk up along one or another of the long gravel bars. As we approached the water in the gathering light, we sometimes perceived all up and down the length of a pool, such as Miner's Bend, the breaking and swirling of a fresh run of steelhead trout. The day before there may have been only occasional fish showing, the vestigial fish, darkened from having already spent some days in fresh water. But on this morning the lower river is alive with new, silvery trout, fresh from the sea. On such a morning as this there is a temptation to dissipate one's attention over too many fish and too much water; one makes a cast above where a broad back has just shown. But even as the drift begins there is a resounding smack on the smooth surface twenty feet upstream. Then two swirls appear forty feet below. Meanwhile your partner clear down at the tail of the slick is backing out of the river, his rod nodding in sweeping arcs, and a gleaming ten-pounder ascends from the water almost into the branches of that overhanging pine on the back opposite him. It is a glorious thing to know the pool is alive with these glancing, diving, finning fish. But at such moments it is well to make an offering in one's heart to the still hour in the redwoods ascending into the sky; and to fish in one place, for one fish at a time. On such mornings, too, one may even catch nothing at all.[23]

But not everyone has Henry Bugbee's poetical gift and his ease of moving between poetry and philosophy. Inept and unschooled attempts at poetry cause embarrassment and sometimes injury to what the poem was meant to present. Such injuries can happen even when the poem is good but the conditions of response are bad. As noted in the previous chapter, deictic discourse extends from the poetical to the political. In political discourse we speak in farther or closer approximation to what finally moves us. It is not always necessary or wise to speak poetically. Speaking by way of approximation is not only warranted by prudence but also by the kinship of significant things. The pool by Miner's Bend on the Gualala River is not unlike many other stretches of rivers in the West, and Western trout streams share certain traits with Eastern streams, untouched streams have characteristics in common with solitary mountains, the splendors of nature are akin to those of music. These generic relations are apparent also in Bugbee's account. Clearly, as we consider and present the traits of wider kinships, our language will become more general. Degrees of generality are natural to deictic discourse. They become detrimental only when generality is arrested at a certain point and congealed into an opaque value. The rule of approximation, on the other hand, is helpful and even indispensable when it is understood that deictic discourse of whatever degree of generality must remain translucent to the concrete things and practices that finally ground and animate such discourse. That significant things and practices are akin to one another is an ultimate given as is each of those things. These kinships are, as we will see in Chapter 25, an important condition for the reform of technology.

Having learned from wilderness and from poetry that is commensurate with it, we must now speak approximately and recollectively about the lessons that are to be drawn from these experiences for a principled reform of technology. This is deictic discourse in the philosophical mode, one that does not testify or appeal directly, as do the poetical and political modes, but reflects on the conditions that eclipse or disclose matters of ultimate concern and on the corresponding possibilities of poetical and political language. Deictic discourse of the philosophical kind is metapoetical and metapolitical. It is at a further remove from what finally matters and therefore in greater danger of becoming uprooted. Still, like poetical and political language, it takes its warrant from the ultimately significant things. It moves at a higher level of reflection and abstraction because it is only here that crucial, perhaps mortal, dangers to ultimate significance become accessible. Philosophical reflection can hope to clear the ground for poetry and politics and thereby for focal things and practices.

We can begin these reflections and preparations by taking up again and continuing the story of the conquest of the North American continent from a slightly different but revealing angle. Leo Marx has traced the literary response, the deictic testimony, as we might say, to the incursion of technology into the natural landscape. In particular he has examined the attempts to reconcile the machine and the garden. He has looked at biographies, fiction, and other literary documents from the beginning of the republic to the first half of this century. He finally puts it this way, speaking of the protagonists in American fiction who have attempted to reconcile the machine with the garden:

> . . . in the end the American hero is either dead or totally alienated from society, alone and powerless, like the evicted shepherd of Virgil's eclogue. And if, at the same time, he pays tribute to the image of a green landscape, it is likely to be ironic and bitter.[24]

I think the analysis of technology which departs from the promise of technology and outlines technology in terms of the device paradigm opens up a more hopeful view. But Leo Marx's findings provide a helpful backdrop.

In Marx's account the symbol of technology is the railroad and the locomotive which ruthlessly invade the countryside with their tracks, noise, and disruption. This view of the matter is no longer adequate for two reasons. Technology is more comprehensive and insinuating than the symbol of the locomotive has it. The machinery of technology can still be obtrusive and disruptive, as in strip mining or highway construction. But technology shapes our lives mostly where its machinery is concealed and only its commodities are apparent. An affluent suburb is seemingly the incarnation of the pastoral garden that Marx's authors see threatened by the incursion of the machine. And yet such a suburb is technological through and through. It is a pretty display of commodities resting on a concealed machinery. There is warmth, food, cleanliness, entertainment, lawns, shrubs, and flowers, all of it procured by underground utilities, cables, station wagons, chemical fertilizers and weed killers, riding lawn mowers, seed tapes, and underground sprinklers. The advanced technological setting is characterized not by the violence of machinery but by the disengagement and distraction of commodities.

The second way in which the relation of nature and technology has changed regards a subtle but important shift of balance. The authors in Marx's book still see nature as the primary context. To be sure, technology defaces and threatens to destroy it. But they see the machine *in* the garden and not the other way round. If we recognize the pervasive and often stealthily transformative power of technology, we come to see technology as the new orthodoxy, the dominant character of reality. Nature in its pristine state now consists of islands in an ocean of technology. This shift changes the nature of wild areas. They now stand out as strictly extraordinary and thus as a roadless challenge to the ordinary ways of reality. One might take a negative and defeatist view of this shift of balance. "The ultimate problem lies in the fact," Rodman says, now quoting Aldo Leopold, "that 'the preservation of some tag-ends of wilderness, as museum pieces' means that 'all conservation of wilderness is self-defeating.' "[25] Certainly, the wilderness as the overpowering and inscrutable setting within which we erect enclosures of civilization is a thing of the past, at least on this continent. Any attempt to treat what is left wild as though it were original wilderness will suffer defeat.

Though it seems at first that to liken wilderness areas to museum pieces is to make a devastating point, one should remember that museums can be salutary places where we are invited to a calm and reverent beholding of great works of art. Such contemplation can call us away from distraction and renew our vigor and confidence.[26] Still, museum pieces have been deracinated and are dead. We will admire a late medieval Pietà, but we will not, in a museum, get down on our knees and share her seven sorrows. Museum pieces are essentially dead even when skillful display gives them a splendor they did not have in their original surrounding. In this sense, of course, the wilderness is not a museum exhibit. It lives and endures where it has existed from time immemorial. Its roots are planted in its native soil. It must be granted however, that there is a gradation between the fullness of wild life and the tokens of what the world was once like.[27] There is a critical size below which an area is a sample rather than a thing in its own right. How are we to define that size? I think a clue lies in the profound and untutored excitement that one feels at the sight of big game in the wild. It is not just the mass and power of a bear or an elk that move us but the experience of seeing the expanse and fertility of the land focused in such a creature. In big game the land shows what it can bring forth, sustain, and shelter. And, obviously, the land in its wildness has been maimed and crippled past a critical point when it can no longer support mountain lions, for instance.[28]

But even where wild areas have retained this vitality, or perhaps precisely when they have retained it, they stand out sharply from the encompassing universe of technology where whatever comes forth is decidedly a human production. The way in which wilderness is now wholly other than techno-logical civilization reminds one of the pretechnological relationship between the sacred and the profane.[29] The shift of balance between nature and culture that was mentioned above can now be seen as an inversion. Whereas in the mythic experience the erection of a sanctuary established a cosmos and habitat in the chaos of wilderness, the wilderness now appears as a sacred place in the disorientation and distraction of the encompassing technology.[30] This in-version, I think, is striking. Before I proceed to its explication, I need to make a point of caution. I do not propose that we transfer the traditional notions of divinity and worship from religion to nature. These concepts and their associated practices have generally become so desiccated that little would be gained in shifting them from one area to another. Rather, I think, it is now a matter of learning again from the ground up what it is to recognize something as other and greater than ourselves and to let something be in its own splendor rather than procuring it for our use. Nor do I claim that pristine nature is the only or the final realm where we can again encounter the divine and learn reverence. I am only saying that in this country the wilderness presents perhaps the clearest beginning.

When we come to know the wilderness, we learn something about technology and ourselves as well. To begin, let us consider a phrase that belonged to the standard rhetoric of the promise of technology when that promise was made most loudly in the middle of the nineteenth century.[31] Technology, so it was said, would annihilate time and space.[32] This was meant, of course, in the impatient spirit of liberation from the constraints of distances and from the burden of having to wait. The annihilation of time and space, that was the hope, would procure the instantaneous and ubiquitous availability of the riches of the world. Today we are becoming aware of the irony of a universe where we have no time and no place. There is still occasionally, as pointed out at the beginning of Chapter 13, exuberance at the thought of having escaped the traditional limits of time and space. But there is growing evidence, considered in Chapter 18, that the annihilation of time and space has been ironically successful in creating emptiness at the center of our lives.

In the wilderness, time and space are restored to us. The time of openness and activity begins with the rising sun which also discloses to us the lay of the land, the four directions of the compass.[33] The sun outlines the time from the first dawn to the brightness of noon and the dusk of night. It assigns our activities their place, rising, breaking camp, hiking, resting, going on, and settling down for the night. The wilderness is also eminently spatial. It is, to begin with, clearly bounded. Though the legal wilderness boundaries are sometimes arbitrarily drawn from an ecological point of view and though there is usually wild country on either side of the line, the boundary nonetheless divides the region where technology is always ready to rearrange matters for more convenient use from the wild area which changes of its own accord in the rhythm of the seasons and at the imperceptible pace of geological development. It is an area that does not speak of human deeds but is eloquent in its own right.[34] Like a temple or a holy precinct, the wilderness is encircled and marked off from the ordinary realm of technology.[35] To enter it, we must cross the threshold at the trailhead where we leave the motorized conveniences of our normal lives behind. Once we have entered the wilderness, we take in and measure its space step-by-step. A mountain is not just a pretty backdrop for our eyes or an obstacle to be skirted or overwhelmed by the highway; it is the majestic rise and elevation of the land to which we pay tribute in the exertion of our legs and lungs and in which we share when our gaze can take in the expanse of the land and when we feel the cooler winds that blow about the peaks. Arriving at the campsite, we settle down at a place that is favored with a dry and level spot, sheltered from the winds, with water nearby. We set up the tent to mark, at least for a time, the center of the wilderness; we establish an abode that constitutes a domestic circle within the precinct of the wilderness.[36]

The wilderness, finally, is eminently deep. A thing is deep if all or most of its physically discernible features are finally significant. Technology takes a shallow view of things and so begins their conversion into resources or devices. Once we look technologically at a pretechnological fireplace, we split off from the fullness of its features the function of procuring warmth as solely and finally significant. All other features are then considered part of the machinery and, being subject to the law of efficiency, become dependent and endlessly changeable. The technological view of a meal reveals an aggregate of tastes, textures, and nutritive features. They alone retain stable significance. How they come to be constituted and placed on the table is determined by the requirements of instantaneity, ubiquity, safety, and ease. When we look at a tree accordingly, we see so much lumber or cellulose fiber; the needles, branches, the bark, and the roots are waste. Rock is 5 percent metal and the rest is spoils. An animal is seen as a machine that produces so much meat. Whichever of its functions fails to serve that purpose is indifferent or bothersome.[37] In the wilderness, however, we let things be in the fullness of their dimensions, and so they are more profoundly alive and eloquent.[38] And as said before, the depth and force of the wilderness come to be focused before us when we see a bear, in its massive and rolling gait, foraging for tubers in the valley bottom, or a hawk circling high in the thermal updrafts, scanning the open slopes for ground squirrels.

In all these experiences of the wilderness we also experience ourselves in a new way.[39] In the wilderness we are not, at least for a time and in relation to what immediately surrounds us, either consumers or conquerors of nature. But neither are we indifferent viewers of the scenery. The land engages not just our eyes but all our senses and indeed our bodily strength, endurance, and sense of balance. In turn, we know ourselves to focus the land more fully than the bear or the hawk. More clearly and deeply than they, we can take in and comprehend the diversity and beauty of the wilderness. We can understand the summer landscape as it has emerged from spring and will drift into fall. We can see the cirque as the work of the glacier and the dense stand of lodgepole pines as the aftermath of a forest fire.

These are the pristine experiences of the wilderness. But there are wistful and sorrowful ones as well. For in the stillness of a mountain meadow we remember the distant noises of technology, and we can see the jet trails overhead. The fact that we had to qualify our experiences in the wilderness by saying that they held "at least for a time" shows that the wilderness is not strictly a thing in its own right but always a thing in the technological universe as well. This troubles the wilderness experience, and we must now trace these troubles more closely to show that they can lead to fruitful measures.

The wilderness, we saw, engages us in the fullness of our capacities, and we in turn comprehend and gather the wilderness in its extent and depth. But this commensuration is contradicted by the frequently made charge that interests of humans and of nature are at odds with one another and that a harmony of interests requires a subordination of human interests to those of nature and of all its species. To put the human species at the center of creation is arrogant; anthropocentrism or homocentrism have become the terms for this sort of species egotism.[40] To this one must reply that there is a sober sense in which the higher animals comprehend and embody the world in greater scope, depth, and concentration than the lower ones, and humans are clearly at the apex of that order.[41] This Aristotelian insight requires, of course, a deictic explanation. It must be conceded that even if human eminence is, in relation to other species, established by measures of complexity, intelligence, memory, or whatever, such eminence may be an indication of intrinsic nobility but is certainly not identical with it. One can easily define measures of eminence by which insects outrank humans. One must, moreover, acknowledge the grain of truth that lies in the charge that humans are guilty of species egotism and imperialism. The point can be put in terms of the rights of humans versus the rights of nature or of natural objects.[42] Rights should be construed as reflections of an entity's significance, and the latter is established in deictic discourse. In a world without humans, rights are arranged in a natural and unproblematic order. Conflicts over rights occur in a human world because human beings not only embody significance but also comprehend it, mediate it as prophets and artists, and make it prevail in statecraft. It can be shown, I believe, if that is necessary, that human beings are more significant than trees and rivers, and so they have greater rights than natural objects. But it is certainly not the case that every conceivable human right takes precedence over every conceivable natural right. It is this latter principle that is acted out in technology when it is held that anything and everything is to be procured for human consumption. This is a perversion of the notion of human rights and a corruption of the significance embodied in human beings. It was the task of Part 2 of this study to show this. Precisely in the experience of the wilderness we can begin to understand that our significance comes fully to life only in the engagement with things that we recognize and respect in their own right. We must distinguish, then, between the base anthropocentrism of mature technology and the higher anthropocentrism of the respect for things in their own right.[43] We can also put the point in Rodman's terms and say that the liberation of nature is inseparable from human liberation.[44]

But more needs to be said about the commensuration of nature and humanity that we experience in the wilderness. Though the latter may engage us fully in our capacities, we cannot help but be aware of the imbalance between our physical needs and what the wilderness supplies. It provides us with water and perhaps firewood, trout, and huckleberries. But what really keeps us warm and nourished in the wilderness of nature are the blessings of technology, hiking boots, backpacks, tents, stoves, freeze-dried foods, and all the other compact, lightweight, and efficient devices that we carry into the wilderness. Without technology we could not venture safely or comfortably into the wilderness. One may take offense at the way the point is expressed here. If the wilderness is truly something like a sacred precinct, one that is a counterplace to technology, then it seems inconsistent or perverse to want to enter it in the technological mode of safety and ease. But it is even clearer that it is immature to court mortal dangers deliberately and needlessly, whether in a technological or natural setting. There is something like a new maturity required of us which recognizes and accepts the fact that in the ordinary and foreseeable circumstances of contemporary life the need to risk one's life has disappeared.

The foregoing reflections imply two points. The first reminds us that when-ever we live today in a physically sustainable way we have always and already accepted technology, be it in the middle of the wilderness or on a homestead where we pretend to live a self-sufficient life. The second point is that this acceptance is required of us. It is the sign, I said, of a new maturity.[45] To grasp the point better, let us consider the difficulties that surround it. If we must accept technology, is there not an ever-present and irrepressible danger that, acting technologically, we will overwhelm the wilderness? This can happen along a gradient from brute force to subtlety. We may road, log, or mine the wilderness; we may build airstrips and hotels in it; or we may venture into it with a packstring and an outfitter who will procure all the conveniences of home in the middle of a mountain meadow; and finally, if too many of us set out for the wilderness at once, even with the best of manners, our footsteps, campsites, and numbers will destroy the wilderness.[46] As regards the brute force of technology, it exists now and cannot be wished away. It would continue to exist as a possibility even in the utterly unlikely case where we would disarm technology to secure the wilderness. Thus respect for the wil-derness will never again be nourished by its formerly indomitable wildness. On the contrary. The wilderness now touches us deeply in being so fragile and vulnerable. This is another aspect of the inversion of nature and culture of which I spoke before. In one respect, the citizens of the technological societies must now achieve the same adulthood in relation to the wilderness that each of us had to attain in regard to our parents. As infants our affection for our parents was informed by our dependence and their power. But as our powers came to equal and in certain ways exceed theirs, we had to learn a new respect. Surely such a respect is more profound for its being extended to the parents in their own right rather than as providers of comfort and security. But neither is it a disinterested general goodwill that we show our parents in our adulthood. Rather we honor in them the embodiment and practice of an order that is greater than ourselves, that has given birth to us, and that we have received with gratitude and want to carry on. One should not overextend the analogy; and here too, as in the case of religion, nature in its pristine state may be more eloquent than parents in a nursing home, and we may have to learn filial reverence through the respect of nature.

Just as the wilderness teaches us to accept technology, so through technology we learn to respect the wilderness, not for its power but for its beauty. It is clear what is meant by power: ferocious animals, steep terrain, high elevations, raging rivers, forbidding snowstorms. All of this technology can overcome. Consistent with my earlier remarks, I use "beauty" as a generic and approximate term for the eloquence of pristine nature as it speaks to us in its splendor and calmness; and as said before, short of hearing that voice directly, it is presented to us most vividly in the speaking of the poet. Technology cannot overcome and secure it. It can procure the beauty of the wilderness only by either killing it or keeping it at bay. Technology kills the wilderness when it develops it through roads, lifts, motels, and camping areas. It keeps the wilderness at bay when, without affecting untouched areas permanently, it insulates us from the engagement with the many dimensions and features of the land, as it does through rides in jet boats or helicopters. Here we can see that technology with its seemingly infinite resourcefulness in procuring anything and everything does have a clear limit. It can procure something that engages us fully and in its own right only at the price of gutting or removing it. Thus the wilderness teaches us not only to accept technology but also to limit it. The limitation of technology is an impossible task when it is undertaken with a view to technology only. But when it takes its measure from engagement, principled and sensible steps are possible. It would be arbitrarily harsh to admit people to the wilderness with at most a coat and a loaf of bread, and it would be inconsistently lenient to allow access to motor vehicles. To require that people (or at most horses and mules) carry in whatever is needed and leave no trash or scars is a rule that balances the mature acceptance of technology with the openness to pristine nature in its deep texture. Thus we become free for the wilderness without courting the danger of disburdenment and disengagement. The burdens of one's gear and of a climb are the ways in which the wilderness discloses itself. They are onerous, to be sure, and taxing. And so they call forth a discipline which is sensibly marked off not only against the strain of labor and the pleasures of consumption but also against the immature pursuit of pretechnological risks.

We can now grasp the significance of the wilderness experience in the midst of technology more generally still. This is necessary since that specific experience is not accessible to many people, and if it were the sole focus for a reform of technology it would permit little hope. It is necessary also to meet the requirement of tolerance; it would be naive or arrogant to expect that the wilderness is equally eloquent for all or that its voice is the only one abroad. A more general statement is possible, as said in the preceding chapter, because there is in fact a kinship among eloquent and focal things.

We can learn from the wilderness that pretechnological things are not mere forlorn remnants of an irretrievable order but attain a new splendor in the midst of technology. They teach us both to accept and to limit technology in a principled and sensible way. They allow us to be more fully human in offering us engagement, in calling forth a new maturity, and in demanding

a rightful discipline. The question now is whether we can give these suggestions a broader grounding and derive from them more specific guidelines
for a reform of technology.

23   Focal Things and Practices

To see that the force of nature can be encountered analogously in many other
places, we must develop the general notions of focal things and practices.
This is the first point of this chapter. The Latin word *focus,* its meaning and
etymology, are our best guides to this task. But once we have learned tentatively to recognize the instances of focal things and practices in our midst,
we must acknowledge their scattered and inconspicuous character too. Their
hidden splendor comes to light when we consider Heidegger's reflections on
simple and eminent things. But an inappropriate nostalgia clings to Heidegger's account. It can be dispelled, so I will argue, when we remember and
realize more fully that the technological environment heightens rather than
denies the radiance of genuine focal things and when we learn to understand
that focal things require a practice to prosper within. These points I will try
to give substance in the subsequent parts of this chapter by calling attention
to the focal concerns of running and of the culture of the table.

The Latin word *focus* means hearth. We came upon it in Chapter 9 where
the device paradigm was first delineated and where the hearth or fireplace, a
thing, was seen as the counterpart to the central heating plant, a device. It
was pointed out that in a pretechnological house the fireplace constituted a
center of warmth, of light, and of daily practices. For the Romans the *focus*
was holy, the place where the housegods resided. In ancient Greece, a baby
was truly joined to the family and household when it was carried about the
hearth and placed before it. The union of a Roman marriage was sanctified
at the hearth. And at least in the early periods the dead were buried by the
hearth. The family ate by the hearth and made sacrifices to the housegods
before and after the meal. The hearth sustained, ordered, and centered house
and family.[1] Reflections of the hearth's significance can yet be seen in the
fireplace of many American homes. The fireplace often has a central location
in the house. Its fire is now symbolical since it rarely furnishes sufficient
warmth. But the radiance, the sounds, and the fragrance of living fire consuming logs that are split, stacked, and felt in their grain have retained their
force. There are no longer images of the ancestral gods placed by the fire;
but there often are pictures of loved ones on or above the mantel, precious
things of the family's history, or a clock, measuring time.[2]

The symbolical center of the house, the living room with the fireplace, often seems forbidding in comparison with the real center, the kitchen with its inviting smells and sounds. Accordingly, the architect Jeremiah Eck has rearranged homes to give them back a hearth, "a place of warmth and activity" that encompasses cooking, eating, and living and so is central to the house whether it literally has a fireplace or not.[3] Thus we can satisfy, he says, "the need for a place of focus in our family lives."[4]

"Focus," in English, is now a technical term of geometry and optics. Johannes Kepler was the first so to use it, and he probably drew on the then already current sense of focus as the "burning point of lens or mirror."[5] Correspondingly, an optic or geometric focus is a point where lines or rays converge or from which they diverge in a regular or lawful way. Hence "focus" is used as a verb in optics to denote moving an object in relation to a lens or modifying a combination of lenses in relation to an object so that a clear and well-defined image is produced.

These technical senses of "focus" have happily converged with the original one in ordinary language. Figuratively they suggest that a focus gathers the relations of its context and radiates into its surroundings and informs them. To focus on something or to bring it into focus is to make it central, clear, and articulate. It is in the context of these historical and living senses of "focus" that I want to speak of focal things and practices. Wilderness on this continent, it now appears, is a focal thing. It provides a center of orientation; when we bring the surrounding technology into it, our relations to technology become clarified and well-defined. But just how strong its gathering and radiating force is requires further reflection. And surely there will be other focal things and practices: music, gardening, the culture of the table, or running.

We might in a tentative way be able to see these things as focal; what we see more clearly and readily is how inconspicuous, homely, and dispersed they are. This is in stark contrast to the focal things of pretechnological times, the Greek temple or the medieval cathedral that we have mentioned before. Martin Heidegger was deeply impressed by the orienting force of the Greek temple. For him, the temple not only gave a center of meaning to its world but had orienting power in the strong sense of first originating or establishing the world, of disclosing the world's essential dimensions and criteria.[6] Whether the thesis so extremely put is defensible or not, the Greek temple was certainly more than a self-sufficient architectural sculpture, more than a jewel of well-articulated and harmoniously balanced elements, more, even, than a shrine for the image of the goddess or the god. As Vincent Scully has shown, a temple or a temple precinct gathered and disclosed the land in which they were situated. The divinity of land and sea was focused in the temple.[7]

To see the work of art as the focus and origin of the world's meaning was a pivotal discovery for Heidegger. He had begun in the modern tradition of Western philosophy where, as suggested in the first chapter of this book, the sense of reality is to be grasped by determining the antecedent and controlling conditions of all there is (the *Bedingungen der Möglichkeit* as Immanuel Kant has it). Heidegger wanted to outdo this tradition in the radicality of his search for the fundamental conditions of being. Perhaps it was the relentlessness of his pursuit that disclosed the ultimate futility of it. At any rate, when the universal conditions are explicated in a suitably general and encompassing way, what truly matters still hangs in the balance because everything depends on how the conditions come to be actualized and instantiated.[8] The preoccupation with antecedent conditions not only leaves this question unanswered; it may even make it inaccessible by leaving the impression that, once the general and fundamental matters are determined, nothing of consequence remains to be considered. Heidegger's early work, however, already contained the seeds of its overcoming. In his determination to grasp reality in its concreteness, Heidegger had found and stressed the inexorable and unsurpassable givenness of human existence, and he had provided analyses of its pretechnological wholeness and its technological distraction though the significance of these descriptions for technology had remained concealed to him.[9] And then he discovered that the unique event of significance in the singular work of art, in the prophet's proclamation, and in the political deed was crucial. This insight was worked out in detail with regard to the artwork. But in an epilogue to the essay that develops this point, Heidegger recognized that the insight comes too late. To be sure, our time has brought forth admirable works of art. "But," Heidegger insists, "the question remains: is art still an essential and necessary way in which that truth happens which is decisive for historical existence, or is art no longer of this character?"[10]

Heidegger began to see technology (in his more or less substantive sense) as the force that has eclipsed the focusing powers of pretechnological times. Technology becomes for him, as mentioned at the end of Chapter 8, the final phase of a long metaphysical development. The philosophical concern with the conditions of the possibility of whatever is now itself seen as a move into the oblivion of what finally matters. But how are we to recover orientation in the oblivious and distracted era of technology when the great embodiments of meaning, the works of art, have lost their focusing power? Amidst the complication of conditions, of the *Bedingungen,* we must uncover the simplicity of things, of the *Dinge.*[11] A jug, an earthen vessel from which we pour wine, is such a thing. It teaches us what it is to hold, to offer, to pour, and to give. In its clay, it gathers for us the earth as it does in containing the wine that has grown from the soil. It gathers the sky whose rain and sun are present in the wine. It refreshes and animates us in our mortality. And in the libation it acknowledges and calls on the divinities. In these ways the thing (in agreement with its etymologically original meaning) gathers and discloses what Heidegger calls the fourfold, the interplay of the crucial dimensions of earth and sky, mortals and divinities.[12] A thing, in Heidegger's eminent sense, is a focus; to speak of focal things is to emphasize the central point twice.

Still, Heidegger's account is but a suggestion fraught with difficulties. When Heidegger described the focusing power of the jug, he might have been thinking of a rural setting where wine jugs embody in their material, form, and craft a long and local tradition; where at noon one goes down to the cellar to draw a jug of table wine whose vintage one knows well; where at the noon meal the wine is thoughtfully poured and gratefully received.[13] Under such circumstances, there might be a gathering and disclosure of the fourfold, one that is for the most part understood and in the background and may come to the fore on festive occasions. But all of this seems as remote to most of us and as muted in its focusing power as the Parthenon or the Cathedral of Chartres. How can so simple a thing as a jug provide that turning point in our relation to technology to which Heidegger is looking forward? Heidegger's proposal for a reform of technology is even more programmatic and terse than his analysis of technology.[14] Both, however, are capable of fruitful development.[15] Two points in Heidegger's consideration of the turn of technology must particularly be noted. The first serves to remind us of arguments already developed which must be kept in mind if we are to make room for focal things and practices. Heidegger says, broadly paraphrased, that the orienting force of simple things will come to the fore only as the rule of technology is raised from its anonymity, is disclosed as the orthodoxy that heretofore has been taken for granted and allowed to remain invisible.[16] As long as we overlook the tightly patterned character of technology and believe that we live in a world of endlessly open and rich opportunities, as long as we ignore the definite ways in which we, acting technologically, have worked out the promise of technology and remain vaguely enthralled by that promise, so long simple things and practices will seem burdensome, confining, and drab. But if we recognize the central vacuity of advanced technology, that emptiness can become the opening for focal things. It works both ways, of course. When we see a focal concern of ours threatened by technology, our sight for the liabilities of mature technology is sharpened.

A second point of Heidegger's is one that we must develop now. The things that gather the fourfold, Heidegger says, are inconspicuous and humble. And when we look at his litany of things, we also see that they are scattered and of yesterday: jug and bench, footbridge and plow, tree and pond, brook and hill, heron and deer, horse and bull, mirror and clasp, book and picture, crown and cross.[17] That focal things and practices are inconspicuous is certainly true; they flourish at the margins of public attention. And they have suffered a diaspora; this too must be accepted, at least for now. That is not to say that a hidden center of these dispersed focuses may not emerge some day to unite them and bring them home. But it would clearly be a forced growth to proclaim such a unity now. A reform of technology that issues from focal concerns will be radical not in imposing a new and unified master plan on the technological universe but in discovering those sources of strength that will nourish principled and confident beginnings, measures, i.e., which will neither rival nor deny technology.

But there are two ways in which we must go beyond Heidegger. One step in the first direction has already been taken. It led us to see in the preceding chapter that the simple things of yesterday attain a new splendor in today's technological context. The suggestion in Heidegger's reflections that we have to seek out pretechnological enclaves to encounter focal things is misleading and dispiriting. Rather we must see any such enclave itself as a focal thing heightened by its technological context. The turn to things cannot be a setting aside and even less an escape from technology but a kind of affirmation of it. The second move beyond Heidegger is in the direction of practice, into the social and, later, the political situation of focal things.[18] Though Heidegger assigns humans their place in the fourfold when he depicts the jug in which the fourfold is focused, we scarcely see the hand that holds the jug, and far less do we see of the social setting in which the pouring of the wine comes to pass. In his consideration of another thing, a bridge, Heidegger notes the human ways and works that are gathered and directed by the bridge.[19] But these remarks too present practices from the viewpoint of the focal thing. What must be shown is that focal things can prosper in human practices only. Before we can build a bridge, Heidegger suggests, we must be able to dwell.[20] But what does that mean concretely?

The consideration of the wilderness has disclosed a center that stands in a fruitful counterposition to technology. The wilderness is beyond the procurement of technology, and our response to it takes us past consumption. But it also teaches us to accept and to appropriate technology. We must now try to discover if such centers of orientation can be found in greater proximity and intimacy to the technological everyday life. And I believe they can be found if we follow up the hints that we have gathered from and against Heidegger, the suggestions that focal things seem humble and scattered but attain splendor in technology if we grasp technology properly, and that focal things require a practice for their welfare. Running and the culture of the table are such focal things and practices. We have all been touched by them in one way or another. If we have not participated in a vigorous or competitive run, we have certainly taken walks; we have felt with surprise, perhaps, the pleasure of touching the earth, of feeling the wind, smelling the rain, of having the blood course through our bodies more steadily. In the preparation of a meal we have enjoyed the simple tasks of washing leaves and cutting bread; we have felt the force and generosity of being served a good wine and homemade bread. Such experiences have been particularly vivid when we came upon them after much sitting and watching indoors, after a surfeit of readily available snacks and drinks. To encounter a few simple things was liberating and invigorating. The normal clutter and distraction fall away when, as the poet says,

> there, in limpid brightness shine,
> on the table, bread and wine.[21]

If such experiences are deeply touching, they are fleeting as well. There seems to be no thought or discourse that would shelter and nurture such events; not in politics certainly, nor in philosophy where the prevailing idiom sanctions and applies equally to lounging and walking, to Twinkies, and to bread, the staff of life. But the reflective care of the good life has not withered away. It has left the profession of philosophy and sprung up among practical people. In fact, there is a tradition in this country of persons who are engaged by life in its concreteness and simplicity and who are so filled with this engagement that they have reached for the pen to become witnesses and teachers, speakers of deictic discourse. Melville and Thoreau are among the great prophets of this tradition. Its present health and extent are evident from the fact that it now has no overpowering heroes but many and various more or less eminent practitioners. Their work embraces a spectrum between down-to-earth instruction and soaring speculation. The span and center of their concerns vary greatly. But they all have their mooring in the attention to tangible and bodily things and practices, and they speak with an enthusiasm that is nourished by these focal concerns. Pirsig's book is an impressive and troubling monument in this tradition, impressive in the freshness of its observations and its pedagogical skill, troubling in its ambitious and failing efforts to deal with the large philosophical issues. Norman Maclean's *A River Runs through It* can be taken as a fly-fishing manual, a virtue that pleases its author.[22] But it is a literary work of art most of all and a reflection on technology inasmuch as it presents the engaging life, both dark and bright, from which we have so recently emerged. Colin Fletcher's treatise of *The Complete Walker* is most narrowly a book of instruction about hiking and backpacking.[23] The focal significance of these things is found in the interstices of equipment and technique; and when the author explicitly engages in deictic discourse he has "an unholy awful time" with it.[24] Roger B. Swain's contemplation of gardening in *Earthly Pleasures* enlightens us in cool and graceful prose about the scientific basis and background of what we witness and undertake in our gardens.[25] Philosophical significance enters unbidden and easily in the reflections on time, purposiveness, and the familiar. Looking at these books, I see a stretch of water that extends beyond my vision, disappearing in the distance. But I can see that it is a strong and steady stream, and it may well have parts that are more magnificent than the ones I know.[26]

To discover more clearly the currents and features of this, the other and more concealed, American mainstream, I take as witnesses two books where enthusiasm suffuses instruction vigorously, Robert Farrar Capon's *The Supper of the Lamb* and George Sheehan's *Running and Being*.[27] Both are centered on focal events, the great run and the great meal. The great run, where one exults in the strength of one's body, in the ease and the length of the stride, where nature speaks powerfully in the hills, the wind, the heat, where one takes endurance to the breaking point, and where one is finally engulfed by the good will of the spectators and the fellow runners.[28] The great meal, the long session as Capon calls it, where the guests are thoughtfully invited, the table has been carefully set, where the food is the culmination of tradition, patience, and skill and the presence of the earth's most delectable textures and tastes, where there is an invocation of divinity at the beginning and memorable conversation throughout.[29]

Such focal events are compact, and if seen only in their immediate temporal and spatial extent they are easily mistaken. They are more mistakable still when they are thought of as experiences in the subjective sense, events that have their real meaning in transporting a person into a certain mental or emotional state. Focal events, so conceived, fall under the rule of technology. For when a subjective state becomes decisive, the search for a machinery that is functionally equivalent to the traditional enactment of that state begins, and it is spurred by endeavors to find machineries that will procure the state more instantaneously, ubiquitously, more assuredly and easily. If, on the other hand, we guard focal things in their depth and integrity, then, to see them fully and truly, we must see them in context. Things that are deprived of their context become ambiguous.[30] The letter "a" by itself means nothing in particular. In the context of "table" it conveys or helps to convey a more definite meaning. But "table" in turn can mean many things. It means something more powerful in the text of Capon's book where he speaks of "The Vesting of the Table."[31] But that text must finally be seen in the context and texture of the world. To say that something becomes ambiguous is to say that it is made to say less, little, or nothing. Thus to elaborate the context of focal events is to grant them their proper eloquence.

"The distance runner," Sheehan says, "is the least of all athletes. His sport the least of all sports."[32] Running is simply to move through time and space, step-by-step. But there is splendor in that simplicity. In a car we move of course much faster, farther, and more comfortably. But we are not moving on our own power and in our own right. We cash in prior labor for present motion. Being beneficiaries of science and engineering and having worked to be able to pay for a car, gasoline, and roads, we now release what has been earned and stored and use it for transportation. But when these past efforts are consumed and consummated in my driving, I can at best take credit for what I have done. What I am doing now, driving, requires no effort, and little or no skill or discipline. I am a divided person; my achievement lies in the past, my enjoyment in the present. But in the runner, effort and joy are one; the split between means and ends, labor and leisure is healed.[33] To be sure, if I have trained conscientiously, my past efforts will bear fruit in a race. But they are not just cashed in. My strength must be risked and enacted in the race which is itself a supreme effort and an occasion to expand my skill.

This unity of achievement and enjoyment, of competence and consummation, is just one aspect of a central wholeness to which running restores us. Good running engages mind and body. Here the mind is more than an intelligence that happens to be housed in a body. Rather the mind is the sensitivity and the endurance of the body.[34] Hence running in its fullness, as Sheehan stresses over and over again, is in principle different from exercise designed to procure physical health. The difference between running and physical exercise is strikingly exhibited in one and the same issue of the *New York Times Magazine*. It contains an account by Peter Wood of how, running the New York City Marathon, he took in the city with body and mind, and it has an account by Alexandra Penney of corporate fitness programs where executives, concerned about their Coronary Risk Factor Profile, run nowhere on treadmills or ride stationary bicycles.[35] In another issue, the *Magazine* shows executives exercising their bodies while busying their dissociated minds with reading.[36] To be sure, unless a runner concentrates on bodily performance, often in an effort to run the best possible race, the mind wanders as the body runs. But as in free association we range about the future and the past, the actual and the possible, our mind, like our breathing, rhythmically gathers itself to the here and now, having spread itself to distant times and faraway places.

It is clear from these reflections that the runner is mindful of the body because the body is intimate with the world. The mind becomes relatively disembodied when the body is severed from the depth of the world, i.e., when the world is split into commodious surfaces and inaccessible machineries. Thus the unity of ends and means, of mind and body, and of body and world is one and the same. It makes itself felt in the vividness with which the runner experiences reality. "Somehow you feel more in touch," Wood says, "with the realities of a massive inner-city housing problem when you are running through it slowly enough to take in the grim details, and, surprisingly, cheered on by the remaining occupants."[37] As this last remark suggests, the wholeness that running establishes embraces the human family too. The experience of that simple event releases an equally simple and profound sympathy. It is a natural goodwill, not in need of drugs nor dependent on a common enemy. It wells up from depths that have been forgotten, and it overwhelms the runners ever and again.[38] As Wood recounts his running through streets normally besieged by crime and violence, he remarks: "But we can only be amazed today at the warmth that emanates from streets usually better known for violent crime." And his response to the spectators' enthusiasm is this: "I feel a great proximity to the crowd, rushing past at all of nine miles per hour; a great affection for them individually; a commitment to run as well as I possibly can, to acknowledge their support."[39] For George

Sheehan, finally, running discloses the divine. When he runs, he wrestles with God.[40] Serious running takes us to the limits of our being. We run into threatening and seemingly unbearable pain. Sometimes, of course, the plunge into that experience gets arrested in ambition and vanity. But it can take us further to the point where in suffering our limits we experience our greatness too. This, surely, is a hopeful place to escape technology, metaphysics, and the God of the philosophers and reach out to the God of Abraham, Isaac, and Jacob.[41]

If running allows us to center our lives by taking in the world through vigor and simplicity, the culture of the table does so by joining simplicity with cosmic wealth. Humans are such complex and capable beings that they can fairly comprehend the world and, containing it, constitute a cosmos in their own right. Because we are standing so eminently over against the world, to come in touch with the world becomes for us a challenge and a momentous event. In one sense, of course, we are always already in the world, breathing the air, touching the ground, feeling the sun. But as we can in another sense withdraw from the actual and present world, contemplating what is past and to come, what is possible and remote, we celebrate correspondingly our intimacy with the world. This we do most fundamentally when in eating we take in the world in its palpable, colorful, nourishing immediacy. Truly human eating is the union of the primal and the cosmic. In the simplicity of bread and wine, of meat and vegetable, the world is gathered.

The great meal of the day, be it at noon or in the evening, is a focal event par excellence. It gathers the scattered family around the table. And on the table it gathers the most delectable things nature has brought forth. But it also recollects and presents a tradition, the immemorial experiences of the race in identifying and cultivating edible plants, in domesticating and butchering animals; it brings into focus closer relations of national or regional customs, and more intimate traditions still of family recipes and dishes. It is evident from the preceding chapters how this living texture is being rent through the procurement of food as a commodity and the replacement of the culture of the table by the food industry. Once food has become freely available, it is only consistent that the gathering of the meal is shattered and disintegrates into snacks, T.V. dinners, bites that are grabbed to be eaten; and eating itself is scattered around television shows, late and early meetings, activities, overtime work, and other business. This is increasingly the normal condition of technological eating. But it is within our power to clear a central space amid the clutter and distraction. We can begin with the simplicity of a meal that has a beginning, a middle, and an end and that breaks through the superficiality of convenience food in the simple steps of beginning with raw ingredients, preparing and transforming them, and bringing them to the table. In this way we can again become freeholders of our culture. We are disfranchised from world citizenship when the foods we eat are mere commodities. Being essentially opaque surfaces, they repel all efforts at extending our sensibility and competence into the deeper reaches of the world. A Big Mac and a Coke can overwhelm our tastebuds and accommodate our hunger. Technology is not, after all, a children's crusade but a principled and skillful enterprise of defining and satisfying human needs. Through the diversion and busyness of consumption we may have unlearned to feel constrained by the shallowness of commodities. But having gotten along for a time and quite well, it seemed, on institutional or convenience food, scales fall from our eyes when we step up to a festively set family table. The foods stand out more clearly, the fragrances are stronger, eating has once more become an occasion that engages and accepts us fully.

To understand the radiance and wealth of a festive meal we must be alive to the interplay of things and humans, of ends and means. At first a meal, once it is on the table, appears to have commodity character since it is now available before us, ready to be consumed without effort or merit. But though there is of course in any eating a moment of mere consuming, in a festive meal eating is one with an order and discipline that challenges and ennobles the participants. The great meal has its structure. It begins with a moment of reflection in which we place ourselves in the presence of the first and last things. It has a sequence of courses; it requires and sponsors memorable conversation; and all this is enacted in the discipline called table manners. They are warranted when they constitute the respectful and skilled response to the great things that are coming to pass in the meal. We can see how order and discipline have collapsed when we eat a Big Mac. In consumption there is the pointlike and inconsequential conflation of a sharply delimited human need with an equally contextless and closely fitting commodity. In a Big Mac the sequence of courses has been compacted into one object and the discipline of table manners has been reduced to grabbing and eating. The social context reaches no further than the pleasant faces and quick hands of the people who run the fast-food outlet. In a festive meal, however, the food is served, one of the most generous gestures human beings are capable of. The serving is of a piece with garnishing; garnishing is the final phase of cooking, and cooking is one with preparing the food. And if we are blessed with rural circumstances, the preparation of food draws near the harvesting and the raising of the vegetables in the garden close by. This context of activities is embodied in persons. The dish and the cook, the vegetable and the gardener tell of one another. Especially when we are guests, much of the meal's deeper context is socially and conversationally mediated. But that mediation has translucence and intelligibility because it extends into the farther and deeper recesses without break and with a bodily immediacy that we too have enacted or at least witnessed firsthand. And what seems to be a mere receiving and consuming of food is in fact the enactment of generosity and gratitude, the affirmation of mutual and perhaps religious obligations. Thus eating in a focal setting differs sharply from the social and cultural anonymity of a fast-food outlet.

The pretechnological world was engaging through and through, and not always positively. There also was ignorance, to be sure, of the final workings of God and king; but even the unknown engaged one through mystery and awe. In this web of engagement, meals already had focal character, certainly as soon as there was anything like a culture of the table.[42] Today, however, the great meal does not gather and order a web of thoroughgoing relations of engagement; within the technological setting it stands out as a place of profound calm, one in which we can leave behind the narrow concentration and one-sided strain of labor and the tiring and elusive diversity of consumption. In the technological setting, the culture of the table not only focuses our life; it is also distinguished as a place of healing, one that restores us to the depth of the world and to the wholeness of our being.

As said before, we all have had occasion to experience the profound pleasure of an invigorating walk or a festive meal. And on such occasions we may have regretted the scarcity of such events; we might have been ready to allow such events a more regular and central place in our lives. But for the most part these events remain occasional, and indeed the ones that still grace us may be slipping from our grasp. In Chapter 18 we have seen various aspects of this malaise, especially its connection with television. But why are we acting against our better insights and aspirations?[43] This at first seems all the more puzzling as the engagement in a focal activity is for most citizens of the technological society an instantaneous and ubiquitous possibility. On any day I can decide to run or to prepare a meal after work. Everyone has some sort of suitable equipment. At worst one has to stop on the way home to pick up this or that. It is of course technology that has opened up these very possibilities. But why are they lying fallow for the most part? There is a convergence of several factors. Labor is exhausting, especially when it is divided. When we come home, we often feel drained and crippled. Diversion and pleasurable consumption appear to be consonant with this sort of disability. They promise to untie the knots and to soothe the aches. And so they do at a shallow level of our existence. At any rate, the call for exertion and engagement seems like a cruel and unjust demand. We have sat in the easy chair, beer at hand and television before us; when we felt stirrings of ambition, we found it easy to ignore our superego.[44] But we also may have had our alibi refuted on occasion when someone to whom we could not say no prevailed on us to put on our coat and to step out into cold and windy weather to take a walk. At first our indignation grew. The discomfort was worse than we had thought. But gradually a transformation set in. Our gait became steady, our blood began to flow vigorously and wash away our tension, we smelled the rain, began thoughtfully to speak with our companion, and finally returned home settled, alert, and with a fatigue that was capable of restful sleep.

But why did such occurrences remain episodes also? The reason lies in the mistaken assumption that the shaping of our lives can be left to a series of individual decisions. Whatever goal in life we entrust to this kind of implementation we in fact surrender to erosion. Such a policy ignores both the frailty and strength of human nature. On the spur of the moment, we normally act out what has been nurtured in our daily practices as they have been shaped by the norms of our time. When we sit in our easy chair and contemplate what to do, we are firmly enmeshed in the framework of technology with our labor behind us and the blessings of our labor about us, the diversions and enrichments of consumption. This arrangement has had our lifelong allegiance, and we know it to have the approval and support of our fellows. It would take superhuman strength to stand up to this order ever and again. If we are to challenge *the rule of technology,* we can do so only through *the practice of engagement.*

The human ability to establish and commit oneself to a practice reflects our capacity to comprehend the world, to harbor it in its expanse as a context that is oriented by its focal points. To found a practice is to guard a focal concern, to shelter it against the vicissitudes of fate and our frailty. John Rawls has pointed out that there is decisive difference between the justification of a practice and of a particular action falling under it.[45] Analogously, it is one thing to decide for a focal practice and quite another to decide for a particular action that appears to have focal character.[46] Putting the matter more clearly, we must say that without a practice an engaging action or event can momentarily light up our life, but it cannot order and orient it focally. Competence, excellence, or virtue, as Aristotle first saw, come into being as an *éthos,* a settled disposition and a way of life.[47] Through a practice, Alasdaire MacIntyre says accordingly, "human powers to achieve excellence, and human conceptions of the ends and goods involved, are systematically extended."[48] Through a practice we are able to accomplish what remains unattainable when aimed at in a series of individual decisions and acts.

How can a practice be established today? Here, as in the case of focal things, it is helpful to consider the foundation of pretechnological practices. In mythic times the latter were often established through the founding and consecrating act of a divine power or mythic ancestor. Such an act, as mentioned in Chapter 22, set up a sacred precinct and center that gave order to a violent and hostile world. A sacred practice, then, consisted in the regular reenactment of the founding act, and so it renewed and sustained the order of the world. Christianity came into being this way; the eucharistic meal, the Supper of the Lamb, is its central event, established with the instruction that it be reenacted. Clearly a focal practice today should have centering and orienting force as well. But it differs in important regards from its grand precursors. A mythic focal practice derived much force from the power of its opposition. The alternative to the preservation of the cosmos was chaos, social and physical disorder and collapse. It is a reduction to see mythic practices merely as coping behavior of high survival value. A myth does not just aid survival; it defines what truly human life is. Still, as in the case of pretechnological morality, economic and social factors were interwoven with mythic practices. Thus the force of brute necessity supported, though it did not define, mythic focal practices. Since a mythic focal practice united in itself the social, the economic, and the cosmic, it was naturally a prominent and public affair. It rested securely in collective memory and in the mutual expectations of the people.

This sketch, of course, fails to consider many other kinds of pretechnological practices. But it does present one important aspect of them and more particularly one that serves well as a backdrop for focal practices in a technological setting. It is evident that technology is itself a sort of practice, and it procures its own kind of order and security. Its history contains great moments of innovation, but it did not arise out of a founding event that would have focal character; nor has it, as argued in Chapter 20, produced focal things. Thus it is not a *focal* practice, and it has indeed, so I have urged, a debilitating tendency to scatter our attention and to clutter our surroundings. A focal practice today, then, meets no tangible or overtly hostile opposition from its context and is so deprived of the wholesome vigor that derives from such opposition. But there is of course an opposition at a more profound and more subtle level. To feel the support of that opposing force one must have experienced the subtly debilitating character of technology, and above all one must understand, explicitly or implicitly, that the peril of technology lies not in this or that of its manifestations but in *the pervasiveness and consistency of its pattern*. There are always occasions where a Big Mac, an exercycle, or a television program are unobjectionable and truly helpful answers to human needs. This makes a case-by-case appraisal of technology so inconclusive. It is when we attempt to take the measure of technologial life in its normal totality that we are distressed by its shallowness. And I believe that the more strongly we sense and the more clearly we understand the coherence and the character of technology, the more evident it becomes to us that technology must be countered by an equally patterned and social commitment, i.e., by a practice.

At this level the opposition of technology does become fruitful to focal practices. They can now be seen as restoring a depth and integrity to our lives that are in principle excluded within the paradigm of technology. MacIntyre, though his foil is the Enlightenment more than technology, captures this point by including in his definition of practice the notion of "goods internal to a practice."[49] These are one with the practice and can only be obtained through that practice. The split between means and ends is healed. In contrast "there are those goods externally and contingently attached" to a practice; and in that case there "are always alternative ways for achieving such goods, and their achievement is never to be had *only* by engaging in some particular kind of practice"[50] Thus practices (in a looser sense) that serve external goods are subvertible by technology. But MacIntyre's point needs to be clarified and extended to include or emphasize not only the essential unity of human being and a particular sort of doing but also the tangible things in which the world comes to be focused. The importance of this point has been suggested by the consideration of running and the culture of the table. There are objections to this suggestion that will be examined in the next chapter. Here I want to advance the thesis by considering Rawls's contention that a practice is defined by rules. We can take a rule as an instruction for a particular domain of life to act in a certain way under specified circumstances. How important is the particular character of the tangible setting of the rules? Though Rawls does not address this question directly he suggests in using baseball for illustration that "a peculiarly shaped piece of wood" and a kind of bag become a bat and base only within the confines defined by the rules of baseball.[51] Rules and the practice they define, we might argue in analogy to what Rawls says about their relation to particular cases, are logically prior to their tangible setting. But the opposite contention seems stronger to me. Clearly the possibilities and challenges of baseball are crucially determined by the layout and the surface of the field, the weight and resilience of the ball, the shape and size of the bat, etc. One might of course reply that there are rules that define the physical circumstances of the game. But this is to take "rule" in broader sense. Moreover it would be more accurate to say that the rules of this latter sort reflect and protect the identity of the original tangible circumstances in which the game grew up. The rules, too, that circumscribe the actions of the players can be taken as ways of securing and ordering the playful challenges that arise in the human interplay with reality. To be sure there are developments and innovations in sporting equipment. But either they quite change the nature of the sport as in pole vaulting, or they are restrained to preserve the identity of the game as in baseball.

It is certainly the purpose of a focal practice to guard in its undiminished depth and identity the thing that is central to the practice, to shield it against the technological diremption into means and end. Like values, rules and practices are recollections, anticipations, and, we can now say, guardians of the concrete things and events that finally matter. Practices protect focal things not only from technological subversion but also against human frailty. It was emphasized in Chapter 21 that the ultimately significant things to which we respond in deictic discourse cannot be possessed or controlled. Hence when we reach out for them, we miss them occasionally and sometimes for quite some time. Running becomes unrelieved pain and cooking a thankless chore. If in the technological mode we insisted on assured results or if more generally we estimated the value of future efforts on the basis of recent experience, focal things would vanish from our lives. A practice keeps faith with focal things and saves for them an opening in our lives. To be sure, eventually the practice needs to be empowered again by the reemergence of the great thing in its splendor. A practice that is not so revived degenerates into an empty and perhaps deadening ritual.

We can now summarize the significance of a focal practice and say that such a practice is required to counter technology in its patterned pervasiveness and to guard focal things in their depth and integrity. Countering technology through a practice is to take account of our susceptibility to technological distraction, and it is also to engage the peculiarly human strength of comprehension, i.e., the power to take in the world in its extent and significance and to respond through an enduring commitment. Practically a focal practice comes into being through resoluteness, either an explicit resolution where one vows regularly to engage in a focal activity from this day on or in a more implicit resolve that is nurtured by a focal thing in favorable circumstances and matures into a settled custom.

   In considering these practical circumstances we must acknowledge a final difference between focal practices today and their eminent pretechnological predecessors. The latter, being public and prominent, commanded elaborate social and physical settings: hierarchies, offices, ceremonies, and choirs; edifices, altars, implements, and vestments. In comparison our focal practices are humble and scattered. Sometimes they can hardly be called practices, being private and limited. Often they begin as a personal regimen and mature into a routine without ever attaining the social richness that distinguishes a practice. Given the often precarious and inchoate nature of focal practices, evidently focal things and practices, for all the splendor of their simplicity and their fruitful opposition to technology, must be further clarified in their relation to our everyday world if they are to be seen as a foundation for the reform of technology.

24   Wealth and the Good Life

Strong claims have been made for focal things and practices. Focal concerns supposedly allow us to center our lives and to launch a reform of technology and so to usher in the good life that has eluded technology. At the end of the preceding chapter we have seen that focal practices today tend to be isolated and rudimentary. But these are marginal deficiencies, due to unfavorable circumstances. Surely there are central problems as well that pertain to focal practices no matter how well developed. Before we can proceed to suggestions about how technology may be reformed to make room for the good life, the most important objections regarding focal practices, the pivots of that reform, must be considered and, if possible, refuted. These disputations are not intended to furnish the impregnable defense of focal concerns which, it was argued in Chapter 21, is neither possible nor to be wished for. The deliberations of this chapter are rather efforts to connect the notion of a focal practice more closely with the prevailing conceptual and social situation and so to advance the standing of focal concerns in our midst. To make the technological universe hospitable to focal things turns out to be the heart of the reform of technology. What follows are first steps in this direction.

Among these, the first in turn requires us to consider the problem of the plurality of focal things and practices. It has a negative and positive aspect; negative because my devotion to a focal concern is rejected or challenged by the commitment of other people to contrary focal practices; positive because the plurality can have the character of a complementary richness in what is called a social union. The latter possibility, however, may be realized in the superficial diversity of various styles of consumption. As a counterforce to such shallowness I will consider in the first half of the present chapter the mode of developing one's faculties which is guided by the so-called Aristotelian Principle. It defines a notion of excellence which revolves about a notion of complexity. The more complex the faculties to whose cultivation we are devoted, the more excellent our life. This turns out to be an ambiguous result. Excellence so defined is no longer a counterforce to technology. On the other hand, it is compatible with a notion of engagement that seems to capture the most important aspirations of focal concerns and at the same time avoids the occasionally, perhaps essentially, constricting effects of the latter. When we measure these findings against an actual focal concern, we will see, however, that it is misguided to think of focal things as being entered in a competition with the concept of engagement and the Aristotelian Principle in a quest to reform technology. Only things that we experience as greater and other than ourselves can move us to judge and change technology in the first place.

Given this clarification of focal concerns we can without fear of misunderstanding explicate their generic features. On the basis of this generic definition of focal things and practices, an explicit definition of the reform of technology becomes possible. A reform so defined is neither the modification nor the rejection of the technological paradigm but the recognition and restraint of the pattern of technology so as to give focal concerns a central place in our lives. The remainder of this chapter provides a twofold application and elaboration of that reform proposal. First and applied to the private an personal realm, it will be seen to engender an intelligently selective attitude toward technology and a life of wealth in a well-defined sense. Second and in regard to traditional excellence and the family, the reform of technology makes possible a revival of these institutions.

First, then, we must consider the question of the plurality of focal commitments. A focal concern, it has been said, centers one's life. It is a final and dominant end which alone truly matters and fulfills and which therefore assigns all other things and activities their rank and place. But it is obvious that the ultimacy and dominance of a focal concern is contradicted by the fact that there are a number of different and apparently competing concerns. It cannot be that both running and fly-fishing matter ultimately. If one does, the other cannot. Focal practices in pretechnological times clearly possessed this dominance and exclusiveness. In the early Middle Ages, everyone went to church on Sundays and holy days, and Hubert, who went hunting, was a sinner for that reason. If focal practices were to become prominent in the life of this country, there surely would be a diversity of them. And would not sympathy require me to question other focal concerns and to win other people over to mine? Even if we heed the counsel of tolerance, the situation would remain unsettled and troubling. In reply we first must note how far removed we are from such a state of affairs and how many salutary measures would have to be taken before a prominent controversy about focal practices could arise.

But let us assume that there will be an evident plurality of focal concerns. How controversial would it be? It may be helpful to begin by considering the origins of that plurality. It became possible in the West when at the beginning of the modern era the unity of the Christian church was shattered through reform movements, scientific and geographical discoveries, and finally through the liberating forces of democracy and technology. In Chapters 6 and 7 we saw that in light of the new scientific laws our actual world appears as one instantiation of all that is physically possible. Similarly, within the context of the immense information and the varied practical possibilities that technology has procured, every actual concern now appears as one surrounded by alternatives. The severing of the ties between focal concerns and social and economic necessity that has been repeatedly noted is just a corollary of this phenomenon.

But we also must remember that we would not want to regain the support of cogency when testifying on behalf of a focal power. This would, on the one hand, compromise the grace and depth of such a power and, on the other, degrade us as respondents to that power. Our parents in their old age, as said before, address us not inasmuch as we are weak and helpless but insofar as we are capable of gratitude and receptive to wisdom, tradition, and mortality. In short, the new adulthood and maturity that are required of us are of a piece with the peculiar radiance and dignity that focal concerns now have. This status of the focal thing has the technological setting for a necessary condition, and it has the plurality of alternative concerns as a compatible background. Perhaps one should take "compatible" in the original and strong sense. We should be able to suffer the contradiction that the background of alternatives constitutes along with the joy that comes from our focal practice. And what we suffer is not just the implicit denial of what matters most to us; we suffer being deprived of great and unreachable things that are sometimes placed not only beyond our time and energy but outside our very comprehension. Sheehan is an eloquent witness:

> I may have difficulty comprehending the grasp that music has on
> its enthusiasts, but I see that as a deficiency in myself, not the

music lovers. When a musician tells me Beethoven's Opus 132 is not simply an hour of music but of universal truth, is in fact a flood of beauty and wisdom, I envy him. I don't label him a nut. And being a city kid, I may be slow to appreciate the impact of nature on those raised differently, but, again, I regret that failure. And when Pablo Casals said, as he did on his ninety-fifth birthday, "I pass hours looking at a tree or a flower. And sometimes I cry at their beauty," I don't think age has finally gotten to old Pablo. I cry for myself.[1]

But can we not instead take the diversity of people's engagements in a positive way? Wilhelm von Humboldt who is one of the authors, as we earlier saw, of the liberal democratic notion of self-realization has also pointed out that no one person can hope to realize all that human beings are capable of; we would in fact weaken our development if we tried. But far from being frustrated by our inevitable one-sidedness, we should embrace and develop our peculiarity and join it with those of others and through this connection experience and enjoy the fullness of humanity.[2] This is the idea of social union which Rawls has rediscovered and elaborated.[3] Clearly, it is an idea that affirms, deepens, and conjoins the notions of sympathy and tolerance.

It appears then that the plurality of focal concerns must be accepted and perhaps can even be seen in a positive light. But the latter possibility must be further pursued and taken to the point where it seems possible clearly to discern a unity underlying the plurality. We can begin with the apparent susceptibility of a social union to technological subversion. One might reply, as Rawls would, that the shallow and distracting diversity of self-realization that the consumption of commodities offers conflicts with the kind of self-development suggested by the Aristotelian Principle which is an integral part of a social union. The Principle says that "other things equal, human beings enjoy the exercise of their realized capacities (their innate or trained abilities), and this enjoyment increases the more the capacity is realized, or the greater its complexity."[4] Accordingly, people will not only prefer chess to checkers, as Rawls has it, but checkers to watching television and cooking a meal from basic ingredients to warming a frozen dinner. Rawls recognizes that the Principle is but a tendency and can be overridden. Yet he is confident that "the tendency postulated should be relatively strong and not easily counterbalanced."[5] But as we have seen in Chapter 18 and elsewhere, technology has not just counterbalanced but very nearly buried it. There is a difference, however, between technological obliteration and subversion. Technology can overcome the wilderness by brute force, but it cannot bring it (easily and obviously) under its rule and procure it as a commodity. Conversely, technology could hardly annihilate values (such as freedom, prosperity, or pleasure), but it can surely subvert them by specifying them in terms of the availability and consumption of commodities. Accordingly, the Aristotelian Principle is not impugned as a counterforce to technology if it can be tech-

nologically overrun so long as it resists technological subversion. But does
it? Clearly the concept of complexity is crucial here. Rawls contends that
"until we have some relatively precise theory and measure of complexity"
we can intuitively grasp the nature of complexity and rank various activities
by complexity in accordance with a principle of inclusiveness where "cases
of greater complexity are those in which one of the activities compared
includes all the skills and discriminations of the other activity and some further
ones in addition."[6] Thus the computer game Defender might rank higher than
fly-fishing since the former requires quicker hand-eye coordination, more
intricate strategy, and evasive as well as aggressive skills. Similarly, exercising
with a Nautilus might be more complex than running since the former allows
one to sense and to work many more muscle groups. Theory here seems to
conflict with considered judgment. Whether both can be saved in their essence
and balanced in a reflective equilibrium is a question that will concern us in
a moment.

Meanwhile let us note that the theory, i.e., the Aristotelian Principle, is
attractive not only in helping to reconcile the variety of human endeavors
within a social union but also in suggesting ways in which the variety of focal
practices can be similarly united. It was pointed out in Chapter 22 that there
is an apparent kinship among significant or focal things; and, symmetrically,
there are common traits to be found among focal practices. These can be seen
when we consider that although both Capon and a fast-food junkie are deeply
concerned with food, Capon, I expect, would have a deeper appreciation of
Sheehan's concern than the junkie's. Unlike the latter, both Capon and Sheehan practice the acquisition of skills, the fidelity to a daily discipline, the
broadening of sensibility, the profound interaction of human beings, and the
preservation and development of tradition. These traits we may bring together
under the heading of engagement. The good life, then, is one of engagement,
and engagement is variously realized by various people. Engagement would
not only harmonize the variety among people but also within the life of one
person. Sheehan, for instance, finds engagement not only in running but also
in literature, and Capon finds it not only in the culture of the table but also
in music.

Engagement is a more flexible and inclusive principle of ordering one's
life, and being so it meets the critique of dominant ends that Rawls puts
forward. If such an end deserves its name and is clearly specified, Rawls
argues, there is a danger of "fanaticism and inhumanity" because the nar-
rowness of the goal does violence to the breadth of human capacities.[7] There
seems to be intuitive confirmation of Rawls's claim. Initially, the firm guidance that a dominant end affords in one's life is appealing, as Rawls notes.[8]
Taking up some thing and practice as a focal and dominant end, one does, as
Sheehan did, experience a sense of clarity and liberation. One is no longer
caught in obliging other people's expectations and in struggling to balance a
plethora of conflicting and confusing aims. Having centered my life in an

ultimate concern, I have clear and principled answers to life's endless and distracting demands. But both Sheehan and Capon testify to the dark night of the soul that settles upon one from time to time, not when one has allowed distraction to erode the core of one's life but just when dedication to the focal thing has been vigorous and faithful.[9] And such darkness, depression, and collapse can be witnessed among people who have dedicated themselves to a cause that is more selfless and sublime than running or the culture of the table. These failures are so much more threatening if not devastating than those that occur under the guidance of inclusive ends because the former case admits of no alibi. One has dedicated oneself to one's highest aspiration and profoundest experience, and one has failed. Where to turn now? In a life of an inclusive end, disappointment here allows one to turn elsewhere for consolation. The question then is whether the collective plurality and the individual restrictiveness of focal concerns can be overcome through the notion of an inclusive end, placed in a social union of persons who shape their lives according to the Aristotelian Principle or according to the concept of engagement. This problem is best approached by connecting it with a still further problem, the question, i.e., whether there can be engagement of an essentially technological or purely mental sort. We have touched on this area in discussing complexity as a mark of excellence in human activities. It seemed that playing the computer game Defender is more excellent in this sense than fly-fishing. Moreover it, or more generally the playing of computer games, seems to satisfy the conditions of engagement. It certainly requires skill, discipline, and endurance; as the games develop technologically, more human capacities are called upon; and the computer game arcades have a social setting of their own and can lead to close human ties.[10] In fact, is not the computer game console a focal thing? It certainly seems to challenge and fulfill the player and to center the player's life. "There's not a lot of fun things in life," says one. "It's taken away my boredom. I've never been as serious about anything as Pac Man."[11]

The status of focal concerns as the basis of a reform of technology is now challenged in two ways. First, it appears that the ultimate givenness of a focal thing as something that unforethinkably addresses us in its own right is denied by the Aristotelian Principle or the concept of engagement. If the latter have independent standing and guiding force, focal things are mere complements that are chosen according to convenience. Second, the essentially metatechnological status of focal things and practices which in the abstract would be compatible with the Aristotelian Principle and the notion of engagement is denied by the apparent existence of essentially technological engagement.[12] Let us try to meet these challenges by pursuing Rawls's goal of achieving a reflective equilibrium and assume to begin with that in our considered judgment fly-fishing is more excellent than playing Defender. Can we align this judgment with the cluster of theories composed of the Aristotelian Principle, the notion of engagement and of a technological focal concern? Fly-fishing is more complex, we might say, because it requires more encompassing and discriminating knowledge. One must know in what season and at what time of day certain insects are hatching and trout are feeding. One must be able to read the water to recognize the riffles and the pools where the big rainbows are lying in wait. There are more intricate bodily skills in casting a line that involves not just the pushing of buttons and the movement of a stick but the harmonious interplay of rod, line, and fly, compensating for the wind, avoiding the willows, using hand, arm, and shoulder while maintaining one's stance in a slippery streambed. And to have a line and finally the fly settle gently on the river, as gently nearly as a real insect might, is one of the most delicate maneuvers humans are capable of. Fly-fishing also centers one's life more clearly and discriminatingly. Just as the grizzly is a symbol of the vastness and power of the open land, so the trout is a focus of the health and fertility of a drainage or even of a continent, considering the ravages of acid rain. To maintain the conditions that are conducive to big fish and to peaceful fishing is to take the measure of the world at large. In contrast, it appears, playing Defender requires a narrow range of highly sharpened skills, and it proceeds in utter indifference to the surrounding world. It is an activity that, given a sufficient store of energy and food, could proceed well underground should the natural environment have become unlivable.

The claim has been made, of course, that computer games allow one to become at home in the computer world. "We have a whole generation growing up," an educational consultant says, "who have no problem at all approaching the computer. They could become the haves."[13] "Kids are becoming masters of the computer," an astrophysicist contends. "When most grown-ups talk about computers, they fear the machines will dominate and displace. But these kids are learning to live and *play* with intelligent machines."[14] What the kids are learning to master is the enjoyment of a commodity; but with the supporting electronic and logical machinery they are as little familiar as consumers are with the substructure of the technological universe.[15]

But what of the people who devote their lives to the design and construction of computers? Surely they have an intimate and competent grasp of what characterizes our era. Tracy Kidder has provided an illuminating account of work at the leading edge of technology, the story of the design and construction of a computer.[16] Such work is among the best technology has to offer. It is challenging and skillful, requiring creativity, enormous dedication, and discipline. Clearly it engages, excites, and fulfills its practitioners. It occupies the center of their lives and enforces profound personal interactions. It is practiced, at least by a good number of the workers, as art for art's sake, without emphasis on remuneration, with seemingly little support from the firm's executives, with no hope of gaining fame in the world at large, and with diffidence or indifference regarding the uses to which the product will be put. Still it seems to me, judging by the evidence of Kidder's book, that computer design is deeply flawed as a focal practice. Some of the flaws are due to unhappy social arrangements. It is at least conceivable that the accomplishments that are rightly celebrated in Kidder's story could come about under socially more balanced and stable circumstances. A more serious flaw is the purely mental and essentially disembodied character of this kind of engagement. But this one-sidedness it has in common with writing music, poetry, and philosophy, with playing chess and reading novels.

Yet the poet in the stillness of writing and in the calm of speaking gathers and presents the world in the comprehensive and intimate ways that distinguish human beings. Through the poet's deictic discourse we come to comprehend the world more fully and are so empowered to inhabit it more appropriately in our tangible and bodily activities. Between poetry and practical engagement there is the complementary rhythm of comprehension and action, of systole and diastole. The focal significance of a mental activity should be judged, I believe, by the force and extent with which it gathers and illuminates the tangible world and our appropriation of it.

Is the design and construction of computers a focal concern by that standard? Not in the setting that Kidder presents. Work on the computer alienates most of the workers from the larger world. And the object of their endeavors to which they devote themselves as an end they know at the same time to be a means for whatever ends. They know that the intoxicating and engaging circumstances of their work have been granted them because for the company and the world at large the new computer will be a mere means. But these again are contingent circumstances. Inasmuch as computers embody and illuminate phenomena such as intelligence, organization, determinism, decidability, system, and the like, they surely have a kind of focal character, and a concern with computers in that sense is focal as well.[17] But the focal significance of work with computers seems precarious to me and requires for its health the essentially complementary concern with things in their own right. Otherwise the world is more likely lost than comprehended.

Have we reached a reflective equilibrium? It may seem as though a more precise inquiry of activities, traditionally thought to be excellent, will show them to be more complex than their more recent and technological rivals. Perhaps this welcome result is due to the fact that a more meticulous scrutiny comes closer to Rawls's "relatively precise theory and measure of complexity" which presumably would settle comparisons conlusively. But all this is semblance. What we have really done is to bring activities back to the things to which we respond in those activities. It is the dignity and greatness of a thing in its own right that give substance and guiding force to the notion of complexity. Complexity by itself and as a formal property is, as we noted in Chapter 22, too flexible a notion to serve as a guide to the value of wild nature; and so it is as a guide to the excellence of human activities.[18] Rawls's Aristotelian Principle is not, to be sure, accidentally tied to a formal notion of complexity.[19] The thrust of *A Theory of Justice*, consistent with its allegiance to the deontological tradition, is to keep the contingent and historical world at bay.[20] Thus Rawls's theory screens out the presence of those things that alone, I believe, can orient our lives. To say this is, of course, to speak approximately and ambiguously. It is after all not finally decisive whether and how we succeed in securing an ordered and excellent life for worldlessly conceived subjects. The point is to remind or to suggest that in all significant reflection of the good life things in their own right have already graced us.

But if this is the pivot of ethics, is it not possible that a technological device or, more generally, a technological invention may someday address us as such a thing, one that, whatever its genesis, has taken on a character of its own, that challenges and fulfills us, that centers and illuminates our world? As said in Chapter 20, it is possible that such an invention will appear and that technology will give birth to a focal thing or event. But none are to be found now, and we must not allow vague promises of technological magnificence to blight the simple splendor of the things that now center and sustain our lives. At the same time we must, in a new kind of maturity and adulthood, accept the plurality of focal concerns, and we can take pleasure in the social union that is fostered by that plurality. But the diverse and complementary nature of our concerns should not be seen as the convergence of the Aristotelian Principle and human finitude. That would diminish focal things to the indifferent furniture of an abstract principle. The threat of one-sidedness that Rawls fears if focal things and practices are taken as dominant ends does not really obtain. Significant or focal things, as pointed out in Chapter 21, have an unsurpassable depth which surely distinguishes them from a dominant end in Rawls's precise sense where such an end "is clearly specified as attaining some objective goal such as political power or material wealth."[21] A dominant end in this sharp conception is more consonant with technology where gifted and ambitious people, dissatisfied with the shallowness of consumption, seek a transcendent goal and yet remain enthralled by technology in choosing a goal that has in principle procurable and controllable, i.e., measurable, character.

There remains one possibility of unity and coherence arising among the dispersed focal concerns. It appears when we remember that the variety of "focal" practices in pretechnological societies was centered about one focus proper, religious in nature. The focus proper did not unite all the subordinate engaging activities as a rule covers its applications. Rather the central focus surpassed the peripheral ones in concreteness, depth, and significance. As suggested in Chapter 23, there may be a hidden focus of that sort now, or one may emerge sometime. But who is to say? To the blight of the enthrallment with technology there corresponds symmetrically the impatient waiting or insistence on the great epiphany of the world's central focus. Instead we should gratefully record the present wealth of focal things and practices, take these things to heart, and work toward a republic of focal concerns.

Having secured, to some extent, a place for the plurality, concreteness and simplicity of focal concerns, we must now show more soberly and specifically how they serve as a basis for the reform of technology. And the first question is: How broad a basis will it be? I have suggested in Chapter 23 that there is a wide and steady, if frequently concealed, current of focal practices that runs through the history of this country. It is the other American mainstream. Its various stretches are linked by the generic features that focal things have in common, and it may be helpful to outline this kinship more formally as a set of traits that focal things and practices exhibit for the most part. These traits are not conditions that are sufficient to qualify something as focal. Nor is each of these traits necessary. Rather these features reflect general recollections and anticipations of focal concerns.

These generic features are divided between the things and practices of focal concern. But the division is not sharp since things and practices are tightly and variously interwoven. The practice of fly-fishing is centered around a definite, independent, and resplendent thing: the trout. The thing in backpacking is expansive, broadly defined, and it exists in its own right: the wilderness. In the practice of running, the thing is always and already there, Sheehan's ocean road, for instance, or the course that the New York City Marathon takes. But it lies there, inconspicuous and indistinct, till the runners bring it into relief. And the great meal and its courses must be prepared and brought forth by the cook and the host. Still we might say this about focal things in general. They are concrete, tangible, and deep, admitting of no functional equivalents; they have a tradition, structure, and rhythm of their own. They are unprocurable and finally beyond our conrol. They engage us in the fullness of our capacities. And they thrive in a technological setting. A focal practice, generally, is the resolute and regular dedication to a focal thing. It sponsors discipline and skill which are exercised in a unity of achievement and enjoyment, of mind, body, and the world, of myself and others, and in a social union.

This is just a summary of issues discussed before. An additional point must now be made. Focal practices are at ease with the natural sciences. Since focal things are concrete and tangible, they are at home in the possibility space that the sciences circumscribe. Because the givenness of these things is so eloquent and articulate, the scientific investigation of such things is not found to be a dissolution but an illumination of them. Correspondingly, the human being, as it is engaged and oriented by great things and is so an eminent focus itself, suffers no threat or diminishment from scientific examination. Capon and Sheehan testify to this openness. They use scientific insight gladly, easily, and often to bring out the splendor and depth of the things that matter to them. It is clear, in light of Chapters 4–7, that the reform of technology would rest on a treacherous foundation if focal things and practices violated or resented the bounds of science.

We now turn explicitly to the reform of technology. It is evident from Chapter 20 that the reform must be one *of* and not merely one *within* the device paradigm. It is reasonable to expect that a reform of the paradigm would involve a restructuring of the device, perhaps the deletion, addition, and rearrangement of internal features. And this would lead, one might think, to the construction of different, perhaps intrinsically and necessarily benign technological devices. But I believe the device paradigm is perfect in its way, and if concrete pefections within the overall pattern are to be achieved, this will be the task of research and development scientists and engineers, not of philosophers. A reform of the paradigm is even less, of course, a dismantling of technology or of the technological universe. It is rather *the recognition and the restraint* of the paradigm. To restrain the paradigm is to restrict it to its proper sphere. Its proper sphere is the background or periphery of focal things and practices. Technology so reformed is no longer the characteristic and dominant way in which we take up with reality; rather it is a way of proceeding that we follow at certain times and up to a point, one that is left behind when we reach the threshold of our focal and final concerns. The concerns that move us to undertake a reform of the paradigm lead to reforms within the paradigm as well. Since a focal practice discloses the significance of things and the dignity of humans, it engenders a concern for the safety and well-being of things and persons. Consequently, focal concerns will stress and support the paradigm's native tendency toward safety, both locally and globally. It will concur with the efforts of consumer advocates and environmentalists, not of course to save and entrench the rule of technology but to provide a secure margin for what matters centrally.

But is this really a radical and remarkable reform proposal? Is it not indistinguishable from all the programs that are worried about the excesses of technology, about the imbalance between means and ends, about the suppression of the value question, and about the enslavement of humankind by its own invention? Would it not be fair to say that these programs have anticipated the goal of the present reform proposal, namely, to restrict technology to the status of a means and to introduce new ends? The question is simply unanswerable because it is deeply ambiguous. If by new ends we mean different commodities, then the present proposal differs sharply from traditional programs of reform. Reform must make room for focal things and practices. In a broad sense, these are the ends that technology should serve. But this broader sense of the means-ends relation is in conflict with the means-ends structure, embodied in the device paradigm. We can put the point at issue clearly, if baldly, this way. Both the common and the present reform proposals revolve about a means-ends distinction. In the common view, the distinction is placed within the device paradigm, in alignment with the machinery-commodity distinction. Thus the role of technology remains invisible and unchallenged. The present proposal is to restrict the entire paradigm, both the machinery and the commodities, to the status of a means and let focal things and practices be our ends. The conflict between these two views is easily overlooked. It is that unresolved conflict that infects the question above with ambiguity. More important, as argued repeatedly and particularly in Chapter 11, the sharpness, pervasiveness, and concealment of the technological means-ends relation exert a nearly irresistible pressure toward resolving the ambiguity in favor of technology. Most traditional reform proposals are finally ensnared by the device paradigm and fail to challenge the rule of technology and its debilitating consequences. Hence a radical reform, as said above, requires *the recognition* and the restraint of the device paradigm, a recognition that is guided by a focal concern. Such recognition can, as suggested in the preceding chapter, shade over into an implicit understanding though explication, it is hoped, would sharpen it.

Let me now draw out the concrete consequences of this kind of reform. I begin with particular illustrations and proceed to broader observations. Sheehan's focal concern is running, but he does not run everywhere he wants to go. To get to work he drives a car. He depends on that technological device and its entire associated machinery of production, service, resources, and roads. Clearly, one in Sheehan's position would want the car to be as perfect a technological device as possible: safe, reliable, easy to operate, free of maintenance. Since runners deeply enjoy the air, the trees, and the open spaces that grace their running, and since human vigor and health are essential to their enterprise, it would be consistent of them to want an environmentally benign car, one that is free of pollution and requires a minimum of resources for its production and operation. Since runners express themselves through running, they would not need to do so through the glitter, size, and newness of their vehicles.[22]

At the threshold of their focal concern, runners leave technology behind, technology, i.e., as a way of taking up with the world. The products of technology remain ubiquitous, of course: clothing, shoes, watches, and the roads. But technology can produce instruments as well as devices, objects that call forth engagement and allow for a more skilled and intimate contact with the world.[23] Runners appreciate shoes that are light, firm, and shock absorbing. They allow one to move faster, farther, and more fluidly. But runners would not want to have such movement procured by a motorcycle, nor would they, on the other side, want to obtain merely the physiological benefit of such bodily movement from a treadmill.

A focal practice engenders an intelligent and selective attitude toward technology. It leads to a simplification and perfection of technology in the background of one's focal concern and to a discerning use of technological products at the center of one's practice. I am not, of course, describing an evident development or state of affairs. It does appear from what little we know statistically of the runners in this country, for instance, that they lead a more engaged, discriminating, and a socially more profound life.[24] I am rather concerned to draw out the consequences that naturally follow for technology from a focal commitment and from a recognition of the device pattern. There is much diffidence, I suspect, among people whose life is centered, even in their work, around a great concern. Music is surely one of these. But at times, it seems to me, musicians confine the radiance, the rhythm, and the order of music and the ennobling competence that it requires to the hours and places of performance. The entrenchment of technology may make it seem quixotic to want to lead a fully musical life or to change the larger technological setting so that it would be more hospitable and attentive to music. Moreover, as social creatures we seek the approval of our fellows according to the prevailing standards. One may be a runner first and most of all; but one wants to prove too that one has been successful in the received sense. Proof requires at least the display, if not the consumption, of expensive commodities. Such inconsistency is regrettable, not because we just have to have reform of technology but because it is a partial disavowal of one's central concern. To have a focal thing radiate transformatively into its environment is not to exact some kind of service from it but to grant it its proper eloquence.

There is of course intuitive evidence for the thesis that a focal commitment leads to an intelligent limitation of technology.[25] There are people who, struck by a focal concern, remove much technological clutter from their lives. In happy situations, the personal and private reforms take three directions. The first is of course to clear a central space for the focal thing, to establish an inviolate time for running, or to establish a hearth in one's home for the culture of the table. And this central clearing goes hand in hand, as just suggested, with a newly discriminating use of technology.[26] The second direction of reform is the simplification of the context that surrounds and supports the focal area. And then there is a third endeavor, that of extending the sphere of engagement as far as possible. Having experienced the depth of things and the pleasure of full-bodied competence at the center, one seeks to extend such excellence to the margins of life. "Do it yourself" is the maxim of this tendency and "self-sufficiency" its goal. But the tendencies for which these titles stand also exhibit the dangers of this third direction of reform. Engagement, however skilled and disciplined, becomes disoriented when it exhausts itself in the building, rebuilding, refinement, and maintenance of stages on which nothing is ever enacted. People finish their basements, fertilize their lawns, fix their cars. What for? The peripheral engagement suffocates the center, and festivity, joy, and humor disappear. Similarly, the striving for self-sufficiency may open up a world of close and intimate relations with things and people. But the demands of the goal draw a narrow and impermeable boundary about that world. There is no time to be a citizen of the cultural and political world at large and no possibility of assuming one's responsibility in it. The antidote to such disorientation and constriction is the appropriate acceptance of technology. In one or another area of one's life one should gratefully accept the disburdenment from daily and time-consuming chores and allow celebration and world citizenship to prosper in the time that has been gained.

What emerges here is a distinct notion of the good life or more precisely the private or personal side of one. Clearly, it will remain crippled if it cannot unfold into the world of labor and the public realm. These aspects will concern us in the next chapter. To begin on the side of leisure and privacy is to acknowledge the presently dispersed and limited standing of focal powers. It is also to avail oneself of the immediate and undeniably large discretion one has in shaping one's free time and private sphere.[27] Even within these boundaries the good life that is centered on focal concerns is distinctive enough. Evidently, it is a favored and prosperous life. It possesses the time and the implements that are needed to devote oneself to a great calling. Technology provides us with the leisure, the space, the books, the instruments, the equipment, and the instruction that allow us to become equal to some great thing that has beckoned us from afar or that has come to us through a tradition. The citizen of the technological society has been spared the abysmal bitterness of knowing himself or herself to be capable of some excellence or achievement and of being at the same time worn-out by poor and endless work, with no time to spare and no possibility of acquiring the implements of one's desire. That bitterness is aggravated when one has a gifted child that is similarly deprived, and is exacerbated further through class distinctions where one sees richer but less gifted and dedicated persons showered with opportunities of excellence. There is prosperity also in knowing that one is able to engage in a focal practice with a great certainty of physical health and economic security. One can be relatively sure that the joy that one receives from a focal thing will not be overshadowed by the sudden loss of a loved one with whom that joy is shared. And one prospers not only in being engaged in a profound and living center but also in having a view of the world at large in its essential political, cultural, and scientific dimensions. Such a life is centrally prosperous, of course, in opening up a familiar world where things stand out clearly and steadily, where life has a rhythm and depth, where we encounter our fellow human beings in the fullness of their capacities, and where we know ourselves to be equal to that world in depth and strength.

This kind of prosperity is made possible by technology, and it is centered in a focal concern. Let us call it wealth to distinguish it from the prosperity that is confined to technology and that I want to call affluence. Affluence consists in the possession and consumption of the most numerous, refined, and varied commodities. This superlative formulation betrays its relative character. "Really" to be affluent is to live now and to rank close to the top of the hierarchy of inequality. All of the citizens of a typical technological society are more affluent than anyone in the Middle Ages. But this affluence, astounding when seen over time, is dimmed or even insensible at any one time for all but those who have a disproportionately large share of it. Affluence, strictly defined, has an undeniable glamour. It is the embodiment of the free, rich, and imperial life that technology has promised. So at least it appears from below whence it is seen by most people. Wealth in comparison is homely, homely in the sense of being plain and simple but homely also in allowing us to be at home in our world, intimate with its great things, and familiar with our fellow human beings. This simplicity, as said before, has its own splendor that is more sustaining than the glamour of affluence which leaves its beneficiaries, so we hear, sad and bored.[28] Wealth is a romantic notion also in that it continues and develops a tradition of concerns and of excellence that is rooted on the other side of the modern divide, i.e., of the Enlightenment. A life of wealth is certainly not romantic in the sense of constituting an uncomprehending rejection of the modern era and a utopian reform proposal.[29]

How wealth can be secured and advanced politically and economically is the topic of the next chapter. I will conclude this chapter by considering the narrower sphere of wealth and by connecting it with the traditional notions of excellence and of the family. In Chapter 18 I suggested that the virtues of world citizenship, of gallantry, musicianship, and charity still command an uneasy sort of allegiance and that it is natural, therefore, to measure the technological culture by these standards. Perhaps people are ready to accept the distressing results of such measurement with a rueful sort of agreement. But obviously the acceptance of the standards, if there is one, is not strong enough to engender the reforms that the pursuit of traditional excellence would demand. This, I believe, is due to the fact that the traditional virtues have for too long been uprooted from the soil that used to nourish them. Values, standards, and rules, I have urged repeatedly, are recollections and anticipations of great things and events. They provide bonds of continuity with past greatness and allow us to ready ourselves and our children for the great things we look forward to. Rules and values inform and are acted out in practices. A virtue is the practiced and accomplished faculty that makes one equal to a great event. From such considerations it is evident that the real circumstances and forces to which the traditional values, virtues, and rules used to answer are all but beyond recollection, and there is little in the technological universe that they can anticipate and ready us for. The peculiar character of technological reality has escaped the attention of the modern students of ethics.

To sketch a notion of excellence that is appropriate to technology is, in one sense, simply to present another version of the reform of technology that has been developed so far. But it is also to uncover and to strengthen ties to a tradition that the modern era has neglected to its peril. As regards world citizenship today, the problem is not confinement but the proliferation of channels of communication and of information. From the mass of available information we select by the criteria of utility and entertainment. We pay attention to information that is useful to the maintenance and advancement of technology, and we consume those news items that divert us. In the latter case the world is shredded into colorful bits of entertainment, and the distracted kind of knowledge that corresponds to that sort of information is the very opposite of the principled appropriation of the world that is meant by world citizenship.[30] The realm of technically useful information does not provide access to world citizenship either. Technical information is taken up primarily in one's work. Since most work in technology is unskilled, the demands on technical knowledge are low, and most people know little of science, engineering, economics, and politics. The people at the leading edge of technology have difficulty in absorbing and integrating the information that pertains to their field.[31] But even if the flood of technical information is appropriately channeled, as I think it can be, its mastery still constitutes knowledge of the social machinery, of the means rather than the ends of life. What is needed if we are to make the world truly and finally ours again is the recovery of a center and a standpoint from which one can tell what matters in the world and what merely clutters it up. A focal concern is that center of orientation. What is at issue here comes to the fore when we compare the simple and authentic world appropriation of someone like Mother Teresa with the shallow and vagrant omniscience of a technocrat.

Gallantry in a life of wealth is the fitness of the human body for the greatness and the playfulness of the world. Thus it has a grounding and a dignity that are lost in traditional gallantry, a loss that leaves the latter open to the technological concept of the perfect body where the body is narcissistically stylized into a glamorous something by whatever scientific means and according to the prevailing fashion. In the case of musicianship the tradition of excellence is unbroken and has expanded into jazz and popular music. What the notion of wealth can contribute to the central splendor and competence of music is to make us sensible to the confinement and the procurement of music. Confinement and procurement are aspects of the same phenomenon. The discipline and the rhythmic grace and order that characterize music are often confined, as said above, to the performance proper and are not allowed to inform the broader environment. This is because the unreformed structure of the technological universe leaves no room for such forces. Accordingly, music is allowed to conform to technology and is procured as a commodity that is widely and inconsequentially consumed. A focal concern for musicianship, then, will curtail the consumption of music and secure a more influential position for the authentic devotion to music.

Finally, one may hope that focal practices will lead to a deepening of charity and compassion. Focal practices provide a profounder commerce with reality and bring us closer to that intensity of experience where the world engages one painfully in hunger, disease, and confinement. A focal practice also discloses fellow human beings more fully and may make us more sensitive to the plight of those persons whose integrity is violated or suppressed. In short, a life of engagement may dispel the astounding callousness that insulates the citizens of the technological societies from the well-known misery in much of the world. The crucial point has been well made by Duane Elgin:

> When people deliberately choose to live closer to the level of material sufficiency, they are brought closer to the reality of material existence for a majority of persons on this planet. There is

not the day-to-day insulation from material poverty that accom-
panies the hypnosis of a culture of affluence.[32]

The plight of the family, finally, consists, as argued in Chapter 18, in the
absorption of its tasks and substance by technology. The reduction of the
household to the family and the growing emptiness of family life leave the
parents bewildered and the children without guidance. Since less and less of
vital significance remains entrusted to the family, the parents have ceased to
embody rightful authority and a tradition of competence, and correspondingly
there is less and less legitimate reason to hold children to any kind of discipline. Parental love is deprived of tangible and serious circumstances in
which to realize itself. Focal practices naturally reside in the family, and the
parents are the ones who should initiate and train their children in them.
Surely parental love is one of the deepest forms of sympathy. But sympathy
needs enthusiasm to have substance. Families, I have found, that we are
willing to call healthy, close, or warm turn out, on closer inspection, to be
centered on a focal concern. And even in families that exhibit the typical
looseness of structure, the diffidence of parents, and the impertinence of
children, we can often discover a bond of respect and deep affection between
parent and youngster, one that is secured in a common concern such as a
sport and keeps the family from being scattered to the winds.

25   Political Affirmation

Assuming that a principled reform of technology can be carried out in the
realm of privacy and of the family, can we take meaningful measures to
reform the national community? This is the final question of our essay. Clearly,
enthusiasm and sympathy require us to seek an affirmative answer, and it is
also clear that appropriate measures of reform must be articulated in public
deictic discourse. But granted that such discourse has the required focus, it
is not clear that it has constructive force as well. It will question the established
order and may yet be unable to replace it. One pivot of this difficulty is the
distinction between legality and morality. The currently clear separation of
these two areas is an indicator of the stability of technology. Is it possible to
undertake a constructive reform by establishing stronger bonds between the
moral and the legal realms? The legal system as far as it pertains to civil and
criminal matters, so I will argue, should be preserved in its morally liberal
character. The factors in the legal system that shape our lives intimately,
inconspicuously, and also unavoidably are the ones that pertain to economics.

To institute a reform of technology by way of economics we must first
delineate the *philosophical* significance of economic reform. This I attempt
to do by showing that there is an opening for economic reform and a clear

goal within that opening. The implementation of reform can then largely be left to economic expertise. But we can go beyond these broad and basic points and show that a kind of technological reform via economics is already going on. To prosper and to become consequential, it requires explication and a collective affirmation. The latter is the constructive culmination of public deictic discourse. The former can depart from the distinction between the standard of living and the quality of life. When the distinction is properly clarified, it will become apparent that we must advance the quality of life at the expense of the standard of living. We can carry this policy into the work world by recognizing and strengthening the distinction between the local and labor-intensive economy and the centralized and highly automated economy. Reforms along these lines will make room for focal concerns in a fruitful and public way. The force of such measures must finally prove itself in regard to two vexing problems of public policy, the restoration of the large cities and the reduction of social injustice. The chapter closes with the consideration of those issues.

Taking up the problem at hand initially and generally, we must ask: How can the reform of technology be extended into the public world and the world of labor? Or more precisely, how can focal concerns be carried into the political realm and into the machinery of technology? Let us begin by noting the constraints on such extensions that are entailed by the findings of the preceding chapters. Since focal things and practices are dispersed and various, the public world cannot be restructured around a central national focus. It would be foolish to proclaim such a focus and totalitarian to impose one. The restriction to the reform of work is just opposite to that which constrains public reform. Labor is devoted to the advancement and maintenance of the technological machinery. The latter has crucial parts that are highly centralized if not truly nationalized. Since we want to preserve and perfect technology as the background and support of focal concerns, it will be impossible to transform the work world entirely in the image of the small-scale, engaging, and socially profound focal practices. Still, incisive and principled reforms in these areas are possible and necessary.

Conceivably, these reforms could arise inconspicuously and unnoticeably, nourished by diverse and implicit concerns. In fact, this is happening to some extent. But it is surely more appropriate to the human condition if profound changes are clearly comprehended and embraced. And this can only occur if there is a discourse that is congenial to the obstacles and goals of those changes. In the present case, the language that is suitable to the understanding of the obstacles of reforms is the one in which the pattern of technology is recognized and criticized. Its suitability to the public arena at first faces only the normal pedagogical problems. Since it is a kind of descriptive or analytical language, it has familiar and accessible character. But the critique of technology finally depends for its direction on the substantive concerns to which we attend in deictic discourse. Deictic discourse, however, is forever contestable, as pointed out in Chapter 21. And the question was raised in that chapter whether the introduction of uncontrollable issues into the public forum would not lead to confusion and paralysis at best. We can throw more light on the difficulty by turning to the subject matter of deictic discourse, i.e., focal concerns. It has been urged that we should be equal to them in testimony and appeal; and there is in fact a literature, as we have seen, that is admirably suited to this task. Yet all this speaking is essentially private. And it can afford to fail because it can count on the stability of the technological background whose fate is not concretely and literally at issue. But assuming that technology itself is drawn into the ken of deictic discourse, are we not jeopardizing the stability of society by subjecting it to inconclusive contests and diverse concerns?

We can approach an answer to this dilemma by considering yet a third way of stating it. To undertake a public reform in terms of deictic discourse is to subject the public realm to moral evaluation and eventually transformation. But such a proposal arouses immediate and profound suspicions. One important expression of the public order is the legal system. And this country is based on the clearest possible separation of legality and morality.[1] This meets the requirement of tolerance and is the achievement of our liberal democratic heritage.[2] Technology of course threatens to succeed all too well in this task and to establish what Stanley calls the libertarian technicist society with its amoral public order of technological rationality. In fact our legal system tends in this direction and assumes, however imperfectly, the pattern of a technological device with an inaccessible and unintelligible machinery that procures, at least for some, commodious security and order. The irony is that this seemingly amoral machinery is far from leaving the question of the good life open and is inextricably coupled with an *éthos*, a definite style of life. In this broader sense of ethics our legal system is as morally charged as any in history though, as seen before, its properly technological fruits resist analysis in traditional moral terms. Yet though technology has begun to pattern the legal system, the latter, like many other forms of present life, has retained traditional features.

The aspect of the interpenetration of the traditional and the technological that concerns us here can be grasped under the title of pluralism. The present system fosters or protects two kinds: the shallow pluralism afforded by the availability of many different commodities and the more profound pluralism of a diversity of focal practices. Certain laws or parts of the Constitution serve both goals, though the former are very differently understood depending on which of the latter they serve. Thus freedom of speech serves shallow pluralism in allowing the mining of taboos on sex and violence for the production of entertainment. In the realm of focal practices freedom of speech guarantees the possibility of testimony and appeal concerning matters of focal significance. The law that requires us to honor contracts is needed for the efficient functioning of the machinery on which shallow pluralism rests. In the more profound pluralism, honoring contracts is of a piece with, if not the same as, the fidelity that characterizes focal practices. This ambiguity of the legal system is quite general and pertains to the legality-morality distinction as well. For shallow pluralism, as suggested above, it is explicated as the machinery-commodity or labor-consumption distinction. In a world of a plurality of focal practices, so it follows from the preceding chapter, legality would secure the generic features that all focal practices have in common whereas morality would be divided among the specifics of the focal practices. In the latter case there would be a continuity and gradation between the legal and the moral with the attendant difficulty of drawing the necessary dividing line between the two.

Inasmuch as our legal system is traditional and not just technological, it exhibits a version of that continuity. Conservatives are aware of it and concerned to protect it against the technological diremption into machinery and commodity. Thus Irving Kristol sketches the "managerial" conception of democracy that is based on the root idea "that democracy is a 'political system' (as they [the social scientists] say) which can be adequately defined in terms of—can be fully reduced to—its mechanical arrangements." To this Kristol objects: "The purpose of democracy cannot possibly be the endless functioning of its own political machinery. The purpose of any political regime is to achieve some version of the good life and the good society."[3] Can the reform of technology find its public extension by taking the conservative clue and in trying to strengthen the bond between legality and morality? Conservatives attempt to do this, as is well known, by promoting moral issues in the area of civil liberties and criminal justice. But as was pointed out in Chapter 14, such endeavors try to make up in legal force what traditional morality has lost in genuine presence and authority; and as suggested in Chapter 20, there are further efforts to shore up the felt weakness of the traditional moral standards by claiming that these standards are necessary for the outward and tangible stability of society.[4] But it follows from Chapter 21 that tolerance requires us to keep civil and criminal justice as liberal as possible, and that requirement, to be sure, has an outward resemblance with the goals of the "managerial" or technologically specified democracy, and it has a genuine affinity with the liberal tradition of democracy. Consequently, when matters of civil and criminal justice are publicly transacted in the kind of language that is appropriate to focal practices, i.e., when these civil and criminal issues are drawn into public deictic discourse, the problem is not that well-established and well-tested social structures will be called into question in an attempt to overturn them; the problem is rather one of securing a new and deeper understanding of the status quo. Such reinterpretations are of course fatuous if they simply layer a new meaning on an old phenomenon without concrete changes taking place anywhere. They are substantial, however, if an old phenomenon is placed in a new context. As said before, to see the context of something is to see its significance. In the present case, civil rights and criminal sanctions must be seen in relation to the focal practices that already exist in the private realm and in relation to public changes to which I now turn.

Conservatives, as pointed out in Chapter 14, do a disservice to morality, not only through their failure to discover its present vigor and by compromising moral authority through attempts at cogency but also by undercutting their moral concern in the area of economic legislation. There is no sharp dividing line between laws that pertain to civil and criminal matters and those that regulate and direct the economy. Still, the latter kind of law is in general more concrete and emphemeral than the former. More important, it touches us more immediately and consequentially than the former. The lives of many of us are not directly affected by legal changes regarding homosexuality, prostitution, abortion, pornography, or wiretapping. This reminder is not to deny the supreme importance of civil liberties but to point out that it is in the economic realm where through legislation we establish the firm, concrete, and specific boundaries that tangibly constrain everyone's life.[5] Conservatives, in pushing hard for the progress of the economy and technology, promote a style of life that suffocates the remainders of traditional morality and one that is inhospitable to the morality of focal concerns, a morality that is in important ways the continuation and development of pretechnological traditions.[6]

But to direct the reform of technology by way of economic legislation is to steer it into quicksand, or so it must seem. The economy is notoriously complex and unmanageable and the economic literature more so by an order of magnitude. Fundamental proposals of social reform regularly expire when the economic profession inspects them and finds them to be impossibly naive and simplistic. It certainly would be foolish to deny that the economic machinery in this country and its attendant scholarship are intricate and difficult to come to grips with. But the difficulties are of two very different kinds. One consists of the technical difficulties which are studied, developed, and jealously guarded by mainstream economists. The other difficulty is philosophical and consists in the task of seeing the economic machinery in context, recognizing it as a mere machinery, and restricting it to its proper place. To extend philosophically the reform of technology into economics is not to suggest ways of tinkering with the economic machinery but to show that there is room for economic reform and to outline concrete goals. If there is an opening for change and if the aims are clear, then it becomes the task of economists and of practical experience to determine the precise and best path from here to those goals.

The opening for reform has several dimensions. Most prosaically, reform requires a certain kind of prosperity, a material surplus that allows us to survive while we contemplate, design, and install new structures and that forgives the mistakes that are inevitably made during reforms. It is well known that absolutely poor people are conservative because they lack the margin necessary for innovation.[7] It is less obvious that an unconditional commitment to affluence, as defined in the previous chapter, is as incapable of reform as poverty. It is capable of progress, of course, and there are technically fundamental innovations in the service of that goal. But every significant effort and surplus is restricted to securing and advancing the standard of living. As long as this commitment is unconditional and largely unspoken, every suggestion to proceed in another direction can be waved aside as unreasonable. Appeals to what is taken for granted by nearly everyone can afford to be simple and brief. An example is provided by Lester C. Thurow who is thought to have provided a ruthlessly honest, tough-minded, provocative, courageous, and insightful analysis of our present economy.[8] But all that incisiveness is confined to the framework of technology whose validity needs only be alluded to in such phrases as: "Man is an acquisitive animal whose wants cannot be satiated. This is not a matter of advertising and conditioning, but a basic fact of existence."[9] It is true that technological voraciousness is not the work of a minority conspiracy but part of a broad and deep agreement as regards the modern approach to reality. Still, it is a historical phenomenon that has come into existence very recently and through a sharp reversal of the human condition. What we know of human culture in its original and longest period, extending over hundreds of millenia, tends to show that material wants were firm and limited and that play and celebration filled the available time rather than relentless production and consumption.[10] And even in more recent and recorded history, the latter two activities appear to have been structured and confined by sanctions and the social order.[11]

Obviously, the technological societies possess the material surplus necessary for reforms. Technology provides the space for its own transformation. But to free that space requires us to uncouple public policy from technology. More concretely, it is clear from recessions that the technological societies can substantially reduce their consumption without suffering genuine material hardships. This, unfortunately, is true in the aggregate only since, especially in this country, the burdens of economic downturns are unequally distributed. Military expenditures, on the other side, show that the industrial countries can afford substantial unconsumable production. In both instances the economic margins that have been removed from consumption are yielded grudgingly or resentfully. One who is engaged in a focal practice, however, can reduce consumption without resentment. Engagement opens up space, takes time, and allows things to emerge and to endure. Thus it stems the voracious and wasteful tide of technology which, haunted by the specter of boredom and due to its shallow contact with any one commodity, requires ever new and more consumption. Not that focal practices inevitably lead to frugality. Raising and training horses, surely a noble and engaging enterprise, makes heavy demands on resources. And as said before, people who center their life in a focal concern may still want to obtain the approval of the larger society by acquiring the trappings of consumption. But it is evident in principle that the wealth of focal practices is in most cases consistent with substantially reduced affluence.[12]

We must be aware here of a seeming inconsistency in the remarks above. It looks as though the frugal aspect of an engaging way of life is used as a premise to argue for the possibility of a reform of technology. In light of the preceding chapters it is obvious that the reform of technology is to serve focal concerns and not vice versa. In a sense this is a matter of emphasis. Focal concern and the reform of technology are one and the same thing. To reform technology is not to address an urgent problem in its own right but to allow focal things to prosper. And the latter task requires us to connect those things with technology in a principled and affirmative way. The kind of reform, then, that is of concern here needs to be properly located and oriented, and this can only happen in public deictic discourse. Since it will be deictic discourse of the political rather than poetic sort, it will speak generally and approximately of the focal things that matter. It must emphasize the point that there is an alternative to consumption and affluence, a life, namely, of engagement and wealth. It will have its forums on the editorial pages, at public hearings, and in legislative assemblies.

Having assured ourselves that the opening for the reform of technology has a material and communicative dimension, we must now ask whether it has a social and empirical one as well. The question is whether there is in fact an inclination on the part of the people to move toward a world of focal things. To move in this direction is to move away from technology. In Chapter 15 we considered empirical and statistical evidence that indicates that underlying the seemingly unconditional allegiance to technology, reflected in Thurow's remarks above, there is ambivalence and uneasiness. But one lets go of the old only if one is prepared to approach something new. Are people ready to do this? There is, as urged in the two preceding chapters, the other American mainstream, a devotion to great things in their own right, a concern with skill and discipline, the practice of a calmer and more engaging life. These indications we can verify in our own experiences, and these again can be amplified through more principled accounts such as Studs Terkel's *American Dreams*.[13] But here too we must balance immediate insight against the broad and scholarly findings of the social scientists. Such evidence is here as always suggestive at best since its representative character is obtained at the price of foregoing preparatory explanations, successively probing questions, challenging counterproposals, etc. By itself the question whether one would be ready to move toward a world of focal things is unintelligible and has not, of course, been put to the public. But there have been surveys on people's readiness to adopt a simpler and calmer way of life. Duane Elgin has surveyed the evidence, and it suggests that there is in fact a substantial popular tendency toward simplicity, one that is endorsed in this country by a majority of two-thirds to three-quarters of the respondents. The people who in fact, knowingly and willingly, practice simplicity constitute perhaps a third of the population. And there appear to be similar trends in some European countries.[14] The firmness and the real springs and principles of these commitments are mixed and cloudy of course. Some of the motives could certainly be accommodated by reforms *within* the paradigm of technology. And of those that aim at a reform *of* the technological framework, some are of the abstract and spiritualistic sort that courts the danger, I believe, of dogmatism and of technological subversion. Still the evidence suffices to show that the unqualified claim of people's unconditional allegiance to technology is indefensible. It seems clear that people are ready to embrace another way of life and that millions have already done so.

But if it is true "that a quiet revolution may be taking place in our national values and aspirations," why is it so well concealed?[15] One reason might be the inertia of technology; once a way of life has become so deeply entrenched, so well articulated, and so widely expressed in our environment, it will for a time continue on its own momentum even when a majority of people have withdrawn their support from it. The concealment of the quiet revolution might also betray the kind of attitude with which people hold their unorthodox convictions. A pollster's question, depending on how it is asked, will put the respondent in a reflective and even magnanimous frame of mind. But the highmindedness of the response will be dissipated in the technological every-day which, as we have seen, has a particularly distracting and disorienting force.[16] But this debility harbors strength as well.

It becomes visible when we turn to the question of how the real but concealed and inarticulate opening for the public reform of technology can be given shape and force. It can only be achieved through a collective affirmation. A collective affirmation is a shared and public commitment to a certain kind of behavior or enterprise. It is to the body politic as a practice is to a group of persons. It allows us as a national community to accomplish tasks that would lie beyond the capacity of individual decisions. A collective affirmation may be informal and is then anchored in mutual expectations and informal sanctions. An example is politeness, sociability, or civility.[17] If every morning or at every encounter I had to decide whether to restrain my frustrations, suppress my resentments, and extend goodwill, I might behave rudely as often as not. And with everyone in this position, life would be brutish and nasty. But in fact I feel constrained by expectations of politeness and put the best face on my troubles. I am strengthened in this commitment by the evenness and cordiality of others and by the fear of being met with raised eyebrows and turned shoulders if I were to be habitually discourteous. A collective affirmation may also be implicit as has emphatically been said of technology. It is a firm and consequential affirmation nonetheless and accounts for the tight coherence and coordination of our various enterprises. The Constitution of this country is one of the most stately collective affirmations. The declaration of war, unhappily, is an example of how a nation becomes capable of efforts and sacrifices that would be impossible to achieve if they were proposed and attempted one by one.[18]

Without a collective affirmation of reform, technology, due to its entrenchment and resourcefulness, will remain the rule. Such an affirmation will have to grow out of public deictic discourse, and its general theme and major forums have already been mentioned. There is a continuum between such fully public discourse and the more dispersed and private speaking that is to be found in the books that are testimonies to focal practices. But is public discourse of the deictic sort just a possibility and a desideratum, or are there more concrete and established issues that bespeak its emergence and can serve its fuller development? I believe that there are such issues and that they can be brought into public focus through the appropriate distinction between the quality of life and the standard of living. That distinction is often made in a way that vaguely parallels the distinction between wealth and affluence as drawn in the preceding chapter. Thus Schumacher uses it to formulate the crucial challenge for socialism: ''What is at stake is not economics but culture; not the standard of living but the quality of life.''[19] Similarly, Louis Harris summarizes his findings about the quiet revolution of aspirations: ''Significant majorities place a higher priority on improving human and social relationships and the quality of American life than on raising the standard of living.''[20]

Lowdon Wingo has defined the quality of life more narrowly as ''the extent to which environments, social and physical, are conducive to a state of happiness.''[21] Some of the physical elements of that quality of life are natural such as mountains, lakes, clean air, and water. Others are human made such as transportation or school systems. Examples of the social elements are freedom from crime, demographic homogeneity, or civility. What all the elements have in common is that they are not commercially producible and cannot be bought individually and privately. Members of a community possess them all at once or not at all.[22] The concept of the quality of life, whether defined broadly or narrowly, is beset with ambiguities. These can be resolved by assimilating the broad sense to wealth, as previously defined, and by accentuating in the narrow sense that aspect that stands for the degree to which the public realm is hospitable to wealth. I am not saying that these ways of resolving the ambiguities lead to a sharply defined notion suitable for cogent arguments of public policy; far from it. What they do is to direct our attention to the focal issues and to those problems of disputation and agreement that are not just technical puzzles and burdens but genuine tasks that we should willingly accept and tolerate if we cannot settle them.

Here the task of public deictic discourse is twofold: to clarify and deepen the parlances and discussions of the quality of life and show that under the latter heading we have already been concerned with the public reform of technology. To see this we must first clarify the tie between wealth and the narrow or public sense of the quality of life. We can depart from the contrast between private luxury and public poverty which Galbraith gave prominence a quarter of a century ago. In a celebrated passage he has us consider a family on an outing, equipped with luxurious devices and commodities and surrounded at the same time by a squalid and decaying environment.[23] That family enjoys a high standard of living and a low quality of life. Again terms are used in various ways; but it is at least consistent and helpful to use synonymously "standard of living," "per capita GNP," and "affluence," the latter defined as the availability of numerous, varied, and refined commodities.[24] In public policy, it would seem, we can either favor that part of the economic machinery whose goal is rising affluence and whose performance is measured as the GNP; or we can favor the production and maintenance of the social and public goods that constitute the quality of life, narrowly understood. I think this is largely true; because it is true, the state of affairs that has so been described provides the most immediate public measure for the reform of technology; because it is true with qualifications only, there is a need first for clarification by way of public deictic discourse and then for more incisive and consequential economic legislation.

To begin with the former task, we must remember from Chapter 18 that the public-private distinction is to be seen in light of the machinery-commodity distinction and that all those public goods that conform to the latter will be secure in the technological society. Specifically, those public goods that are indispensable parts of the productive machinery we will maintain reasonably well, if grudgingly so; this holds of the interstate highway system, air traffic guidance and safety systems, scientific and technical research and education, water supply systems, and so on. Public goods that can be procured as commodities are prospering. Examples are radio and television programs which, as urged above, surely have public and social character. The joys that are now to be had in National Parks clearly could be converted into commodities; and naturally those who consider that an obvious and desirable goal would largely turn the parks over to the corporations that are expert at constructing the necessary machinery of procurement. Some of these public and social concerns are necessary and salutary, others are frivolous or pernicious; they are all *within* the framework of technology. Public policy tends toward a reform *of* technology when it guards and nourishes things in their own right, those which we do not consume but meet with respect and engagement. Setting aside wilderness areas, keeping rivers free-flowing, rehabilitating lakes, saving endangered species, promoting the arts, literature, and the useless sciences, supporting education as a means of achieving world citizenship and the excellence of an engaging life—these measures advance the quality of life appropriate to wealth. Using "quality of life" in this appropriate sense, as I henceforth will be, one can say that there is already in public policy an awareness of the need to decide either in favor of the quality of life at the expense of the standard of living or vice versa. As in private life there are occasions of decision where we affirm or revoke our allegiance to technology, so there are forums of decision in public policy. The debates of the federal and state budgets are the broadest and most consequential of these forums. Narrower ones are hearings on utility siting, on forest management, wilderness areas, etc. What clouds the public awareness of the decisions at issue is the inclination of the advocates of wealth and the quality of life to disguise their concern, so it was said in Chapters 20 and 22, as one for affluence and the standard of living. Not that deictic discourse should be used to the exclusion of technological arguments if the latter are sound. It would be heartless to challenge a legislature to save the timber wolf out of concern for the quality of life or not at all. That may well lead to the extinction of the wolf. Rather one should begin by getting a hearing for deictic discourse.

But eventually one must hope to go further in word and deed, for the alternative between the quality of life and the standard of living is more profound than it at first appears. Although the necessity of choosing one at the expense of the other is due to the limits of our resources, that necessity is more significantly anchored in the general finitude of our world. Even if we had limitless means of transforming our environment, the world will finally have to be of one sort rather than another, and we will accordingly respond to it this way or that. The crucial question is how prominent and far-reaching a position we will secure in our world for engagement. So far I have suggested how we may make and are in fact already making room for the things that center or inspire our focal practices. Clearly, we should go much further in that direction, and, if we did, the face of the technological universe would look much different. There would be more open space, more academies and concert halls, more preservation of historical treasures. And such a shift toward the quality of life would, as urged above, entail a certain shrinking in the production and consumption of commodities. But though the productive machinery of the technological society would so be reduced to a certain extent, its character and tendency would remain intact. This has the consequence, as seen in Chapter 17, that a large proportion of the adult population would have either mindless and stultifying work or, increasingly, no work at all. But in that chapter we also noted that, in the Western world, work is still considered one of the significant ways, perhaps the crucial one, in which we are engaged with the world. It is through work that each of us should be able to secure a free and prosperous life for all of us. Surely the engaging life remains an illusion if no engagement can be found in work.

In certain settings of the pretechnological world, work was an engaging activity and in fact had focal character in a pretechnological sense. This is suggested by the sketch of the wheelwright's work, drawn in Chapter 9 from Sturt's book. Such work was centered on carts and wagons that gathered and disclosed the land and the people. It had a unity of achievement and enjoyment, requiring skill and forging deep personal bonds. But Sturt also makes vivid the fact that as the world of things becomes technologically transformed, its focus, the wheelwright's shop, becomes blurred and finally extinguished. There have been recent attempts to revive the arts and crafts and to make them prevail in a technological setting. People who make custom furniture, weave rugs, throw pots, or establish local bakeries are the practitioners of this new tradition. It has an approximate heading in the expression "local, labor-intensive industry," and I will use this title though it needs clarification. Clearly, that kind of industry exists and is developing, like other reforms of technology, at the inconspicuous margins of public attention, and it contrasts with the centralized and highly or fully automated industry which is paradigmatic of technology. The reform of technology requires that we recognize, politically affirm, and promote this distinction, and accordingly establish a two-sector economy. Let me work out the details of this proposal in two stages. The first clarifies the notion of the two-sector economy, considering similar suggestions that have been made by others. The second elaborates the requirements and consequences that this part of the reform of technology would bring with it.

Galbraith has shown that we already have a two-sector economy. One is composed of a thousand gigantic corporations which dominate half of the economy; the other half is composed of 12 million small firms.[25] There are no clear quantitative criteria, Galbraith says, that would unfailingly allow us to assign a firm to one sector or the other. "But there is a sharp conceptual difference," he insists, "between the enterprise that is fully under the command of an individual and owes its success to this circumstance and the firm which, without entirely excluding the influence of individuals, could not exist without organization."[26] The one sector Galbraith calls the market system, the other the planning system. What accounts for the division of the economy? The planning system has absorbed all business except where it is "unstandardized or geographically dispersed."[27] In those cases large-scale planning and organization are to no avail. In distinguishing the market from the planning system, Galbraith delimits that realm of the economy that has an affinity with the kinds of businesses that the proponents of appropriate technology call for, those that allow for self-determination, work on a small scale, and are likely to adjust their enterprise to local circumstances. But like the proposals of appropriate technology, Galbraith's market system lacks a vital center. It is defined in reaction to the planning system. The former can call its own only what the planning system has been unable to arrogate. Though the tasks of the market system may be recalcitrant to total absorption by centralized and automated machinery, clearly technology will not rest until all tasks are taken over according to its paradigmatic approach. And just as Galbraith's division leaves the domain of the market system insecure, so it leaves the quality of work within it unexamined and unprotected. The task, then, is to elaborate a version of the division that is firmer and more consequential and one that is guided by insight into technology and engagement.

Galbraith is at pains to highlight the distinction between the market and planning systems to expose the neglect that the former has suffered, which in turn has greatly reduced the economic security and rewards in that part of

the economy. Here Galbraith is guided by the liberal democratic, technologically specified notion of social justice.[28] Lewis Mumford, being more critical
of technology, also is more inclined to see the differences that the predomi-
nance of one or the other system makes to the good life. Mumford's distinction, though closely related to Galbraith's, has a large historical sweep. "My
thesis, to put it bluntly," he says, "is that from late neolithic times in the
Near East, right down to our own day, two technologies have recurrently
existed side by side: One authoritarian, the other democratic, the first system-
centered, immensely powerful, but inherently unstable, the other man-
centered, relatively weak, but resourceful and durable."[29] I do not share
Mumford's demonic conception of the modern variant of authoritarian technology, nor can I accept his intimations that it has a tendency toward instability.[30] I think he is right, however, in seeing that democratic technology
proceeds on a surveyable and familiar scale, fosters skill and social union,
and is more respectful of nature.[31]

At an earlier stage of his writing, when Mumford was still more hopeful
of the prospect of technology, he had proposed a division of work that affords
a further clue for the reform of technology. "Work for Automaton and Amateur," he called it.[32] Obviously it parallels his later distinction and constitutes
a modern version of it. It suggests that a critical return to the promise of
technology requires us to deal with both the degradation and elimination of
work.

> The chief benefit the rational use of the machine promises is
> certainly not the elimination of work: what it promises is some-
> thing quite different—the elimination of *servile* work or *slavery:*
> those types of work that deform the body, cramp the mind, deaden
> the spirit.[33]

Automation, as we saw in Chapter 17, extends the promise of this kind of
liberation. It provides work of its own kind, the exacting and demanding
work of its associated technostructure and the work of what Mumford calls
"machine-tending," which is at least not as deadening as strictly divided
labor since it "often calls for alertness, non-repetitive movement, and general
intelligence."[34] But did we not also find in Chapter 17 that the automatic
liberation from servile work would result in the elimination of much if not
most work? In his later article Mumford argues like Galbraith that "significant
forms of work" would remain for democratic technology because they would
remain "unprofitable or technically impossible under mass production: work
dependent upon special skill, knowledge, aesthetic sense."[35] In the earlier
book he even thought that the work of the amateur would remain indispensable
to the automated machine processes themselves because the former alone
could provide the educational basis, the discoveries, and the flexibility of

production that the welfare of the latter would require. But these are precarious hopes.

We must go further then in defining and securing a space for engaging work. As in the case of leisure, one should not think of focal practices as remnants of a pretechnological era but as engagements in their own right which attain a splendor of their own in technology if only we make room for them. The many people who devote themselves to arts and crafts against forbidding economic odds testify to the technologically unsurpassable dignity of work that engages us fully.[36] But as in the case of leisurely focal practices, those of work show real significance if they stand in a discriminating and affirmative relationship to the technological setting of the highly automated industry. Engaging work is largely and inevitably dependent on the latter for tools, machines, energy, materials, transportation, and communication. But it will not adopt technological devices indiscriminately. The criterion will be whether a device is helpful or detrimental to the worker's skill and to the focal depth of the work. By the focal depth of a piece of work or a service I mean the extent to which they tangibly gather and embody the capacities of the worker, the aspirations of the recipient, the natural features and cultural tradition of the local setting. We should affirm the dignity of such engagement by making room for it as work, not as a hobby, not as "Work for the Amateur," the way Mumford has it. We should come to depend on the fruits of that work, and the workers should be respected in our expectations. Thus we can avail ourselves of the circumstance that such work is not only complementary to the disengagement of technology but, being labor intensive, to the technological elimination of labor as well. Local and labor-intensive industry can at least in principle absorb the workers whom automation leaves unemployed.[37]

Though Galbraith's reform proposals divide the economy in a different way and for different reasons than here proposed, one can only agree with his statement of the first requirement of reform: "The emancipation of belief is the most formidable of the tasks of reform and the one on which all else depends."[38] The emancipation in this essay is from the belief that technology must be the rule of life, and the emancipation can be achieved, if at all, through public deictic discourse. In such discourse we must explicate people's misgivings about technology by illuminating them through the device paradigm. We must encourage one another's dedication to focal practices. We must speak up at forums of decision to clarify the fundamental choice at issue and speak on behalf of the quality of life. More specifically regarding work, we must emphasize the benefits of engagement and employment. But extolling these virtues will be misleading if the distinction between wealth and affluence is not made. Without it, the two-sector economy will be taken, as most economic reform proposals rightly are, to be a design in support of affluence. The critics who have invested themselves in technology will quickly see and point out that the two-sector economy will reduce affluence, and they will brand the proposal as mistaken or fraudulent. Hence it must be recognized all along that a reform of technology will diminish affluence but increase wealth.

When social theorists, and philosophers particularly, contemplate the implementation of reform, they often envisage a moratorium on public action during which the reform is publicly proposed, discussed, and accepted. But such an event is unlikely and unnecessary. Political conversations and actions will proceed side by side, unevenly, and sometimes inconsistently. We have already taken political steps in the direction of a reform of technology. But it seems in this case unlikely to me that the reform will get very far without a public deictic conversation catching up with it and then running ahead of it. Only in this way can we achieve a collective affirmation of wealth at the expense of affluence, and only through a collective affirmation can we attain the endurance and resourcefulness required to translate it into a political affirmation, i.e., one which after trials and false starts has found expression and some permanence in our laws and institutions.

Let me emphasize again that the importance of public deictic discourse does not derive from the assumption that it alone will give us the reform of technology that presumably is needed so desperately. Discourse on behalf of focal concerns does not claim to be the most promising entrant in the competition to reform technology. Its significance lies in allowing us to be true to our deepest experiences and aspirations and to make these prevail against technology. Hence we must in the public arena be attentive to the poets and prophets who speak of focal concerns most adequately. The unique things and forces of which they speak are connected by bonds of kinship. When talking about the latter, we speak at some distance about what finally matters, but we also speak about general issues that allow us to agree and to act politically. In fact, where the reform of technology is transacted politically, we not only deal with the generic features and the general well-being of diverse focal practices but also with concerns of reform that have no focal origin and are motivated by more or less articulate conceptions of security, peace, equity, ecology, and the like. I find these difficult or impossible to understand as foundations for the good life; yet it would be sectarian to insist that people not only set out jointly in the right direction but also share the final goal. Principled alliances for reform and common action of diverse groups are possible if there is clarity and tolerance regarding goals. The first measures of reform are the most ambiguous since, though they may all be departures from technology, they can lead to very different final points. Being most ambiguous they can also be accepted by the greatest number of people. As the reforms proceed, the ambiguities are more and more resolved toward an ever smaller subset of the initial array of goals. To the extent that such resolutions become more difficult, reform slows down and finally reaches a point of stability somewhere between the extremes of the strictly technological universe on the one side and a world structured around one great focus on the other. The point of stability is also one of balance between the desire to see one's focal concern prevail and the respect for the focal concerns of others, an equilibrium, i.e., of sympathy and tolerance.

What then is needed and feasible in the political arena to promote the two-sector economy and engaging work in particular? First there must be a collective agreement that the production of certain goods and services is to be entrusted to local, labor-intensive industries. The goods should lend themselves to engaging work and be capable of focal depth. We know from experience that these would include food, furniture, clothing, health care, education, and instruction in music, the arts, and sports.[39] It is not a matter, obviously, of establishing an appropriate industry but of recognizing and promoting politically the one that already exists. Appropriate legislation may have a preamble about the virtues of truly engaging work, but it will not be able to capture such work in criteria and regulations. The law as always must be simpler and broader than the causes it serves. Thus we must agree on serviceable definitions of local ownership and labor intensity, and if these secure for the most part the kind of work that concerns us, nothing more need be done. If the definitions fail, we must tighten them and include criteria of size, consumption of energy, capital investment per worker, or whatever. In addition to broadly delimiting engaging work, legislation must contain mechanisms of support. These must be strong enough to nurture and protect local and labor-intensive industry as a populous and productive sector of the economy. At the same time they should provide for as smooth a transition and rest as lightly on the economy as possible. It would be burdensome to impose prohibitions, quotas, or embargoes on the centralized and automated industry in order to shift production to the other sector. Rather the local and labor-intensive sector should be favored through tax and credit measures to the point where its goods and services prevail in the market through relatively lower prices.[40]

The centralized and more and more automated sector of the economy will retain three tasks. The first is the maintenance and improvement of the infrastructure of transportation, utilities, and communication. The second is the production of certain goods and services such as machine tools, cars, appliances, raw materials, insurance, and finance. The third is research and development. In this sector we affirm and advance today's inevitably technological setting of the human condition. But technology should be taken here as the context, not the rule or center, of life. Thus we have to strive in the large for the perfection and simplification of technology that a person, engaged in a focal practice, will effect in the private sphere.

These hints raise as many questions as they answer. The divisions that have been drawn leave parts of the economy between the two sectors. There are problems of foreign trade and of internal, regional imbalances, problems of transition, coordination, and feasibility. Perhaps they are insuperable. They should, however, not be thought so because of the supposed court of last appeal to which mainstream economists are wont to resort: the costs of such changes and people's unwillingness to change. The arguments that have been put forward about the definiteness and vacuity of the good life that technology has procured, about people's uneasiness regarding technology, about their readiness for an engaging way of life, about the economic discretion that wealth provides as opposed to affluence, all these arguments may be flawed; but they have to be met in their own right before the possibility of reforming technology publicly and economically can be rejected.

We can summarize the character of the world in which technology has been reformed by adapting remarks of Duane Elgin's which in turn have been inspired ecologically. He has proposed a world that is balanced between differentiation and integration or diversity and connectedness and so avoids both monotony and chaos.[41] Clearly, the local and labor-intensive industry would serve the former goals and the centralized and automated industry the latter. But this summary, along with the previous features, still lacks consideration of two crucial public problems: the fate of the large cities and of social justice. Here, as in the case of the economy, the tasks are limited: to show how from the viewpoint of technology and engagement paths become visible toward more vital cities and a more just society.

The big cities constitute the eminently technological spaces. They grew up with modern technology as the standard human dwelling places. Technology made them possible and needs them. They contain the greater and, globally, a still growing share of the population. They harbor the inventive and productive forces of technology. They exhibit most starkly the division between labor and leisure with its gigantic daily transition of commuting. Life in the big cities is marked, as Louis Wirth has emphasized, by the "superficiality, anonymity, and the transitory character of urban social relations," and so manifests paradigmatically what we found disturbing about the rule of technology.[42]

The components of the currently perfect technological city are obvious. The leisure area is composed of suburbs where, as remarked in Chapter 22, we find a natural veneer of cedar shakes and lawns layered over a thoroughly technological substructure. Labor is most typically housed in the downtown high-rise office buildings which, as noted in Chapter 11, constitute imposing and disengaged containers of technological space. The realms of leisure and labor are connected by a rapid and convenient transportation link. But the technological version of the city is unstable in principle and in fact. It is so in principle because, so we saw in Chapter 10, the consumption of commodities can be stylized, to be sure, in the image of the household in the manor or on the ranch. But consumption needs neither household nor family and fits, when suitably refined and attenuated, into an apartment as well as a single family home. And the machinery of labor can change radically in size and location as more efficient modes of procurement are discovered and developed. The technological city is unstable in fact because nowhere has technology failed its own standards more obviously and painfully than in the overall organization of the urban setting. That is particularly true in this country. Acting technologically, we have failed for the most part to procure clean air, security, and ease of transportation for ourselves. And the cities contain in the starkest and most concentrated forms the people with whom the broad middle class has been unconcerned to share the standard blessings of technology.

These instabilities and imbalances, however, are less than scandalous from the technological point of view. We have seen in Chapter 18 that consumption has an intrinsic tendency toward privacy, and so the decay of civility and of the public realm is not thought to be a crucial danger as long as it does not threaten the integrity of private consumption and the functioning and expansion of the productive machinery. When a point of such danger is approached, the metadevice of politics comes into play and initiates the necessary repairs. But these instabilities of principle and fact do scandalize one who is concerned about the loss of the public and bodily dimensions of our lives. A corresponding reform must wrest public spaces that can be bodily inhabited from crime and from technology. Violent crime can be combated technologically through the establishment of more or less private fortresses and thus only through the surrender of the public domain. If the latter is to be regained for civility, it is not enough to ward off the forces of crime; they must be reconciled with the body politic, and that involves the question of social justice to which I will turn in a moment.

The big cities still contain public places. But most of them are bequests of early modern or pretechnological times. Surprisingly, however, the large technological structures that shape the urban setting have a native countertendency to technology. David P. Billington, as we saw in Chapter 11, contrasts their enduring, massive, site-specific, and slowly evolving nature with the machines that have the transient, mobile, and ubiquitous character of technological devices. But as Billington also points out, structures can be standardized, thoughtless, and impenetrable, impressive in a brute and imposing manner that repels inhabitation and appropriation.[43] The curtain-wall skyscraper is the archetype of this kind of structure. It makes space technologically available. It is essentially a device for human storage. The all but overwhelming tendency in the way the inner cities change is toward the expansion of the machinery that furnishes technologically available space. To counteract this tendency and to recover public and inhabitable spaces in the city, three linked turns must be taken.

The first consists, as Billington urges, in opening up structures such as "roads, bridges, terminals, dams, harbors, waterworks, power plants, office towers, and public housing blocks."[44] To open them up is to give them an intelligible design, to adjust them to their location, and above all to invite humans to walk along, across, and through them, to rest and linger in them, and to allow people to comprehend the structures from various angles and at various levels. This provides for an appropriation of structures which, like running, is both simple and profound. It is a minimal requirement to demand of a structure that it welcome us as bodily creatures, moving about and perceiving things in our own right. Yet measured and attentive walking has since the beginning of architecture been the appropriate human response to great buildings.

But an aggregate of intelligible and accessible structures is not yet a city in the eminent sense. As Kent C. Bloomer and Charles W. Moore point out, a city is a memorable place if it is oriented by nature, history, divinity, or a great and common task.[45] A memorable place is a focal thing writ large. It gathers and focuses the crucial dimensions of the world. Orientation in the inner cities does not have to be invented or produced; it needs discovery and nurture, the restoration of historic buildings and the preservation of open space around them, the recovery of green areas along river banks and lake shores, and the connection of these focal points through pleasant walkways. But especially in places where this second turn has been taken with care and on a grand scale it leaves one vaguely dissatisfied. Why? There are cities, especially in Europe, where the churches, palaces, city gates, and convents have been restored with lavish attention, where the inner city has been made a pedestrian enclave and adorned with paintings, benches, varied pavements, bridges, and fountains. People are milling and sitting about, visiting museums, admiring cathedrals, taking pictures, eating, shopping, going to concerts and plays. Is this not an excellent life and urban culture at its best? It would be zealotry to deny the real pleasures and profound experiences that are to be had in such a setting. Still, it has a passive and distracting air about it. To see it more clearly one must distinguish between culture as scenery and culture as enactment. Culture as scenery is something that is taken in by looking or listening. However different the circumstances from which buildings, paintings, and concertos have arisen, they are just so many cultural values or attractions. They have different rankings as established by art history and tourism, but they are all "taken in" the same inconsequential way. A Greek temple, a medieval castle, a baroque orchestral suite were created and appropriated in totally different but equally engaging ways, that is to say, they were enacted as culture. They are now enjoyed in one and the same passive manner. They have congealed into magnificent stages on which nothing of consequence is enacted. The final turn then that we must take toward a life of public excellence is one that encourages the enactment of culture. As said before, this cannot be done as an affair of the state. What we can do is to reshape our cities so that they provide prominent and thoughtfully designed places for the exercise of the various focal practices that have engaged us, for sports, music, the arts, worship, and engaging work.[46]

Finally, we come to the problem of social justice. Unlike focal practices that are presently confined to the margins and shadows of the technological society, social justice needs no special recollection and affirmation. It is a clear and central concern of the liberal democratic tradition. What the reform of technology has to contribute to this problem is the consideration of the obstacles and opportunities that come into relief once the pattern of technology and its decisive counterforces are recognized. The crucial obstacle or, better, deflection of social equality derives from the fact, first, that liberal democracy allowed technology to specify the kind of life to be secured for all, and, second, that technology, once its rule was unchallenged, put the historically given inequality in the service of its stability and advancement. More specifically and less misleading, once the broad middle class that should have been the basis of social reforms had agreed upon the technological approach to reality, its members thought, mistakenly, that a hierarchy of inequality would provide for them individually the ladder to the fullest blessings of technology. That was the argument of Chapters 13–16. Only a cataclysmic turn of economic events would be able to rupture the tie between technology and inequality that we find in Western democracies.[47] The energy crisis might bring about such a turn, but it is not likely as suggested in Chapter 19. However, instead of seeing the hold that technology has on the social structure being broken through an external and violent blow, we may loosen it by revoking from within our allegiance to technology. Equality then becomes accessible in a new way. And such an emancipation from technology is of course the goal of reform.

What does that mean concretely? If we center ourselves in focal practices, the worth of our lives will no longer be measured by the standard of living. The standard of excellence is now wealth of engagement. Thus the standard of living loses both its constricting and invidious forces. In losing the former, it frees the means for social reform; in losing the latter it yields to an ideal of excellence that is more generally affordable and attainable. The culture of the table in the early modern period used to be the property of all people, and the contributions of the relatively poor to this heritage are as noble as those of the rich.[48] Running is open to everyone; so is gardening, music, and poetry. Wealth, of course, requires a certain level of affluence, one that is denied at least to those that the government recognizes as poor. To provide for them the standard of living that is needed for an engaging life, affluence must be shifted from the middle to the lower class. This can only be done if enough of us have come to understand the good life as one of wealth so that we gladly let go of the affluence that is in excess of wealth and a distraction to it. And as suggested in Chapter 21, the focal thing that graces our lives with wealth and enthusiasm will issue in sympathy as well. Thus the reduction of affluence in one's life springs not only from a concern to strengthen one's personal focal practice but also from a desire to share that possibility with others. Those others are the people in this country, but they are the poor around the globe as well.

These suggestions, drawn from the analysis of technology and the experience of engagement, are mere hints, of course. But they shed new light, I believe, on a problem that has become puzzling and untractable within the liberal democratic tradition. They are essentially consonant, however, with the proposals to achieve greater social justice as they have been formulated by the best proponents of that tradition, for example, Rawls, Thurow, Galbraith. They bring into relief the center or pivot that remains indistinct in the liberal design. As in the case of the two-sector economy, the renewal of the cities and the advancement of social justice must proceed in an interplay of collective affirmation and legislation. Here too a collective affirmation must provide the basis for the experiments and trials that we must pass through to attain a political affirmation of the truly civic and just society.

26   The Recovery of the Promise of Technology

The promise of technology was one of liberty and prosperity. But the brilliance and joy of life that are implied in the promise have not come about in spite of two centuries of gigantic efforts. The technological measures that have freed us from hunger, disease, and illiteracy have become part of the inconspicuous periphery of everyday life. The commodities that fill the center of our lives with entertainment and diversion gratify us in a passing and shallow way. We take justified pride in the intricacy and power of the technological machinery that we have constructed and continue to improve. But this confidence about the means goes hand in hand with great diffidence about the ends in which they issue.

There is no doubt that modern technology has brought forth the most complex and the most imposing creations in human history. The ingenuity, coordination, and devotion that have come to be embodied in the technological achievements are of epochal rank and deserve admiration. One who plays an authentic role in these accomplishments can, as did the engineers of Tracy Kidder's story, take satisfaction simply in the completion of a singularly demanding task. But to be human is to recognize and appropriate one's world. Hence the context of the uses to which technological work is devoted cannot in the end be denied. There is satisfaction to be had in this wider scope as well. Medical technology provides healing and wholeness where otherwise there would be insufferable pain and crippling disfiguration. Media technology allows us to consider all things and to be enlightened about the world in an intelligent and compassionate way. But once restored to health and well informed, we are now able to take up life. And here it is no good to cling to the preparatory and the exceptional. Rather we must ask: What kind of life have we secured for ourselves *typically and willingly?* Can engineers, managers, lawyers, and all the other members of the technostructure be content in their work if they must admit that it serves a life that often is ruled at its center by triviality and frivolity? Sometimes there is a temptation to embrace openly and proudly what Langdon Winner has called the rule of instrumentality.[1] One wants to elevate the machinery to the central and crucial position and reduce the so-called ends to mere obstacles and occasions for the development and celebration of technological devices. We would then welcome accidents and premature deaths because they allow us to maintain and improve an impressive insurance industry which in turn would give us a reason to construct something as breathtaking as the Sears Tower. We would be glad of the boredom that quickly overtakes the latest video games because it is the spur to designing still more sophisticated games which in turn permits us to search for more sophisticated computer technology. Cancer would be considered a blessing because it occasions an admirable medical technology. But at least in our reflective moments we hold to the traditional understanding of means and ends.[2]

Not only the machinery of technology and the work out of which it grew are being demeaned through the kind of consumption that is typically final and central today. There is a related degradation of commodities too. Normally earthbound people who take a charter flight to a distant country are visibly enthralled by the power and speed of the takeoff and openly appreciate the care they receive in flight. Yet there is scarcely more sullen and surly, if not sober, company than one composed of people who once more are jetting from here to there. A shower in the routine of technological life is a chore to be done along with brushing one's teeth and taking the garbage out. But after a run through cold, wet, and muddy conditions, a shower is an ablution that heals and elevates.

The reform of technology that has been suggested so far would prune back the excesses of technology and restrict it to a supporting role. That suggestion does not stem from ill will toward technology but from the experience that there are forces that rightfully claim our engagement and truly grace our lives and from the concomitant experience that to procure these things technologically is to eviscerate them; finally, it springs from the experience that the joys that technology is able to furnish seem to have a parasitic and voracious character: they require as a contrast pretechnological limits and contours, and they seem to draw vitality from the firmness of pretechnological life by devouring and displacing it. But the focal things and practices that we have considered in Chapters 23 and 24 are not pretechnological, i.e., mere remnants of an earlier culture. Nor are they antitechnological, i.e., practices that defy or reject technology. Rather they unfold their significance in an affirmative and intelligent acceptance of technology. We may call them metatechnological things and practices. As such they provide an enduring counterposition to technology. They provide a contrast against which the experience of specifically technological liberty and prosperity remains alive and appreciated. Not only do focal concerns attain their proper splendor in the context of technology;

the context of technology too is restored to the dignity of its original promise through the focal concerns at its center.

Let me make the point more concrete through examples first and more general reflections then. As has been hinted just now, if we inhabit a place faithfully and know its features and seasons from bodily appropriation, then to rise high above it and to leave it at an instant is to regain it in a larger and illuminating context. Doing bodily battle with the heat of the day and chill of night, with the steepness and hardness of the ground in hiking or running teaches one to marvel at the ease and assuredness of technological comforts.[3] For one who practices a sport or plays an instrument, it is an inspiring and gratefully accepted experience to see the best perform on television. Given the counterweight of an engaging practice, televised performances need no brutality, carnal danger, promises of new records, or the spice of financial rewards for which the performers are made to fight.

Generally, the local and bodily intensity of focal engagements preserves our sensitivity for the wide-ranging and effortless way in which technology provides a context of security, comfort, and enlightenment. It also sharpens our sensitivity; engagement provides resonance for those commodities that represent and support excellence, and, finding no echo in the trivial and frivolous, it ignores banal commodities and helps to reduce them. So counterbalanced, technology can fulfill the promise of a new kind of freedom and richness. If our lives are centered in a focal concern, technology uniquely opens up the depth and extent of the world and allows us to be genuine world citizens. It frees us from the accidental limits of shortness of time, lack of equipment, or weakness of health so that we can turn to the great things of the world in their own right. It frees us for the genuine limits of our endurance, fortitude, and fidelity; and if we fail, we fail where we ought to fail and where we can hope to grow.

An important part of genuine world citizenship today is scientific and technological literacy. Here too one may hope that an appreciation of the force of technology, nourished by metatechnological practices, would inspire the attention and dedication that are needed to appropriate the scientific and engineering principles on which the technological machinery rests. Neither the resentful, if dutiful, service to the technological machinery that we discharge in labor nor the distracted pleasure of consumption are conducive to the study of technology. But the voluntary discipline that one exercises in a focal practice, the sustained appreciation of technology, and the desire to join the two in order to regain the cosmopolitan franchise may be helpful to the pursuit of scientific and technological education.

What, in conclusion, is the likelihood of a vigorous and visible reform of technology? Or more generally, what will likely be the fate of technology? There is one point that I want to insist on and another that I feel easy about. I want to insist that the destiny of the focal things, the one thing that matters should one emerge at length, is the fulcrum of change. We should measure the significance of the developments about us by the degree to which focal concerns are beginning to flourish openly or continue to live in hiding. All other changes will be variants of technological concerns. Not that the latter are unimportant. The ultimate calamity would be the complete destruction of technology; it would be the eradication of all hope. The preservation and improvement of technology, however, is a penultimate success at best. But I am not anxious about whether focal concerns will in fact prosper. One would rightly be nervous about the possibility that a great thing may fail accidentally, that the kingdom may be lost for want of a nail. But our focal concern will languish or prosper for essential reasons. I hope it will prevail, and it sustains my hope.

Notes

ACKNOWLEDGMENTS

1. The preparatory stages of my arguments are evident from my essays listed below. Their material is incorporated in this volume.

"Technology and Reality," *Man and World* 4 (1971):59–69.

"Orientation in Technology," *Philosophy Today* 16 (1972):135–47.

"Functionalism in Science and Technology," in *Proceedings of the XVth World Congress of Philosophy* (Sofia, Bulgaria, 1973–75), 6:31–36.

"Mind, Body, and World," *Philosophical Forum* 8 (1976):68–86.

"The Explanation of Technology," *Research in Philosophy and Technology* 1 (1978):99–118.

"Freedom and Determinism in a Technological Setting," *Research in Philosophy and Technology* 2 (1979):79–90.

"Should Montana Share Its Coal? Technology and Public Policy," *Research in Philosophy and Technology* 3 (1980):287–311.

"Review of William Barrett, *The Illusion of Technique*," *Man and World* 13 (1980):458–65.

"Review of Don Ihde, *Technics and Praxis*," *Philosophical Topics* 12 (1982):190–94.

"Review of Edward G. Ballard, *Man and Technology* and of Donald M. Borchert and David Stewart, eds., *Being Human in a Technological Age*," *Man and World* 15 (1982):107–15.

"Technology and Nature in Europe and America," in *International Dimensions of the Environmental Crisis*, ed. Richard N. Barrett (Boulder, Colo., 1982), pp. 3–20.

"The Good Life and Appropriate Technology," *Research in Philosophy and Technology* 6 (1983):11–19.

"Technology and Democracy," *Research in Philosophy and Technology* 7 (1984).

CHAPTER 1

1. See Aristotle, *Nicomachean Ethics*, Book 10, chapters 7 and 8. I will also use "theory" to designate the enterprise of working out such a final vision.

2. On this phenomenon see Martin Heidegger, *Being and Time*, trans. John Macquarrie and Edward Robinson (New York, 1962), pp. 210–24.

3. The founder of this approach is Immanuel Kant. A more recent monument of it is *The Linguistic Turn*, ed. Richard Rorty (Chicago, 1967).

CHAPTER 2

1. Carl Mitcham begins his survey of "Types of Technology" by distinguishing this sense as the narrow and engineering sense from the broad social science sense. See *Research in Philosophy and Technology* 1 (1978):229–31. Further discussion of Mitcham's survey in Chapter 3 below.

2. Charles Suskind's *Understanding Technology* (Baltimore, 1973) is guided by this sense and an example of the very tentative orientation such a sense provides.

3. In this vein W. Norris Clarke has wondered "what detailed or precise contributions philosophers as such can make to the problem of technology." See his

"Reflections on the 15th World Congress of Philosophy," *International Philosophical Quarterly* 14 (1974):117. See my "Orientation in Technology," *Philosophy Today* 16 (1972):135–36. Arguments for the need of philosophy of technology along with a survey of approaches has been provided by Marx W. Wartofsky in "Philosophy of Technology," in *Current Research in Philosophy of Science,* ed. Peter D. Asquith and Henry E. Kyburg, Jr. (East Lansing, Mich., 1979), pp. 171–84.

4. Such as "the space age," "the postindustrial society," "the atomic age," "future shock," "the technetronic age," "the new industrial state," and others.

5. A comprehensive study of this position has been provided by Langdon Winner, *Autonomous Technology: Technics-Out-of-Control as a Theme in Political Thought* (Cambridge, Mass., 1977). See also his remarks on typologies of technology, pp. 176–77.

6. See Carl Mitcham and Robert Mackey, "Introduction: Technology as a Philosophical Problem," in *Philosophy and Technology,* ed. Mitcham and Mackey (New York, 1972), pp. 5–7; Donald W. Shriver, Jr., "Man and His Machines: Four Angles of Vision," *Technology and Culture* 13 (1972):534–38.

7. See Samuel C. Florman, "In Praise of Technology," *Harper's Magazine* 251 (November 1975):53–72.

8. See William Leiss, "The Social Consequences of Technological Progress: Critical Comments on Recent Theories," *Canadian Public Administration* 13 (1970): 248–53.

9. See Jacques Ellul, *The Technological Society,* trans. John Wilkinson (New York, 1964), pp. 18–22.

10. See Mitcham and Mackey, "Jacques Ellul and the Technological Society," *Philosophy Today* 15 (1971):102–21.

11. According to Ellul's explicit framework, the power and peculiarity of modern technique become apparent in the analyses of the encounter between the technical phenomenon and society (pp. 61–64). That framework stipulates society as an independent force that interacts with technology. But in the actual analyses, society appears as an entirely passive partner in the interaction with technique. See Mitcham and Mackey, "Jacques Ellul," pp. 107–10.

12. See Ellul, p. 20.

13. Ibid., pp. xxv, 21, 133–47, 171–77, 263–66, 388. See Mitcham and Mackey, "Jacques Ellul," pp. 111–12.

14. See Ellul, pp. 79–147.

15. See Florman, "In Praise of Technology" and Mitcham and Mackey's list of reviews of Ellul in "Jacques Ellul," p. 120, n. 5.

16. John Kenneth Galbraith, *The New Industrial State,* 2d ed. (Boston, 1972). See Ellul, pp. 183–227 and 248–318.

17. Winner's book (n. 5 above) is important in elaborating the force of Ellul's position through a comprehensive and circumspective analysis of consonant and competing findings by other authors.

18. See Mitcham and Mackey, "Introduction," pp. 4–5.

19. Ibid., pp. 2–4.

20. See Shriver, pp. 532–34.

21. This issue and the following ones are examined in detail in Chapters 13–16 below.

22. See Leiss, "The Social Consequences."

23. See Shriver, pp. 538–41.

24. See Paul T. Durbin, "Technology and Values: A Philosopher's Perspective," *Technology and Culture* 13 (1972):556–76.

25. See Shriver, pp. 541–47. An example is Victor C. Ferkiss, *Technological Man: The Myth and the Reality* (New York, 1969).

CHAPTER 3

1. See n. 1 of Chapter 2. In "Philosophy of Technology" (*A Guide to the Culture of Science, Technology, and Medicine,* ed. Paul T. Durbin [New York, 1980], pp. 282–363), Mitcham has further elaborated the significance of his typology and used it to review the pertinent literature. This article presents the best survey of the field to date.

2. See Langdon Winner's review in *Science* 102 (October 6, 1978):44–45.

3. See Mitcham, "Types of Technology," p. 232.

4. Ibid.

5. Hannah Arendt, *The Human Condition* (Chicago, 1958).

6. See Mitcham, "Types of Technology," pp. 233, 234, and n. 11 on p. 271. On p. 232 he speaks of "a structural and/or phenomenological analysis." What phenomenologists, at one important level of investigation, are concerned with are *éide* or essences.

7. See Jacques Ellul, *The Technological Society,* trans. John Wilkinson (New York, 1964), p. 43; Martin Heidegger, *The Question Concerning Technology,* trans. William Lovitt (New York, 1977), pp. 14–31; William Leiss, *The Domination of Nature* (New York, 1972).

8. See Mitcham, "Philosophy and the History of Technology," in *The History and Philosophy of Technology,* ed. George Bugliarello (Urbana, Ill., 1979), 163–201.

9. See Mitcham, "Types of Technology," p. 233.

10. Ibid., p. 242.

11. Ibid., p. 258.

12. Ibid., p. 260.

13. Ibid., p. 259. Technology-as-volition is also important as a focus of traditional scholarship. See Mitcham and Jim Grote, "Philosophy of Technology," in *Encyclopedia of Bioethics,* ed. Warren T. Reich (New York, 1978), p. 1620.

CHAPTER 4

1. See G. Ray Funkhouser, "Public Understanding of Science: The Data We Have," in *Workshop on "Goals and Methods of Assessing the Public's Understanding of Science"* (University Park, Pa., 1973), pp. 11–18; Amitai Etzioni and Clyde Nunn, "The Public Appreciation of Science in Contemporary America," *Daedalus* 103, no. 3 (Summer 1974):201; L. John Martin, "Science and the Successful Society," *Public Opinion* 4 (June/July 1981):19 and 55.

2. See Etzioni and Nunn, pp. 195–96.

3. See Todd R. La Porte and Daniel Metlay, "Technology Observed: Attitudes of a Wary Public," *Science,* 188 (April 11, 1975):121–27; Nicholas Wade, "Contrary to Fears, Public is High on Science," *Science* 199 (March 31, 1978):1421.

4. See Funkhouser, pp. 18–31; La Porte and Metlay, p. 122; Wade, pp. 1420–21; Etzioni and Nunn, pp. 191–95; Nunn, "Is There a Crisis of Confidence in Science?" *Science* 198 (December 9, 1977):995; Martin, p. 17.

5. Funkhouser, p. 24; Etzioni and Nunn, pp. 196–97.

6. See Clyde Z. Nunn, John Kosa, and Joel J. Alpert, "Causal Locus of Illness and Adaptation to Family Disruptions," *Journal for the Scientific Study of Religion* 7 (1968):210–18. Note also this summary provided by Daniel Yankelovich:

> In 1970, 30% of the public believed that "everything has a logical sci-entific explanation"; another 42% said they used to believe that all the mysteries of life would eventually be explained by science but now believed that some things could only be understood in a non-rational way; 28% said they believed that life as we know it is controlled by "strange and mysterious forces that decide our fate." It is interesting to note the direction of the changes that have occurred in these perspectives within the last decade. There has been a modest reduction in the size of the group believing that everything has a logical scientific explanation (30% to 27%), while the group of people saying they used to believe that the mysteries of life would eventually be explained by science, but no longer do, grew from 42% to 48%.

In "Changing Public Attitudes to Science and the Quality of Life," *Science, Technology, and Human Values* 7 (Spring 1982):25.

7. Such an equipoise is not unlike John Rawls's "reflective equilibrium." See *A Theory of Justice* (Cambridge, Mass., 1971), pp. 20–21, 48–51.

8. See Yankelovich, *New Rules* (Toronto, 1982), p. 52; and "Changing Public Attitudes," pp. 23 and 26–27.

CHAPTER 5

1. See H. J. Phaff, M. W. Miller, and E. M. Mark, *The Life of Yeasts* (Cambridge, Mass., 1966).

2. Ibid., p. 2.

3. See M. A. Amerine and M. A. Joslyn, *Table Wines: The Technology of Their Production,* 2d ed. (Berkeley, Calif., 1970), p. 177.

4. See Phaff et al., p. 4; Amerine and Joslyn, pp. 177–78.

5. See Phaff et al., pp. 4–5.

6. Ibid., pp. 5–6; and Amerine and Joslyn, pp. 178–80.

7. See Phaff et al., pp. 5–6; Amerine and Joslyn, p. 178 n. 2.

8. In the fourth book of *Metaphysics*.

9. In the transcendental deduction of the pure concepts of understanding in the *Critique of Pure Reason*.

10. See Kant, *Critique of Pure Reason*, A 321–32; Aristotle, *Posterior Analytics,* Book 2, chapters 11 and 12 and throughout the *Analytics*.

11. See Carl G. Hempel, *Aspects of Scientific Explanation* (New York, 1965), pp. 331–496.

12. This explanation sketch is problematic in at least two ways. (1) The second premise contains more than is required for a deduction, namely, something like a bridge law or a redescription of the explanandum, and the latter are imperfect at best since must is more than a sugar solution. (2) The conclusion suffers from similar problems since wine is more than a mixture of water and alcohol and more than must in which (part of) the sugar has been converted into alcohol. Some of these problems will be addressed in the following chapter.

13. See Michael Friedman, "Explanation and Scientific Understanding," *Journal of Philosophy* 71 (1974):16–19.

14. See Ernan McMullin, "Structural Explanation," *American Philosophical Quarterly* 15 (1978):147.

CHAPTER 6

1. Such an event will always only violate, or fall outside of, some of the laws of nature as they are presently known. If it violated them all at once, it could not be understood or experienced by us in any sense.

2. For surveys of this controversy see Rudolph H. Weingartner, "The Quarrel about Historical Explanation [1961]," *Philosophical Problems of Science and Technology,* ed. Alex C. Michalos (Boston, 1974), pp. 165–80; and Howard Cohen, "*Das Verstehen* and Historical Knowledge," *American Philosophical Quarterly* 10 (1973):299–306.

3. See Carl G. Hempel, *Aspects of Scientific Explanation* (New York, 1965), pp. 334, 351, 361, 421–22; and Danny Steinberg, "Nickles on Intensionality and the Covering Law Model," *Philosophy of Science* 40 (1973):406.

4. See Michael E. Levin and Margarita Rosa Levin, "Flagpoles, Shadows and Deductive Explanation," *Philosophical Studies* 32 (1977):293–99.

5. See Hempel, p. 337.

6. See Wesley C. Salmon, "Theoretical Explanation," in *Explanation,* ed. Stephan Körner (New Haven, 1975), pp. 118–45. As Salmon points out, factors can be relevant to the occurrence of an event and therefore have explanatory power even when they do not suggest that the event was to be expected. This is so in certain statistical or inductive explanations. These are not specifically discussed here since the crucial points under consideration apply, *mutatis mutandis,* to them as well.

7. See Levin and Levin; and also Peter Achinstein, "The Object of Explanation," in Körner, pp. 1–45; Paul Snyder, *Toward One Science* (New York, 1978), pp. 71–73, 91–96.

8. The example is adapted from Levin and Levin and ultimately goes back to Bromberger.

9. This is Levin and Levin's thesis.

10. See Marx W. Wartofsky, "Is Science Rational?" in *Science, Technology, and Freedom,* ed. Willis H. Truitt and T. W. Graham Solomons (Boston, 1974), pp. 204–6.

11. After the breakthrough, it may even be difficult to see the original problem. See Wartofsky, "All Fall Down: The Development of the Concept of Motion from Aristotle to Galileo," in *Conceptual Foundations of Scientific Thought* (New York, 1968), pp. 419–73, pp. 449 and 456 in particular. See also Alasdair MacIntyre, *After Virtue* (Notre Dame, Ind., 1981), pp. 89–91.

12. See Thomas S. Kuhn, *The Structure of Scientific Revolutions,* 2d ed. (Chicago, 1970); also "Logic of Discovery or Psychology of Research?" in *Criticism and the Growth of Knowledge,* ed. Imre Lakatos and Alan Musgrave (Cambridge, 1970), pp. 1–23; and "Reflections on my Critics," ibid., pp. 231–78.

13. See Paul Feyerabend, "Consolations for the Specialist," in Lakatos and Musgrave, p. 202. Strictly speaking, incommensurability would make even change unnoticeable and unstatable.

14. Kuhn sees the ontological question but does not believe that a clear answer can be given. See his "Reflections," p. 265; and *Scientific Revolutions,* pp. 184 and 206–7.

15. With Feyerabend's exception, this is stressed in one way or another by all contributors to the Lakatos and Musgrave anthology.

16. For details see Wartofsky's "All Fall Down." Wartofsky does not share the thesis presently to be developed. But much of his account is compatible with it and illustrates it.

17. Strictly speaking, the revolutionary scientist's work also has deictic significance. We may call it *global* deictic significance to distinguish it from the poet's singular deictic explanations.

CHAPTER 7

1. For a more detailed and qualified account of the relation of modern science and technology, see Mario Bunge, "Toward a Philosophy of Technology," in *Philosophy and Technology,* ed. Carl Mitcham and Robert Mackey (New York, 1972), pp. 62–76.

2. For details see Thomas S. Kuhn, *The Structure of Scientific Revolutions,* 2d ed. (Chicago, 1970); and Imre Lakatos, "Falsification and the Methodology of Scientific Research Programmes," in *Criticism and the Growth of Knowledge,* ed. Imre Lakatos and Alan Musgrave (Cambridge, 1970), pp. 91–196.

3. See Chapter 10 for further illustration and discussion.

4. See Gerald Holton, "On Being Caught between Dionysians and Apollonians," *Daedalus* 103, no. 3 (Summer 1974):65–81. Judging on the evidence mentioned in Chapter 4, the public attitude at large is soberly positive.

5. Sometimes liberation harbors new enslavement. See Paul K. Feyerabend, "On the Improvement of the Sciences and the Arts, and the Possible Identity of the Two," in *Boston Studies in the Philosophy of Science,* ed. Robert S. Cohen and Marx W. Wartofsky, (Dordrecht, 1967), 3:387–415.

6. See Paolo Rossi, *Philosophy, Technology and the Arts in the Early Modern Era,* trans. Salvator Attanasio (New York, 1970); and Wartofsky, "Is Science Rational?" in *Science, Technology, and Freedom,* ed. Willis H. Truit and T. W. Graham Solomons (Boston, 1974), pp. 202–10.

7. For arguments pro and con see the selections by Leo Tolstoy, Jacob Bronowski, Karl Deutsch, Joseph Wood Krutch, and Herbert J. Muller in *The New Technology and Values,* ed. John G. Burke (Belmont, Calif., 1966), pp. 24–49. For discussion see Wartofsky, *Conceptual Foundations of Scientific Thought* (New York, 1968), pp. 403–15.

8. See José M. R. Delgado, *Physical Control of the Mind: Toward a Psychocivilized Society* (New York, 1969); B. F. Skinner, *Beyond Freedom and Dignity* (New York, 1971); and R. Buckminster Fuller, *Operating Manual for Spaceship Earth* (New York, n.d. [first published in 1969]).

9. See his "On the Improvement of the Sciences and the Arts," p. 404.

10. For illustrations, see n. 7 above.

11. See Hans Jonas, "The Scientific and Technological Revolutions: Their History and Meaning," *Philosophy Today* 15 (1971):76–101. (A revised version is given in Jonas's *Philosophical Essays* [Englewood Cliffs, N.J., 1974], pp. 45–80.)

12. See Boris Hessen, "The Social and Economic Roots of Newton's Principia," in Truitt and Solomons, pp. 89–99.

13. Paul T. Durbin, "Toward a Social Philosophy of Technology," *Research in Philosophy and Technology* 1 (1978):67–97.

14. Joseph Agassi, "The Confusion between Science and Technology in the Standard Philosophies of Science," *Technology and Culture* 7 (1966):348–66. For Bunge see n. 1 above.

15. Science must be something more than an instrument if it has the kind of power Jonas ascribes to it. He speaks in fact of "the ontological breakthrough" at the beginning of the modern age and modern science (p. 77). But Jonas speaks like an instrumentalist when he compares the scientific view with the view of the life world (pp. 87, 88–89, 90). Jonas is similarly divided on the question of whether the new scientific world view has dissolved human spontaneity or rendered it omnipotent (pp. 92–94).

CHAPTER 8

1. See Richard Rorty, "Keeping Philosophy Pure," *Yale Review* 65 (1976): 342, 352. Thomas S. Kuhn is also concerned with the inaccessibility of paradigms though it is usually of a different sort; the paradigm is not invisible but inaccessible to a formulation in a set of rules. See *The Structure of Scientific Revolutions*, 2d ed. (Chicago, 1970), pp. 191–98. Langdon Winner stresses the invisibility of technology in *Autonomous Technology* (Cambridge, Mass., 1977), p. 6.

2. See Francis Bacon, *The New Organon and Related Writings*, ed. Fulton H. Anderson (Indianapolis, 1960), pp. 3–4; René Descartes, *Discourse on Method*, trans. Laurence J. Lafleur (Indianapolis, 1956), pp. 4, 39.

3. See Bacon, *The New Organon*, p. 16.

4. See Descartes, *Discourse*, p. 40.

5. For background and a discussion of this notion, see William Leiss, *The Domination of Nature* (New York, 1972).

6. See Descartes, *Discourse*, p. 40.

7. Quoted by Mulford Q. Sibley in *Technology and Utopian Thought* (Minneapolis, 1971), p. 40.

8. See Karl Polanyi, *The Great Transformation* (New York, 1944).

9. See Granville Stuart, *Forty Years on the Frontier*, ed. Paul C. Phillips (Cleveland, 1925), 1:159.

10. Ibid., p. 160.

11. Ibid., p. 161.

12. See Eugene S. Ferguson, "The American-ness of American Technology," *Technology and Culture* 20 (1979):16.

13. Ibid. For a reflective and perceptive statement of the promise of technology see Langdon Gilkey, "The Religious Dilemma of a Scientific Culture," in *Being Human in a Technological Age*, ed. Donald M. Borchert and David Stewart (Athens, Ohio, 1979), pp. 74–78. As the second quotation from Ferguson indicates, in the United States particularly the notion of democracy and technology became intertwined. See Hugo A. Meier, "Technology and Democracy," *Mississippi Historical Review* 43 (1957):618–40; and Carroll Pursell, "The American Ideal of a Democratic Technology," in *The Technological Imagination*, ed. Teresa De Lauretis, Andreas Huyssen,

and Kathleen Woodward (Madison, Wis., 1980), pp. 11–25. This relationship is analyzed in Chapters 14 and 16. For further American versions of the promise of technology, see Leo Marx, *The Machine in the Garden* (Oxford, 1964), pp. 181–242.

14. On p. 11 of that issue. The promise of technology takes its commonest but also its vaguest and most confusing form in the notion of scientific and technological progress.

15. In *Passages* (November 1979):111.

16. In the *New York Times Magazine*, 4 November 1979, p. 69.

17. In *Frontier* (May/June 1978):1. This example now seems to be obsolete since one can now have "sixteen pads that transmit computerized impulses to stimulate muscle groups. Lying still, you obtain the benefits of 970 sit ups, 970 push ups, 1940 lateral twists, or jogging 12 miles." See *Missoulian* (August 7, 1982): A-7.

18. See the *Wall Street Journal*, 13 April 1976, p. 11. Ferguson's faith in technology (taken broadly) is not unqualified either. See his article, pp. 23–24.

19. See the *Wall Street Journal*, 13 April 1976, p. 11.

20. Ibid. Wiesner gives a longer and more qualified statement of his view on technology in "Technology is for Mankind," *Technology Review* 75, no. 6 (May 1973):10–13.

21. A brief sketch can be found in Mitcham's article, cited in n. 1 of Chapter 3, pp. 282–85. See also his "Philosophy and the History of Technology" in *The History and Philosophy of Technology*, ed. George Bugliarello and Dean B. Stoner (Urbana, Ill., 1979), pp. 163–201. Important materials are assembled in Lewis Mumford, *Technics and Civilization* (New York, 1963); and in Paolo Rossi, *Philosophy, Technology, and the Arts in the Early Modern Era*, trans. Salvator Attanasio (New York, 1970).

22. In "The Question of Heidegger and Technology," a paper I wrote with Carl Mitcham (forthcoming in *Philosophy Today*), references and further discussion can be found.

23. Here I have Otto Pöggeler on my side. See his *Philosophie und Politik bei Heidegger* (Freiburg, 1972), pp. 45 and 62.

CHAPTER 9

1. Earlier versions of this notion of technology can be found in "Technology and Reality," *Man and World* 4 (1971):59–69; "Orientation in Technology," *Philosophy Today* 16 (1972):135–47; "The Explanation of Technology," *Research in Philosophy and Technology* 1 (1978):99–118. Daniel J. Boorstin similarly describes the character of everyday America in terms of availability and its constituents. See his *Democracy and Its Discontents* (New York, 1975).

2. See Emmanuel G. Mesthene, *Technological Change* (New York, 1970), p. 28.

3. See Melvin M. Rotsch, "The Home Environment," in *Technology in Western Civilization*, ed. Melvin Kranzberg and Carroll W. Pursell, Jr. (New York, 1967), 2:226–28. For the development of the kitchen stove (the other branch into which the original fireplace or stove developed), see Siegfried Giedion, *Mechanization Takes Command* (New York, 1969 [first published in 1948]), pp. 527–47.

4. See George Sturt's description of the sawyers in *The Wheelwright's Shop* (Cambridge, 1974 [first published in 1923]), pp. 32–40.

5. In economics, "commodity" is a technical term for a tradable (and usually movable) economic good. In social science, it has become a technical term as a translation of Marx's *Ware* (merchandise). Marx's use and the use here suggested and to be developed agree inasmuch as both are intended to capture a novel and ultimately detrimental transformation of a traditional (pretechnological) phenomenon. For Marx, a commodity of the negative sort is the result of the reification of social relations, in particular of the reification of the workers' labor power, into something tradable and exchangeable which is then wrongfully appropriated by the capitalists and used against the workers. This constitutes the exploitation of the workers and their alienation from their work. It finally leads to their pauperization. As stressed in Chapters 13–16, I disagree that this transformation is at the center of gravity of the modern social order. The crucial change is rather the splitting of the pretechnological fabric of life into machinery and commodity according to the device paradigm. Though I concede and, in Chapter 25, stress the tradable and exchangeable character of commodities, as I use the term, their primary character, here intended, is their commodious and consumable availability with the technological machinery as their basis and with disengagement and distraction as their recent consequences. On Marx's notion of commodity and commodity fetishism, see Paul M. Sweezy, *The Theory of Capitalist Development* (New York, 1968), pp. 34–40.

6. See Morton Kaplan, "Means/Ends Rationality," *Ethics* 87 (1976):61–65.

7. Martin Heidegger gives a careful account of the interpenetration of means and ends in the pretechnological disclosure of reality. But when he turns to the technological disclosure of being *(das Gestell)* and to the device in particular *(das Gerät)*, he never points out the peculiar technological diremption of means and ends though he does mention the instability of the machine within technology. Heidegger's emphasis is perhaps due to his concern to show that technology as a whole is not a means or an instrument. See his "The Question Concerning Technology," in *The Question Concerning Technology and Other Essays*, trans. William Lovitt (New York, 1977), pp. 3–35, pp. 6–12 and 17 in particular.

8. It also turns out that a generally rising standard of living makes personal services disproportionately expensive. See Staffan B. Linder, *The Harried Leisure Class* (New York, 1970), pp. 34–37.

9. See Sturt, *The Wheelwright's Shop*, p. 132; see also pp. 31 and 38.

10. Ibid., p. 66.

11. Ibid., p. 23.

12. Ibid., p. 25.

13. Ibid., p. 45.

14. Ibid., p. 31.

15. Ibid., p. 24.

16. Ibid., p. 192.

17. Ibid., pp. 17–18.

18. Ibid., p. 41.

19. See Peter Laslett, *The World We Have Lost* (New York, 1965), pp. 22–52.

20. See Sturt, p. 25.

21. Ibid., p. 28. See also the portrait of the sawyers, pp. 32–40.

22. Ibid., pp. 30, 43, 175–81.

23. Ibid., pp. 53 and 200.
24. Ibid., pp. 53–55.
25. Ibid., p. 23.
26. Ibid., p. 45.
27. Ibid., p. 153; see also pp. 201–2.
28. Ibid., pp. 201–2.
29. Ibid., p. 201.
30. Ibid., p. 113.
31. Ibid., pp. 154, 201.
32. Ibid., p. 201.

33. A sketch and an analysis of technological illiteracy can be found in Langdon Winner, *Autonomous Technology* (Cambridge, Mass., 1977), pp. 282–95. While ignorance (of the machinery) is to be admitted and stressed, one must add that this ignorance goes hand in hand with an understanding (discussed below) of the overall pattern of technology.

34. Robert M. Pirsig describes this aversion to technology and contends that we can find wholeness at the center of technology if we begin to understand, maintain, and care for our devices. See his *Zen and the Art of Motorcycle Maintenance* (New York, 1974), pp. 11–35, 49–50, 97–106, 276, 290–92, 300–326. For further discussion see Chapter 20 below.

35. Joseph Weizenbaum argues that certain computer programs have altogether escaped comprehensibility. See his *Computer Power and Human Reason* (San Francisco, 1976), pp. 228–57.

36. See "Wonders of '89," *Newsweek,* 19 November 1979, p. 151; and "And Man Created the Chip," *Newsweek,* 30 June 1980, p. 50. Further discussion of microelectronics can be found in Chapter 19.

37. See Weizenbaum, *Computer Power,* p. 103.

CHAPTER 10

1. See Judson Gooding, "Hot off the Vine," *New York Times Magazine,* 1 August 1976, pp. 16–20.

2. Ibid., pp. 18–20.
3. Ibid., p. 20.
4. Ibid., p. 18.
5. In *Consumer Reports* 37 (1972):746.

6. Like "commodity," "device," and other familiar terms, I am using "consumption" in a narrow and definite sense which is developed and determined within the device paradigm and made to serve the clarifying and critical function of the paradigm. Still, the explication of the term's meaning captures, I believe, a large and crucial sense of what we usually mean by consumption.

7. In the *New York Times Magazine,* 4 November 1979, pp. 68–69. Jeffrey Schrank has gathered interesting observations on the decomposition and artificial reconstitution of food and of other phenomena and on the disorienting character of that development. But he wrongly suggests that corporate greed is the major cause and that overt harms (such as poor nutrition) are the major effect. He does not see how deeply grounded this transformation is, nor does he see the extent of people's agreement with this large and profound tendency. See his *Snap, Crackle, and Popular Taste: The Illusion of Free Choice in America* (New York, 1977).

Notes to Pages 52–59

261

8. See Daniel J. Boorstin, *Democracy and Its Discontents* (New York, 1975), p. 28.

9. See Stephen Kline and William Leiss, "Advertising, Needs, and 'Commodity Fetishism,'" *Canadian Journal of Political and Social Theory* 2 (1978):21–22; John Kenneth Galbraith, *The New Industrial State,* 2d ed. (Boston, 1972), pp. 204–7.

10. See Stuart Ewen, *Captains of Consciousness: Advertising and the Social Roots of the Consumer Culture* (New York, 1976).

11. See Galbraith, pp. 59–71 and passim.

12. Boorstin's contribution to the laying bare of those roots can be found in *The Americans: The Democratic Experience* (New York, 1973), pp. 89–164.

13. See Kline and Leiss, pp. 17–18.

14. Ibid., p. 17.

15. Ibid., pp. 17–18 and 25.

16. Ibid., p. 25.

17. See Leiss, *The Limits to Satisfaction* (Toronto, 1976), p. 63.

18. See Kline and Leiss, pp. 22–25.

19. In *Time,* 1 March 1976, inside back cover.

20. See Alvin Toffler, *Future Shock* (New York, 1970), pp. 219–37, 303–22.

21. See Gooding, p. 18; and the advertisement referred to in n. 7 above.

22. See Kline and Leiss, p. 23; and Ewen, pp. 95–102.

23. "Attenuation of experience" is Boorstin's term, and he describes the phenomenon in *Democracy and Its Discontents,* pp. 103–12 and 119–20.

24. See Martin H. Krieger, "What's Wrong with Plastic Trees?" *Science* 179 (February 2, 1973):446–55; Toffler, pp. 219–37.

CHAPTER 11

1. See Herbert L. Sussman, *Victorians and the Machine* (Cambridge, Mass., 1968), pp. 4–5.

2. See Hugo A. Meier, "Technology and Democracy, 1800–1860," *Mississippi Valley Historical Review* 43 (March 1957):633.

3. See Leo Marx, *The Machine in the Garden* (Oxford, 1964).

4. Quoted in Leo Marx, p. 178. Henry David Thoreau said similarly: "We do not ride the railroad; it rides upon us." See *Walden and Other Writings,* ed. Brooks Atkinson (New York, 1950), p. 83.

5. See Hannah Arendt, *The Human Condition* (Chicago, 1958).

6. Ibid., p. 152.

7. Ibid., p. 153. Martin Heidegger makes the same point in his portrayal of the silversmith at work in *The Question Concerning Technology,* trans. William Lovitt (New York, 1977), pp. 7–9.

8. See Arendt, p. 145.

9. See Thomas Carlyle, "Signs of the Times," in *Critical and Miscellaneous Essays* (New York, 1869), 1:465.

10. See Timothy Walker, "Defense of Mechanical Philosophy," in *Readings in Technology and American Life,* ed. Carroll W. Pursell (New York, 1969), p. 72 (first published in 1831).

11. See Carlyle, p. 465.

12. Ibid., p. 466.

13. See Langdon Winner, *Autonomous Technology* (Cambridge, Mass., 1977), pp. 230–36.

14. See Carlyle, p. 474.

15. Ibid., p. 468.

16. See Walker, pp. 68 and 72.

17. See, e.g., Robert Dorfman, "An Afterword: Humane Values and Environmental Decisions," in *When Values Conflict*, ed. Laurence H. Tribe, Corinne S. Schelling, and John Voss (Cambridge, Mass., 1976), p. 160; Laurence H. Tribe, "Technology Assessment and the Fourth Discontinuity: The Limits of Instrumental Rationality," *Southern California Law Review* 46 (1973):620–21; Winner, *Autonomous Technology*, pp. 226–51.

18. See also Tribe's "Policy Science: Analysis or Ideology?" *Philosophy and Public Affairs* 2 (1972):66–110; and "Ways Not to Think about Plastic Trees," *Yale Law Journal* 83 (1974):1315–48.

19. See Tribe, "Technology Assessment," pp. 625–30.

20. See Winner, *Autonomous Technology*, pp. 234–36.

21. Ibid., p. 229.

22. See Tribe, "Technology Assessment," pp. 620–23; see "Ways Not to Think about Plastic Trees," pp. 1323–25.

23. See Tribe, "Technology Assessment," p. 642.

24. Ibid., p. 641–57.

25. Ibid., p. 651 n. 117.

26. Ibid., pp. 645 and 647–48.

27. Ibid., p. 650 n. 115.

28. See Winner, *Autonomous Technology*, pp. 232–36.

29. Ibid., p. 234.

30. Ibid., p. 235.

31. Ibid., p. 301.

32. See Walker, "Defence of Mechanical Philosophy," p. 70. For antecedents see Paolo Rossi, *Philosophy, Technology, and the Arts in the Early Modern Era*, trans. Salvator Attanasio (New York, 1970), pp. 137–45.

33. See Leo Marx, *The Machine in the Garden*, pp. 190–209.

34. See Lewis Mumford, *Technics and Civilization* (New York, 1963), pp. 321–63, where Mumford is still eager to see a new order manifest itself in the machine though there is an admixture of doubt even then.

35. See Le Corbusier (Charles Édouard Jeanneret-Gris), *Towards a New Architecture*, trans. Frederick Etchells (London, 1931), p. 1.

36. Ibid., p. 14.

37. Quoted by Reyner Banham in *Theory and Design in the First Machine Age* (New York, 1960), p. 326.

38. Ibid., p. 303.

39. See Percival Goodman and Paul Goodman, *Communitas* (Chicago, 1947), p. 40. See also R. Buckminster Fuller and Robert Marks, *The Dymaxion World of Buckminster Fuller* (Garden City, N.Y., 1973), pp. 18–23 and 116–41.

40. See Charles Jencks, *Architecture 2000* (New York, 1971), p. 59. See also Kent C. Bloomer and Charles W. Moore, *Body, Memory, and Architecture* (New Haven, 1977), pp. 74–75.

41. See Le Corbusier, *Towards a New Architecture*, pp. 4, 95, 108.

42. See David P. Billington, "Structures and Machines: The Two Sides of Technology," *Soundings* 57 (1974):275. Detailed arguments and illustrations in support of the central thesis are provided in Billington's *Structures and the Urban Environment* (Princeton, N.J., 1978) which also, on pp. 149–53, contains a summary and extension of the article cited above. Billington's distinction between structures and machines is foreshadowed by Lewis Mumford's between utilities and machines. See *Technics and Civilization*, pp. 9–12.

43. See Billington, "Structures and Machines," pp. 275–76.

44. But to the external articulation corresponds (intended) internal vacuity.

45. For a discussion of uncertain exceptions see Bloomer and Moore, pp. 131–38.

46. See Robert H. Socolow, "Failures of Discourse: Obstacles to the Integration of Environmental Values into Natural Resource Policy," in *When Values Conflict*, ed. Tribe, Schelling, and Voss, p. 14.

CHAPTER 12

1. See David Layzer, "The Arrow of Time," *Scientific American* 233 (December 1975):58–59.

2. See F. H. C. Crick, "Thinking about the Brain," *Scientific American* 241 (September 1979):222.

3. See Herbert G. Reid and Ernest J. Yanarella, "Toward a Post-Modern Theory of American Political Science and Culture," *Cultural Hermeneutics* 2 (1974):91–166; Richard J. Bernstein, *The Restructuring of Social and Political Theory* (New York, 1976); and Alasdair MacIntyre, *After Virtue* (Notre Dame, Ind., 1981), pp. 84–102.

4. See Thomas S. Kuhn, *The Structure of Scientific Revolutions*, 2d ed. (Chicago, 1970).

5. See Imre Lakatos and Alan Musgrave, eds., *Criticism and the Growth of Knowledge* (Cambridge, 1970); and Bernstein, *The Restructuring of Social and Political Theory*, pp. 84–93.

6. See Anne C. Minas, "Why 'Paradigms' Don't Prove Anything," *Philosophy and Rhetoric* 10 (1977):217–31.

7. Cf. Sheldon S. Wolin's list of paradigms in "Paradigms and Political Theories," in *Politics and Experience*, ed. Preston King and B. C. Parekh (Cambridge, 1968), p. 134.

8. C. B. Macpherson uses "model" in the sense in which I use "paradigm," and he underscores a model's lack of explanatory self-sufficiency thus: "The definition of a model depends on value judgments about what *are* the essentials, and those judgments cannot be defended merely by invoking a definition." See *The Life and Times of Liberal Democracy* (Oxford, 1977), p. 9.

9. For support of this point see Wolin's article quoted in n. 7 above; Macpherson's book in the preceding note, pp. 1–9; John G. Gunnell, "Social Science and Political Reality: The Problem of Explanation," *Social Research* 35 (1968):159–201; and John Rodman, "Paradigm Change in Political Science: An Ecological Perspective," *American Behavioral Scientist* 24 (1980):49–78.

10. For a similar but more elaborate and comprehensive view of the irony in the development of technology see Manfred Stanley, *The Technological Conscience* (New York, 1978), pp. 18–52.

11. The relation of the increasing prominence of commodities to the increasing

unobtrusiveness of machineries parallels and may be taken as a generalized version of the amplification-reduction structure that Don Ihde uncovers in his stimulating analyses of technologically informed instrumentation and perception in *Technics and Praxis* (Dordrecht, 1979), pp. 3–50, 56–57, 74–77. A generalization and radicalization of this structure allows us, I believe, to tie it to substantive concerns and thus to determine in just what way the structure is "nonneutral" and leads to "significant transformations." See ibid., pp. 54 and 66. See also my review of Ihde, cited in the note to the Acknowledgments.

12. Commodities are really neither things, nor properties, nor social relations but ontological items of a novel sort. Therefore one might proceed more ambitiously and try to develop the thesis that the traditional world of substantial things is, in the rise of the modern period, being dissolved into functions, that the description of our world in terms of the traditional substances is misleading, and that a new vocabulary of functions, systems, mechanisms, and structures is required. This is the thesis of Heinrich Rombach, *Substanz, System, Struktur: Die Ontologie des Funktionalismus* (Freiburg, 1965). I regard this problem, like the problem of the origin of technology touched on in Chapter 8, as significant and challenging but beyond the pale of my present concerns.

CHAPTER 13

1. E.g., Daniel J. Boorstin, *Democracy and Its Discontents* (New York, 1975); Jürgen Habermas, *Legitimation Crisis,* trans. Thomas McCarthy (Boston, 1975); August Heckscher, *The Public Happiness* (New York, 1962); Robert L. Heilbroner, *An Inquiry into the Human Prospect,* 2d ed. (New York, 1980); Walter Kerr, *The Decline of Pleasure* (New York, 1962); Staffan B. Linder, *The Harried Leisure Class* (New York, 1970); Tibor Scitovsky, *The Joyless Economy* (Oxford, 1976).

2. See *The Oxford English Dictionary.*

3. See R. Buckminster Fuller, *Operating Manual for Spaceship Earth* (New York, n.d. [first published in 1969]), pp. 130–31.

4. See W. Norris Clarke, "Technology and Man: A Christian Vision," in *Philosophy and Technology,* ed. Carl Mitcham and Robert Mackey (New York, 1972), pp. 249–50 and 257–58. See also the anthology *Values and the Future: The Impact of Technological Change on American Values,* ed. Kurt Baier and Nicholas Rescher (New York, 1969) which proceeds from the assumption that the value question is fundamental.

5. See his "What Is Value? An Analysis of the Concept," in Baier and Rescher, p. 40.

6. Ibid., p. 38.

7. Ibid., p. 40.

8. Ibid.

9. See Clarke, p. 257.

10. See Baier, p. 48. An example of how general values are and how susceptible to technological specification can be found in the tables of values in Milton Rokeach, *The Nature of Human Values* (New York, 1973), pp. 57–71.

11. See the anthology edited by Tribe et al., cited in n. 17 of Chapter 11.

12. See, e.g., "America: Out to Eat," *Newsweek,* 3 October 1977, pp. 86–89.

13. See Stuart Ewen, *Captains of Consciousness* (New York, 1976), pp. 31, 42, 52, 54, 190.

14. See G. William Domhoff, *The Higher Circles: The Governing Class in America* (New York, 1971). For the varying numerical estimates of the governing class, see pp. 34, 72, 93, 250, 307. For further discussion of this issue and a review of a later book of Domhoff's, see Andrew Hacker, "What Rules America?" *New York Review of Books,* 1 May 1975, pp. 9–13.

15. John Kenneth Galbraith, *The New Industrial State,* 2d ed. (Boston, 1972), pp. 115–16. See also Hacker's article of the previous note. On the emergence of the division between ownership and control, see Alfred C. Chandler, Jr., *The Visible Hand: The Managerial Revolution in American Business* (Cambridge, Mass., 1977).

16. See Langdon Winner, *Autonomous Technology* (Cambridge, Mass., 1977), p. 41.

17. Paul A. Baran and Paul M. Sweezy, no friends of the very rich, admit that their conspicuous consumption has decreased. See *Monopoly Capital* (New York, 1968), pp. 44–45; see also p. 35.

18. According to Baran and Sweezy, capitalists' consumption has been decreasing as a share of profits and even more so as a share of total output. See *Monopoly Capital,* pp. 79–81.

19. See Herbert Marcuse, *One-Dimensional Man* (Boston, 1964).

20. See Harry Braverman, *Labor and Monopoly Capital: The Degradation of Work in the Twentieth Century* (New York, 1974).

21. See Marcuse, *One-Dimensional Man,* pp. xvi and 235. On Marcuse's ambivalence and its resolution, see Jürgen Habermas, "Technology and Science as 'Ideology,'" in *Toward a Rational Society,* trans. Jeremy J. Shapiro (Boston, 1970), pp. 81–122; William Leiss, "Technological Rationality: Marcuse and His Critics," in *The Domination of Nature* (New York, 1972), pp. 199–212. On Marcuse's trust in the perfectibility of technology, see Reinhart Maurer, "Der angewandte Heidegger: Herbert Marcuse und das akademische Proletariat," *Philosophisches Jahrbuch* 70 (1970):238–59; and Hans Sachsse, "Die Technik in der Sicht Herbert Marcuses und Martin Heideggers," in *Proceedings of the XVth World Congress of Philosophy* (Sofia, Bulgaria, 1973), 1:371–75. On the uncritical acceptance of technology by Marxists generally, see Langdon Winner, "The Political Philosophy of Alternative Technology," in *Technology and Man's Future,* 3d ed., ed. Albert H. Teich (New York, 1981), pp. 376–77.

22. There is a last desperate move that Marxists sometimes make, and that is to claim that people's very consciousness has been appropriated by the capitalists so that people's consciousness needs first to be freed for liberation. But to regard people as so malleable is to take a dubious view of human nature. On that view reform becomes indistinguishable from manipulation. See Robert L. Heilbroner, *An Inquiry into the Human Prospect,* 2d ed. (New York, 1980), pp. 136–48.

23. See Baran and Sweezy, *Monopoly Capital,* pp. 363–67; Marcuse, *One-Dimensional Man,* pp. xii–xiii and 225–46.

24. See Galbraith, *The New Industrial State,* 2d ed., pp. 47–49.

25. See Marcuse, *One-Dimensional Man,* pp. 2, 16, 18, 235. New departures can be found in Marcuse's *The Aesthetic Dimension* (Boston, 1978) which is an attempt to break away from the technological one-dimensionality, and William Leiss's *The Limits to Satisfaction* (Toronto, 1976).

CHAPTER 14

1. John Stuart Mill, *On Liberty*, ed. Currin V. Shields (Indianapolis, 1956), title page of the treatise.

2. See Mill's *Autobiography* (New York, 1944), pp. 178–80. See C. B. Macpherson, "Democratic Theory: Ontology and Technology," in *Philosophy and Technology*, ed. Carl Mitcham and Robert Mackey (New York, 1972), p. 166.

3. One should not think that Humboldt expects each individual to develop all possible faculties. Rather each is to be free to develop those capacities in which he or she feels naturally gifted; diversity is achieved and completed socially when we enjoy one another's developed talents in what John Rawls calls a social union in his *A Theory of Justice* (Cambridge, Mass., 1971), pp. 520–29. For the original statement see Wilhelm von Humboldt, "Ideen zu einem Versuch, die Gränzen der Wirksamkeit des Staats zu bestimmen," in *Werke*, ed. Andreas Flitner and Klaus Giel (Stuttgart, 1960–64), 1:64–69. For further discussion see Chapter 24.

4. See C. B. Macpherson, *The Life and Times of Liberal Democracy* (Oxford, 1977), p. 1.

5. Ibid.

6. Ibid., p. 2.

7. See Ronald Dworkin, "Liberalism," in *Public and Private Morality*, ed. Stuart Hampshire (New York, 1978), pp. 130–33.

8. See Macpherson, *The Life and Times*, p. 47.

9. Ibid., p. 99.

10. See Ronald Dworkin, "Liberalism," p. 127.

11. Ibid.

12. Ibid., p. 142.

13. See Gerald Dworkin, "Paternalism," in *Morality and the Law*, ed. Richard A. Wasserstrom (Belmont, Calif., 1971), pp. 107–26.

14. See Macpherson, *The Life and Times*, pp. 9–10; and Mulford Q. Sibley, *Technology and Utopian Thought* (Minneapolis, 1971).

15. See Macpherson, *The Life and Times*, pp. 10–12.

16. See Daniel J. Boorstin, *Democracy and Its Discontents* (New York, 1975), p. 28.

17. Ibid., p. 36.

18. Ibid., p. 102. Boorstin speaks very similarly in "The Republic of Technology," in *The Republic of Technology* (New York, 1978), pp. 1–12. His thesis must be seen against the background of his detailed study of *The Americans: The Democratic Experience* (New York, 1973). It must also be stressed that Boorstin's view of democracy or technology is complex. Deep misgivings are woven into his approval and hope.

19. See Christopher Jencks, *Who Gets Ahead? The Determinants of Economic Success in America* (New York, 1979); and Richard P. Coleman and Lee Rainwater, *Social Standing in America* (New York, 1978).

20. E.g., Eugene S. Ferguson, "The American-ness of American Technology," *Technology and Culture* 20 (1979):3–24; Bertrand de Jouvenel, "Technology as a Means," in *Values and the Future*, ed. Kurt Baier and Nicholas Rescher (New York, 1969), pp. 217–32; and Boorstin's essay quoted in n. 18 above. Scandinavia and Western Europe are better examples of universal if unequal prosperity than the United States.

21. See Gerald Dworkin, "Paternalism," p. 118.

22. Ibid., pp. 123 and 124.

23. See Irving Kristol, "Pornography, Obscenity, and the Case for Censorship," in *Philosophy of Law,* ed. Joel Feinberg and Hyman Gross (Encino, Calif., 1975), pp. 165–71.

24. See Jürgen Habermas, *Legitimation Crisis,* trans. Thomas McCarthy (Boston, 1975), pp. 105–10.

25. See Ronald Dworkin, "Liberalism," p. 142.

26. Ibid., p. 143.

27. Ibid.

28. That the mind is a dubious fundament for the adjudication of value problems I have argued in "Mind, Body, and World," *Philosophical Forum* 8 (1976):68–86.

29. See his "What Liberalism Isn't," *New York Review of Books,* 20 January 1983, pp. 47–50.

30. See his "Why Liberals Should Believe in Equality," *New York Review of Books,* 3 February 1983, pp. 32–34.

31. See Dworkin, "What Liberalism Isn't," pp. 33 and 34; and "Why Liberals Should Believe," p. 47.

32. See John Rawls, *A Theory of Justice* (Cambridge, Mass., 1971).

33. Ibid., pp. 395–97.

34. See, e.g., Adina Schwartz, "Moral Neutrality and Primary Goods," *Ethics* 83 (1973):294–307; Michael Teitelman, "The Limits of Individualism," *Journal of Philosophy* 69 (1972):545–56; Thomas Nagel, "Rawls on Justice," in *Reading Rawls,* ed. Norman Daniels (New York, n.d.), pp. 9–10; Benjamin R. Barber, "Justifying Justice," in ibid., pp. 292–318.

35. See Rawls, *A Theory of Justice,* pp. 121, 126, and throughout.

36. Ibid., p. 92 and at countless other places.

37. Ibid., pp. 198–99.

38. I am using "opportunities" in a sense that is both broader and more concrete than Rawls's and includes not only what he calls powers and opportunities, and income and wealth, but also those concrete institutions that inevitably define the opportunities to whose use income and wealth entitle us.

39. See Rawls, "Fairness to Goodness," *Philosophical Review* 84 (1975): 536–54.

40. Rawls's book is admirably circumspect and thoughtful. Hence one can hardly raise an objection to it that Rawls has not considered and to some degree conceded. Thus he grants that the means to pursue a conception of the good may not be neutral (pp. 415 and 416), and he recognizes that wealth beyond a certain point can be distracting and tempt one to lead an empty life (p. 290). But though Rawls acknowledges these problems, he does not pursue them.

41. See Rawls, "A Kantian Conception of Equality," in *Property, Profits, and Economic Justice,* ed. Virginia Held (Belmont, Calif., 1980), p. 201; and *A Theory of Justice,* p. 259.

42. See Rawls, *A Theory of Justice,* pp. 328–29; and "Fairness to Goodness," p. 544.

43. See Macpherson, *The Life and Times of Liberal Democracy,* p. 99; see also his "Democratic Theory," pp. 168–70.

44. See Macpherson, *The Life and Times,* p. 100.

45. Ibid., pp. 102–8.

46. In "Democratic Theory: Ontology and Technology," Macpherson's unresolved difficulties in his view of democracy and technology are plain. He suggests that technology can serve as an instrument in advancing the liberal democratic ideal of self-development for all. But the facile instrumentalist approach is not open to Macpherson because he takes the notion of the person as the consumer, derived from capitalism, as opposed to truly liberal democracy. Thus technology can aid self-development only through the reduction of labor (p. 169). Macpherson sees clearly that in the sphere of leisure improved technology will lead to increased consumption, a counterforce to liberal democracy in his sense (p. 170). Thus technology turns out to be both the servant and the enemy of liberal democracy.

47. See Jürgen Habermas, "Technology and Science as 'Ideology,'" in *Toward a Rational Society*, trans. Jeremy J. Shapiro (Boston, 1970), pp. 103, 112, 113. Again I cannot do justice to the continuously evolving thinking of Habermas. I am concerned here merely with some striking and helpful objections from Habermas's pen.

48. Ibid., p. 90.

49. Ibid., p. 91. "Choice" may suggest that work establishes ends as well as it employs means. But Habermas makes it clear that work proceeds only from given ends or preferences. Work is essentially instrumental. In *Legitimation Crisis*, p. 141, the rationality of work is treated in more detail, being distinguished into purposive and systems rationality. The distinction is not crucial to what follows.

50. See Habermas, "Technology and Science," p. 92.

51. Ibid., pp. 94–95.

52. Ibid., pp. 98–99; see *Legitimation Crisis*, pp. 17–26.

53. See Habermas, "Technology and Science," p. 99.

54. Ibid., p. 104. This point has been developed carefully by Mario Bunge in "Toward a Philosophy of Technology," in *Philosophy and Technology*, ed. Carl Mitcham and Robert Mackey (New York, 1972), pp. 62–76.

55. See Habermas, "Technology and Science," pp. 106–7.

56. Ibid., pp. 119–20.

57. See Habermas, "Towards a Theory of Communicative Competence," *Inquiry* 13 (1970):371–72. A similar set of conditions has been set down by Milton R. Wessel under the heading of *The Rule of Reason: A New Approach to Corporate Litigation* (Reading, Mass., 1976), pp. 19–24. The fact that Wessel urges acceptance of the rule of reason because it "is essential to corporate success and even corporate survival in its present form" and "must be adopted as a matter of sound business practice and economic well-being" shows how ambiguous and subvertible Habermas's suggestion is.

58. See Richard J. Bernstein, *The Restructuring of Social and Political Theory* (New York, 1978), pp. 223–24.

59. Ibid., pp. 224–25.

60. See Chapter 11 above for discussion and nn. 5–8 in that chapter for reference.

61. See Habermas, "Technology and Science," p. 94; see also p. 114.

62. See Otto von Simson's account of the construction and dedication of the abbey of St. Denis in *The Gothic Cathedral* (Princeton, N.J., 1974), pp. 61–141. See William Leiss, "Needs, Exchanges and the Fetishism of Objects," *Canadian Journal of Political and Social Theory* 2 (1978):27–48, on the discontinuities of norms in pretechnological cultures and also on the danger of overemphasizing them.

63. See Habermas, "Technology and Science," p. 98.

64. Ibid., pp. 100–101, 119, 120; see *Legitimation Crisis*, pp. 36–37 and passim.

65. See Habermas, "Technology and Science," pp. 102–3; and *Legitimation Crisis*, pp. 60, 61, and 135.

66. See Habermas, "Technology and Science," pp. 107–10.

67. Ibid., p. 109; and *Legitimation Crisis*, p. 73.

68. See Habermas, "Technology and Science," p. 107.

69. Ibid., pp. 118–19.

70. This is so if we take the outline of communicative competence as the specification of necessary conditions for a desirable society.

71. See Habermas, "Technology and Science," pp. 113 and 119; and *Legitimation Crisis*, pp. 142–43.

72. This would be so even if discussions were not merely unrestrained but took place "under conditions of individuation" and achieved "full complementarity of expectations." See "Towards a Theory of Communicative Competence," pp. 371–72. Kai Nielsen recognizes how thin the norms of communicative competence are and seeks to strengthen them through additional features. This shows that there is still a common fund of values and experiences that we can tap in speaking of fairness, solidarity, reasonableness, and finally perhaps of communicative competence. In Chapter 11 I have tried to explain my reservations about values as fundaments of reform. See Nielsen, "Technology as Ideology," *Research in Philosophy and Technology* 1 (1978):143–46.

CHAPTER 15

1. See Langdon Winner, *Autonomous Technology* (Cambridge, Mass., 1977), p. 46. William Leiss also criticizes frequent inconsistencies in the scholarly concepts of technology in "The Social Consequences of Technological Progress," *Canadian Public Administration* 13 (1970):246–62.

2. For elaboration see my "Freedom and Determinism in a Technological Setting," *Research in Philosophy and Technology* 2 (1979):79–90. The notion of "capacity for significance" is similar to Manfred Stanley's concept of human dignity. See *The Technological Conscience* (New York, 1978), pp. 53–75.

3. For the scholarly setting in which such a view of the basis of the social order is to be located, see Stanley, pp. 101–5.

4. For evidence of people's sense of loss and grief in the face of the social changes that accompany technological progress, see Daniel Yankelovich, *New Rules* (New York, 1982), p. 103. For a discussion of those changes see Chapter 18. As regards the growing uneasiness in people's complicity with technology, see Duane Elgin, *Voluntary Simplicity* (New York, 1981), pp. 126–34.

5. See Irene Taviss, "A Survey of Popular Attitudes toward Technology," *Technology and Culture* 13 (1972):609; Todd R. La Porte and Daniel Metlay, "Technology Observed: Attitudes of a Wary Public," *Science* 188 (April 11, 1975):123; see also the same authors' "Public Attitudes toward Present and Future Technologies: Satisfactions and Apprehensions," *Social Studies of Science* 5 (1975):375, 379, 397.

6. See La Porte and Metlay, "Technology Observed," p. 123.

7. Ibid., p. 121; Taviss, p. 607; La Porte and Metlay, "Public Attitudes," pp. 373, 375, 396; and Yankelovich, p. 103.

8. See Taviss, p. 609; La Porte and Metlay, "Technology Observed," p. 123.

9. See Taviss, p. 608; La Porte and Metlay, "Technology Observed," pp. 123–24; and "Public Attitudes," p. 379.

10. See Richard A. Easterlin, "Does Money Buy Happiness?" *Public Interest,* no. 30 (1973):3–10; and "Does Economic Growth Improve the Human Lot?" in *Nations and Households in Economic Growth,* ed. Paul A. David and Melvin W. Reder (New York, 1974), pp. 89–125.

11. See Lee Rainwater, *What Money Buys: Inequality and the Social Meanings of Income* (New York, 1974), pp. 88–93; Easterlin, "Does Money Buy Happiness?" p. 10.

12. See La Porte and Metlay, "Public Attitudes," pp. 393 and 396.

13. See Albert H. Cantril and Charles W. Roll, Jr., *Hopes and Fears of the American People* (New York, 1971), pp. 19 and 23; Nicholas Rescher, "A Questionnaire Study of American Values by 2000 A.D.," in *Values and the Future,* ed. Kurt Baier and Rescher (New York, 1969), p. 136.

14. See Taviss, pp. 613 and 621. For evidence that confidence in technology has recently been decreasing, see Yankelovich, "Changing Public Attitudes to Science and the Quality of Life," *Science, Technology, and Human Values* 7, no. 39 (Spring 1982): 25.

15. E.g., Rainwater's study, referred to in n. 11 above; and Lillian Breslow Rubin, *Worlds of Pain: Life in the Working Class Family* (New York, 1976).

16. See Richard Sennett and Jonathan Cobb, *The Hidden Injuries of Class* (New York, 1973).

17. Ibid., p. 107.

18. Ibid., p. 110.

19. Ibid., p.117.

CHAPTER 16

1. See Jürgen Habermas, *Legitimation Crisis,* trans. Thomas McCarthy (Boston, 1975), pp. 60, 61, 135.

2. Ibid., pp. 64 and 68.

3. See John Kenneth Galbraith, *The New Industrial State,* 2d ed. (Boston, 1972), pp. 1–10.

4. See Aldous Huxley, *Brave New World* (New York, 1958 [first published in 1932]); Manfred Stanley, *The Technological Conscience* (New York, 1978), pp. 39–42.

5. Cf. Todd R. La Porte and Daniel Metlay, "Public Attitudes toward Present and Future Technologies," *Social Studies of Science* 5 (1975):382 in particular.

6. See Normal H. Nie, Sidney Verba, and John R. Petrocik, *The Changing American Voter* (Cambridge, Mass., 1976).

7. See Arthur T. Hadley, *The Empty Polling Booth* (Englewood Cliffs, N.J., 1978), pp. 15–26.

8. They constitute 35 percent of those who refrain from voting; the poor and uneducated represent 13 percent, the alienated 22 percent.

9. See Donald J. Devine, *The Attentive Public: Polyarchical Democracy* (Chicago, 1970); and La Porte and Metlay, "Technology Observed," *Science* 188, 11 April 1975, p. 125.

10. The force of the democratic call for equality makes itself felt in cycles as Samuel P. Huntington has pointed out in *The Crisis of Democracy,* by Michael Crozier,

Huntington, and Joji Watanuki (New York, 1975), pp. 59–118, p. 112 in particular.

11. Immanuel Kant, *Foundations of the Metaphysics of Morals*, trans. Lewis White Beck (Indianapolis, 1959), pp. 51–53. See Andrew Hacker, "Creating American Inequality," *New York Review of Books*, 20 March 1980.

12. See Lester C. Thurow, "Tax Wealth, Not Income," *New York Times Magazine*, 11 April 1976; and *The Zero-Sum Society* (Middlesex, 1981), pp. 168–69.

13. See Richard A. Posner, "Economic Justice and the Economist," *Public Interest*, no. 33 (1973):116–18.

14. Equality has equal rights as necessary or formal conditions. But the substantive degree (or the sufficiency of the conditions) of equality is measured by income (or wealth). Societies are of course conceivable where equality of wealth or income is not correlated with equality of one's standing in society, and there is some slack in this country between income or wealth and one's life-style and prestige. Education and occupation are differentiating factors independent, to some extent, of income. But their force seems to be declining while that of income seems to be rising (see Daniel Yankelovich, *New Rules* [New York, 1982], pp. 142–43; and Richard P. Coleman and Lee Rainwater, *Social Standing in America* [New York, 1978], pp. 18, 24, 26, 28–46).

15. See Thurow, "Toward a Definition of Economic Justice," *Public Interest*, no. 31 (1973):56–63; and Posner, pp. 114–16.

16. See Thurow, "Toward a Definition," p. 77.

17. See Hacker, "Creating American Inequality," p. 21. The families whose income is $50,000 or higher constitute, as said before, 3.6 percent.

18. See Peter Laslett, *The World We Have Lost* (New York, 1965); Macpherson, *The Life and Times of Liberal Democracy* (Oxford, 1977), pp. 9–43; Thurow, "Toward a Definition," pp. 68–69.

19. See Hacker, "Creating American Inequality," p. 21; and Thurow, "Tax Wealth, Not Income," p. 32.

20. See Thurow's puzzlement in "Tax Wealth, Not Income," pp. 102–3.

21. See Hacker, "Creating American Inequality," pp. 20–26.

22. See Thurow, "Toward a Definition," pp. 75–77; and *The Zero-Sum Society*, p. 168.

23. See Easterlin's studies, referred to in n. 10 of Chapter 15; and Thurow, "Toward a Definition," pp. 65–67.

24. See Thurow, "Tax Wealth, Not Income," pp. 102–3.

25. This diachronic equality of affluence has also been called "dynamic egalitarianism." See Fred Hirsch, *Social Limits to Growth* (Cambridge, Mass., 1976), pp. 166–67.

26. On the shifting line of poverty see Lillian Breslow Rubin, *Worlds of Pain* (New York, 1976), pp. 8, 29–31, 47–48, 169–70, 206. On the gradation and acceptance of inequality see Coleman and Rainwater, *Social Standing in America*, pp. 24, 119–221; and Yankelovich, *New Rules*, pp. 134–43. In a socialist country, almost everyone is affected by an economic decline. Hence, Heilbroner to the contrary, it seems that capitalist countries are structurally better able, in the short run at least, to cope with economic and energy crises. See Robert L. Heilbroner, *An Inquiry into the Human Prospect*, 2d ed. (New York, 1980), pp. 77–111.

27. See Jacques Ellul, *The Technological Society*, trans. John Wilkinson (New York, 1964), pp. 229–318.

CHAPTER 17

1. See Georges Friedmann, "Leisure and Technological Civilization," *International Social Science Journal* 12 (1960):509–21; and E. P. Thompson, "Time, Work-Discipline, and Industrial Capitalism," *Past and Present*, no. 38 (1967): 60–61.

2. The present work-labor distinction is not to be confused with Arendt's that was touched on in Chapter 11. See nn. 5–8 in that chapter. Even prior to the advent of modern technology, work was sometimes taken as a mere means in an attitude of instrumentalism. See Alasdair Clayre, *Work and Play* (New York, 1974), pp. 103–12. But one must distinguish between subjective and objective instrumentalism. The former is a matter of attitude and individual disposition, the latter is built into the work process. The former can be changed through an improvement of individual attitude. The latter can be concealed or ignored through the thinking of pious thoughts, but it can never be overcome by an individual.

3. See Sebastian de Grazia, *Of Time, Work, and Leisure* (New York, 1964), pp. 75, 189, 300–302. The loss of good work is chronicled in part by Thompson (see n. 1 above) and by Herbert G. Gutman, "Work, Culture, and Society in Industrializing America, 1815–1919," *American Historical Review* 78 (1973):531–88.

4. See George Sturt, *The Wheelwright's Shop* (Cambridge, 1974), pp. 12, 14, 15, 31, 47.

5. See William H. Form, "Auto Workers and Their Machines: A Study of Work, Factory, and Job Satisfaction in Four Countries," *Social Forces* 52 (1973):2. A historical account of work from the grim viewpoint has been given by Melvin Kranzberg and Joseph Gies, *By the Sweat of Thy Brow: Work in the Western World* (New York, 1975).

6. See Adam Smith, *The Wealth of Nations*, ed. Edwin Cannan (New York, 1937), pp. 3–21.

7. See Harry Braverman, *Labor and Monopoly Capital: The Degradation of Work in the Twentieth Century* (New York, 1974), pp. 75–77. See also Hannah Arendt, *The Human Condition* (Chicago, 1958), pp. 123–26.

8. See John Kenneth Galbraith, *The New Industrial State*, 2d ed. (Boston, 1972), pp. 59–71.

9. See Siegfried Giedion, *Mechanization Takes Command* (New York, 1969), pp. 79–96.

10. See Adam Smith, pp. 7–10.

11. See Braverman, pp. 169 and 185–87; and Bernard Gendron and Nancy Holmstrom, "Marx, Machinery, and Alienation," *Research in Philosophy and Technology* 2 (1979):120.

12. See Giedion, pp. 96–106; and Braverman, pp. 85–123.

13. See Giedion, pp. 130–246.

14. See Daniel J. Boorstin, *The Americans: The Democratic Experience* (New York, 1973), pp. 91–100, 173–87, 263–67, 309–36, 546–55.

15. Beyond the suggestions in the text, the challenge of showing how the device paradigm fits organizations is one that I cannot take up in this essay. Pertinent work in this direction has been devoted to the analysis of bureaucracy. See especially Max Weber, *Economy and Society*, ed. Guenther Roth and Claus Wittich, 3 vols. (New York, 1968), 3:956–1005; and also Roberto Mangabeira Unger, *Knowledge and Politics* (New York, 1976), pp. 145–90, particularly pp. 170–74; and Alasdair MacIntyre, *After Virtue* (Notre Dame, Ind., 1981), pp. 33 and 68.

16. "Division" and "device" are etymologically cognate; but that is a mere curiosity today.

17. See Giedion, pp. 152–55, 222–28, 452–67; and Boorstin, pp. 175–80, 309–16; Caroll W. Pursell, Jr., "Cyrus Hall McCormick and the Mechanization of Agriculture," in *Technology in America,* ed. Pursell (Cambridge, Mass., 1981), pp. 71–79.

18. See Lewis Mumford, *Technics and Civilization* (New York, 1963), pp. 173–74.

19. See Braverman, pp. 155–68 and 236–48.

20. See De Grazia, pp. 1–56. Adina Schwartz, in "Meaningful Work," *Ethics* 92 (1982):634–46, has rightly argued that we have a moral obligation to provide good work for all. But her reform proposal, which resembles Lauterburg's, discussed below, does not go far enough.

21. See Eugene S. Ferguson, "The American-ness of American Technology," *Technology and Culture* 20 (1979):16.

22. See Boorstin, *Democracy and Its Discontents* (New York, 1975), pp. 112–14. Fred Hirsch similarly reminds us that going to the barber can be more than a mere means of being shaved; see his *Social Limits to Growth* (Cambridge, Mass., 1976), pp. 73–74.

23. See Boorstin, *The Americans: The Democratic Experience,* pp. 347–51, for the need and benefits of modern water supply systems.

24. Quoted by Braverman on p. 424 where further illustration is provided.

25. Ibid., pp. 426–35.

26. Ibid., pp. 430 and 433–34.

27. See Hirsch, pp. 45–51.

28. See Braverman, pp. 438–39.

29. See Randall Collins, *The Credential Society* (New York, 1979).

30. See Eli Ginzberg and George J. Vojta, "The Service Sector of the U.S. Economy," *Scientific American* 244 (March 1981):48–49.

31. Ibid., p. 50.

32. Ibid., pp. 50–51.

33. See Braverman, pp. 330–38.

34. See the Thompson and Gutman papers cited in nn. 1 and 3 above.

35. See Braverman, pp. 11–13.

36. Gendron and Holmstrom attempt to construct such an argument in the article cited in n. 11 above.

37. Ibid., p. 128.

38. Thompson quoting a Methodist lay preacher, p. 75.

39. Ibid., pp. 83–88.

40. See de Grazia, pp. 131–45; Braverman, pp. 139–52; and J. B. Schneewind, "Technology, Ways of Living, and Values in 19th Century England," in *Values and the Future,* ed. Kurt Baier and Nicholas Rescher (New York, 1971), pp. 125–32.

41. See Form's article cited in n. 5 above.

42. See Louis E. Davis and Albert B. Cherns, eds., *The Quality of Working Life* (New York, 1975), p. 14; and in the same anthology Stanley E. Seashore, "Defining and Measuring the Quality of Working Life," pp. 107–8.

43. On the duality of responses, see John P. Robinson, *How Americans Use Time* (New York, 1977), pp. 125 and 128. For in-depth testimonies on the draining and stultifying nature of divided labor, see Studs Terkel, *Working* (New York, 1974).

A survey of findings on work dissatisfaction in the United States can be found in *Work in America,* prepared by a Special Task Force of the Secretary of Health, Education, and Welfare (Cambridge, Mass., 1973), pp. 10–23 and 29–56.

44. See Christoph Lauterburg, *Vor dem Ende der Hierarchie,* 2d ed. (Düsseldorf, 1980), p. 52.

45. See "The Robot Revolution," *Time,* 8 December 1980, quoting James S. Albus on p. 73. Further materials on microelectronics and labor in Tom Forester, ed., *The Microelectronics Revolution* (Cambridge, Mass., 1981), pp. 290–355.

46. See Lauterburg, p. 49.

47. See "Robots Join the Labor Force," *Business Week,* 9 June 1980, p. 63; see also "The Robot Revolution," in *Time,* 8 December 1980, p. 78; and Colin Norman, *Microelectronics at Work: Productivity and Jobs in the World Economy* (Washington, D.C., 1980), p. 6.

48. See Lauterburg, pp. 20–31 and 43–47.

49. On the growth and the necessity of hierarchical organization in American business and industry, see Alfred D. Chandler, Jr., *The Visible Hand: The Managerial Revolution in American Business* (Cambridge, Mass., 1977.)

50. See *Time,* 8 December 1980, p. 73; *Business Week,* 9 June 1980, p. 64.

51. See *Business Week,* 9 June 1980, p. 63. See Norman, pp. 29–40. A progress report on the way to automation has been given in *Scientific American* 247 (September 1982) which is devoted to the mechanization of work.

52. See Norman, pp. 21–29, *Business Week,* 9 June 1980, pp. 62–63, *Newsweek,* 30 June 1980, p. 51. See also "A New Era for Management," *Business Week,* 25 April 1983, pp. 50–80.

53. See *Business Week,* June 9, 1980, p. 63.

54. Ibid., p. 68.

55. For beginnings of this trend, see Hans Berglind, "Unemployment and Redundancy in a 'Post-Industrial' Labor Market," in *Work and Technology,* ed. Marie R. Haug and Jacques Dofny (London, 1977), pp. 195–213. See also "The Disenchantment of the Middle Class," *Business Week,* 25 April 1983, pp. 82–86.

CHAPTER 18

1. See Ivan Illich, *Tools for Conviviality* (New York, 1973), pp. 1–8.

2. See Tibor Scitovsky, *The Joyless Economy* (New York, 1976), pp. 165–70.

3. See "The Robot Revolution," *Time,* 8 December 1980, p. 83; see also "And Man Created the Chip," *Newsweek,* 30 June 1980, pp. 51 and 56; and Alvin Toffler, *The Third Wave* (New York, 1981), pp. 155–67 and 380–91.

4. Walter Kerr, *The Decline of Pleasure* (New York, 1962); Staffan B. Linder, *The Harried Leisure Class* (New York, 1970); Scitovsky, *The Joyless Economy.* Studies in the same vein with less indicative titles are August Heckscher, *The Public Happiness* (New York, 1962); Sebastian de Grazia, *Of Time, Work, and Leisure* (Garden City, N.Y., 1964); Fred Hirsch, *Social Limits to Growth* (Cambridge, Mass., 1976); Daniel Bell, *The Cultural Contradictions of Capitalism* (New York, 1976); William Leiss, *The Limits to Satisfaction* (Toronto, 1976). See n. 1 in Chapter 13.

5. Two *loci classici* of this ideal are Plato's allegory of the cave in *The Republic,* 514A-517A, and the beginning of Aristotle's *Metaphysics,* 980a22-983a24. World citizenship is of course the result of education in the profound sense.

6. Gallantry corresponds to the Greek ideal of being *kalòs kagathòs* and to the Roman principle of *mens sana in sano corpore.*

7. "Above all," says de Grazia, "the Greeks were and wished to be musicians." See *Of Time, Work, and Leisure*, p. 15.

8. See Hannah Arendt, *The Human Condition* (Chicago, 1958), pp. 236–43.

9. What I am asserting is, more technically put, that underlying the ethics of rules, which is dominant today, the older ethics of virtues is still weakly alive and can to some extent be appealed to. On the demise of the morality of virtues, see Alasdair MacIntyre's illuminating book *After Virtue* (Notre Dame, Ind., 1981). MacIntyre argues that the older morality has survived in unintelligible fragments only and that no equally viable and consistent ethics has taken its place. It is clear from MacIntyre's study that the drawing up of a list of virtues is difficult in the best of circumstances. But whether the list above is sound or not is finally less than decisive since, as I want to show in Part 3, Chapter 24 in particular, the tradition of virtues must be revived from the ground up.

10. On the modern demise of world citizenship, see Richard Sennett, *The Fall of Public Man* (New York, 1977).

11. See de Grazia, pp. 59 and 419.

12. Ibid., pp. 59–74.

13. See Daniel Yankelovich, *New Rules* (New York, 1982), p. 18.

14. See Lee Rainwater, *What Money Buys* (New York, 1974), p. 46.

15. See Linder, pp. 135–37.

16. See John P. Robinson, *How Americans Use Time* (New York, 1977), pp. 89–91; and de Grazia, pp. 57–83.

17. See Robinson, pp. 98, 102, 107.

18. See the references in n. 4 above and also Angus Campbell, Phillip E. Converse, and Willard L. Rodgers, *The Quality of American Life* (New York, 1976)

19. See Robinson, pp. 92, 102, and 173–79; and de Grazia, pp. 106–8 and 422.

20. See Bertrand de Jouvenel, "Technology as a Means," in *Values and the Future*, ed. Kurt Baier and Nicholas Rescher (New York, 1969), p. 217. Very similar remarks by Emmanuel G. Mesthene can be found in his "Technology and Wisdom," in *Philosophy and Technology*, ed. Mitcham and Mackey (New York, 1972), pp. 110–11.

21. See de Jouvenel, p. 232.

22. See Chapter 8.

23. See Chapter 10.

24. See Howard Mumford Jones, *The Pursuit of Happiness* (Ithaca, N.Y., 1966).

25. See ibid., pp. 74–80; Leo Marx, *The Machine in the Garden* (London, 1964), pp. 117–50; and Hugo A. Meier, "Thomas Jefferson and a Democratic Technology," in *Technology in America*, ed. Caroll W. Pursell, Jr. (Cambridge, Mass., 1981), pp. 17–33.

26. See Richard A. Easterlin, "Does Economic Growth Improve the Human Lot?" *Nations and Households in Economic Growth*, ed. Paul A. David and Melvin W. Reder (New York, 1974), pp. 89–125; and "Does Money Buy Happiness?" *Public Interest*, no. 30 (1973), pp. 3–10; Hirsch, pp. 111–14; and Nicholas Rescher, *Unpopular Essays on Technological Progress* (Pittsburgh, 1980), pp. 3–22.

27. See Scitovsky, pp. 59–79.

28. Ibid., pp. 204–47.

29. Ibid., p. 234.

30. Ibid., pp. 150 and 234.

31. Ibid., pp. 149–203 and passim.

32. See ibid., pp. 234 and 254–55.

33. See Hirsch, pp. 117–58, 128–29, and p. 141 in particular.

34. Ibid., pp. 111–13.

35. Ibid., pp. 55–60.

36. See Karl Marx and Friedrich Engels, *The Communist Manifesto* (New York, 1955 [first published in 1848]), pp. 9–15.

37. See Hirsch, p. 167.

38. Richard Sennett quotes Raymond Hood, "one of the presiding geniuses of the Rockefeller Center development," as saying: "Congestion is good. . . . New York is the first place in the world where a man can work within a ten-minute walk of a quarter of a million people. . . . " In "Giants of the Market. *The Skyscraper*. By Paul Goldberger," *New York Times Book Review*, 29 November 1981, p. 15.

39. See Michael R. Real, "The Super Bowl: Mythic Spectacle," in *Television: The Critical View*, ed. Horace Newcomb, 2d ed. (New York, 1979), pp. 170–203.

40. See Hirsch, pp. 95–101.

41. Hirsch provides indirect support for this view by pointing out that the effectiveness of the supporting morality "does not require neighborly love to exist, but only action *as if* it exists" (p. 142; see also pp. 146–47). An as-if-instruction invokes a familiar pattern to secure an as-yet unfamiliar behavior. But there is always some excess and deficiency in the familiar pattern which through repeated use in the unfamiliar setting are gradually adjusted. Finally, the new behavior is familiar and is seen to have its own character. There are numerous examples of this in sports and music. Here the shift is perhaps from as-if-altruism to the acceptance of the device paradigm.

42. See Hirsch, pp. 7–83; and Scitovsky, pp. 170–81 and 236–47.

43. See Peter Laslett, *The World We Have Lost* (New York, 1965), pp. 1–106; John Demos, "The American Family in Past Time," *American Scholar* 43 (1974): 422–46; Mary Jo Bane, *Here to Stay: American Families in the Twentieth Century* (New York, 1976), p. 37; Ruth S. Cowan, "The 'Industrial Revolution' in the Home: Household Technology and Social Change in the 20th Century," *Technology and Culture* 17 (1976):1–3.

44. See Christopher Lasch, *Haven in a Heartless World* (New York, 1979).

45. Ibid., pp. 22–43. Perhaps the ultimate dissolution of the household is reached when the companion is further reduced to a procurer of the commodities required to satisfy the spouse's "emotional needs." Andrew Hacker quotes Andrew Cherlin as saying that "husbands and wives are more likely today than in the past to evaluate their marriage primarily according to how well it satisfied their emotional needs." See "Farewell to the Family?" *New York Review of Books*, 18 March 1982, p. 38.

46. See Lasch, pp. 62–110.

47. See Urie Bronfenbrenner, "The Disturbing Changes in the American Family," *Search* 2, no. 1 (Fall 1976):4–10; and Hacker, "Farewell to the Family?" pp. 37–44.

48. On the stability of the family, see the Bane and Hacker references in nn. 43 and 47 above.

49. See John Kenneth Galbraith, *Economics and the Public Purpose* (Boston, 1973), pp. 233–40.

50. See Cowan, p. 21. The manipulation and exploitation of women has remained a prominent feature of advertising to this day.

51. See Grace Hechinger, "Happy Mother's Day," *Newsweek,* 11 May 1981, p. 19.

52. See Lillian Breslow Rubin, *Worlds of Pain: Life in the Working Class Family* (New York, 1976), p. 169.

53. See Myra Marx Ferree, "The Confused American Housewife," *Psychology Today* 10, no. 4 (September 1976):76–80.

54. See Daniel Yankelovich, *New Rules* (New York, 1982), pp. 93 and 101.

55. "Defensive products" is Ralph Hawtrey's term, quoted and explained by Scitovsky, pp. 108–9; Hirsch, pp. 55–60, speaks of regrettable necessities; and Rescher, in *Unpopular Essays,* pp. 5–6, uses the expression "negative benefits."

56. For these and other examples, see "And Man Created the Chip," *Newsweek,* 30 June 1980, p. 50; Myron Berger, "Enter the Computer," *New York Times Magazine,* pt. 2, 27 September 1981; and George O'Brien, "Living with Electronics," ibid., pp. 25–37.

57. There is of course Linder's problem of harriedness where a hectic and unhappy life results from cramming more and more consumption into the necessarily limited leisure time (see n. 4 for reference). A critique, similar to that of Scitovsky and Hirsch, is needed here, and it would have to make these points. Harriedness as a problem *within* technology will have our full attention and the benefit of technological resourcefulness. By means of scheduling, innovation, variety, and arranging for "quality time," we can secure at least the semblance of a solution. While harriedness can so be alleviated, the problem of disengagement and distraction is exacerbated at the same time.

58. See Real's article referred to in n. 39 above.

59. This tendency is well illustrated by the reaction of parents to teenage pregnancy which they commonly bemoan as a technical, not a moral, failure.

60. See Marie Winn, *The Plug-in Drug* (New York, 1978); and Neil Postman, "Childhood's End: The Tragedy of the Television Age," *American Educator* 5, no. 3 (1981):20–25 and 37.

61. See Robinson, *How Americans Use Time,* pp. 105–7.

62. See Winn, pp. 179–83.

63. Ibid., pp. 189–92.

64. See Dennis Porter, "Soap Time: Thoughts on a Commodity Art Form," in *Television,* ed. Newcomb, pp. 87–96.

65. Quoted by Winn on p. 129.

66. See Paul M. Hirsch, "The Role of Television and Popular Culture in Contemporary Society," in *Television,* ed. Newcomb, p. 263.

67. Ibid., p. 261.

68. See Winn, pp.12, 17–18, 25, 160–61, 166, 191–92, 232, and passim. Robinson on the other hand reports (on p. 179) that not many Americans "feel that the television programs they watch are a waste of time." Whence this inconsistency? As in surveys on work satisfaction, the evaluation in the responses may depend heavily on the setting and the scope of the question. See the preceding chapter and nn. 41–43 in that chapter.

69. See Robinson, p. 173.

70. Ibid., p. 116.

71. See Winn, pp. 215–44.

72. Ibid., pp. 228–29 and passim.

CHAPTER 19

1. See Robert L. Heilbroner, *An Inquiry into the Human Prospect,* 2d ed. (New York, 1980), pp. 18–19. Note that for Heilbroner scientific technology is the driving force of the time whose prospect he considers (pp. 56, 74–75, 92, 108). See also Warren Johnson, *Muddling toward Frugality* (Boulder, Colo., 1979), pp. 13 and 233–34.

2. See my review of Edward Goodwin Ballard, *Man and Technology* (Pittsburgh, 1978), and of Donald M. Borchert and David Stewart, eds., *Being Human in a Technological Age* (Athens, Ohio, 1979), in *Man and World* 15 (1982):112–14 for references and discussion.

3. See E. F. Schumacher, *Small Is Beautiful* (New York, 1973), pp. 31, 32, 37, 46, 101, 263.

4. See Chapter 2 for discussion of the substantive notion of technology and n. 7 in that chapter for a reference to Florman who lays bare the weaknesses of that concept.

5. See the review cited in n. 2 for examples and discussion.

6. See Staffan B. Linder, *The Harried Leisure Class* (New York, 1970). Duane Elgin argues that there are forbidding bureaucratic limits to growth. See his *Voluntary Simplicity* (New York, 1981), pp. 251–71. See n. 57 in the preceding chapter for discussion.

7. See Schumacher, pp. 20 and 147. See also Ivan Illich, *Tools for Conviviality* (New York, 1973), pp. 71 and 85.

8. See Schumacher, pp. 113, 159, 262; and Illich, pp. 13, 48, 51–54, 108; and the review referred to in n. 2 above. A classic statement of the pessimistic view is given by S. R. Eyre, "Man the Pest: The Dim Chance of Survival," *New York Review of Books,* 18 November 1971, pp. 18–27.

9. See Johnson, pp. 69–90; and Heilbroner, pp. 47–55 and 68–74.

10. Heilbroner's distress is genuine. He mourns the passing of technological affluence and its blessings (p. 175).

11. See Schumacher, p. 20.

12. That evidence has been summarized by Johnson, pp. 69–90; and Heilbroner, pp. 47–55 and 68–74.

13. See R. Buckminster Fuller, *Operating Manual for Spaceship Earth* (New York, n.d. [first published in 1969]), p. 52.

14. See Christopher D. Stone, *Should Trees Have Standing?* (Los Altos, Calif., 1974), p. 53.

15. See Lawrence H. Tribe, "Technology Assessment," *Southern California Law Review* 46 (1973):620. For discussion and eloquent expressions of this view by Archibald MacLeish and Anne Morrow Lindbergh, see Ronald Weber, "The View from Space: Notes on Space Exploration and Recent Writing," *Georgia Review* 33, (1979):280–96, pp. 283, 288, and 289 in particular.

16. See Donella H. Meadows et al., eds., *The Limits to Growth: A Report for the Club of Rome's Project on the Predicament of Mankind* (New York, 1972), p. 19.

17. Ibid., p. 35. We found that same device helpful in Chapter 9 where the device paradigm was first outlined.

18. See Robert Stobaugh and Daniel Yergin, eds., *Energy Future* (New York, 1980).

19. See *Newsweek*, 30 June 1980; and *Time*, 8 December 1980.

20. Quoted in Colin Norman, *Microelectronics at Work: Productivity and Jobs in the World Economy* (Washington, D.C., 1980), p. 5. See also Herbert A. Simon, "What Computers Mean for Man and Society," in *The Microelectronics Revolution*, ed. Tom Forester (Cambridge, Mass., 1981), pp. 419–33. Further appraisals can be found in Forester's anthology on pp. 3–64 and 434–96.

21. See *Newsweek*, 30 June 1980, p. 51.

22. See Alvin Toffler's account of how quickly and easily he came to master a simple computer used as a word processor in *The Third Wave* (New York, 1981), p. 189.

23. See Daniel Yankelovich, *New Rules* (New York, 1982), p. 18.

24. See *Information Please Almanac*, ed. Ann Golenpaul (New York, 1975), pp. 80 and 87.

25. See *Newsweek*, 30 June 1980, p. 50.

26. Ibid.

27. See pt. 2 of the *New York Times Magazine* of 27 September 1981, which was devoted to the issue of "Living with Electronics"; and Toffler's book referred to in n. 22.

28. Toffler in *The Third Wave*, pp. 265–88, argues that the consumer will more and more become a producer too, thus constituting a "prosumer." But it is clear from the majority of his examples that prosuming is the typically unencumbered and unskilled, if newly busy, consuming which is guided by and rests on an impenetrable productive machinery.

29. See Tony Schwartz, "The TV Pornography Boom," *New York Times Magazine*, 13 September 1981.

30. See Daniel Bell, *The Coming of Post-Industrial Society* (New York, 1973), pp. 477–80; and then the elaboration of this scheme (with the addition of the polity as a third and relatively independent force) in Bell's *The Cultural Contradictions of Capitalism* (New York, 1976).

31. On the dominance of culture, see Bell, *The Cultural Contradictions*, pp. 33–35.

32. See Bell, "The Social Framework of the Information Society," in *The Microelectronics Revolution*, ed. Forester, p. 509.

33. Ibid., pp. 517–19.

34. Ibid., pp. 532 and 533. Joe Weizenbaum, in a reply to Bell, stresses that while the (narrowly) technological dream has been realized, "the cultural dream was cruelly mocked in *its* realization." See his "Once More, the Computer Revolution," in *The Microelectronics Revolution*, ed. Forester, pp. 550–70, p. 553 in particular.

35. Ibid., pp. 525–26.

36. Ibid., p. 539.

37. Ibid., p. 545.

38. Ibid.

CHAPTER 20

1. See R. R. Wilson, "The Humanness of Physics," in *Being Human in a Technological Age*, ed. Donald M. Borchert and David Stewart (Athens, Ohio, 1979), p. 31.

2. Ibid., p. 4.

3. See John Noble Wilford, "Space and the American Vision," *New York Times Magazine,* 5 April 1981, p. 53.

4. See "In Space to Stay," *Newsweek,* 27 April 1981, pp. 22 and 24.

5. See Erwin Panofsky, *Gothic Architecture and Scholasticism* (New York, 1976 [first published in 1957]); and Otto von Simson, *The Gothic Cathedral* (Princeton, N.J., 1972 [first published in 1956]).

6. See Ronald Weber, "The View from Space," *Georgia Review* 33 (1979): 281.

7. See Robert M. Pirsig, *Zen and the Art of Motorcycle Maintenance: An Inquiry into Values* (New York, 1974).

8. See Eugen Herrigel, *Zen in the Art of Archery,* trans. R. F. C. Hull (New York, 1953).

9. See Pirsig, p. 26.

10. Ibid., pp. 12–14, 27–28.

11. Ibid., pp. 18–26 and passim.

12. Ibid., pp. 32–35.

13. Ibid., pp. 97–104.

14. Ibid., p. 102.

15. Ibid., pp. 54–93.

16. Ibid., pp. 174–241.

17. Ibid., p. 255.

18. Ibid., pp. 274–326.

19. Ibid., p. 297.

20. Ibid., pp. 399–412.

21. This distinction and its pivotal status have been discovered and discussed by environmentalists. But the debate has become too intricate and ramified for fruitful reference in our context. A survey of the discussion has been provided by George Sessions, "Shallow and Deep Ecology," in *Ecological Consciousness,* ed. J. Donald Hughes and Robert C. Schultz (Washington, D.C., 1981).

22. See Alvin M. Weinberg, "Can Technology Replace Social Engineering?" in *Technology and Man's Future,* 3d ed., ed. Albert H. Teich (New York, 1981), pp. 30 and 34. The essay was first published in 1966.

23. Ibid., p. 35. Weinberg's suggestion springs from more than a little social pessimism. See ibid., p. 32.

24. Ibid, pp. 31–33.

25. Ibid., pp. 33–36.

26. Ibid., p. 35.

27. Ibid., p. 36.

28. See Amory B. Lovins, "Energy Strategy: The Road Not Taken?" *Foreign Affairs* 55, no. 1 (October 1976): 65–96.

29. See Warren Johnson, *Muddling toward Frugality* (Boulder, Colo., 1979), p. 14.

30. See E. F. Schumacher, *Small Is Beautiful* (New York, 1973); and *Good Work* (New York, 1979). He remarks specifically on the terminology of "intermediate" vs. "appropriate" in *Good Work,* pp. 130–31. For discussion of the terminology, see J. van Brakel, "Appropriate Technology: Facts and Values," *Research in Philosophy and Technology* 3 (1980): 385–402.

31. See, e.g., the proposals in *Energy Future,* ed. Robert Stobaugh and Daniel Yergin (New York, 1979), pp. 287–304. For discussion, see Langdon Winner, "The Political Philosophy of Alternative Technology," *Technology and Man's Future,* ed. Teich, pp. 369–85, pp. 377–83 in particular.

32. A monument to such efforts is *Where We Agree: Report of the National Coal Policy Project, Summary and Synthesis* (Washington, D.C., n.d.) which issued from a meeting of industrialists and environmentalists.

33. See Schmacher, *Small Is Beautiful,* pp. 21, 112, 156.

34. Ibid., pp. 23, 93, 101, and passim; Johnson, pp. 13, 187, 233–34; Lovins, p. 94; Ivan Illich, *Tools for Conviviality* (New York, 1973), p. xiii; Duane Elgin, *Voluntary Simplicity* (New York, 1981).

35. See Schumacher, *Small Is Beautiful,* pp. 155–57; and Johnson, p. 9.

36. See Illich, p. 13; Schumacher, *Small Is Beautiful,* p. 34; Johnson, p. 12; Elgin, pp. 162–215.

37. See Illich, pp. xii–xiii.

38. Ibid. See also p. 11.

39. See ibid., pp. 23 and 69.

40. Ibid., p. 69.

41. Ibid., pp. 39–42.

42. See Barry Cohen, "Future Bikes," *New York Times Magazine,* 10 August 1980; and Albert C. Gross et al., "The Aerodynamics of Human-powered Land Vehicles," *Scientific American* 249 (December 1983): 142–52.

43. See Schumacher, *Small Is Beautiful,* p. 95.

44. Ibid., pp. 96–101.

45. See Johnson, p. 182.

46. Ibid., pp. 218–19. Village life is similarly appreciated by Peter Laslett in *The World We Have Lost* (New York, 1965), pp. 53–80; and by Lewis Mumford in *The Myth of the Machine: Technics and Human Development* (New York, 1967), pp. 156–62.

47. See Fred Hirsch's reminders of how cloying and oppressive close association can be in *Social Limits to Growth* (Cambridge, Mass., 1976), pp. 81–82 and 139–40.

CHAPTER 21

1. See Roberto Mangabeira Unger, *Knowledge and Politics* (New York, 1975), p. 7.

2. See Alasdair MacIntyre, *After Virtue* (Notre Dame, Ind., 1981), p. 112.

3. Ibid., p. 33.

4. See Manfred Stanley, *The Technological Conscience* (New York, 1978), pp. 40 and 42.

5. Ibid., p. 42.

6. Ibid.

7. See MacIntyre, pp. 6–7 and 227–37.

8. See this exchange:

"We can't be a pitiful helpless giant. We gotta show 'em we're number one."
"Are you number one?"
A pause. "I'm number nothin'."

In Studs Terkel, *American Dreams: Lost and Found* (New York, 1980), p. xxv.

9. MacIntyre says of emotivism, a version of this seemingly unbounded freedom, "that to a large degree people now think, talk and act *as if* emotivism were true, no matter what their avowed theoretical stand-point may be." (See p. 21 of *After Virtue.*) I agree that people talk that way; but they think and act according to a definite pattern.

10. See "Big Game Farms Booming in Montana," *Missoulian,* 4 November 1979, p. 1.

11. Ibid.

12. A fine example can be found in the *New York Times Magazine,* 20 February 1983, p. 3, where we read: "All these years you've been doing for others. Summer camp. Orthodontists. Ballet lessons. Tuitions. Now it's time to do something for you . . . the two of you. A beautiful 1983 Cadillac! And it's all you hoped it would be . . . in comfort . . . ride . . . and luxury. Isn't it time you did something just for you?"

13. The reproving part of the appropriate idiom has been furnished along with the critique of technology and includes such terms as "disengagement," "distraction," "loneliness," "disorientation," "domination," "procurement," "debilitation," "shallowness," "complicity," etc. The approving part is provided in Chapters 23 and 24 and contains terms such as "engagement," "skill," "discipline," "fidelity," "celebration," "resolve," etc., and the terms of traditional excellence in a revived sense. The terms of deictic discourse, presented in this chapter, also belong to the approving part. Any one of this idiom's terms is of course unintelligible or ambiguous outside of the context of the overall argument.

14. See Stanley, p. 42.

15. See John Stuart Mill, "Utilitarianism [1863]," in *Ethical Theories,* ed. A. I. Melden (Englewood Cliffs, N.J., 1967), pp. 391–434, p. 403 in particular.

16. See John Rawls, *A Theory of Justice* (Cambridge, Mass., 1971), pp. 17–22 in particular. The point needs more qualification; but Rawls's intention to make "the original position" as reasonable and uncontroversial as possible is clear.

17. See Blaise Pascal, *Pensées,* ed. Victor Giraud (Paris, 1935), pp. 95–98; and Anselm of Canterbury, "Proslogium," in *Basic Writings,* 2d ed., trans. S. N. Deane (La Salle, Ill., 1962), pp. 9–10. It is remarkable that both of these attempts at cogent discourse are embedded in deictic discourse of the first order. But even if we could convict people of inconsistency, we might, as Robert Nozick has pointed out, achieve a hollow victory since one may gladly live (with) an inconsistency. See Nozick's *Philosophical Explanations* (Cambridge, Mass., 1981), pp. 405–9.

18. Some of what follows is akin to and informed by Paul Tillich's concept of ultimate concern. But it will also be clear from the sequel that I cannot accept the ahistorical and abstract sense of Tillich's notion. See his *Dynamics of Faith* (New York, 1958).

19. Deictic discourse has a kinship too with Habermas's communicative competence. But an ideal and abstract character distinguishes the latter from the former. For discussion and references, see Chapter 14, n. 57 in particular.

20. Enthusiasm is related to what Nozick calls ethical push, tolerance to ethical pull; sympathy is balanced between the two. See his *Philosophical Explanations,* pp. 399–504. These relations allow one to see how the suggestions above connect with

traditional ethics. An alternative but congenial and much more circumspect account of the contestability and legitimacy of discourse on ultimate concerns has been given by Manfred Stanley, pp. 83–135.

21. See Tillich, pp. 16–22.

22. See Fred Hirsch, *Social Limits to Growth* (Cambridge, Mass., 1976), pp. 81–82 and 139–40.

23. See Chapters 5 and 12 above.

24. See Otto von Simson, *The Gothic Cathedral* (Princeton, N.J., 1974), pp. 162–63.

25. See Norman Malcolm, "Wittgenstein's Philosophical Investigations," *Philosophical Review* 63 (1954): 543–47.

26. The distinction between active and declarative assent parallels John Henry Newman's between real and notional assent in *A Grammar of Assent,* ed. Charles Frederick Harrold (New York, 1947).

27. Robert Nozick has recently urged that philosophical explanations should not be coercive and has refused to furnish a coercive argument in support of his suggestion. But I believe we can take the issue further than he does. See his *Philosophical Explanations,* pp. 4–8.

28. See MacIntyre, pp. 54–57. We can also say, with Holmes Rolston III, that "an 'ought' is not so much *derived* from an 'is' as discovered simultaneously with it." See his "Is There an Ecological Ethic?" *Ethics* 85 (1975): 101.

29. The reader who wants to see a picture of deictic explanation will find a striking one in Steve Dunwell and David McCord, *Harvard* (Little Compton, R.I., 1982), p. 48.

CHAPTER 22

1. On the definition of wilderness and on the origin of the concept, see John C. Hendee, George H. Stankey, and Robert C. Lucas, *Wilderness Management* (Washington, D.C.: U.S. Department of Agriculture, 1978), pp. 9–10.

2. See Daniel J. Boorstin, "From the Land to the Machine," in *The Republic of Technology* (New York, 1978), pp. 37–48.

3. See Leo Marx, *The Machine in the Garden: Technology and the Pastoral Ideal in America* (New York, 1964), pp. 36–40. For the late medieval tradition of the pastoral ideal, see J. Huizinga, *The Waning of the Middle Ages* (Garden City, N.Y., 1954 [first published in 1924]), pp. 128–38.

4. See Leo Marx, pp. 75–86.

5. See Roderick Nash, *Wilderness and the American Mind,* 2d ed. (New Haven, 1978), pp. 8–43.

6. See Nash, "International Concepts of Wilderness Preservation," in Hendee, Stankey, and Lucas, pp. 43–59.

7. It gathered momentum from the end of the eighteenth to the middle of the nineteenth century and then reached its take-off point. See Leo Marx, pp. 145–226; and Alfred D. Chandler, Jr., *The Visible Hand* (Cambridge, Mass., 1977), pp. 75–78.

8. See Eugene S. Ferguson, "The American-ness of American Technology," *Technology and Culture* 20 (1979): 4–6; and Frederick Jackson Turner's celebrated essay on "The Significance of the Frontier in American History," in *The Frontier in American History* (New York, 1958), pp. 1–38.

9. See Wendell Berry, *The Unsettling of America* (New York, 1978), pp. 3–48.

10. See Ferguson, pp. 7–14.

11. For the contemporary result of these developments, see Vance Packard, *A Nation of Strangers* (New York, 1972); and Alvin Toffler, *Future Shock* (New York, 1974), pp. 7–181.

12. See Nash, *Wilderness and the American Mind,* pp. 44–83.

13. See Aldo Leopold, "Wilderness," in *A Sand County Almanac and Sketches Here and There* (London, 1968), pp. 188–201.

14. See Christopher D. Stone, *Should Trees Have Standing?* (Los Altos, Calif., 1974), p. 43.

15. See Robert H. Socolow, "Failures of Discourse: Obstacles to the Integration of Environmental Values into Natural Resource Policy," *When Values Conflict,* ed. Laurence H. Tribe et al. (Cambridge, Mass., 1976), pp. 20–21.

16. See Tribe, "Ways Not to Think about Plastic Trees," *Yale Law Journal* 83 (1974): 1330–31; and John Rodman, "The Liberation of Nature?" *Inquiry* 20 (1977): 83–84.

17. See "Public Participation in Outdoor Activities and Attitudes toward Wilderness—1977," *Research Recap* (of the American Forest Institute), no. 10 (December 1977): 1–4.

18. See Rodman's reference to Peter Singer, "a moral philosopher who hopes to lead us, not 'by sentimental appeals for sympathy' but by vigorous [rigorous?] moral reasoning, to make 'a mental switch' in our 'attitudes towards a very large group of beings: members of species other than our own.'" See Rodman, p. 84.

19. See Rodman, pp. 115 and 117.

20. See Duane Elgin, *Voluntary Simplicity* (New York, 1981), pp. 21, 35, 37, and 41.

21. See, e.g., Holmes Rolston III, "Is There an Ecological Ethic?" *Ethics* 85 (1975): 106 and 108.

22. See Colleen D. Clements, "Stasis: The Unnatural Value," *Ethics* 86 (1976): 136–44.

23. See Henry G. Bugbee, *The Inward Morning* (State College, Pa., 1958), p. 86.

24. See Leo Marx, p. 364.

25. See Rodman, p. 111.

26. One should note that Leopold actually pleaded for the preservation of museum pieces and saw a self-defeating tendency only in the destructive crowding of wilderness lovers.

27. See Leopold, pp. 189–92.

28. Sometimes it is suggested that the minimal size of a wilderness area is one that would allow or require a hiker to camp in it. See Hendee, Stankey, and Lucas, p. 9.

29. Since, in what follows, I will be drawing heavily on Mircea Eliade's *The Sacred and the Profane* (New York, 1961) I must say a word to distinguish my view from Eliade's. It differs in two respects. First, it seems to me that Eliade overstresses the discontinuity ("solution of continuity" as he calls it, pp. 25 and 68) between the sacred and the profane. Though the realms are clearly separated, they do not in general, I believe, deny one another but rather complement each other. The holy sanctifies the

profane; the profane surrounds the holy with an allowance for human distraction and fallibility. Eliade, in fact, often points up bridges across the gap between the two realms, especially in regards to time (pp. 68–113). Second, it seems to me that Eliade is to some extent an unwitting hostage to the metaphysical distinction between the phenomenal and the ideal, the material and the spiritual, the immanent and the transcendent, and to other versions of it. Though mythic people certainly distinguished different realms and realities, they saw an interpenetration of them that we easily mistake metaphysically. This metaphysical mistake informs, I believe, Eliade's rejection of what he calls "naturism" (pp. 118 and 121), the claim that a natural object is divine in being natural.

30. See Eliade, pp. 29–30.

31. See Leo Marx, pp. 180–226.

32. Ibid., p. 54.

33. See Eliade, pp. 45–47. An eminent disclosure of this kind has been given by Black Elk in *Black Elk Speaks* (Lincoln, Neb., 1961), pp. 20–47 and 166–80. And, in general, much is to be learned from the Native Americans as regards the eloquence of nature on this continent.

34. See Eliade, p. 165.

35. Ibid., pp. 58–62.

36. Ibid., pp. 21–26.

37. See Rodman, p. 100.

38. Ibid., p. 94.

39. Ibid., p. 113.

40. See Stone, pp. 42–54.

41. Human existence, as the anthropic principle has it, also may be at the center of the universe in the sense that the character or specificity of the cosmos comes to be focused in humanity; more particularly, among all the physically possible worlds, the peculiarity of the actual world is most evident from the specific requirements it has met to make possible the evolution of intelligent life. For exposition, see George Gale, "The Anthropic Principle," *Scientific American* 245 (December 1981): 154–71; for discussion, see John Leslie, "Anthropic Principle, World Ensemble, Design," *American Philosophical Quarterly* 19 (1982): 141–51; see also Eric Chaisson, "The Broadest View of the Biggest Picture," *Harvard Magazine* (January-February 1982): 21–25.

42. See the Stone, Rodman, and Rolston essays; and Arne Naess's seminal sketch, "The Shallow and the Deep, Long-Range Ecology Movement," *Inquiry* 16 (1973): 95–100.

43. See Rolston, p. 104.

44. See Rodman, pp. 104–5.

45. See Hans Jonas, *Das Prinzip Verantwortung* (Frankfurt am Main, 1979).

46. Cf. Leopold, p. 101; and Nash, *Wilderness and the American Mind*, pp. 263–73.

CHAPTER 23

1. See *Paulys Realencyclopädie der classischen Altertumswissenschaft* (Stuttgart, 1893–1963), 15:615–17; See also Fustel de Coulanges, "The Sacred Fire," in *The Ancient City*, trans. Willard Small (Garden City, N.Y., n.d. [first published in 1864]), pp. 25–33.

2. See Kent C. Bloomer and Charles W. Moore, *Body, Memory, and Architecture* (New Haven, 1977), pp. 2–3 and 50–51.

3. See Jeremiah Eck, "Home Is Where the Hearth Is," *Quest* 3 (April 1979): 12.

4. Ibid., p. 11.

5. See *The Oxford English Dictionary*.

6. See Martin Heidegger, "The Origin of the Work of Art," in *Poetry, Language, Thought,* trans. Albert Hofstadter (New York, 1971), pp. 15–87.

7. See Vincent Scully, *The Earth, the Temple, and the Gods* (New Haven, 1962).

8. See my *The Philosophy of Language* (The Hague, 1974), pp. 126–31.

9. See Heidegger, *Being and Time,* trans. John Macquarrie and Edward Robinson (New York, 1962), pp. 95–107, 163–68, 210–24.

10. See Heidegger, "The Origin of the Work of Art," p 80.

11. See Heidegger, "The Thing," in *Poetry, Language, Thought,* pp. 163–82. Heidegger alludes to the turn from the *Bedingungen* to the *Dinge* on p. 179 of the original, "Das Ding," in *Vorträge und Aufsätze* (Pfullingen, 1959). He alludes to the turn from technology to (focal) things in "The Question Concerning Technology," in *The Question Concerning Technology and Other Essays,* trans. William Lovitt (New York, 1977), p. 43.

12. See Heidegger, "The Thing."

13. See M. F. K. Fisher, *The Cooking of Provincial France* (New York, 1968), p. 50.

14. Though there are seeds for a reform of technology to be found in Heidegger as I want to show, Heidegger insists that "philosophy will not be able to effect an immediate transformation of the present condition of the world. Only a god can save us." See "Only a God Can Save Us: Der Spiegel's Interview with Martin Heidegger," trans. Maria P. Alter and John D. Caputo, *Philosophy Today* 20 (1976): 277.

15. I am not concerned to establish or defend the claim that my account of Heidegger or my development of his views are authoritative. It is merely a matter here of acknowledging a debt.

16. See Heidegger, "The Question Concerning Technology," p. 43; Langdon Winner makes a similar point in "The Political Philosophy of Alternative Technology," in *Technology and Man's Future,* ed. Albert H. Teich, 3d ed. (New York, 1981), pp. 369–73.

17. See Heidegger, "The Thing," pp. 180–82.

18. The need of complementing Heidegger's notion of the thing with the notion of practice was brought home to me by Hubert L. Dreyfus's essay, "Holism and Hermeneutics," *Review of Metaphysics* 34 (1980): 22–23.

19. See Heidegger, "Building Dwelling Thinking," in *Poetry, Language, Thought,* pp. 152-53.

20. Ibid., pp. 148–49.

21. Georg Trakl, quoted by Heidegger in "Language," in *Poetry, Language, Thought,* pp. 194–95 (I have taken some liberty with Hofstadter's translation).

22. See Norman Maclean, *A River Runs through It and Other Stories* (Chicago, 1976). Only the first of the three stories instructs the reader about fly fishing.

23. See Colin Fletcher, *The Complete Walker* (New York, 1971).

24. Ibid., p. 9.

25. See Roger B. Swain, *Earthly Pleasures: Tales from a Biologist's Garden* (New York, 1981).

26. Here are a few more: Wendell Berry, *Farming: A Handbook* (New York, 1970); Stephen Kiesling, *The Shell Game: Reflections on Rowing and the Pursuit of Excellence* (New York, 1982); John Richard Young, *Schooling for Young Riders* (Norman, Okla., 1970); W. Timothy Gallwey, *The Inner Game of Tennis* (New York, 1974); Ruedi Bear, *Pianta Su: Ski Like the Best* (Boston, 1976). Such books must be sharply distinguished from those that promise to teach accomplishments without effort and in no time. The latter kind of book is technological in intent and fraudulent in fact.

27. See Robert Farrar Capon, *The Supper of the Lamb: A Culinary Reflection* (Garden City, N.Y., 1969); and George Sheehan, *Running and Being: The Total Experience* (New York, 1978).

28. See Sheehan, pp. 211–20 and elsewhere.

29. See Capon, pp. 167–181.

30. See my "Mind, Body, and World," *Philosophical Forum* 8 (1976): 76–79. The intentional ambiguity of commodities has been discussed in Chapter 10.

31. See Capon, pp. 176–77.

32. See Sheehan, p. 127.

33. On the unity of achievement and enjoyment, see Alasdair MacIntyre, *After Virtue* (Notre Dame, Ind., 1981), p. 184.

34. See my "Mind, Body, and World," pp. 68–86.

35. See Peter Wood, "Seeing New York on the Run," *New York Times Magazine*, 7 October 1979; Alexandra Penney, "Health and Grooming: Shaping Up the Corporate Image," ibid.

36. See *New York Times Magazine*, 3 August 1980, pp. 20–21.

37. See Wood, p. 112.

38. See Sheehan, pp. 211–17.

39. See Wood, p. 116.

40. See Sheehan, pp. 221–31 and passim.

41. There is substantial anthropological evidence to show that running has been a profound focal practice in certain pretechnological cultures. I am unable to discuss it here. Nor have I discussed the problem, here and elsewhere touched upon, of technology and religion. The present study, I believe, has important implications for that issue, but to draw them out would require more space and circumspection than are available now. I have made attempts to provide an explication in "Christianity and the Cultural Center of Gravity," *Listening* 18 (1983): 93–102; and in "Prospects for the Theology of Technology," *Theology and Technology*, ed. Carl Mitcham and Jim Grote (Lanham, Md., 1984), pp. 305–22.

42. See M. F. K. Fisher, pp. 9–31.

43. For what social and empirical basis there is to this question see Chapter 24.

44. Some therapists advise lying down till these stirrings go away.

45. See John Rawls, "Two Concepts of Rules," *Philosophical Review* 64 (1955): 3–32.

46. Conversely, it is one thing to break a practice and quite another to omit a particular action. For we define ourselves and our lives in our practices; hence to break a practice is to jeopardize one's identity while omitting a particular action is relatively inconsequential.

47. See Aristotle's *Nicomachean Ethics*, the beginning of Book Two in particular.

48. See MacIntyre, p. 175.

49. Ibid., pp. 175–77.

50. Ibid., p. 176.

51. See Rawls, p. 25.

CHAPTER 24

1. See George Sheehan, *Running and Being* (New York, 1978), p. 102.

2. See Wilhelm von Humboldt, "Ideen zu einem Versuch, die Gränzen der Wirksamkeit des Staats zu bestimmen," in *Werke,* ed. Andreas Flitner and Klaus Giel (Stuttgart, 1960–64), 1:64–69.

3. John Rawls, *A Theory of Justice* (Cambridge, Mass., 1971), pp. 520–29.

4. Ibid., p. 426.

5. Ibid., p. 429.

6. Ibid., p. 427.

7. Ibid., p. 554.

8. Ibid., p. 552.

9. See Robert Farrar Capon, *The Supper of the Lamb* (Garden City, N.Y., 1969), pp. 182–91; and Sheehan, pp. 238–40.

10. See Aaron Latham, "Video Games Star War," *New York Times Magazine,* 25 October 1981; "Invasion of the Video Creatures," *Newsweek,* 16 November 1981, pp. 90–94; "Games That Play People," *Time,* 18 January 1982, pp. 50–58.

11. See *Time,* p. 56.

12. How can there be technological engagement if technology is defined as disengaging? The answer is that technology in this essay is defined according to the device paradigm, and so defined it becomes disengaging primarily (*a*) in consumption and (*b*) in the mature phase after it has taken the ironical turn. Hence the possibility of technological engagement suggests that technology could achieve an alternative maturity.

There is already technological engagement in the sense that certain activities essentially depend on technological products as alpine skiing or bicycle racing do. But note that the technological devices do not procure but mediate engagement. The engagement is finally with slopes, snow conditions, courses, turns, etc. And there is full and skilled bodily engagement too.

13. See *Newsweek,* 16 November 1981, p. 94.

14. Ibid., p. 90.

15. Along similar lines one could show that running is more excellent than exercising with a Nautilus.

16. See Tracy Kidder, *The Soul of a New Machine* (Boston, 1981).

17. Remember Daniel Bell's remark, referred to in Chapter 19 (see n. 32 there), that the computer is the "thing" in which the postindustrial society is coming to be symbolized. For a treatise in support of the thesis, see Douglas R. Hofstadter, *Gödel, Escher, Bach: An Eternal Golden Braid* (New York, 1979).

18. Engagement, too, taken as a formal notion or as a concept of a certain sort of worldlessly conceived human existence, fails as a guide to enduring excellence. But understood as a term that recollects and anticipates the human response to focal things, it is a helpful vocable, and I will continue so to use it.

19. Aristotle's Principle is not so dependent on complexity since it is balanced by the rightful assumption and careful explication of a definite and articulate world. See Chapter 6 above.

20. Rawls attempts to control the empirical world by admitting it into the design of the just society in an orderly sequence of four stages (see *A Theory of Justice*, pp. 195–201). This procedure does succeed in occluding the good life of focal things and practices. The apparent opening, so Rawls hopes, will be filled with the good life that springs from rationality, the Aristotelian Principle, and social union. But as we saw, the hope is not fulfilled. Instead, as argued in Chapter 14, the technological society emerges as the only possible but unacknowledged realization of Rawls' just society. One might argue, incidentally, that technology is not only an indispensable aid but also a guide for Rawls's theory which is designed to make justice available in the technological sense. I believe, however, that, appearances to the contrary, the formidable machinery of Rawls's theory bespeaks a commitment to fairness, openness, and compassion primarily and secondarily, at most, to technology.

21. See Rawls, p. 554.

22. On the general rise and decline of the car as a symbol of success, see Daniel Yankelovich, *New Rules: Searching for Self-Fulfillment in a World Turned Upside Down* (Toronto, 1982), pp. 36–39.

23. Although these technological instruments are translucent relative to the world and so permit engagement with the world, they still possess an opaque machinery that mediates engagement but is not itself experienced either directly or through social mediation. See also the remarks in n. 12 above.

24. See "Who Is the American Runner?" *Runner's World* 15 (December 1980): 36–42.

25. The statistical empirical evidence will be considered in the next chapter.

26. Capon's book is the most impressive document of such discriminating use of technology.

27. A point that is emphatically made by E. F. Schumacher in *Small Is Beautiful* (New York, 1973) and in *Good Work* (New York, 1979); by Duane Elgin in *Voluntary Simplicity* (New York, 1981); and by Yankelovich in *New Rules*.

28. See Roger Rosenblatt, "The Sad Truth about Big Spenders," *Time*, 8 December 1980, pp. 84 and 89.

29. On the confusions that beset romanticism in its opposition to technology, see Lewis Mumford, *Technics and Civilization* (New York, 1963), pp. 285–303.

30. See Daniel J. Boorstin, *Democracy and Its Discontents* (New York, 1975), pp. 12–25.

31. See Elgin, pp. 251–71. In believing that the mass of complex technical information poses a mortal threat to bureaucracies, Elgin, it seems to me, indulges in the unwarranted pessimism of the optimists.

32. Ibid., p. 71.

CHAPTER 25

1. Sometimes I will use "legality" to mean *legal system* and at other times to mean, in the more common sense, *set of conditions that something must meet to be legal or a law.* Similarly for "morality.' This ambiguity is harmless since the context resolves it. More important, the ambiguity, as is apparent from prior remarks, corresponds to a gradation from the abstract (the values of justice) to the concrete (the

practices and institutions in which justice eminently comes to pass) and does not indicate an equivocation. The legality-morality distinction overlaps with that between the constitutional or just society on the one hand and the good society on the other. See Chapter 14 above.

2. For a dissenting and critical view, see Roberto Mangabeira Unger, *Knowledge and Politics* (New York, 1976), pp. 83–103.

3. See Irving Kristol, "Pornography, Obscenity, and the Case for Censorship," in *Philosophy of Law*, ed. Joel Feinberg and Hyman Gross (Encino, Calif., 1975), p. 169.

4. There are traces of this argument in Kristol also on pp. 165 and 168–69.

5. See John Rawls, *A Theory of Justice* (Cambridge, Mass., 1971), pp. 195–99 and 258–65.

6. To capture this inconsistency, Erhard Eppler has distinguished between a conservatism of values and a conservatism of (economic) structures. See his *Wege aus der Gefahr* (Reinbeck, 1981), pp. 101–6, where he also discusses similar findings of other authors.

7. See John Kenneth Galbraith, "Poverty and the Way People Behave," in *Economics, Peace, and Laughter* (New York, 1972), pp. 168–69.

8. So quotations on the covers of the paperback edition inform us. See Lester C. Thurow, *The Zero-Sum Society: Distribution and the Possibilities for Economic Change* (Middlesex, 1981).

9. Thurow, p. 120; see also p. 197. For discussion, see William Leiss, *The Limits to Satisfaction* (Toronto, 1976), pp. 24–27.

10. See Warren Johnson, *Muddling toward Frugality* (Boulder, Colo., 1979), pp. 32–38 where references to further sources can be found.

11. See Jürgen Habermas, "Technology and Science as 'Ideology,'" in *Toward a Rational Society*, trans. Jeremy J. Shapiro (Boston, 1970), pp. 94–95; Jacques Ellul, *The Technological Society*, trans. John Wilkinson (New York, 1964), pp. 23–42; Carl Mitcham, "Philosophy of Technology," *A Guide to the Culture of Science, Technology, and Medicine*, ed. Paul T. Durbin (New York, 1980), pp. 309–10.

12. On simplicity as a condition for reform, see Duane Elgin, *Voluntary Simplicity* (New York, 1981), p. 37.

13. See Studs Terkel, *American Dreams: Lost and Found* (New York, 1981).

14. See Elgin, pp. 129–31. A willing acceptance of simplicity is the attitude closest to the reform here proposed though even it is not unambiguously one of focal concern. There are other indications of a popular desire for basic reform though these indications and the accounts given of them are uneasily located on the line that divides reforms within and of the framework of technology. See especially Daniel Yankelovich, *New Rules* (Toronto, 1982); and the success of such books in Europe as Niels I. Meyer, K. Helveg Petersen, and Villy Sörensen, *Revolt from the Centre*, trans. from the Danish by Christine Hauch (Lawrence, Mass., 1981); and Eppler's book cited in n. 6 above.

15. See Duane Elgin, quoting Louis Harris on p. 128.

16. This view is supported by Yankelovich, p. 174. But I am not sure that regarding this dividedness one should, as Yankelovich does, place people's wholehearted alliance on the side of a high and rising standard of living.

17. See Fred Hirsch, *Social Limits to Growth* (Cambridge, Mass., 1976), pp. 71–83; and Tibor Scitovsky, *The Joyless Economy* (Oxford, 1976), pp. 173–74. The

reasoning that leads one to support a collective affirmation and cooperative action is always balanced, if not outweighed, by a calculation that counsels one to prefer individual advantage. Game theory explores the settings, structures, and strategies of this problem. For discussion and references, see Robert Nozick, *Philosophical Explanations* (Cambridge, Mass., 1981), pp. 542–43 and n. 118 on p. 742. I want to urge that the unhappy tension between the calculus of social and individual advantage can be overcome through enthusiasm and sympathy. See also Rawls, pp. 240 and 267–70.

18. On the tie between collective affirmation ("final acceptance" as he calls it) and reform, see Warren Johnson, p. 157. An interesting study of the rise of a collective affirmation and a reform of technology is Noel Perrin's *Giving Up the Gun: Japan's Reversion to the Sword* (Boston, 1979).

19. See E. F. Schumacher, *Small Is Beautiful* (New York, 1973), p. 260; see his *Good Work* (New York, 1979), p. 126.

20. Quoted by Duane Elgin on p. 128.

21. See Lowdon Wingo, "The Quality of Life: Toward a Microeconomic Definition," *Urban Studies* 10 (1973): 4 n. 2, see also p. 7.

22. The truly rich can buy many of the elements of the quality of life except one: genuine membership and respect in a community. Ordinary folk have some individual choice in the quality of life through mobility

23. See John Kenneth Galbraith, *The Affluent Society* (New York, 1958), pp. 199–200.

24. Following Hirsch, we have seen in Chapter 18 (see n. 35 there) that the GNP is a dubious measure of social prosperity. Accordingly, Thurow (p. 5) refuses to identify per capita GNP with the standard of living. Still, the behavior of most mainstream economists and politicians regarding the GNP allows one to hold to the suggested synonymy.

25. See John Kenneth Galbraith, *Economics and the Public Purpose* (Boston, 1973), pp. 43–44.

26. Ibid., p. 44.

27. Ibid., p. 41.

28. That Galbraith accepts the technological specification of liberal democracy is most evident in Chapter 23 of *Economics* (pp. 233–40). That his acceptance is not uncritical is clear from pp. 225–26.

29. See Lewis Mumford, "Authoritarian and Democratic Technics," *Technology and Culture* 5 (1964): 2. See also Carroll Pursell, "The American Ideal of a Democratic Technology," in *The Technological Imagination*, ed. Teresa De Lauretis et al. (Madison, Wis., 1980), pp. 11–25.

30. For discussion, see Langdon Winner, "Do Artifacts Have Politics?" *Daedalus* 109, no. 1 (Winter 1980): 121–36.

31. See Mumford, pp. 2–3.

32. See Lewis Mumford, *Technics and Civilization* (New York, 1963 [first published in 1934]), pp. 410–17.

33. Ibid., p. 414.

34. Ibid., p. 411. Empirical support has been gathered by Ruth Tenne and Bilha Mannheim in "The Effect of the Level of Production Technology on Workers' Orientations and Responses to the Work Situation," in *Work and Technology*, ed. Marie R. Haug and Jacques Dofny (London, 1977), pp. 61–79.

35. See Mumford, "Authoritarian and Democratic Technics," p. 8.

36. Elgin and Schumacher talk about such people, and so does Peter N. Gillingham, "The Making of Good Work" in Schumacher's *Good Work*, pp. 147–218.

37. I do not want to imply that the two-sector economy will solve the problem of the degradation or lack of work completely or quickly. It provides a long-term and hopeful goal. Meanwhile, the government should, as Thurow urges on pp. 203–6, take immediate measures to deal with the lack of work.

38. See Galbraith, *Economics*, p. 223.

39. See Mumford's suggestions in *Technics*, p. 415; and Elgin's on p. 287.

40. We should use regulations that directly influence prices rather than aim at definite quantities and assignments in the production of goods. See Thurow, pp. 150–51.

41. See Elgin, pp. 283–86. Similar proposals have been made by Gillingham, pp. 191–203; and by William Irwin Thompson in *Darkness and Scattered Light* (Garden City, N.Y., 1978), pp. 53–103.

42. See Louis Wirth, "Urbanism as a Way of Life," in *On Cities and Social Life,* ed. Albert J. Reiss, Jr. (Chicago, 1964), p. 71.

43. See David P. Billington, *Structures and the Urban Environment* (Princeton, N.J., 1978), especially pp. 149–53. See also Kent C. Bloomer and Charles W. Moore, *Body, Memory, and Architecture* (New Haven, 1977), and in it Robert J. Yudell's essay "Body Movement," pp. 57–76.

44. See Billington, p. 149.

45. See Bloomer and Moore, pp. 105–30. These memorable places include buildings as well as towns or cities.

46. Note George Sheehan's remark that "the city must primarily be a playground." In *Running and Being* (New York, 1978), p. 91. On the distinction between culture as scenery and as enactment, see Ina-Maria Greverus, "Denkmalräume oder Lebensräume?" in *Auf der Suche nach Heimat* (Munich, 1979), pp. 182–98. There are large social or communal gaps, of course, between the family, centered around a focal practice, and the larger communities that celebrate their focal concerns in the cities. And there is a still larger gap between these communities of focal concern and the nation. My concern is not to outline all the social structures that are likely or desirable in a setting of reformed technology but to point up the openings for and the centers of such structures. For suggestions on such structures, see Elgin, pp. 282–95; and William Irwin Thompson, pp. 53–103.

47. See Thurow, pp. 199–200.

48. See Robert Farrar Capon, *The Supper of the Lamb* (Garden City, N.Y., 1969), pp. 22–34.

CHAPTER 26

1. See Langdon Winner, *Autonomous Technology* (Cambridge, Mass., 1978), pp. 229–31; see also Chapter 11 above.

2. Edward G. Ballard does believe that the balance of means and ends has been fatally and radically upset. "Feeding the poor," he says, "generally improving the lot of men, is to be justified by the contribution these humanitarian activities make to the advance of technology." *Man and Technology* (Pittsburgh, 1978), p. 203.

3. See Colin Fletcher, *The Complete Walker* (New York, 1971), p. 7.

Index

84-3243

303.483
B64

Borgmann, Albert.
Technology and the character of
contemporary life.

The Patrick and Beatrice Haggerty

Library

Mount Mary College

Milwaukee, Wisconsin 53222

DEMCO